INVENTING ENTREPRENEURS

TECHNOLOGY INNOVATORS AND THEIR ENTREPRENEURIAL JOURNEY

Gerard George

Tanaka Business School
Imperial College London
United Kingdom

Adam J. Bock

Tanaka Business School
Imperial College London
United Kingdom

PEARSON

Prentice
Hall

UPPER SADDLE RIVER, NEW JERSEY 07458

Library of Congress Cataloging-in-Publication Data

George, Gerard.
   Inventing entrepreneurs : technology innovators and their entrepreneurial journey/
Gerard George, Adam J. Bock.
      p. cm.
   Includes bibliographical references.
   ISBN-13: 978-0-13-157470-0 (pbk.)
   ISBN-10: 0-13-157470-1 (pbk.)
   1. Technological innovations.   2. Inventions.   3. New products.
   4. Entrepreneurship. I. Bock, Adam J.   II. Title.

   T212.G46 2009
   658.4'21—dc22
                                                           2007047252

Editor-in-Chief: *David Parker*
Acquisitions Editor: *Jennifer M. Collins*
Product Development Manager: *Ashley Santora*
Editorial Assistant: *Elizabeth Davis*
Marketing Assistant: *Ian Gold*
Associate Managing Editor: *Suzanne Grappi*
Project Manager, Production: *Ann Pulido*
Permissions Project Manager: *Charles Morris*
Senior Operations Supervisor: *Arnold Vila*
Operations Specialist: *Carol O'Rourke*
Senior Art Director: *Janet Slowik*
Cover Design: *Karen Quigley*
Cover Photo: *Angelo Cavalli/Digital Vision/Getty Images*
Composition: *ICC Macmillan Inc.*
Full-Service Project Management: *Winifred Sanchez/ICC Macmillan Inc.*
Printer/Binder: *STP/RR Donnelley/Harrisonburg*
Typeface: *10/12 Times Ten Roman*

Credits and acknowledgments borrowed from other sources and reproduced, with permission, in this textbook appear on appropriate page within text.

Pearson Education Ltd., London
Pearson Education, Canada, Ltd.
Pearson Education Australia PTY, Limited
Pearson Educación de Mexico, S.A. de C.V.

Pearson Education Singapore, Pte. Ltd.
Pearson Education–Japan
Pearson Education North Asia Ltd.
Pearson Education Malaysia, Pte. Ltd.

10   9   8   7   6   5   4   3   2   1
ISBN-13: 978-0-13-157470-0
ISBN-10:   0-13-157470-1

BRIEF CONTENTS

Chapter 1   Inventing Entrepreneurs   1

PART I   DISCOVERING ENTREPRENEURIAL OPTIONS   11

Chapter 2   Entrepreneurial Purpose   13
Chapter 3   Inventing Entrepreneurial Options   31
Chapter 4   Technology Licensing   43
Chapter 5   Lifestyle Businesses   57

PART II   CULTIVATING AN ENTREPRENEURIAL IDENTITY   69

Chapter 6   The Entrepreneurial Academic   71
Chapter 7   Entrepreneurial Journey Model   81
Chapter 8   Sample Journeys   95

PART III   ASSEMBLING THE ENTREPRENEURIAL TOOL KIT   117

Chapter 9   Understanding Industry Context   119
Chapter 10   Accumulating Business Skills and Knowledge   145
Chapter 11   Primer on Financing the Technology-Based Growth Company   185

PART IV   VISUALIZING THE ROAD AHEAD   205

Chapter 12   The Managerial Challenge   207
Chapter 13   Preparing for Growth   229
Chapter 14   Exit   243

PART V   PRESERVING IDENTITY   261

Chapter 15   Identity, Growth, and Learning on the Journey   263

Name Index   277
Subject Index   281

CONTENTS

Preface   xi

About the Authors   xv

CHAPTER 1   Inventing Entrepreneurs   1

Overview   1

Entrepreneurs as Agents of Change   3

Scientific Innovation and Entrepreneurship   4

Defining the Inventing Entrepreneur   5

Preconditions   6

Organization of This Book   7

Endnotes   9

PART I   DISCOVERING ENTREPRENEURIAL OPTIONS   11

CHAPTER 2   Entrepreneurial Purpose   13

Overview   13

The Decision to Propagate Innovation   13

Introduction to the Commercial Venture Process   14

Foundations of Entrepreneurial Purpose   18

Visualizing the Ultimate Goal   20

Grasping the Significance of the Technology   22

Understanding the Inventor's Affinity Threshold for the Technology   24

*Estimating the Benefits Associated with Commercializing
a Technology   25*

Setting Boundaries for the Need to Control the Technology   26

Conclusions and Summary   29

Endnotes   29

CHAPTER 3   Inventing Entrepreneurial Options   31

Overview   31

Entrepreneurial Intent, Capacity, and Value Creation   31

The "File Drawer Idea" (Low Market Potential, Low
Entrepreneurial Capacity)   34

The Reluctant Entrepreneur (High Market Potential, Low
Entrepreneurial Capacity)   35

The Lifestyle Entrepreneur (Low Market Potential, High
Entrepreneurial Capacity)   35

The Inventing Entrepreneur (High Market Potential, High
Entrepreneurial Capacity)   36

The Inherent Value of Intellectual Property   39

Conclusions and Summary   40

Endnotes   40

CHAPTER 4   Technology Licensing   43

Overview   43

The Technology Transfer Process   45

WARF: A Technology Transfer Office Example   48

Licensing: The TTO Perspective   49

When and Why to License a Technology   51

Conclusions and Summary   53

Endnotes   54

Recommended Readings   55

CHAPTER 5   Lifestyle Businesses   57

Overview   57

The Start-Up Option   57

What Is a Lifestyle Business?   60

The TTO and Lifestyle Businesses   62

Considerations for a Lifestyle Business   63

Entrepreneurial Options   65

Conclusions and Summary   66

Endnotes   67

**PART II   CULTIVATING AN ENTREPRENEURIAL
IDENTITY   69**

CHAPTER 6   The Entrepreneurial Academic   71

Overview   71

Who Are Academic Entrepreneurs?   72

The Intellectual Challenge of Entrepreneurship   73

Business Challenges   74

Access to Mentorship   75
Access to Basic Business Knowledge   76

Personal Challenges   76
Prioritizing Goals   76
*Repercussions Within the Academic Environment—Conflict
     of Interest   77*

Conclusions and Summary   79

Endnotes   80

CHAPTER 7   Entrepreneurial Journey Model   81

Overview   81

Entrepreneurial Identities   82

The Entrepreneurial Journey Model   85

Case Study: TomoTherapy   88

Application of the Journey Model   90

Conclusions and Summary   93

Exercise   94

Endnotes   94

CHAPTER 8   Sample Journeys   95

Overview   95

Journey 1: The Research Transfer Entrepreneur   96

Journey 2: The Sabbatical Entrepreneur   97

Journey 3: The Research-Driven Inventing
Entrepreneur   99

Journey 4: The Dual-Role Inventing Entrepreneur   101

Journey 5: The Corporate Entrepreneur   105

Journey 6: The Business-Focused Inventing Entrepreneur   108

Lessons from the Journey Model   109
*The Venture Path Is Not the Same As the Entrepreneur's
     Journey   110*
Every Journey Is Unique and Personal   110
Is There an Optimal Path?   111
*Capital Intensity and the Viability of Adopting Multiple
     Role Identities   112*
The Journey Transforms the Inventor   113

Conclusions and Summary   114

Exercise   114

Endnotes   115

PART III ASSEMBLING THE ENTREPRENEURIAL TOOL KIT 117

CHAPTER 9 Understanding Industry Context 119

Overview 119

Industries and Markets 120

Industry Attractiveness and the Value Chain 122

Disruptive Technologies 131

Start-Up Location Choices and Their Implications 132

Cost and Differentiation Strategies 134

The New Business Road Test 137

Checking the Basic Premise 138

Conclusions and Summary 141

Endnotes 141

Recommended Readings 143

CHAPTER 10 Accumulating Business Skills and Knowledge 145

Overview 145

Forming the Business 146
> *Timing: When Do You Form a Start-Up? 146*
> *Choice of Legal Entity 147*
> *Allocation of Ownership 150*
> *Selecting Officers and Directors 151*
> *Service Providers 152*

Writing and Using the Business Plan 155
> *Purpose of the Business Plan 156*
> *Preparing to Write the Full Business Plan 156*
> *The Nuts and Bolts of Business Plans 158*
> *Exit Events 166*
> *Getting Help 168*
> *Appendices, Documentation, and Other Issues 168*

Realistic Analyses 169
> *Realistic Customer Analysis 172*
> *Realistic Market Analysis 173*
> *Realistic Competitor Analysis 174*
> *Realistic Budgeting 175*
> *Realistic Revenue Projections 176*

Introduction to Start-Up Financing 177

Conclusions and Summary 180

Endnotes 181

Recommended Readings 183

CHAPTER 11 **Primer on Financing the Technology-Based Growth Company** **185**

Overview 185

Growth Financing 186

Layers of Funding 190

Milestone-Based Financing 192

Obtaining Private Financing 193

Beyond Seed-Stage Financing 199

Conclusions and Summary 201

Endnotes 202

Recommended Reading 203

PART IV VISUALIZING THE ROAD AHEAD **205**

CHAPTER 12 **The Managerial Challenge** **207**

Overview 207

Why Management Is Important 208
Vision and Implementation 211
Management Characteristics and External Perception 212
Risk Reduction 213

Management Models 214

Interacting with Professional Management 216
Natural Conflicts between Founders and Professional Management 216
Creating Mutual Incentives for Success 218
Separating Personal Issues from Business Issues 219

The Inventor as Manager 220
Conflict of Interest 220
Augmenting the Managerial Skill Set 221
Prioritization and Time Constraints 222

Conclusions and Summary 226

Endnotes 227

CHAPTER 13 **Preparing for Growth** **229**

Overview 229

Understanding the Growth Strategy or Growth Type of the Business 230

Transitioning from Project Management to Business Administration 234

Crossing Moore's Chasm 238

The Changing Role of the Inventing Entrepreneur/Founder 240

Conclusions and Summary   241

Endnotes   242

CHAPTER 14   Exit   243

Overview   243

What Is an "Exit"?   245

Types of Exits   246
Financial Exits   246
Participatory Exits   247
Ownership/Control Exits   249

Less Than Perfect Exits   250
A Simplified Negative Exit Example   250
Control of the Organization at Failure   252
Control of the Intellectual Property at Failure   253
Long-Term Outcomes for Inventing Entrepreneurs   254

What Will I Do After the Exit?   255

Conclusions and Summary   257

Endnotes   257

PART V   PRESERVING IDENTITY   261

CHAPTER 15   Identity, Growth, and Learning on the Journey   263

Overview   263

Scientific Identity: Back to the Basics   264

The Underlying Characteristics of Inventing Entrepreneurs   270

Common Experiences of Inventing Entrepreneurs   272
The Importance of Luck   272
The Importance of the Team   273
The Search for Challenge and Growth   274

Conclusions and Summary   275

Endnote   275

Name Index   277

Subject Index   281

PREFACE

You are an inventor. Perhaps you are a biochemist or an electrical engineer or training to be one. Perhaps you're in an academic setting or in a corporate environment. You might be investigating high-energy physics at a government facility, or researching novel plastics for a specialized chemicals company. Perhaps you sometimes conduct basic research investigating naturally occurring phenomena. Or perhaps you are improving on existing technologies or products. You might be a student, you might have prior business experience, or you might be currently managing a research lab with dozens of students and employees. You might be involved in commercializing other innovations or perhaps you are observing other innovators participating in technology commercialization.

Eureka! You've discovered something interesting! You are convinced that your discovery has the potential to create value. You believe that your discovery could benefit companies, industry, individuals, the environment, or the world. *You want to make sure that your innovation is used.*

Can the development of this innovation be a reasonable part of your professional career? Do you have the freedom and resources to commercialize a novel technology? Will you be able to balance the demands of research, development, and commercialization with your family obligations and personal goals? Do you have the experience to bring a product to market? You are concerned that others might have similar inventions. You might also wonder if this is, after all, worth your time, effort, and resources.

You are likely contemplating an entrepreneurial option. Could you start a company? Should you license the technology to another organization? Should you give it away for free? Thousands of innovators have asked these questions, considered these options, made these decisions, and embarked on *entrepreneurial journeys.* You are one of these innovators, someone we refer to as an *inventing entrepreneur*.

IN THIS BOOK

This text summarizes our research on inventing entrepreneurs. We started with our own experiences; they led us around the world and across many scientific disciplines. We met with inventing entrepreneurs who changed the world, and others who never saw their technologies reach the market. Some are chief executive officers (CEOs), professors, corporate scientists; some are retired. We explain in this book the critical factors that spark and fuel these entrepreneurial journeys. In doing so, we identify trends and patterns in the entrepreneurial journey: the underlying decisions, commonalities, and contrasting outcomes.

No two inventing entrepreneurs' journeys are the same. Although most inventing entrepreneurs will pass through similar decision points—many of which have limited options—the path you take will change you, profoundly, in ways and degrees that will vary dramatically from the experiences of everyone else. Idiosyncratic backgrounds, technologies, motivations, and objectives result in unique, personal journeys.

The entrepreneurial journey is not necessarily the same as the commercialization path of the technology. Although some inventing entrepreneurs participate actively in commercialization (e.g., by forming their own company, serving as a consultant to a licensee, or propagating technology from within a research laboratory), many others participate peripherally, or not at all. They hand off the commercialization to market experts, which allows them to focus on new innovations.

OUR PURPOSE

Our purpose, then, is not to tell you how to walk the path—though we hope the collective wisdom of other innovators will help you identify and systematically evaluate your options. Instead, we illustrate the plurality of outcomes that you may experience, and prepare you for some of the surprises that lie ahead.

We believe the biggest surprise will be how the entrepreneurial experience will radically change your life. Nearly every inventing entrepreneur we spoke with talked about the transformative power of entrepreneurship, whether seen from the perspective of the academic scientist advising the commercialization process or from the perspective of the CEO of a high-risk venture. Most inventing entrepreneurs identify with their innovations, and participate closely in the ups and downs of adoption and propagation. Understanding your own definitions of success will help prepare you for the success or failure of your inventions.

To start this book, we review the personal and commercial factors that drive the entrepreneurial decision. We discuss individual purpose, its influence in propagating novel technologies, and the entrepreneurial options available. The core of this book focuses on the researchers and scientists who made an entrepreneurial decision to either work closely with the companies that commercialize technology, become founders of new ventures, or become founders and executive management of new ventures. We discuss *entrepreneurial capacity*—the question of whether individual characteristics and skills match the requirements for a new venture. And we look specifically at the *entrepreneurial academic*—university scientists who have had success in entrepreneurship. We propose a simple framework for mapping *entrepreneurial journeys,* so that you can learn from the experience of other peers and colleagues. We provide tools and insights that help you on your journey. Finally, we revert to a discussion on the individual's *role identity* to see how inventing entrepreneurs can preserve their scientific identity through the entrepreneurial transformation.

We hope you'll find us effective advisors. Between us, we have cofounded five technology companies, extensively researched and studied technology entrepreneurship, evaluated numerous business plans, facilitated significant amounts of venture funding, and interviewed a considerable number of scientists, engineers, researchers, inventors, and entrepreneurs. Regardless of what decisions you make in your entrepreneurial journey—and regardless of the outcome of those decisions—we are inspired to share with you the excitement of being an inventing entrepreneur. Bon voyage!

ABOUT THE AUTHORS

Gerard (Gerry) George is professor and chair of Innovation and Entrepreneurship at Imperial College London, where he serves as the founding director of the Rajiv Gandhi Centre. The Centre facilitates Imperial College's strategic commitments in India for joint research initiatives, technology commercialization, and educational programs in innovation and entrepreneurship. Professor George is an Innovation Fellow of the Advanced Institute of Management (Economic and Social Research Council), UK. The fellowship supports his research on technology entrepreneurship in the UK and elsewhere. He is an expert on managing innovation in technology-based companies and has successfully launched ventures of his own. He serves on the boards of high-technology companies and is actively engaged in guiding start-ups and large companies in technology venturing and entrepreneurship.

Before joining Imperial College, Professor George held tenured positions at the London Business School, where he served as Faculty Director of the Institute of Technology, and at the University of Wisconsin–Madison, where he directed the Applied Ventures in Entrepreneurship Program.

Apart from his work on scientist entrepreneurs, he studies the global diffusion of human embryonic stem cells as well as innovation patterns in the biotechnology industry. Previously, he was chair of the Research Committee (Entrepreneurship Division, Academy of Management) from 2005–2007. He serves on the editorial boards of the *Academy of Management Journal, Journal of Business Venturing,* and *Strategic Entrepreneurship Journal.*

An award-winning researcher and teacher, Professor George has published several articles in leading scholarly journals on the topics of resource constraints in entrepreneurial firms, value creation, absorptive capacity and innovation in large and small organizations.

He lives in London with his wife, Hema, and two daughters, Vivian and Maegan.

Adam J. Bock is currently reading for his Ph.D. at Imperial College London. He has cofounded two early-stage medical device companies and served as interim CEO of a third; all three companies were spin-outs of university research. He spent four years facilitating angel investments in high-technology companies, reviewing more than 1,000 early-stage business plans; this work resulted in nearly $10 million in private investment. Bock has taught entrepreneurship at the University of Wisconsin–Madison School of Business MBA program and has given dozens of seminars on technology evaluation and private financing. He has consulted on technology transfer and the venture start-up process, both for universities and entrepreneurs. For ten years, he has served in an advisory and consulting capacity for The SEED

Foundation, a nonprofit organization in Washington, D.C., that runs the only public boarding schools for underprivileged children in the United States. Prior to receiving his MBA, Bock worked as a consultant for Monitor Group, the strategy consulting firm started by Professor Michael Porter.

Bock earned a BS in Aeronautical Engineering and a BA in Economics from Stanford University, as well as an MBA from the University of Wisconsin–Madison. He lives in Wisconsin with his wife Lynn, son Taran, and daughter Kenna.

CHAPTER 1

INVENTING ENTREPRENEURS

OVERVIEW

We live in an age of entrepreneurship, a period when transformative social changes stem from fundamental inventions and innovations. Extensive research has measured the impact of entrepreneurship on industry growth and on the economy. We know that the majority of job creation comes from entrepreneurial firms and that the list of the world's richest people is becoming almost synonymous with the list of successful growth firms.

Despite the spotlight that has played on entrepreneurship and entrepreneurs, one group of innovators has remained relatively unknown and unstudied—the scientific inventors, the researchers who solve fundamental problems and optimize technological solutions. Historically, these individuals have not generally been the driving force behind commercialization and market development. Within the last 25 years, however, greater numbers of these researchers have taken on the responsibility for bringing innovations to markets. These are inventing entrepreneurs.

We define the inventing entrepreneur as a scientific researcher who works to commercialize his innovations. Consider the case of John Hennessy—currently the president of Stanford University. He was a young addition to the Stanford electrical engineering faculty when his research on reduced instruction set computer (RISC) architecture caught the attention of forward-thinking researchers and entrepreneurs. Rather than focusing solely on the research within the university structure, Hennessy was instrumental in founding a company to commercialize the technology (see Profile 1-1). As a cofounder of MIPS Technologies, Inc. in the early 1980s, he was an early example of the faculty researcher who brought technology out of the university into the commercial world via the mechanism of

---

Professor John Hennessy

John Hennessy, the President of Stanford University, describes himself as a reluctant entrepreneur, but one for whom the entrepreneurial experience was truly transformative. Hennessy now looks back with a critical but enthusiastic eye on founding MIPS Computer Systems, the company that first commercialized RISC architecture. Hennessy states that inspiration for starting a company came from C. Gordon Bell, one of the pioneers of the computer industry:

> Industry was extremely skeptical, extremely skeptical. People said, "You're crazy, have you forged these results?" We were sitting there doing the usual thing, sharing information with people who were interested. There was interest at the Digital Equipment Corporation local research lab on the West Coast. By and large, the mainstream was ignoring us. Gordon Bell came by and said, "You guys should start a company to build this technology, because if you don't, it's going to sit on the shelf. It's too disruptive to the established players for them to do it."

As a young academic, Hennessy hadn't really wanted to start a company, and he planned to return to Stanford:

> My role [chief scientist] was always the same from the beginning my notion was that I was going to go back to the university after spending about a year full time on it, then be involved on a part-time, consulting, summer basis.

But that year (which became a year and a half) and Hennessy's subsequent experiences with entrepreneurship had a significant impact on him:

> It probably was the single most formative year of my life. Coming to Stanford and being a faculty member was more important overall for my career, but if I take just one year, that year was absolutely transforming. I learned so much in that year. People who are in engineering disciplines and spend their whole time in academia really don't understand what it's like in companies. They don't understand how people make decisions. You realize the difference between a product and something you have in a laboratory. You learn about leading people and managing teams; you learn a lot about focus. And you learn that there is a great reward when you build a product and people use it.

One of the most fascinating aspects of Hennessy's experience was its impact on his perceptions about technology transfer:

> More often than not, the right technology-transfer path for a new innovation was a start-up rather than an existing company. The more disruptive the technology is, the higher the probably it has to be transferred by a start-up. You see that time and time again. If you have a discovery that is directly useful for some company's product line, that's fine—then they know how to license it. If you have something that represents a new opportunity for them to establish a whole new product line, that's much harder for them.

Hennessy has firsthand experience of the entrepreneurial roller coaster. The experience of founding a technology-based start-up brings responsibilities and learning opportunities. For Hennessy, founding a start-up was essentially a short detour from a professional career that has led from his first faculty position at Stanford in 1977 to the university president's office. But it was a detour that helped him develop skills, and it's not unreasonable to believe that this short, formative experience contributed to his taking on more responsibilities—responsibilities that include administrative leadership roles at Stanford and a seat on the board of directors of both Cisco and Google:

> Learning to be a professor is important. But all the other skills that I learned from being an administrator, dean, provost, and president, I probably learned more from the time I spent [in the start-up] and subsequent [entrepreneurial activities] than I did anywhere else. Decision making, hiring people, evaluating people—these are things most academics don't do [as] much.

There are few experiences quite like starting a technology-based spin-out of a university research project. Hennessy never doubted his long-term role at the University, but he knows the value of the start-up environment, and its impact on the founders:

> If you're a founder in a company, with that comes a certain mantle of responsibility that puts you in a position of doing things that force you to learn how to navigate in very stormy waters. Those are things that prepare you very well to do that on a larger scale subsequently. It also prepares you to focus and make decisions. At small companies, you have to decide. That's a skill set that's absolutely crucial: to be able to make decisions on less than perfect information—and it happens all the time.

a start-up company. Today, he emphasizes that the world of the high-tech start-up entrepreneur is not always a glamorous one:

> You do everything. I did everything. I wiped counters; I picked up donuts for the guys.... I hired people, I did cold calls, I was the technical evangelist, I went on the road and did cold calls all the time.

In the end, he returned to his faculty role at the university, and eventually to administration. While this isn't always the case, it is useful to hear President Hennessy's comments about why he came back, and why he has remained at Stanford instead of pursuing other entrepreneurial or corporate roles:

> I could have served in any of the senior officer positions, any time I wanted it. But I just loved being an academic, I loved the students. Would I rather [be a CEO than be president of Stanford]? No.... It has to do with breadth and mental stimulation. There is no CEO job in the entire world that has the breadth of this job, because no company has this breadth.

Our goal in this book is to talk about the experience of individuals like Hennessy—individuals who are inventing entrepreneurs.

ENTREPRENEURS AS AGENTS OF CHANGE

Entrepreneurs have always been fundamental change agents in societies. Entrepreneurs recognize opportunities in a market or identify the opportunity to create a new market, and capitalize upon these opportunities by securing resources and methodically building a new business. In many ways, entrepreneurs inspire action and change by figuring out new ways of doing things that either save money or improve productivity. Whether it is cutting blocks of ice from frozen ponds in Boston and shipping them by rail (the railroad network made this novel "ice" industry geographically competitive) to the southern parts of the United States in the late 1800s—or writing software code that enables a graphic user interface—entrepreneurship has evolved from a simple arbitrage or trade enterprise to a complex process of invention, product development, and commercialization. The complexity of these challenges also requires more nuanced explanations of how the process from invention to commercialization unfolds.

In the popular imagination, an entrepreneur is someone who experiences an epiphany, a flash of genius that cannot be resisted. Many popular books pursue this idea and view entrepreneurs as inspired individuals who amass their riches by being visionaries who risk everything and toil for the pursuit of wealth. While this approach has intuitive merits and reflects the story of some successful entrepreneurs, focusing exclusively on successes and the underlying entrepreneurial "philosophy" ignores large segments of the entrepreneur population. In particular, it misses entrepreneurs who methodically incubate a venture from a lab bench discovery to a viable product. In addition, any attention that is focused on these "inventing entrepreneurs" usually targets the technology and the market opportunity (i.e., the potential to treat Alzheimer's disease), rather than the entrepreneur's journey. These entrepreneurs create a company because their invention holds a greater purpose of societal benefit; they are impelled to act because larger companies do not find an appropriate use for their invention or it does not fit the companies' existing business model. Perhaps these entrepreneurs even have an internal passion that cannot be quenched in their existing jobs or roles.

SCIENTIFIC INNOVATION AND ENTREPRENEURSHIP

In this book, we describe people whose inventions were the culmination of years of hard work—opportunities that have taken time in the making. This type of entrepreneur propagates technology not by launching grand plans or by envisioning opportunities but by systematically exploring alternatives that may be moderately risky but whose perception of societal and economic benefit exceeds the risk associated with the attempt. It is important to understand not only the product concept that creates a business but also how the business transforms the individual. In this book, we capture entrepreneurial journeys and describe how these scientists and inventors have propagated novel technologies—usually by creating and sustaining fledgling enterprises that have transformed their lives.

Our observations and conclusions are based on a comprehensive and systematic research project conducted over a five-year period. We interviewed scientists and innovators to identify the drivers underlying the adoption of an entrepreneurial identity: how scientists form their identity as entrepreneurs in addition to their core identity as scientists or inventors. In all cases, our research team invested a substantial amount of time in background research on each scientist, which provided us with information on the individual's inventive activity and entrepreneurial ventures. We conducted detailed interviews with academic technology-transfer managers, business people, and administrators to better understand the broader context of technology commercialization. We also examined historical interviews of inventors from the past and conducted surveys of scientists. By comparing the common impediments to and enablers of technology entrepreneurship, we can identify the influence of personal disposition on the venture-creation process. This book also effectively translates published academic articles in this subject area that have been written by the authors and other leading researchers.

DEFINING THE INVENTING ENTREPRENEUR

We have chosen to focus on and clarify the myths surrounding **inventing entrepreneurs**—the individuals, usually scientists and/or researchers, who have developed new technologies (inventions) or technology applications (innovations) in order to solve unmet market needs or create new markets. These individuals may work at research universities or at corporations focused on research and development (R&D); or in some cases, they may independently pursue invention as a hobby. All these individuals, whatever their primary career realize that the technology will need resources and perhaps a base outside the originating institution to reach its full potential. The paths available to these entrepreneurs, at least initially, are limited. The technology can remain in the parent institution indefinitely; it can be "spun out" into a start-up company; it can be licensed or sold to an existing third party; or it can be given away or abandoned. An entrepreneur is someone who is willing and eager to create a new venture in order to present a concept to the marketplace, whether in a start-up context or in an established organization (private, public, or nonprofit). We extend this definition to encompass the inventing entrepreneur as a technology innovator or developer who is willing and eager to see her technology solve problems in the broader market or establish entirely new markets.

Inventing entrepreneurs are distinct from traditional entrepreneurs exemplified by such icons as Henry Ford, George Soros, or Bill Gates. Inventing entrepreneurs come from an entirely different training paradigm, and often have no intention of creating wealth or even commercially viable products or services. The vast majority of inventing entrepreneurs were initially driven by the desire to solve a problem or extend the reach of scientific knowledge as appropriate challenges in and of themselves. These innovators bring to the creative process a sense of organized skepticism[1]—an extension of the scientific method in which dispassionate inquiry may generate results that overturn established thinking or expectations. Within the research context, the scientist assumes that any novel technology or innovation won't solve a problem until empirical data show otherwise. At some level, this philosophy is only partly viable in a commercial setting where conviction in the technology and product is paramount for gaining customer confidence and securing resources for business growth.

Entrepreneurship is often referred to as the pursuit of opportunities without regard to the resources at hand—a process that for most academic researchers would be somewhat difficult to envision or execute. Scientists tend to be inherently more cautious than traditional entrepreneurs because of the critical nature of scientific peer review and the fact that they are trained to methodically search for new solutions with a sense of detachment and skepticism. This process of scientific research creates a generally slower commercial process—with fewer novel ideas entering into the "market" (because more have been reviewed and rejected on a "premarket" basis). Commerce requires a higher risk tolerance, a willingness to take chances, be wrong, and try again. Consider what is implied by the difference between failure in the market and failure within the scientific community. We all have stories and examples of business executives who failed one or more times before hitting a huge success, or who succeeded, only to fail and eventually succeed again. Within the scientific community, however, such failure is anathema; consider the example of Fleishman and Pons, whose cold-fusion controversy has become a generic name for unproven, extraordinary results.[2]

In another sense, academic researchers may have the specialized skills and knowledge to take advantage of entrepreneurial opportunities. Entrepreneurship is broadly defined as the process of creating value by bringing together a unique combination of resources to exploit an opportunity.[3,4] Inventing entrepreneurs are uniquely positioned to see possible technological solutions as well as market applications, even if the latter are often identified at the highest level of abstraction (i.e., a broad market need, such as hydrogen power) rather than at the level of customer need where the actual purchase takes place (i.e., a specific application, such as long-lasting laptop batteries for business travelers, that solves problems for a clearly identified group of end users). We infer that inventing entrepreneurs undergo philosophical transformations in their entrepreneurial journey that range from tolerance of commercial uncertainty to the enthusiastic adoption of entrepreneurial beliefs and behaviors.

In this book, we suggest that inventing entrepreneurs employ a genuine "local" optimism tempered with a "global" skepticism.[5] Inventing entrepreneurs do not give up their broadest adherence to scientific principles or rational skepticism. Instead, most come to grips with some of the additional uncertainty inherent in the business environment and the reality that the market often rewards significant leaps of faith. The inventing entrepreneur, therefore, may need to come to terms with having to make decisions on the basis of information that is less than adequate for taking the new venture through an often challenging obstacle course.

PRECONDITIONS

To initiate our investigation into the journeys of inventing entrepreneurs, it is useful to briefly examine the preconditions that must exist.

An *inventing entrepreneur* has developed a new technology or technological advance.

An *inventing entrepreneur* believes that the marketplace, in one form or another, is the final test of technology-based applications.

An *inventing entrepreneur* may or may not lead the endeavor to commercialize a new technology but shares in some incentive for the success of that commercialization.

It would be relatively easy to extrapolate from these definitions either that greed is a necessary component of entrepreneurship or that entrepreneurship requires a renunciation of scientific ethos—but neither is correct. Many inventing entrepreneurs never leave their primary institutions, and many do not anticipate financial rewards from their inventions (some do not receive financial rewards for a variety of reasons). In fact, our own research suggests that while many inventing entrepreneurs are now aware of the potential for financial rewards, such rewards are not the primary driver of their work.[6]

When we asked Dr. Michael Sussman if he would be upset to receive little financial benefit from his seven years of consistent effort in starting and supporting NimbleGen Systems (a developer of advanced tools for genomics analysis), he responded with an emphatic "No." "I did this because of the scientific and intellectual challenge," he explained, "and because the research had the potential to help so many other researchers, and eventually the health-care community." At the same time, some inventing entrepreneurs leave their "ivory tower" for the capitalist battlefield and never return. What we saw in our research is that there are several viable paths for an inventing entrepreneur, and each path has its own risks and rewards. In most cases, individuals tend to contemplate and pursue a path that fits best with their ultimate purpose for entering the entrepreneurial fray.

ORGANIZATION OF THIS BOOK

To understand and evaluate this entrepreneurial process that starts with an invention and ends with commercialization, we highlight five specific milestones in the entrepreneurial journey. The entrepreneurial process is triggered by an idea or invention. Consequently, the inventors face a distinct choice about how to proceed—about whether to create a start-up or perhaps license the technology. If the decision is to create a start-up, then the inventor elects to become an inventing entrepreneur. If successful, the venture may experience stages of maturation. The "growth" stage represents a series of challenges as well as opportunities to expand the market for the newly generated venture. The "exit" stage may offer options for harvesting value to owners, usually by the sale of the company or its assets to another firm. In Figure 1-1 these milestones are connected by the underlying five specific subprocesses that comprise the larger entrepreneurial process.

For the inventing entrepreneur, the entrepreneurial process from idea to exit can be unpacked into the subprocesses of discovering entrepreneurial options, cultivating an entrepreneurial identity, assembling a tool kit to build the business,

FIGURE 1-1 Stages in the Entrepreneurial Process

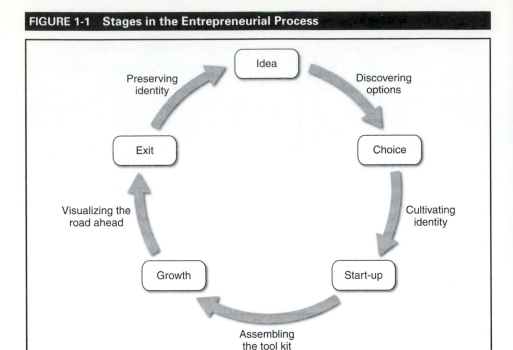

and visualizing a growth plan. By contrast with entrepreneurs who are not primarily research scientists, the inventing entrepreneur attempts to preserve her original scientific identity after her exit from the business and reverts, in many cases, back to her academic or technological background. We conceptualize this entire process of idea to exit to return to the lab as an **entrepreneurial journey** during which the inventor manages her social identity as both an inventor and entrepreneur in order to succeed at this new venture. For further clarity, this book is subdivided into five sections that reflect these subprocesses of the entrepreneurial journey.

In this book, we hope to shed light on one of the most fascinating developments in the business world: the rise in prominence of the academic or scientific entrepreneur. While not all inventing entrepreneurs are academics, our focus is on innovators with scientific training. The unique training and experience that defines these individuals suggest they may experience entrepreneurship and the entire commercialization process differently than traditional entrepreneurs. We encourage innovators reading this book to be introspective and honest in evaluating their intentions and goals. Only the aspiring entrepreneur can evaluate these issues for herself. Once the journey has begun, especially if a commercial venture has been initiated, it becomes much more difficult to implement significant changes to accommodate revised goals.

Endnotes

1. Merton, R. K. 1973. *The Sociology of Science: Theoretical and Empirical Investigation.* Chicago: University of Chicago Press.
2. www.en.wikipedia.org/wiki/Cold_fusion
3. Kirzner, I. 1973. *Competition and Entrepreneurship.* Chicago: University of Chicago Press.
4. Shane, S. 2000. Prior knowledge and the discovery of entrepreneurial opportunities. *Organization Science,* 11(4): 448–469.
5. "Think globally, act locally" is a maxim credited to Rene Dubos, a French-born American microbiologist, experimental pathologist, environmentalist, humanist, and Pulitzer Prize–winning author.
6. George, G., Jain, S., & Maltarich, M. 2005. Academics or entrepreneurs? Entrepreneurial identity and invention disclosure behavior of university scientists. Paper presented at the Academy of Management Meeting, Honolulu, Hawaii.

DISCOVERING ENTREPRENEURIAL OPTIONS

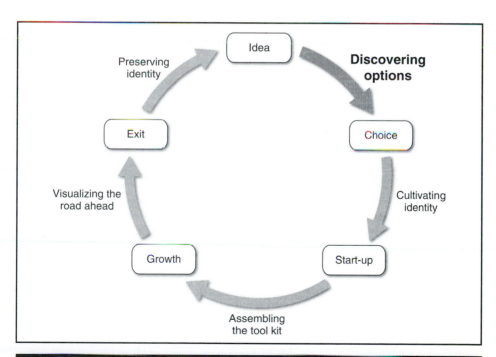

Stages in the Entrepreneurial Process

CHAPTER 2

ENTREPRENEURIAL PURPOSE

OVERVIEW

Entrepreneurs approach the role of change agent from many perspectives. For inventing entrepreneurs, the *personal role* or *purpose* of entrepreneurial activity necessarily incorporates consideration of the broad principles of scientific discovery, ownership of innovation, and commercialization intent. As part opener figure shows, the inventor must consider the options available once the idea has been developed. In this chapter, we discuss some of the common factors that influence entrepreneurial purpose.

THE DECISION TO PROPAGATE INNOVATION

For most inventing entrepreneurs, the purpose of research on innovative technology is to expand the reach of human knowledge or to solve intellectually challenging problems within a specific field of expertise. While some inventing entrepreneurs are aware of a potential commercial application for their inventions, many (if not most) conduct scientific research without specific commercial intent in mind. At some point, however, each inventing entrepreneur realizes that the impact of his innovation extends beyond the laboratory into the world of commerce. At this juncture, the inventing entrepreneur decides to propagate or widely disseminate a technology using commercial means (corporations, licensing, and product development) rather than academic means (journal publications or free distribution of biological or software materials to academic peers). By initiating this process, the innovator implicitly develops a secondary purpose, which could include the widespread dissemination of technology, financial rewards, or other goals.

The propagation decision is the point at which the innovator determines that the innovation has commercial value. Most inventing entrepreneurs we've spoken with described the propagation decision to be, in retrospect, strikingly complex and ill defined. Yet many made their decisions based on a single factor that was almost always be directly associated with their perspective on propagation. ("The university wanted us to form a company." "I didn't want to see my technology licensed to a big corporation where it wouldn't receive the attention it deserves." "The only way I could get this into the market was by moving it into a different organization." "I was the only person who could bring this to the market.") Realistically, many of these decisions appear to be made either informally or simply by default. In addition, as the incidence of university start-ups becomes pervasive, more scientists have begun to see such start-ups as a means by which to benefit fairly and appropriately from years of hard work. But few inventing entrepreneurs we talked to really understood what the lifestyle and workplace implications would be at the time of the decision. Most entrepreneurs fail to realistically estimate the time commitments and legal implications that follow from commercialization decisions. Most inventors also receive limited (if any) mentoring from other inventing entrepreneurs; strikingly few have business experience or knowledge of the basic administrative steps associated with bringing a new product or service to market.

INTRODUCTION TO THE COMMERCIAL VENTURE PROCESS

Although we'll discuss in detail the various commercialization options in Chapter 3, some notes on creating a start-up venture are warranted here. The increased visibility of private finance for start-up technology companies (primarily venture capital and angel capital), combined with the significant success of some university spin-outs, has resulted in a dramatic shift in technology transfer policies at major research universities.[1,2] Partly as a consequence of these factors, the activities and goals of major university technology transfer offices (TTOs) have been redirected toward equity ownership in start-ups (as opposed to near-term cash or royalty revenues), suggesting to many university researchers that the start-up is the preferred mechanism for commercialization.[3,4] For example, one of the most successful technology transfer organizations in Europe is housed at Imperial College, London. Imperial College has bundled its intellectual property and created a publicly traded company, Imperial Innovations Ltd. The funds raised from this capital market listing are being used to fund more than 60 technology start-ups.

Regardless of whether the start-up is the best vehicle for commercialization, it is useful to note that successful technology-based growth businesses generate the greatest financial rewards for the financiers—which are often venture-capital firms and their investors. Founding scientists can become wealthy from the success of start-ups but not by owning a majority share of the companies they start.

John Nesheim discovered in his research: "Founders other than the CEO rarely owned more than 4% [of the company] at IPO time."[5,6] In most of the IPO examples that Nesheim reviewed, the venture capitalists and other private financiers owned 30% to 80% of the company at the time of IPO.[7] Despite these data, our interviews suggested that most inventing entrepreneurs did not see their innovations and ventures as vehicles through which venture capitalists could generate significant financial rewards, nor did they immediately realize that they would likely be relatively small stakeholders at the time of a significant exit event (i.e., acquisition of the company or IPO). For the most part, inventing entrepreneurs are not naïve; many hope to create personal wealth from their ventures. Regardless, wealth creation tends not to be the primary driver for starting a new business.

Some university scientists (and possibly corporate R&D scientists) are surprised to discover that their innovations may need to pass through a *commercial process* that rewards highly resourced industry participants rather than the creators of inventions disseminated for the "common good." But we did find examples of researchers with very different visions. Professor Miron Livny, the developer of the Condor distributed computing technology, believes that this technology has a broad purpose in the democratization of computing resources. His entrepreneurial vision has resulted in a large academic program at the University of Wisconsin–Madison, developing and supporting the technology for a wide variety of corporate and academic users in a not-for-profit context. Professor Livny's experience and his unique vision for technology commercialization are depicted in Profile 2-1.

INVENTING ENTREPRENEUR PROFILE 2-1

Miron Livny and Condor

Professor Miron Livny provides an example of the successful inventing entrepreneur within the academic environment. The Condor technology, a pioneering distributed computing system,[8] remains rooted in the Computer Science department at the University of Wisconsin–Madison—while being used by thousands of clients worldwide, including Fortune 100 companies. The multi-million dollar program has grown to nearly 35 staff in every functional area: systems theory, software engineering and development, and customer support. In the broadest sense, the Condor technology solves a deceptively simple problem. Professor Livny explains:

> Having a customer waiting for a resource, and having a resource available, and not bringing them together doesn't make sense. That's what Condor is designed to do…. The reason we can do this after 20 years without being accused of being senile or crazy is the underlying principle beyond the technology. Today we're doing it with data and storage. Another component that is fundamental to Condor is the concept of matchmaking. If you are in a situation where someone wants computational power, and someone else is willing to allocate excess capacity, then you have a match. But you must still ask, "What is the purpose of the engagement?"

(continues)

But this also represents a point of departure for the commercialization potential of the technology. There can be no question of the value of "matchmaking" information technology resources with needs (SETI@Home and Folding@Home are popular desktop examples), but Professor Livny's personal mission doesn't necessarily incorporate the commercial profit motive that would drive a traditional business model. When asked about the applications for the technology, his response shows his focus on problem solving, rather than market-making:

> As a computer scientist, at some level you don't care. If you come and say, "Look, I have an application here and a resource here, how do I bring them together?"—we start realizing that workstations are becoming common technology, we start introducing the concept of distributed ownership.... The bottom line is what we are trying to do, at least to do it right, is to motivate things by principles that are independent of technology.

Professor Livny isn't unaware of the commercial markets, or the value of technology to the university. The technology has been made available for commercial licensing under various circumstances, and was licensed to IBM. A start-up company licensed the technology and attempted to establish a more market-facing model for distributing and supporting the software. In the end, however, Professor Livny believes that this particular commercialization effort (via the start-up) may have been doomed to fail.

The motivation for the continuing development of the Condor system has been rooted in the information technology (IT) support model. IT has become a fundamental building block for nearly every branch of scientific research. And there is a natural tension between the need for processing and modeling power and the cost of that power. As Moore's Law has held true decade after decade,[9] the desktop availability of what was once supercomputer power creates both freedom and dependence. Livny describes the tension between computing capacity and the way that capacity is utilized:

> Technology is definitely a very strong motivator here—which is the reduction in the cost/performance ratio of computing capacity and networking. This is a computing trend, but this is also a meta-trend. Computing power is getting cheaper and cheaper; networking is becoming more and more powerful and available; and we can build communities.... That's the technology part. When we start implementing these types of communities, then we have to worry about the principles.... Science is becoming more and more dependent on IT.... Today, it's almost scary how dependent more and more scientists are on computing technology. If we disappeared, there are very few people who could just do it with paper and pencil and a wet lab.

Professor Livny sees the mission as a significant effort to enable advancement in the various sciences. And his own interpretation of the value of the software system provides a fascinating insight into some of his own motivations and rationale for propagating the technology:

> Software doesn't have real value. What has value is the software with the people. Software is a living entity, and therefore we have a problem with the university structure, because we're not well positioned to sell. You have to sell the package. It's not like a patent: You take it, you define it, you own it. The inventor can go and do something completely different and the patent stays.... It was fascinating to work with [the TTO]. What do we give you? Do we give you the version of today? What about the version of tomorrow? What does it mean to give the right [to use or sell the technology] to the company? Is it today's technology, tomorrow's

technology? And [the TTO] doesn't know what to do with it. It's a hard problem. So when you're trying to create a legal relationship between a commercial entity and an activity within the university, it requires creativity and ingenuity that were not there. I still believe that the only way to [commercialize this technology] is for the university to do it.

Of course, the logistics of a functioning software development and support system operating entirely within the academic environment presents a series of challenges and issues. In this sense, Professor Livny's perspective varies widely from that of many of his colleagues who have actively commercialized their innovations. Professor Livny even has his own perspective on the role of the intellectual property and technology transfer office. But he's also had to adjust to the loss of certain freedoms in managing the growth of his group:

> There were two problems—it's very different, computer science, the scientific community in general and computer science as the special case—it's not used to long-term support of software. What also was difficult was that in the '90s everyone was into high-performance computing; how to sustain Condor became more and more difficult. What also became clear was that people were taking advantage of our technology in a way that made us less competitive in the academic market. Today I'm bringing in $4–5 million a year; so you're running a business, and competing in the market. It's a business. Condor helps the biologists, and the result is that they are coming up with another patent, and that helps the university. I'm not certain that people are thinking about it this way, but we should be thinking about it strategically.

The continuing success of the Condor group is a strong testament to the vision and drive that Professor Livny brings to the computer science world. He is philosophical about the alternate paths he could have taken but his fundamental passion for the purpose and value of information technology is unshaken. In addition, Professor Livny has an overriding respect for the academic mission in general. He also respects competent business people, but he feels strongly that the two may not be easily combined:

> I think that it taught me about the "ins and outs" of managing a business—but that it also taught me about the need for complete separation. I don't think there is a middle way—the worlds are so fundamentally different—the commercial and academic worlds. If there's anyone in the world doing this better, then we should stop doing it. We should do something we are the best at or stop doing it at all.

Professor Livny describes his belief in the power of information technology as "almost a religion." That faith has clearly been a seminal factor in his efforts to propagate the Condor technology for its broadest possible benefits:

> How important is it for us to be enablers for other scientists? Part of my mission in being in the university is to enable a researcher in biotech to do his science. There was another group that offered us money in terms of having a partnership, but we weren't interested because part of the motivation of Condor is that the software should be available for everyone to use, because that's the only way you can enable small groups to come together to create a significant computing environment. I argue that distributed systems support democratization of computing. So there is open availability of the software built into the religion, so to speak. We aren't doing it just because we like the technology; we also believe we're doing something right!

Despite the surprises, miscalculations, and disillusionments experienced by some inventing entrepreneurs who choose the start-up route, most feel good about the journey—even the ones who experience partial or total failure in their commercial venture. In our research, nearly all inventing entrepreneurs described their journey as a learning process; an opportunity to be challenged and tested. Therefore, certain aspects of the academic researchers' mindset—especially those related to the development of novel solutions—are well adapted to the intellectual rigor of entrepreneurship, regardless of the level of involvement the inventing entrepreneur assumes.

FOUNDATIONS OF ENTREPRENEURIAL PURPOSE

The path to commercial success usually provokes concerns about control and decision making even among the most seasoned inventors. Our investigations suggest that these concerns most often stem from the inventing entrepreneur's failure to clarify her ultimate entrepreneurial purpose. Entrepreneurial purpose can be made even more complex and confusing when a team of inventing entrepreneurs is involved, rather than just an individual. Recently, one of us was asked to meet with a team of academic researchers looking to commercialize a novel water purification technology. It quickly became apparent that the three team members had dramatically different definitions of commercial success. One was close to retirement and wanted a nest egg or inheritance for his grandchildren. The second simply wanted to pay off his mortgages. The third team member was hoping to see the technology improve quality of life in impoverished third-world communities that have limited access to clean water. It should be self-evident that differences in purpose *within* teams of inventing entrepreneurs can make the commercialization process more complicated.

In this section, we articulate five strategic dimensions as the foundations of entrepreneurial purpose. The inventor will need clarity about each dimension to determine whether to strive to become an inventing entrepreneur. Individuals contemplating entrepreneurship are strongly encouraged to consider the "Five Foundations of Entrepreneurial Purpose" listed in Table 2-1 to evaluate their own goals and needs, and to prepare themselves for some of the changes and conflicts that the commercialization process will entail. To facilitate dialog, we have provided representative questions in Table 2-1. The inventor's responses to these questions are important because they shape the individual's perception of the commercialization process as well as attitude toward the entrepreneurial process and its potential outcomes.

Consider again the case of Professor Miron Livny, someone who has propagated the Condor technology from within the university structure rather than through corporate licensing or start-ups. In part, Professor Livny believes in focusing on his own strengths as an academic as well as on his academic mission:

TABLE 2-1 **Five Foundations of Entrepreneurial Purpose**	
Foundations	*Representative Questions*
Visualizing the ultimate goal	• What is your long-term goal for the innovation? • Are you attempting to solve a problem or encourage the use of a specific innovation? • What must happen for you to consider the innovation successful?
Grasping the significance of the technology	• Can you realistically assess the potential impact of the innovation on specific markets or industries? • Are there social implications (utilization by underserved populations, wealth distribution, and ecological impacts)?
Understanding the inventor's affinity threshold for the technology	• Do you attribute your own success or worth to the success of your research and/or innovations? • Do you expect others to evaluate your success based on the validity or success of your research and/or innovations? • Do you closely identify yourself with people and institutions focused on this area of research and innovation? • If this particular innovation were invalidated or unsuccessful in the market, would it impact your assessment of your personal success?
Estimating the benefits associated with commercializing a technology	• Who should benefit most from the potential success of your innovation? • Will there be significant financial benefits? • Are those financial benefits associated with cost reductions, new applications, or new markets? • Will there be social or other significant benefits not directly associated with sales?
Setting boundaries for the need to control the technology	• Who should have the right to determine how the technology is utilized? • Who should be involved in managing day-to-day operations of the commercialization entity? • Who should be involved in long-term strategic decisions relating to technology development and application?

I believe in the model that we should do what we are good at — being academicians. People who want to do business should do business if they are good at it. We can talk about why we should do it in the university: Should we stop doing Condor and do something else because it is not in our academic mission? I believe it is our mission and I think we are fortunate to be one of the very few to do it.

VISUALIZING THE ULTIMATE GOAL

For many traditional entrepreneurs, the ultimate goal combines the adoption of a novel product by the market with the prospect of financial success. Inventing entrepreneurs (at least, in their first iteration) often initiate their journey with slightly different purposes. Some inventing entrepreneurs aspire to make a positive impact on society through their inventions, whereas others see the commercial and technology application as the successful culmination of their long-term scientific research stream. Social benefit, career actualization, and intellectual challenge are often combined into an overarching goal as well. Some inventing entrepreneurs maintain altruistic ideals throughout the journey, while others add more commercial and financial outcomes to their set purpose.

Professor Ron Raines, for example, has developed a complex set of intertwining goals around the commercialization of technologies developed both in his own and related biochemistry labs. Raines specifically wants to develop novel therapeutics, both because the technologies present unique product development options but also because of the challenge and scope of the endeavor. In addition, he wants to impact local economic development, partly because of his affinity to the community. Profile 2-2 describes Professor Raines' experience, including some of the unusual factors that led him to become an inventing entrepreneur.

INVENTING ENTREPRENEUR PROFILE 2-2

Professor Ron Raines and Quintessence

For Professor Ron Raines, one of the most formative experiences leading to his entrepreneurial efforts was a summer spent at Chiron Corporation. Raines was enrolled in a postdoctoral program at the University of California at San Francisco (UCSF), working in Bill Rutter's lab. Rutter was one of the founders of Chiron. Raines remembers:

> He ran the company as well as running a research lab that was as big or bigger than mine, which is kind of amazing. I think it was hard to do both in a really conscientious way. I spent a summer or six months at Chiron while I was a post-doc. I asked Bill if I could have a desk at Chiron, and he said "sure." And because I worked for the boss I had keys to the place and I was treated very well, and I basically had my run of the place.... It was great. For four to six months, it was really beneficial, and I met all the scientists and I found out what it was like in a biotech company. That basically taught me that it could be done and that I could do it.

That entrepreneurial vision lay dormant for many years, but Raines stayed connected to the corporate world. After taking a position at the University of Wisconsin–Madison, Raines made a point of learning about the local biotechnology community:

> I made efforts to get to know people in local [biotech] companies.... Early on, within my first two or three years, I had already befriended people and written Small Business Innovation Research [SBIR] grants with them, which brought me some collaboration and equipment, and I think I just branched out from there. I was interested enough in start-ups that I invested in [a local biotech start-up], and I got to know those guys as well. Then, I saw some of my colleagues do a start-up, and I thought, "I can do this too."

Technologies in his lab and a related lab appeared to have commercial promise. They included neobiopolymers for metastasizing chemical reactions and cancer-cell-killing ribonucleases, along with three other technologies from Raines' research. Raines formed Quintessence Biosciences, Inc. and licensed the technologies from the Wisconsin Alumni Research Foundation (WARF). Then he went on sabbatical to try to get the company off the ground:

> We actually have a suite of technologies that are related only in the broadest sense; they are all biochemical. I like the fact that my lab is very broad and diverse because of that—we have a suite of technologies that could allow a company a lot of flexibility in development. If something looks like it isn't working out, we can shift resources. If something is on the backburner, but turned out to be super-hot because of development elsewhere, we can take it off the backburner and put it on the frontburner. We hired a graduate student, Laura Strong, and she has always been entrepreneurial. We hired her to be the first employee, and she helped with those initial phases—helping me raise money from the angel group, present at venture fairs, talk to venture capitalists.... We paid her out of our pockets.

But the process was slow. Raines attributes part of the problem to the company's breadth of technology:

> This leads to some difficulties.... In terms of funding, a lot of people want to see you focus on one thing; they can truly understand what this company is about. Another way to think about it is that the investor would have to trust management because there would be these decisions to make to meet the challenges.

Raines was also learning that seeking venture funds was, as he put it, "not something I wanted to do for a living." Raines states that, in the end, the most important thing that came out of the sabbatical was his hiring of an experienced chief executive officer (CEO), a serial entrepreneur in the biotechnology space that Ron had originally approached as a potential investor.

For Raines, the "I can do this" thought engendered in a Chiron lab evolved into a more mature perspective about his own goals:

> I don't think I could be [the CEO]. I think he has a unique skill set. He has an amazing skill set. He is great at being the CEO. As for me, I think being CEO is hard.... With the science, it's me against nature—there are no other people involved. In talking to VCs [venture capitalists], the experience was really interesting. A lot of the VCs are really smart, which was kind of a surprise to me. A lot of them were shockingly smart. They knew about science and a lot about funding. That was really enlightening to me. But what was difficult about it was—that the decision-making process they used—I thought there was arbitrariness to it that I just didn't understand . . . and couldn't control. I really like academic research. At the company you have to be so focused on applications you can't really do basic science. I like basic science.

Not that Raines has reduced his vision for the business. His knowledge about how the industry functions helped shape his commercial thinking:

> I wanted to develop a therapeutic.... There are three products that biotech companies sell. Reagents—you might put them on the lowest tier in that there's no barrier to entry but there's intense competition. Diagnostics would be the next level, where there are some barriers to entry; there might be some FDA approval [to obtain]. The highest level, therapeutics, is the billion-dollar molecule that really brings in the big bucks; you have to sell an awful lot of chemical assay kits to equal one Prozac.

Inventing entrepreneurs need to identify commercialization paths that best match their goals. We suspect that post hoc rationalization allows many entrepreneurs to justify decisions that were the result of naiveté, lack of introspection, or just lack of information. We believe, however, that inventing entrepreneurs who explicate clear "end states" have the greatest potential for self-actualization. The following list summarizes key issues inventing entrepreneurs need to consider as they evaluate personal purpose:

- Personal long-term goals and needs (e.g., visibility, financial security, achievement)
- Career stage (e.g., tenured full professor) or research phase (e.g., established lab)
- Enthusiasm for the technology and its future development trajectory
- Desire to give back to the community and ability to define both what it means to give back and how it should be done
- Recognition from the community for contributions and an understanding of the best way to achieve it

Understanding and appreciating these factors should help the novice inventing entrepreneur evaluate his commitment to the entrepreneurial process. This is critical because the vast majority of research scientists do not necessarily define success based on a new venture. Professor James Thomson, the pioneer of embryonic stem cells, emphasized the importance of that type of academic ideal:

> Ultimately, you go into academics because you love a certain area. It's very good to keep track of the fact that what you do does have commercial interest. It's important when you publish that you actually think it through a little bit and ask, "Does this have commercial value?" The process of going through [the tech transfer office] is pretty painless, and it doesn't take a lot of your time to file something, but at the end of the day that's probably not why you're at the university—and that's a good thing.

Thomson's comments underscore our emphasis on visualizing the goal. Most inventing entrepreneurs tend to hold the pursuit of science above the commercial potential of their research. It is important to acknowledge that inventions from the lab bench can have commercial potential, because truly innovative technologies are likely to be commercialized by *someone,* even if it is not the inventor.

GRASPING THE SIGNIFICANCE OF THE TECHNOLOGY

Entrepreneurs tend to be optimists—individuals who instinctively say "let's make it happen."[10] Presented with the fact that most technology-based start-ups fail, entrepreneurs are likely to simply respond, "Not mine." Our anecdotal experience is that the inventing entrepreneur, like the traditional entrepreneur, usually allows her own technology affinity to bias evaluation of commercial potential. Some technologies are truly revolutionary (or the application of the technology is revolutionary), but the waste bins of venture capitalists (VCs) and angel networks are littered with the business plans of inventing entrepreneurs who all committed the same error: overestimating the market potential of the technology.

In many cases, technology is developed based on an application hypothesis (e.g., "I've come up with a novel technology based on resolving a fundamental research question. I've heard this could be useful in a given industry—let me see if I can figure out how someone could use it"). These "products in search of markets" can succeed, but such single-minded pursuit often focuses on evolving technology development, rather than product development. A common problem for these entrepreneurs is simply a lack of direct interaction with customers that would help establish likely commercial potential. Will the technology improve or replace existing products and technologies? Is this a "marginal" or "radical" departure from existing technologies or technological infrastructure? Inventing entrepreneurs would do well to note that many successful technology companies don't derive their greatest success from their first product. This also explains why investors have so much at stake when it comes to the qualifications of the management team—investors know that success may likely emerge from nimbly meeting market needs rather than doggedly pushing a specific technology solution despite negative market feedback.

Professor Hector DeLuca is one of the pioneers of vitamin D innovations and the cofounder of Bone Care International, a company commercializing some of the therapeutics that he developed. DeLuca notes that although the company initially targeted osteoporosis, a dramatic change in direction toward targeting end-stage renal failure eventually drove the success of the business.[11] This is not an uncommon occurrence for growth technology companies; sometimes the best market opportunity is discovered or revealed through a process of time and effort.

Sometimes the significance of the technology may exceed even the entrepreneurs' expectations. In these cases, the entrepreneur may fail to calculate the resource requirements, potentially dooming the venture to constrained growth or even total failure. In Figure 2-2, we depict a stylistic model of the relationship

FIGURE 2-2 Technology-Based Start-Up Company Complexity

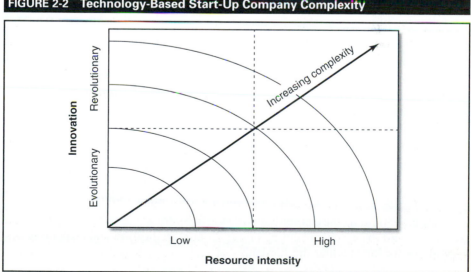

between the radical nature of the innovation and its resource requirements. For example, when Stanford's John Hennessy approached venture capitalists about his new computer processor design, everyone knew that development and manufacturing would be resource intensive. Professor Hennessy also believed the technology was revolutionary, because it redesigned the processor from the ground up, on the basis of a reduced instruction set. This combination of high design and manufacturing cost meant that the business would have a high level of resource intensity. On the other hand, Genetics Computer Group, one of the first companies to provide bioinformatics software, may have represented a relatively low resource-intensive opportunity (as many software technologies do, at least initially), even though it represented an important step forward in the automation of genetic sequencing.[12]

Revolutionary technologies, in general, tend to present greater difficulties with regard to market assessment. Industry-changing technologies usually face extensive barriers to adoption. More resource-intensive technologies will require greater investment (usually in the form of outside capital) to reach commercialization. An inventing entrepreneur may be able to gauge the relative complexity or difficulty of propagation by considering the resource intensity of the development, manufacturing, and distribution processes and the extent to which adoption would require a change in the mindset of customers and industry.

UNDERSTANDING THE INVENTOR'S AFFINITY THRESHOLD FOR THE TECHNOLOGY

In adapting the concept of "affinity threshold" from biochemistry, we hope to reinforce the analogous conceptual elements of protein binding. Just as enzymes have relative binding affinities to certain molecules, some researchers uniquely identify with a specific research stream or technology innovation. The identity of the inventor is enmeshed with the development and success of the innovation (or, in some cases, the target application).[13] Affinity may incorporate one or more of the following binding factors:

- The inventor's sense of social identity is directly tied to the area of research, the technological innovation, or the use-application.

- The inventor's internal evaluation of success is determined in part or wholly by the validity of the discovery/innovation and/or the ultimate successful application of the technology.

- The inventor's external evaluation of success is determined in part or wholly by the broad acceptance of the validity of the discovery/innovation and/or the ultimate successful application of the technology.

- The inventor's external validation of success is determined in part or wholly by the knowledge that she was responsible for the technology.

The more binding the elements linking the inventor to the technology, the more passionate and driven the inventing entrepreneur. Dedication and zeal are necessary elements for tackling the hardships of technology-based entrepreneurship;

but an overly narrow focus can limit an entrepreneur's ability to objectively evaluate changing markets and real-world hurdles. The entrepreneur unwilling to believe that he can be wrong, that his technology might fail, or that the market wants something different, may not be adaptive enough to bring viable products to fruition. In the face of necessary strategic changes, some high-affinity entrepreneurs may become disenchanted, frustrated, and uninterested. At the extreme, high-affinity inventors do not differentiate between the adoption of the technology and their own self-actualization. We believe that "founder's syndrome" (a term that usually refers to situations in which company founders refuse to give up control of the technology and/or the business, even when their own participation becomes detrimental) can often be traced to extremely high inventor-technology affinity.

ESTIMATING THE BENEFITS ASSOCIATED WITH COMMERCIALIZING A TECHNOLOGY

The benefits stemming from technology commercialization can be separated into financial and nonfinancial categories. While some might argue that any benefit could ultimately be reduced to financial gain, our purpose is to focus on the entrepreneurial intent rather than the broader global consequences. Thus we consider benefits as they are likely to be evaluated by the inventing entrepreneur (instead of, for example, by an economist or a Wall Street analyst):

- Direct global/social benefit accruing from improved quality of life across a number of criteria (improvements in health, longevity, environmental impact, etc.)
- Indirect benefits accruing from efficiencies gained by users of the technology (customer experience with regard to reduced waste, improved products, etc.)
- Financial benefits to the entrepreneur
- Financial benefits to other individuals associated with the venture

The majority of inventing entrepreneurs we researched were focused entirely on the impact their ideas would have on society and/or on their own finances. This is, arguably, a natural reaction. Most inventing entrepreneurs (especially first-time entrepreneurs) hope to commercialize a new technology to solve a specific (usually broad-based societal) problem. The opportunity to generate financial returns, however, is usually the second consideration; very few of our interviewees specifically mentioned the desire to generate financial returns for their investors (other than as a necessary evil) or to improve the businesses of suppliers, vendors, or related businesses.

Professor James Thomson reflected on this issue: "In my own case, I decided not to accept any ownership in [a licensor company] or accept any fees from them, so there was a kind of discordance in where the rewards were going. For me, I don't mind doing work in the public interest for which I don't directly get compensated, but if somebody else is earning a large profit on [my work] that seems a little wrong to me."[14] Early on, Thomson made significant efforts to distance himself from the commercial applications of his path-breaking stem-cell technology: Because he believes that such research could save human lives, he was driven not by the technology's commercial potential, but rather by its potential to generate broad scientific acceptance for stem-cell applications. Initially, the technology transfer office drove the licensing process, and Thomson interacted with the corporations that had licenses to the technology. Subsequently, there were certain applications for the technology that were best suited for a start-up, so Thomson and a few of his colleagues founded new ventures to pursue the commercialization process. As significant and active participants, they chose to be shareholders of these start-up companies. Such overlaps between socially oriented goals and the individual's commercial interest are more the norm than the exception among inventing entrepreneurs.

Inventors considering the long-term commercialization process would do well to consider at least some of these factors. Statistically, technology-based companies that have a successful IPO generate the most benefits for the venture-capital firms and late-stage institutional investors; individual founders usually own less than 10% of the entity at that time. In other words, the largest financial gains are, in general, realized by the cash investments of the financial backers rather than by the sweat equity and intellectual capital of the scientific founders and managers. Some inventing entrepreneurs, therefore, eschew venture capital in favor of bootstrapping. Jeff Cernohaus, a former 3M Corporation (3M) scientist, founded Inter-Facial Solutions without external capital. He took an in-kind investment from Phillips Plastics Corporation to have access to sophisticated laboratory space:

> Things weren't moving as fast as I hoped, and I basically had a one-year window for my company to become profitable. Within weeks of being out, I called a couple retired guys from 3M and talked to them about seed money. They were pretty conservative; they didn't want to invest so soon. The network helped me; they turned me on to [person] at Phillips Plastics. So after one meeting, [the investor] said, I want you to come and work in my tech center, my new accelerator, and I'll pay your costs. We worked on a handshake arrangement.

But once his own inventions began generating revenue, Cernohaus immediately negotiated to buy back the stock he'd given to Phillips.

Though there is some research evidence that entrepreneurial firms tend to be resource constrained,[15] there are no systematic published studies comparing the relative success of bootstrapped versus venture-funded technology businesses. Anecdotal data from our own research and the popular press suggest that bootstrapped technology companies often suffer from resource limitations that can slow the commercialization process.

SETTING BOUNDARIES FOR THE NEED TO CONTROL THE TECHNOLOGY

Many inventing entrepreneurs express strong concerns about maintaining control over the technology, the development and commercialization processes, and the venture entity itself. The decision to retain majority control (i.e., at least

50.1% stock ownership) usually carries a price: limitations on external financing and/or other resources (expertise, whether business or scientific) that could be obtained via stock sales or stock-option grants. This restriction is more complex than it appears, because limitations on any resource can translate into slower progress. While there may be no optimal commercialization path, some commercialization strategies may be more efficient than others, and some delayed paths may suffer from late market entry and reduced financial rewards. The long-term trade-offs associated with maintaining control are extremely difficult to evaluate.

In the case of technology-driven ventures, "control" really encompasses a number of factors: day-to-day management of the company, long-term strategic direction for the company, disposition of the underlying technology (possibly including new technological developments), and disposition of the company itself. We briefly note each element of control, and the most common issues.

DAY-TO-DAY MANAGEMENT OF THE COMPANY

This factor was commonly commingled, inaccurately, with the issue of stock ownership. Inventing entrepreneurs (along with many traditional entrepreneurs) commonly fail to appreciate the administrative intricacies of running a growth business (especially without the centralized administrative infrastructure that an academic research laboratory takes for granted). Research professors sometimes take on the chief executive officer/chief operating officer (CEO/COO) role of the company, simply because "I'm the only one who can do it." As a counterexample, consider Professor Richard Burgess, who hired Sal Braico (a recent MBA) to serve as the operational manager of ConjuGon, Burgess's start-up commercializing a novel bacterial conjugation technology. A significant amount of the work associated with getting the business off the ground involved corporate documentation, preparation of an off-campus laboratory, administration of a private round of financing, human-resource administration, accounting, and other "nonscientific" activities. Although each of these was critical to the day-to-day functioning of the business, Professor Burgess believed the best use of his own time was being in the university laboratory and providing scientific oversight. He focused his efforts on the ongoing research and the "top end" of the business functions—making final hiring decisions (after screening), closing investors (instead of writing the actual business plan), and approving the lab plan (rather than creating it). It's useful to note that as ConjuGon moved toward clinical applications, the company hired a CEO with direct clinical experience.

LONG-TERM STRATEGIC DIRECTION OF THE COMPANY

While most inventing entrepreneurs understand the direct connection between control of the company and long-term strategy, they may or may not have the experience and mindset to evaluate and execute corporate business planning. The inventor of a novel biofuel technology may have a vision for replacing fossil fuels use, but he may not appreciate the complexity of the tactical steps needed to achieve that goal. Understanding this distinction is critical.

There are examples of inventing entrepreneurs who successfully tackle both. John Devereux, who founded Genetics Computer Group, one of the first bioinformatics software businesses, successfully led the company through eight years of growth to acquisition by Oxford Molecular. Several entrepreneurs in our interviews reflected on the philosophical differences between a university research lab and a corporate entity—which suggests that in some cases inventing entrepreneurs will struggle with a long-term strategy that is driven by changing consumer markets instead of underlying research goals.

There are, of course, examples of inventing entrepreneurs who did not possess the necessary strategic perspective to lead long-term commercialization efforts. We encourage inventors and nascent inventing entrepreneurs to carefully evaluate their own skill sets and try to find mentors who can help them consider whether an executive management role is appropriate or even warranted.

Inventing entrepreneurs should not confuse strategic planning with business administration. Many inventing entrepreneurs want to maintain direct control of or at least contribute to the strategic planning process, but most individuals that we interviewed were less enthusiastic about oversight and involvement in the day-to-day company administration.

DISPOSITION OF THE TECHNOLOGY

The disposition (or end-user application) of the technology is, for inventing entrepreneurs, the most commonly misunderstood aspect of control. Many inventing entrepreneurs tend to believe that ensuring the "proper" disposition of the technology (i.e., the ultimate application of the technology in the market, or the transfer of the technology to another entity for distribution) requires the innovator to maintain active management and oversight throughout the process, often in the form of being majority stockholder and part of executive management. The reality is more subtle, and, ironically, more conducive to the success of the business and the innovator. The long-term adoption of the innovation may not utilize the specific technology under license; the impact of the innovation may not be limited to its use by the technology licensor.

The disposition of technology can differ significantly from product commercialization. Most of the technology-based businesses that we reviewed utilized technologies licensed from research organizations where the terms of the license agreement established parameters for technology disposition. Specifically, a protein therapeutic licensed into a company solely for use in addressing multiple sclerosis cannot be redirected as a cure for Alzheimer's without the approval of the licensing agency. Some licenses are written more broadly than this, authorizing commercialization (the utilization) of the technology within the parameters of the license as the ultimate goal, rather than the specific application of the technology to a limited target. Thus the act of licensing the technology into a corporate entity legally defines the commercialization purpose, whether such purpose is in line with the innovator's intent or not.

In addition, many technology-driven companies (especially in life-science fields) accept third-party investments to fund premarket development and testing work. In doing so, companies accept another, totally disparate legal obligation. The company has a fiduciary duty to act for the benefit of those investors. In the event that the licensee reaches a decision point where the value of the technology can be maximized through disposition that is opposed to the innovator's intent, the corporation has a legal obligation to maximize shareholder value rather than pursue personal goals (so long as the parameters of license are not breached).[16] This aspect of external accountability trumping internal aspirations may not always be immediately obvious to first-time inventing entrepreneurs.

DISPOSITION OF THE COMPANY

In most cases, majority stockholder control is the primary determinant of company disposition. It should be noted, however, that fiduciary duty is a relevant issue, and that exit processes can be dramatically more complex than they appear. In the long term, it is rare for inventing entrepreneurs to maintain control over the disposition of the company (i.e., by having more than 50% stock ownership), especially for high-tech growth companies that require extensive external financing. Nesheim notes that investors dominate ownership; their proportion often exceeds 70% just before the IPO. Interestingly, there was no significant correlation between percentage sold to investors versus the amount of capital raised—in other words, the outcome of limited control for inventing entrepreneurs may be independent of how much capital the venture requires. It is unrealistic for an inventing entrepreneur to expect to maintain long-term control over the disposition of a company commercializing licensed technology, unless she intends to operate a lifestyle business (see Chapter 4).

Conclusions and Summary

For the scientist, entrepreneurial purpose often begins as a relatively simple goal: the pursuit of innovation and perhaps propagation of novel technology.[17] The realities of the corporate environment will likely complicate this vision. Issues relating to ownership, financial rewards, and even appropriate technology use may create confusing or even conflicting incentives for the entrepreneur. In this chapter, we have outlined five foundations of entrepreneurial purpose: visualizing the ultimate goal, grasping the significance of the technology, understanding the inventor's affinity threshold for the technology, estimating the benefits of commercializing the technology, and setting boundaries for control of the technology. As inventors contemplate the decision to start a new venture to commercialize their technology, it is important to contemplate these issues and exhaustively question one's motives and purpose for creating a new venture.

Endnotes

1. Shane, S. 2004. *Academic Entrepreneurship: University Spinoffs and Wealth Creation.* Northampton, MA: Edward Elgar.
2. Wright, M., Clarysse, B., Mustar, P., & Lockett, A. 2007. *Academic Entrepreneurship in Europe.* Cheltenham, UK: Edward Elgar.
3. Shane, S. 2002. Selling university technology: Patterns from MIT. *Management Science,* 48(1): 122–137.

4. Siegel, D., Waldman, D., & Link, A. 2003. Assessing the impact of organizational practices on the relative productivity of university technology transfer offices: An exploratory study. *Research Policy,* 32(1): 27–48.
5. IPO is an abbreviation for Initial Public Offering.
6. Nesheim, J. 2000. *High-Tech Startup.* New York: Free Press, p. 129.
7. Certain notable exceptions include Microsoft (5%) and Oracle (8%). See Nesheim for more details.
8. The Condor technology enables "pools" of computing resources to made available on an as-needed basis for high-intensity computing needs. From the Condor Web site: "The key to HTC is effective management and exploitation of all available computing resources. Since the computing needs of most scientists can be satisfied these days by commodity CPUs and memory, high efficiency is not playing a major role in a HTC environment. The main challenge a typical HTC environment faces is how to maximize the amount of resources accessible to its customers. Distributed ownership of computing resources is the major obstacle such an environment has to overcome in order to expand the pool of resources it can draw from. Recent trends in the cost/performance ratio of computer hardware have placed the control (ownership) over powerful computing resources in the hands of individuals and small groups. These distributed owners will be willing to include their resources in an HTC environment only after they are convinced that their needs will be addressed and their rights protected."
9. In his 1965 paper published in *Electronics Magazine,* Moore states that the number of transistors that can be placed on an integrated circuit doubles about every two years. This suggests that the cost of computational power drops exponentially over time. Moore, G. 1965. *Electronics Magazine,* 38(8).
10. Baum, J. R. & Locke, E. A. 2004. The relationship of entrepreneurial traits, skill, and motivation to subsequent venture growth. *Journal of Applied Psychology,* 89(4): 587–598.
11. Bone Care International was acquired by Genzyme in 2005 for approximately $600 million.
12. www.ebi.ac.uk/2can/glossary/index.php?letter=G
13. At this stage, we still differentiate between the "inventor" and the "inventing entrepreneur" because the evaluation of affinity can take place separately from the propagation decision or the inventor's decision to actively participate in the commercialization process.
14. Jain, S. & George, G. 2007. Building legitimacy for novel technologies: The case of Wisconsin Alumni Research Foundation and human embryonic stem cells. *Industrial and Corporate Change,* 16(4): 535–567.
15. Holtz-Eakin, D. & Joulfaian, D. 1994. Sticking it out: Entrepreneurial survival and liquidity constraints. *Journal of Political Economy,* 102(1): 53–75.
16. However, in some cases, the opportunities of maximum value may, in fact, occur outside the jurisdiction of the license, because the original technology developed within the academic institution is no longer the best option for commercialization.
17. For some inventing entrepreneurs, simply disseminating the technology, whether primarily within the scientific community or to the broader market, represents an appropriate level of commercialization effort. We will focus primarily on active commercialization in this book, since the opportunity to create start-up spin-out ventures remains relatively new and undocumented.

INVENTING ENTREPRENEURIAL OPTIONS

OVERVIEW

This chapter will focus on the entrepreneurial options available to the technology innovator. We'll provide a straightforward series of questions and issues to help the innovator consider a foray into entrepreneurship. The chapter describes four basic types of technology-focused entrepreneurs. The types are differentiated based on individual characteristics, such as entrepreneurial intent and capacity, as well as the new venture's potential to create value.

Technology entrepreneurs present a spectrum of entrepreneurial modes and paths. Our discussion, thus far, has focused on one specific type of technology entrepreneur, namely, the inventing entrepreneur. Taking a step back, it is useful to consider all the different forms of technology entrepreneurs and distinguish between their characteristics. We hope this process helps innovators evaluate their own opportunities by enabling them to compare personal characteristics and commercialization paths with the heuristics and examples provided.

ENTREPRENEURIAL INTENT, CAPACITY, AND VALUE CREATION

To make distinctions between the different types of technology entrepreneurs, let us consider one exogenous (market-driven) and two related endogenous (individual) factors: the **value creation potential** of an opportunity and **entrepreneurial intent and capacity.** Value creation potential represents a broad

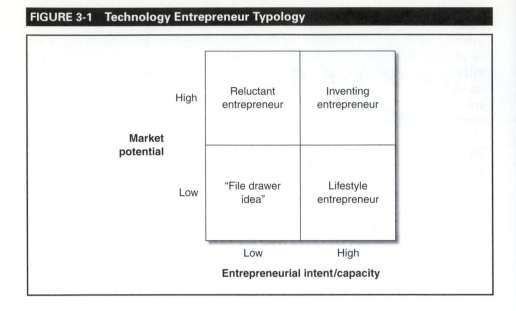

FIGURE 3-1 Technology Entrepreneur Typology

measure of whether the innovation can generate substantial financial (wealth) or social benefits. Entrepreneurial intent reflects the inventor's propensity to undertake commercially related activity. Entrepreneurial capacity captures the inventor's skills or capabilities to undertake commercially related activity. Because *intent* and *capacity* may be interdependent, we choose to simplify the analysis by combining them into a single endogenous factor.[1] We can then map these two factors in a simple matrix (shown in Figure 3-1) to distinguish between the most likely entrepreneurial options. We will review each quadrant and provide examples for clarity.

Some academic researchers have more than one opportunity; every opportunity inhabits a unique place on the intent/value matrix. The story of Professor Rock Mackie and Paul Reckwerdt is a useful illustration of this situation. The first innovation from their research, the Pinnacle picture archiving and communication system (PACS) for medical imaging, represented a growth opportunity in a medium-sized market.[2] A start-up company (Geometrix) was formed, and one of the graduate students on the project left the university to manage it:

> Reckwerdt: It was decided over beers at the [student union]. We were talking at this meeting about doing guerilla marketing, sending software to universities and then providing upgrades and concurrently gaining FDA approval—it was crazy! We finally said, "We really need to start a company, let's get a real license agreement, let's get lawyers involved."

Neither Reckwerdt nor Mackie were emotionally tied to the Pinnacle technology. Both believed that the ongoing, long-term research on radiation therapy being developed in Mackie's medical physics laboratory held greater promise. It may not be that unusual for technology innovators to consider trade-offs between entrepreneurial opportunities. In this case, Mackie and Reckwerdt had the capacity and even some of the intent to commercialize Pinnacle. But they believed that the value creation potential for the radiation therapy technology was greater, and their intent clearly centered on helping cancer victims. They turned over the Pinnacle opportunity to the entrepreneurs who had the right intent to lead that effort.

The radiation therapy opportunity took much longer to gestate. Funded by General Electric (GE) for a number of years, the opportunity emerged when internal issues at GE left the academic team without support:

> Mackie: We'd heard rumblings that [the project] was in trouble [at GE]. Nobody was paying attention to us anymore; we thought we were doing everything right, but what was happening was that GE was folding up the tents in radiotherapy. I made a trip to France. I was told by the last manager, "We're closing radiotherapy and we just have to figure out what to do with you."

For Mackie and Reckwerdt, this turned out to be the decision point for creating TomoTherapy, a standalone company developing an innovative medical imaging and radiation treatment system that would leapfrog existing market technologies. Nearly 20 million radiation treatments are provided each year, and billions of dollars are spent on new radiation treatment machines each year, resulting in a high-potential value creation opportunity. TomoTherapy is Reckwerdt and Mackie's passion, exemplifying high entrepreneurial intent.

The relative spectra of "entrepreneurial intent" and "value creation potential" are broad and multifaceted. While the inherent value of an innovation (measured generally in terms of long-term revenue, profits, or even net present value) has been subject to extensive scrutiny and analysis, effective valuation of any technological advance, especially particular embodiments of such an advance, remains somewhat an art form. Entrepreneurial intent and capacity must be evaluated on an individual basis without the benefit of established measures or criteria. Our goal, therefore, is not to provide a quantitative "test" for potential entrepreneurs, but to encourage self-reflection and conscious decision making. We hope to initiate a discussion, both at the theoretical level and in the practical world of technology commercialization. Studies reveal three primary modes of entrepreneurial intent[3,4]:

- Lack of commercialization intent, usually combined with either the lack of commercialization experience or a disinterest in commercialization due to philosophical or lifestyle preferences
- Significant commercialization intent, usually triggered by prior experience in a commercial setting or vicariously from another successful inventing entrepreneur
- Learned commercialization intent, based on prior personal commercialization experience

For our purposes, the latter two are functionally similar, since we are focused on the practical decision-making process for the nascent inventing entrepreneur, rather than on the drivers for intent.

In addition, we have purposely chosen to explore "value creation potential" rather than measures such as market size or net present value (a financial measure that theoretically reflects the current cash value of a technology or business opportunity). Recommending supposedly precise measures would falsely advocate an inappropriate level of theoretical accuracy to the nascent entrepreneur. In the vast majority of cases, it will not be possible to calculate a precise monetary value of the opportunity in this early phase. To highlight this issue, let us consider human embryonic stem-cell research, a high-profile and controversial innovation. While numerous analyses of market opportunities and net present value have been developed by a variety of organizations (including state governments, technology transfer offices, venture capitalists, and entrepreneurs), such analyses remain speculative. To date, no government-approved human embryonic stem cell–based product has reached an end-user market. Clearly, this hasn't prevented the proliferation of stem-cell based technology companies, so we must accept that the uncertainty in early value creation measures is inherent to innovative technology entrepreneurship. Consequently, the technology entrepreneur typology must serve as a useful tool for understanding the categories of entrepreneurs rather than act as a precise classification matrix. Let us now consider each cell in the typology.

THE "FILE DRAWER IDEA" (LOW MARKET POTENTIAL, LOW ENTREPRENEURIAL CAPACITY)

These are, generally, dead-end situations. Realistically, a significant portion of long-term research programs generate ideas, technologies, and solutions that don't have a direct market impact. The output from these research programs may push the boundaries of scientific knowledge without having implications for day-to-day life. Much research that appears to have promising implications for industry or society simply doesn't yield anticipated or useful results, and ends up tucked away in a file drawer. The technology or innovation may be fascinating, clever, sophisticated, and totally novel, but it may have a limited end-user market, and consequently, limited value creation potential. Perhaps the innovation can be mimicked by a dramatically less expensive technology. For instance, a new test for measuring gasoline octane with spectacular precision may appear to have a huge market, but not if the oil companies or their gasoline distribution systems do not need higher precision—especially if federal and state governments don't mandate it. Perhaps the market for the technology does not exist because complementary products aren't available.

In this cell of the typology the scientist is also uninterested in pursuing the opportunity, whether because of the limited market potential or the simple lack of commercialization interest.

THE RELUCTANT ENTREPRENEUR (HIGH MARKET POTENTIAL, LOW ENTREPRENEURIAL CAPACITY)

In this scenario, the scientist has developed a novel technology with significant market potential. At the same time, although the scientist's expertise, reputation, and enthusiasm may be necessary components of a successful commercialization effort, the scientist may be unwilling or unqualified to lead it. Alternatively, the scientist might not have even considered commercialization seriously.

Professor Stephen Rao found himself at the leading edge of functional magnetic resonance imaging (fMRI) in the late 1990s. His clinical background in neuropathology gave him unique insight into fMRI's capacity to evaluate both the pathology of neurological diseases and the effectiveness of existing and new drugs on those diseases. But he hadn't considered commercialization issues until approached by the technology transfer office. Dr. Rao is the first person to admit he knew little about starting a business, much less financing and running a tech-based growth business. He notes that without the intervention of a local incubator (TechStar), Neurognostics Inc. might not have been formed at all. Another excellent example is Professor Hennessy (President of Stanford University, profiled in Chapter 1), who stated:

> I was in some ways the reluctant entrepreneur. Not so reluctant that I wouldn't do it, but the basic argument somebody said was, "This is revolutionary technology; if you don't do it, it's not going to happen."

THE LIFESTYLE ENTREPRENEUR (LOW MARKET POTENTIAL, HIGH ENTREPRENEURIAL CAPACITY)

Opportunities in this quadrant are characterized by an enthusiastic, potentially capable entrepreneur, but also by a limited market opportunity. Although the technology may solve a real problem in industry, the product may not offer a significant revenue stream and/or there may not be an opportunity to create a new market addressing undeveloped customer needs. Success stories result from entrepreneurs who build a business to serve the niche opportunity, leveraging their unique expertise and/or technological innovation into specialized products with high margins. For example, Tyler Research Corporation of Alberta, Canada supplies experimental antimicrobial film testing kits—an almost one-of-a-kind application for a very limited group of businesses that need to test for microbial adherence and biofilm formation on specialty surfaces. Each testing kit has to be handmade for the specific application, and relatively few companies require these systems. This is, therefore, a lifestyle business—it's how Dr. Tyler makes his living, and yes, he does answer the phone when you call the 800 number. Recently, this field has been expanding based on increased use of implanted medical devices designed to limit biofilm adhesion and thus reduce bacterial infections.

Dr. Tyler may have the option to expand his business. But to date, the kind of growth available to his company has been limited by the technology processes and the market opportunity, and possibly by his own intent.

An alternate circumstance occurs when the resource requirements don't match the market rewards. Perhaps the classic examples of these opportunities are "orphan drugs." These are therapeutics that, if approved, would serve very small populations of patients. For example, the Centers for Disease Control (CDC) estimates that while 23 million Americans have some form of heart disease,[5] only 30,000 Americans have ALS (Lou Gehrig's disease).[6] Without regard to any ethical questions, heart disease is a larger, more attractive market. Since the cost of bringing a new drug to market ranges from $50 million to over $1 billion, the scientist-entrepreneur creating this type of business may need to be seeking more altruistic rewards than financial ones.[7]

Failures in this quadrant usually stem from overestimating the market opportunity. Growth financing isn't often appropriate for these businesses, and may lead to significant ownership dilution if the business can't meet investor expectations. In 2001, we were approached by an inventing entrepreneur (working independently) who had developed a novel rain gauge that dramatically increased the accuracy of rainfall measurements by eliminating collection errors associated with wind effects. The invention was both innovative and simple, and the U.S. Patent Office issued a patent to cover the technology. At this point, however, the entrepreneur failed to effectively evaluate the market need. He believed that the target market was the general public, rather than specialized weather measurement purposes. The entrepreneur was seeking venture financing, hoping to build a large business quickly. Realistically, the technology may well fit a lifestyle business by selling a niche product at a premium price to specialty organizations (weather stations, farmers, irrigation system managers, etc.). In our opinion, it simply was not possible to build a major commercial success on this technology platform. The entrepreneur did not secure financing from professional investors.

THE INVENTING ENTREPRENEUR (HIGH MARKET POTENTIAL, HIGH ENTREPRENEURIAL CAPACITY)

Most of this book focuses on "inventing entrepreneurs," the scientists and researchers who develop novel technologies with significant market potential. Many venture capital–funded businesses fall into this category—where the opportunity for value creation is substantial and the inventor is an enthusiastic supporter or organizer of the venture. Technology transfer offices at universities and corporations often encourage these high-potential ventures as well.

You will read more on inventing entrepreneurs and their entrepreneurial journeys in subsequent chapters. Profile 3-1 provides one of the most fascinating and rewarding examples of inventing entrepreneurs, in part because the two inventing entrepreneurs took different paths as part of the same venture.

Professor Rock Mackie, Paul Reckwerdt, and TomoTherapy

The TomoTherapy story provides insight into nearly every aspect of the inventing entrepreneurial experience. One of the two founders remained in academia while the other became a senior manager at the start-up company. The founders invested significant amounts of their personal worth into the business, and eventually raised institutional venture capital. Success has been a long time coming, and there have been numerous moments on the brink. In May 2007, TomoTherapy became a publicly traded company (i.e., had its initial public offering (IPO)), and there is general agreement that the company's technology has set a new standard in cancer treatment.

We are not suggesting that the TomoTherapy story is typical or even necessarily a model to follow. But the experiences of Paul Reckwerdt and Dr. Rock Mackie offer a window to the world of the inventing entrepreneur that began when they decided not to get actively involved in commercializing an earlier technology.

Mackie and Reckwerdt were both in the medical physics department at the University of Wisconsin–Madison. In the late '80s, Reckwerdt, along with a graduate student named Mark Gehring, had developed code for the Pinnacle picture archival and communications system (PACS) for medical imaging modalities. At that time, transferring the technology to the market turned out to be unexpectedly tricky:

Mackie: We had great software and we wanted the world to use it but we couldn't do it [the FDA had a prohibition on university software leaving the state]. So then we thought, well, what do we do? We thought about licensing it, but the trouble was no one really wanted to license it because it had too many [university-dependent] idiosyncrasies; a lot of value had to be added before it could be a commercial product—and before you know it, we were talking about starting our own company.

The team reached a crossroads—who would go to work at the company?

Reckwerdt: At that time, we had the ownership arrangement and how people fit in, and Cam [Sanders] and Mark [Gehring] asked Rock and I, "Why don't you split off and do this," and Rock and I already had the first passes at the Tomo thing, and we thought—we said—well, we think this Tomo thing is going to be 10 times bigger, and they didn't believe it . . . they didn't see the vision we did.

The team founded Geometrics, with financial support from a California company called ADAC Laboratories, Inc. Gehring and Sanders took on the management of the start-up, while Mackie and Reckwerdt stayed at the university to work on "this Tomo thing." Geometrics was eventually bought out by ADAC,[8] and the Pinnacle system developed by Geometrics is still used in nearly half of all the world's medical imaging systems.

TomoTherapy represents a major advance in radiation cancer treatment. A modulated radiation source revolves entirely around the patient's body, and travels along the transverse axis of the patient, as well. Advanced optimization software controls the strength of the radiation beam and the speed the source travels, simultaneously modulating the cross-sectional shape of the beam. This complex process dramatically

(continues)

minimizes irradiation of innocent tissue around the tumor, allowing the clinician to irradiate complex shapes and surfaces, such as the interior surface of the lung.[9]

The development of the technology required significant resources; General Electric agreed to sponsor the necessary research at the University, which would cost millions of dollars. Despite the commercial success in process at Geometrics, Mackie and Reckwerdt were just happy to keep the TomoTherapy concept moving forward.

> Mackie: GE was funding it. GE potentially would have owned all the goodies, if they had stuck to it. Paul and I were still academics, we're sitting back saying Tomo's such a great idea, it's going to be such a big thing, the good of mankind . . .

But the arrangement with GE eventually ran aground. GE was divesting its radiotherapy businesses, and the technology devolved back to the university. At that point, Mackie and Reckwerdt decided a start-up company was their best option. Following the sale of Geometrics, they had access to some funds—but TomoTherapy was, at heart, a completely different animal, and would have to be funded differently. Geometrics was a true software play, requiring little capital equipment. TomoTherapy was all about capital equipment, from big server arrays to multi-ton gantries and small linear accelerators, all of which would require concrete bunkers for testing. TomoTherapy would need venture capital.

> Mackie: We did a road show for 18 months . . . West Coast, East Coast, Midwest. In California, no one wanted to fund us here in the Midwest—they wanted us to move. Most didn't want to fund us because we were capital intensive . . . .
>
> Reckwerdt: We required a lot of capital—they didn't like equipment—they liked software. One of them said—we really like you guys, we like the idea, we just have one big problem—you can never do this in Wisconsin. Why? You can't manufacture in Wisconsin. I guess he didn't know that GE was here and that this is a world headquarters for medical devices. I asked him, "Do you know where the largest medical device manufacturer is in the world? New Berlin, WI. This is the ideal place to do it." The real reason was he didn't want to fly out here.

TomoTherapy was eventually funded by a syndicate of midwestern VCs. Mackie remained at the university, while Reckwerdt became the CEO of the newly funded business. Following an additional financing round, the VC group brought in an industry CEO. Reckwerdt remained as president of the company, the role he still holds today.

Throughout the growth of the business, Mackie and Reckwerdt have focused on the importance of people. From the time of the founding of the company to its current success, they have noted situations and circumstances that directly reflect the people involved, including their own partnership:

> Reckwerdt: Be very aware of who you partner with—it really is a marriage. We get on each other's nerves and we bash each other all the time but intrinsically we trust each other; we understand each other well enough to know what our hot buttons are—but we also know that we're honest. You've got to trust each other at a basic level.

But the most powerful story about the team came at a time when the company's fate hung in the balance:

> Reckwerdt: Before the second round, we were really broke. We were delayed on shipping—the first machine was a prototype, so it wasn't being used for clinical, so we weren't getting anything we could show to people. We were running out of cash, our credit cards were maxed out, Rock

and I had mortgaged our houses, and it was very close to closing the doors. And at that point—this is a key factor: We were always very open about the state of our business with our employees. They all came in and said, "Don't pay us. We can survive for three months if you don't pay us, we know you don't have any money." And I was crying . . . they had all come together and said "We don't need the money, don't pay us, we'll do this for free for three months, we know you'll get the money." And the next day we got a check from London Ontario [the first commercial sale]. But these guys will never forget this team—they'll all be millionaires—but the fact is that they had faith and the fact is that they knew we'd pull it off . . . .

The entrepreneurial journeys of these two founders took very different directions, even though they shared the path of their company. Mackie notes the skills that would be beneficial to bring to corporate administration and is honest about his own style:

Mackie: Good management of an university group and project development are probably good. I would never ever claim to be a good project manager. I think I ran a relatively slipshod project management (within the university), but it was a very creative one. You have to evolve to a company; you need to have very well-defined procedures; you have to document everything very well—and that runs a little counter to how it goes at the university.

But Reckwerdt made that transition, and the impact on his identity has been significant:

Reckwerdt: I've had the largest transformation. Rock has the luxury of continuing to work on things 10 years out at the university. And I can't. And I've lost a lot of the identity of a scientist, which in some ways I really miss. But I also realize—we're not bad at business. Business is not rocket science. And so I've learned a new skill set. And it can actually pay me a lot more than research. And I'm really pretty good at the business end in a lot of ways. I have weaknesses of course. I'd love to go back to invention—not so much the grind of follow-through, but the raw, the first-invention stuff—those were really exciting times.

THE INHERENT VALUE OF INTELLECTUAL PROPERTY

A significant aspect of high-potential ventures depends upon the inherent value of intellectual property associated with innovation. In most cases, "intellectual property" (IP) refers to patents (approved or pending), copyrights (often the case with software), and sometimes trade secrets (information not generally available to the industry). Regardless of the form of intellectual property, the process of technology transfer (whether via license to an established organization or a start-up) involves the transmission of the rights to the intellectual property to an organization positioned to bring products to market. As such, the value of any given portfolio of intellectual property varies widely. For example, the value of a patent on an FDA-approved therapeutic for a major illness or disease could be worth billions of dollars. That same patent 10 years earlier, when the drug target was still unproven, could have been nearly worthless.

Valuation of intellectual property, especially early-stage intellectual property, is a nontrivial exercise.[10] Regardless, the determination of value for any given intellectual property is, in part, at best a precursor activity, because some organization or individual must still convert the intellectual property into a marketable product or service.[11] In this book, we focus less on intellectual property and more on the process of commercialization as experienced by inventing entrepreneurs. To that end, we offer up these comments from Professor George Church, who has developed some of the most valuable intellectual property covered in our research:[12]

> A good business idea will trump controlling technology. You don't want to have a good business idea and get thrown out of the market because someone else patented it. Solera, in my field, didn't have any intellectual property. Microsoft didn't have much in the way of intellectual property. I think a clear business idea is better. Now scientists will tend not to get involved unless they have IP, but I think that's one thing that should be communicated to them—that they shouldn't get too infatuated with their invention to think that's going to be sufficient, or even necessary.

Conclusions and Summary

The initial conditions of any entrepreneurial venture bear implications for the final outcome. For inventing entrepreneurs, the initial conditions include personal and lifestyle characteristics that bear special consideration. No model could effectively predict the transformational experience of any one inventing entrepreneur. We believe the Technology Entrepreneur Typology (Figure 3-1) provides a starting point for nascent entrepreneurs as they consider their own circumstances and goals. Then they can begin a realistic evaluation of the commercial potential and resource requirements of not only the innovation in question but the entire commercialization process.

Endnotes

1. This simplification puts the burden on the technology innovator to self-evaluate the combination of intent and capacity. Our investigations suggest that most research scientists have strong self-reflection capacities, especially in regards to personal goals and purpose. But measuring "entrepreneurial capacity" is likely a novel and challenging undertaking for the scientifically trained innovator. In our opinion, external evaluation and peer review will likely be more useful for evaluating "entrepreneurial capacity" than self-appraisal will.
2. While such measures are always relative, in this case the PACS market was growing from tens of millions to hundreds of millions of dollars.
3. Samsom, K. 1990. Scientists as Entrepreneurs: Organizational Performance in Scientist-Started New Ventures. London: Kluwer.
4. George, G., Jain, S., & Maltarich, M. 2005. Academics or entrepreneurs? Entrepreneurial identity and invention disclosure behavior of university scientists. Paper presented at the Academy of Management Meeting, Honolulu, Hawaii.

5. www.cdc.gov/nchs/fastats/heart.htm

6. www.alsa.org/als/facts.cfm?CFID=881432&CFTOKEN=86307063

7. The FDA, in conjunction with the CDC and the IRS, has attempted to encourage research on "orphan drugs" by creating fast-track approval processes and even significant tax incentives for research on "orphan" ailments. Despite this, the vast majority of venture-capital investments in therapeutics target heart disease, Alzheimer's, and cancer.

8. ADAC was eventually acquired by Phillips for $426 million.

9. "The TomoTherapy Hi Art System® is a new, revolutionary way to treat cancer with radiation. With the TomoTherapy Hi Art System®, the physician can check the location of the patient's tumor before each treatment, then deliver painless and precise radiation therapy based on a carefully customized plan. TomoTherapy combines precise 3-D imaging from computerized tomography (CT scanning) with highly targeted radiation beams." "The TomoTherapy Hi Art System® combines IMRT with a helical delivery pattern to deliver the radiation treatment. Photon radiation is produced by a linear accelerator, which travels in multiple circles around the gantry ring as the couch moves through the gantry. The linac moves in unison with a *multileaf collimator,* or MLC, which constantly modulates the radiation beam as it leaves the accelerator." From the www.Tomotherapy.com Web site.

10. Razgaitis, R. 2003. *Valuation and Pricing of Technology-Based Intellectual Property*. New York: Wiley.

11. Hanel, P. 2006. Intellectual property rights business management practices: A survey of the literature. *Technovation,* 26(8): 895–931.

12. More information about Professor Church will be provided later in the book, but suffice to say that Professor Church was one of the founders of genomic sequencing, including helping initiate the human genome project.

CHAPTER 4

TECHNOLOGY LICENSING

OVERVIEW

Technology transfer is the process by which one organization empowers another organization to access proprietary technology. In most cases, the legal transaction is embodied in a license or sale, and the licensee or acquirer anticipates some commercial activities based on the right to utilize that technology. An extensive literature exists on the technology transfer process,[1] including patenting,[2] technology valuation,[3] negotiation, licensing,[4] and commercialization.[5] Our discussion will focus on technology transfer from academic research facilities to commercial entities, with specific emphasis on early stage or start-up businesses. In these circumstances the inventing entrepreneur plays a critical role—she is likely to be the primary catalyst for the transition of research innovation into commercial technology or products.

Professor George Church at Harvard University has had more experience with this process than most. His first experience with technology transfer came in 1977, when his DNA sequence reader technology caught the attention of Bio-Rad, a biotechnology company. No transaction developed from that first interaction. In our conversation with him, Professor Church reflected on how unfamiliar and awkward that process can be for an academic researcher:

> I wasn't quite sure what the appropriate interaction between an
> academic and a company was. I was very gung-ho, but I didn't know
> what the rules were. It was a learning experience; it was very valuable.
> If we had both buckled down and had a lot of resources, we might have
> brought DNA sequencing to market much earlier.

For many academic researchers, the technology transfer process emerges by necessity, as innovations capture the attention of commercial entities. Some academic research institutions now provide extensive resources and education to faculty to support and encourage early consideration of technology transfer and commercialization potential. Faculty members, especially those managing significant research programs, often can't set aside enough time from teaching, research, and administrative responsibilities to become experts on the technology transfer process at their institution. Profile 4-1 describes Harvard Professor George Church's entrepreneurial journey. As one of the founders of the modern field of genomics, Professor Church has a unique perspective on both the entrepreneurial process and the evolution of one of the most important scientific undertakings of the last century—the quest for the human genome.

INVENTING ENTREPRENEUR PROFILE 4-1

Professor George Church

Professor George Church has never been tempted to start his own company. His research accomplishments are significant: He is one of the original developers of genome sequencing along with numerous other technologies, including molecular multiplexing and tags, homologous recombination methods, and DNA array synthesizers. His technologies have been licensed to industry, and he has served as an advisor to at least 22 different companies. In some ways, Church might have been a perfect candidate for the start-up commercialization route. Wally Gilbert, the founder of Biogen, was Church's Ph.D. advisor, and Church even spent six months working at Biogen while completing his degree. But when the time came to consider commercialization options for his multiplex sequencing technology, Church wasn't in a position to consider starting his own venture or other non-traditional commercialization options:

> The first real patent that got issued was on multiplex sequencing, and that got licensed to Millipore. I was going with however the Harvard licensing office wanted to go. I figured they had more experience than I did—this was my first real-time commercialization exposure. I had watched Biogen happen; I hadn't really seen how they had done it.

Church remained actively interested in technology transfer, but tenure was "the logical route . . . the CEO role didn't appeal to me and still doesn't appeal to me; I prefer to keep the academic position where I can invent freely on a variety of subjects."

More opportunities have emerged since then, and Church has been a more active participant in getting technologies placed into the market, including into start-up companies. The best example might be Codon Devices, Inc. This venture-capital funded start-up is commercializing processes for synthesizing large DNA strings from DNA chips. Again, however, Church had no interest in leading the endeavor himself. Serendipitous timing led to the formation of Codon Devices, in part because of the availability of a colleague at the Massachusetts Institute of Technology (MIT) with the necessary corporate leadership skills:

> We didn't feel there was a company ready to use this. Joe [Jacobson] was available and a known quantity, and one of the only other people in the field, and it was a coincidence that he

was geographically close. It didn't seem there was another alternative, and we both have a close connection to Flagship [a Boston-based venture-capital firm].

Of the academic entrepreneurs we interviewed, Church is one of the ones most certain about his contribution and its limitations. He clearly and convincingly notes the difficulty in transitioning from the role of academic researcher to corporate management, especially via the start-up vehicle:

> [Codon] raised my expectations, but I would still prefer not to be CEO. It's not so much interest as it is the skill set. The company depends on the CEO being skillful at CEO-like things, and I'm better at inventing—at recruiting scientists from academia and writing academic articles, which in a certain sense is advertising for the company—I think I'm good at it and I enjoy it. Of the scientists I've seen become CEOs, overall I've not been impressed, and I don't feel any luckier than they are, so I don't feel like I want to push my luck. If approached for advice by a junior colleague about taking on a start-up CEO role, I would probably start with some descriptions of famous scientists he or she knew who have been ineffective as CEOs. Do you really like travel and being away from your family a lot—do you really like hiring and firing people, and deciding on benefits? Do you feel like your vision isn't going to be communicated if you are chairman of the company's scientific advisory board? Do they have delusions about what fraction of the company the CEO can get? A scientific founder can get very good equity without being CEO, and there might be some confusion there.

Church is even clearer about the issue of control. Unlike the academic entrepreneurs who lead commercialization efforts, Church advocates a hard-nosed approach to understanding the reasons for taking the lead on commercializing a technology:

> It's an inexperienced gambler's game. It doesn't mean you can't do it. You should do it from the point of having a lot of knowledge. It's not something you should do with your gut. You should really know what it takes to be a CEO before you do it, and have a good reason for doing it that way. Not just "I'm infatuated with the technology and I want to have total control over it and never lose control . . .." That's risky and sounds ill thought out.

THE TECHNOLOGY TRANSFER PROCESS

Technology transfer[6] can be a complicated process. As a first step, a scientist approaches the technology transfer entity[7] with an invention. In most cases, the scientist discusses research results with a representative of the technology transfer office to make sure that the innovation merits further discussion.[8] If so, the inventor usually provides basic written information about the innovation. This submission, called a "disclosure," may include notes, drawings, a proposed journal manuscript, or raw experiment output and/or other data. Though technology transfer offices vary significantly in their practices, the inventing entrepreneur may want to consider some of the sample disclosure questions identified in Table 4-1. Though Table 4-1 highlights different scenarios with relatively simplistic questions and answers, inventors should note that the overall process is quite complex; protecting novel technologies is a nonobvious exercise—with sometimes unpredictable outcomes. Even technology experts are occasionally wrong; the default should be to disclose your invention to the TTO. The TTO will then inform you of your options.

TABLE 4-1 When to Disclose?

Status	*Disclose?*
The science is novel, nonobvious to someone in the same field, and potentially useful.	Yes; even if you do not know what applications would be useful, it is recommended to disclose.
The invention merits publication in a leading scientific journal.	Yes; quality of science is an important factor in the ability to license a technology or create a start-up.
The invention is a process, machine, article of manufacture, composition of matter, or an improvement on any of the previous ones.	Yes; these are different categories of utility patents issued by the U.S. Patent and Trademark Office.
I am planning to share my results in a publication. Should I disclose now?	Yes; there are complex rules in the United States and the rest of the world regarding who is first to invent and who is first to publish an invention.
I have asexually reproduced plant varieties and designs.	Check with the TTO; certain plant varieties are patentable.
I think I have made a new discovery, but other colleagues at different institutions are also working on the same process.	Check with the TTO; the colleagues may not have patented or their work could be slightly different.
Can I write up a document and share it with a researcher at a different university not on my research team—or share it with the sponsoring company—before I disclose to my TTO?	This is not recommended. Please check with the TTO first because this may impact your ability to patent the technology.
I have some initial results on my research that are intriguing. Should I disclose?	Yes; it may be a bit early but the TTO should make the decision about whether they want to have more data before they patent. They may ask you to come back later with more concrete data.
My research is federally funded and I have made an invention. Should I disclose to my TTO?	Yes; you are required to do so under the 1980 Bayh-Dole Act.

A TTO employee then assesses this disclosure for patentability and its potential economic value. Presuming the TTO determines that the technology can be protected and is of reasonable significance, TTO staff will likely direct patent counsel to prepare to file a patent.[9] The TTO staff then interacts with patent and trademark offices around the world to ensure that the patent has adequate coverage. The relevant patent office (such as the U.S. Patent and Trademark Office) returns queries called "office actions" that are attended to by patent counsel. These office actions, among other things, may include rewriting claims made in the patent or responding to requests for additional data. The patent is subsequently issued or denied. If it is issued, the licensing personnel may then take up the patent (or a portfolio of patents) and shop it around to private or public entities. Studies suggest that the likelihood of licensing is significantly higher when the technology is patented because then companies have a legal claim that protects the invention from competitors.[10]

Patent protection can generate commercial value for inventions by providing the inventor, the TTO, and its licensees the ability to exclude other organizations from copying specific inventions. An imitator (competitor) could attempt to sell similar products, utilize the underlying technology in different products, or even attempt to sue the inventors or owners on matters of ownership, control, or marketing rights. Excluding competitors provides a mechanism by which a company may offset the potentially staggering costs of product development in markets such as biopharmaceuticals or semiconductors.[11] A company (or another research entity) then enters into a license agreement with the technology transfer office and agrees to pay royalties to use the patented invention. The technology transfer office, for its part, assumes the responsibility for protecting the patented technology through litigation with those who infringe upon the claims made in the patent. While this brief description serves as a basic overview of the process, there are other mechanisms — (an important one being entrepreneurial start-ups) through which technology is transferred to private entities.

Figure 4-1 presents a stylized diagram of the process from disclosure to licensing. There's a natural winnowing process that occurs from the time of the

FIGURE 4-1   A Simplified Licensing Process Model

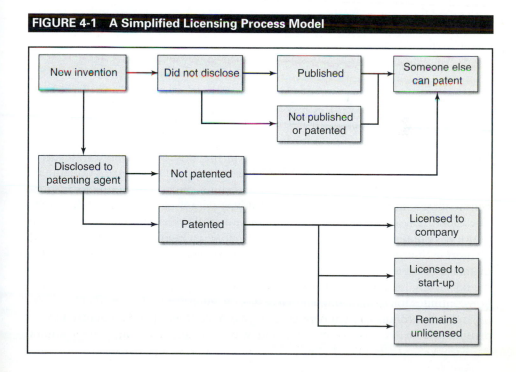

initial research and innovations to the point at which disclosures and patent filings are made. For example, we can expect that about 30 to 70 percent of disclosures are patented. Of these patents, it is possible, on average, that about 10 to 30 percent of the TTO's patent portfolio will be licensed to a private company. Occasionally, it is possible for disclosures to go through a licensing process even without a patent filing (especially, for example, in the case of information that could be subject to copyright law or of biological materials that could be used for specific test services). However, the focus of most TTOs is on licensing patented and "patent pending" technologies. Because of this licensing process, TTOs over the past three decades have become sophisticated with regard to technology-based value creation and the structure of licensing agreements that increase financial returns to the inventor and the university.[12]

Patent protection may confer on the inventor and to the university right to continue to work in a given technological space, and ultimately to market products for a limited time without direct competition. For example, a patent on a given chemical compound with intriguing medical benefits (such as the ability to limit or reverse cancerous tumor growth) might offer protection against other firms developing and marketing the same or similar compounds without upfront research costs.[13]

Such rights may be essential. Unscrupulous private organizations, commonly referred to as **patent trolls,** have found mechanisms by which to trap R&D-intensive companies in patent infringement lawsuits in order to receive damage awards for the illegitimate use of the technology discovered or developed by the firm that performed the original R&D work.[14] Patent trolls can impede research in an area if they obtain patent rights that some individuals may have consciously or unknowingly foregone.

WARF: A TECHNOLOGY TRANSFER OFFICE EXAMPLE

One successful technology transfer office is the Wisconsin Alumni Research Foundation (WARF). Since 1925, WARF has successfully transferred valuable inventions from university labs to private and other public entities. WARF's first major success story was the commercial development of a vitamin D discovery. The widespread commercial availability of vitamin D offered the first real opportunity to virtually eliminate rickets. WARF fulfilled a humanitarian mission while furthering the research mission of the university of Wisconsin by converting the financial benefits of licensing activities into scientific grants and awards within the university. Its most recent success is human embryonic stem cells. The foundation continues to cultivate ongoing successes by patenting and licensing University of Wisconsin–Madison technologies each year. WARF has been recognized for its pivotal role in technology transfer and was a recipient of the 2003 National

Medal of Technology, an annual award conferred by the President of the United States that recognizes significant and lasting contributions to the country's economic, environmental, and social well-being implemented through the development and commercialization of technology. Its managing director, Dr. Carl Gulbrandsen, commented:

> We have a succinct mission—to foster research at the University of Wisconsin. There are two things we do really well—patenting and licensing. We are good at protecting inventions and we should continue to be expert in that. We are good at licensing and at finding a home for the invention so that someone finds good use for our technologies. The real purpose is not to make the most money and squeeze every penny out of every invention. We are proactive about licensing. Our best source for leads is the faculty member; they know the market and the people. It is an efficient way of getting to the right leads. We go on marketing trips all over the world. Our goal is that people are not sitting at their desks; they are out visiting companies; they are constantly prospecting and looking for leads.

LICENSING: THE TTO PERSPECTIVE

Licensing an invention to a third party with commercialization resources already in place remains the predominant choice of inventors and is the first, most direct, and most viable option for getting the invention to the marketplace. This licensing process is handled through an organizational intermediary, such as WARF for the University of Wisconsin–Madison. For instance, WARF manages around 1,000 issued and 800 pending patents and signs more than 200 license agreements each year. By any performance yardstick, WARF is successful at technology transfer through patenting and licensing. However, not every technology gets licensed. Approximately 30 percent of WARF's technology portfolio is licensed to other corporate entities. Using a random sample of 60 patents, we generated the probability (hazard rate) of licensing a patent at any given point in time (see Figure 4-2).

We see that the probability of a technology being licensed is highest between years 2 and 4 (at about 6% probability of being licensed that year) after the patent application has been filed. The probability that a technology gets licensed after year 6 is sharply lower. WARF bears the risk associated with licensing a technology and shares a certain percentage of the licensing revenues with the inventor, the inventor's lab, and the university.

In an internal report, WARF estimated the cost of patenting at approximately $33,000 for an unlicensed patent and $54,000 for a licensed patent in 2005. A comparable cost if the patent was secured independent of WARF was estimated at approximately $39,000 and $70,000 respectively. In a 2003 newsletter,[15] Johns

FIGURE 4-2   **Likelihood of Licensing a Patent**

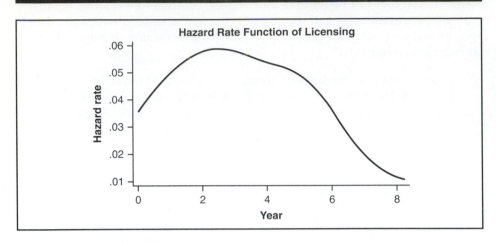

Hopkins University's licensing office calculated a sample cost of patent at approximately $31,500. They used an example of an unlicensed U.S. patent application filed for a neurologically related diagnostic that appeared to be a good business risk at the time of its preparation. Preparation and filing of the case cost approximately $15,680. Downstream patenting efforts spanning five years effectively doubled their cash outlay for the invention, which at that time had still not been approved by the U.S. Patent and Trademark Office! Nowadays, there is the opportunity to outsource patenting paperwork at low cost to other countries but that also carries uncertainties regarding the quality of the application filed or the coordination costs between the inventor and the patent attorney.

There are several important issues that inventors need to understand:

- The probability of licensing a patent, on average, tends to be higher when the technology is bundled as a portfolio of patents.
- Experienced TTOs may be able to cross-sell technologies along with other inventions in their portfolio to potential corporations, thereby increasing the probability that a technology will be licensed.
- Most "leads" for a licensing deal come from the inventor who met a prospective licensor at a conference or through a research contact.
- The TTOs spend their time and effort in prosecuting a patent and getting the patent issued—and in most cases, at no up-front cost to the inventor.
- In return for the invention, the TTO shares a percentage of any licensing revenues with the inventor (ranging from 20 to 40 percent net of costs incurred).

WHEN AND WHY TO LICENSE A TECHNOLOGY

The decision to license a technology to a commercial organization is usually driven primarily by the technology transfer office. Most academic institutions, however, will not license a technology to a commercial enterprise without some consultation with the inventor. Most research institutions at least offer the option to actively participate in the licensing of a technology. Professor Jo Handelsman is a perfect example. She described her goals of improving agricultural yields while decreasing dependence on deleterious pesticide agents. But she's equally clear that she does not want to start her own company to see the technologies propagated:

> There's no way I can imagine starting a company; the large-scale synthesis and fermentation equipment would require a huge capital investment. You have to find out what you're good at in life, and I don't know if I would be good at [starting and running a company]. My life serves its purpose of education and teaching. I like to be able to dig in really deeply to specific experiments, and I like to take a longer view than is afforded in the commercial world. I don't need to see results immediately—I can take four years to work with a student I have faith in, and see the results at the end.

Professor George Church notes some of the other critical pieces of the puzzle, such as the presence of competent, resourced companies in the industry, or the availability of a competent team to lead a start-up:

> Start-ups are very challenging; licensing has the advantage that if the company has some money or experience, you can leverage that. You don't get quite as much ownership of it, but it has its advantages. Start-ups are great when you think you have a wonderful team for some reason or other. It's all about teamwork; if you get a dysfunctional team, then there's no reason to even start the start-up.

Many factors drive the decision to license a technology; some may be personal and some may be practical. In Table 4-2, we have created a limited set of issues and questions that can help the inventing entrepreneur consider the situation.

There may be a single factor that drives the decision (e.g., an inventor does not want to be involved in commercialization). For example, some inventors simply prefer not to be involved in the commercialization process. Otherwise, inventors that respond "Yes" to a majority of the "Questions/Factors to Consider," should focus on working with the relevant technology transfer authority to license the technology to an unrelated third party. Now let us consider the commercial issues in licensing (see Table 4-3).

TABLE 4-2 Considering Technology Licensing: A Personal Perspective

Personal (Purpose)	*Questions/Factors to Consider*
Visualizing the ultimate goal	• Do I plan to stay in my current job/position in the short term? • Do I plan to stay in my current job/position in the long term? • Is there external expertise that would help bring this technology to market?
Grasping the significance of my technology	• Is the technology likely to be of interest to a third party? • Does the technology offer potential for a third party to generate revenues and profits? • Is the technology more likely to succeed with people who have commercialized similar technologies in the past?
Understanding my personal affinity for the technology	• Do I need to control the outcome or applications of the technology? • Am I comfortable with the possibility that the technology may reach the market in a format or product I haven't considered?
Estimating the benefits associated with commercializing my technology	• Am I comfortable with a significant majority of the financial rewards from this technology resting with a third party? • Would I prefer to participate financially via a consulting role (more upfront remuneration, less downstream remuneration) than via ownership?
Setting boundaries for the need to control my technology	• Can I accept that someone else may make the decisions about how the technology is developed and marketed? • Am I comfortable with the possibility that people with less technological expertise may fail to bring the technology to market?

Complementary assets are defined as resources that are needed to effectively use the technological innovation so that it can create value or profits.[16] In Table 4-2, there may be a single factor that drives the decision (e.g., the complementary assets required are far greater than those afforded by a small start-up). For example, in some cases the cost of acquiring the assets necessary to bring a technology to market will exceed the financing options available to a start-up company.[17] Inventors that respond "Yes" to a majority of the "Questions/Factors to Consider" in Table 4-2 should again focus on working with the relevant technology transfer authority to license the technology to an unrelated third party.

TABLE 4-3 Considering Technology Licensing: A Commercial Perspective	
Commercialization (Opportunity)	*Questions/Factors to Consider*
Complementary assets	• Does my technology need significant complementary assets (i.e., capital equipment, other intellectual property, etc.) to make it viable?
	• Is there a large production volume required before the technology is viable?
	• Will commercialization require significant expertise in related fields or functions that will be expensive to access?
	• Will replicating the necessary assets impose a cost burden on a new company trying to commercialize the technology (e.g., the cost of new equipment, compared to the cost of existing infrastructure, reduces or eliminates the value obtained from the new technology)?
	• Is the value creation from my technology dependent on other products and/or services?
	• Will the value creation from my technology be limited by a small sales and distribution infrastructure?
Intellectual property	• Is my technology limited by "freedom to operate" issues (e.g., do any other companies have blocking patents, or do any other companies have control of enabling patents)?
	• Will my technology's value creation be limited if it isn't augmented by significant R&D expenditures in related fields, or in continuous novel developments?

Conclusions and Summary

The technology innovator requires at least a rudimentary knowledge of the technology transfer process because many start-ups are formed by licensing an innovation from a technology transfer office. The role of the technology transfer office is critical, because the mission of the TTO may not necessarily be the same as the personal and professional goals of the innovator. The inventor considering the world of technology commercialization, especially one who may assume the role of an inventing entrepreneur, should carefully and objectively evaluate both the technology potential and his own motivations as preparation for entering the licensing process.

Endnotes

1. Chapple, W., Lockett, A., Siegel, D., & Wright, M. 2005. Assessing the relative performance of UK university technology transfer offices: Parametric and nonparametric evidence. *Research Policy,* 34(3): 369–384; Etzkowitz, H. 2002. *MIT and the Rise of Entrepreneurial Science.* New York: Routledge; Roberts, E. 1991. Entrepreneurs in High Technology. Oxford, UK: Oxford University Press; Siegel, D., Waldman, D., & Link, A. 2003. Assessing the impact of organizational practices on the relative productivity of university technology transfer offices: An exploratory study. *Research Policy,* 32(1): 27–48.

2. Henderson, R., Jaffe, A. B., & Trajtenberg, M. 1998. Universities as a source of commercial technology: A detailed analysis of university patenting, 1965–1988. *Review of Economics and Statistics,* 80(1): 119–127; Mowery, D. C., Nelson, R., Sampat, B., & Ziedonis, A. 2004. *Ivory Tower and Industrial Innovation: University Technology Transfer Before and After the Bayh-Dole Act.* Palo Alto, CA: Stanford University Press; Owen-Smith, J. & Powell, W. W. 2001. To patent or not: Faculty decisions and institutional success at technology transfer. *Journal of Technology Transfer,* 26: 99–114; Ding, W. W., Murray, F., & Stuart, T. E. 2006. Gender differences in patenting in the academic life sciences. *Science,* 313(5787): 665–667.

3. Razgaitis, R. 2003. *Valuation and Pricing of Technology-Based Intellectual Property.* New York: Wiley.

4. George, G. 2005. Learning to be capable: Patenting and licensing at the Wisconsin Alumni Research Foundation 1925–2002. *Industrial and Corporate Change,* 14(1): 119–151.

5. Stuart, T. E. & Ding, W. W. 2006. When do scientists become entrepreneurs? The social structural antecedents of commercial activity in the academic life sciences. *American Journal of Sociology,* 112(1): 97–144; Feldman, M., Feller, I., Bercovitz, J., & Burton, R. 2002. Equity and the technology transfer strategies of American research universities. *Management Science,* 48: 105–121; Di Gregorio, D. & Shane, S. 2003. Why do some universities generate more start-ups than others? *Research Policy,* 32(2): 209–227; George, G., Zahra, S. A., & Wood, D. R. 2002. The effects of business-university alliances on innovative output and financial performance: A study of publicly traded biotechnology companies. *Journal of Business Venturing,* 17(6): 577–609; Shane, S. & Stuart, T. E. 2002. Organizational endowments and the performance of university start-ups. *Management Science,* 48(1): 154–170.

6. There are several similarities across countries with regard to technology transfer. However, our discussion on technology transfer will focus on practices and circumstances relevant to Western academic research facilities, and in particular to U.S. academic research facilities.

7. At most research universities, there is a dedicated technology transfer office (TTO). Occasionally it is the provost for Academic Affairs or an office dedicated to managing research grants and funding.

8. At every stage, the TTO must continuously draw relatively rapid conclusions as to whether the innovation is both significant and can be protected. If the technology fails either test, then expending resources may be inappropriate. At this "predisclosure" stage, most TTOs will operate "optimistically," encouraging the disclosure process. But even the well-resourced TTOs would be overwhelmed if every novel research result were "disclosed" for evaluation.

9. Some TTOs have in-house patent attorneys, and some outsource nearly all patent prosecution to private intellectual property law firms.

10. Fosfuri, A. 2006. The licensing dilemma: Understanding the determinants of the rate of technology licensing. *Strategic Management Journal,* 27(12): 1141–1158.
11. The unique right to market a product, protected by country specific patent rights, is purposefully designed to offer limited monopoly power to the owner of the patent, specifically to enable the owner to obtain profits in a non-competitive environment to offset those development costs. An effective patenting infrastructure is thus intended to spur innovation with the promise of monopoly profits.
12. M. Edwards, F. Murray & R. Yu (2003). Value creation and sharing among universities, biotechnology and pharma. *Nature Biotechnology,* 21(6): 618–624.
13. The ability to "copy" the research performed by another firm could enable a competitor to enter a market with a lower cost structure (because the firm would not need to recoup prior or ongoing research and development costs) and thus with a lower price. Such a situation could effectively penalize the companies that invest in long-term research and development.
14. Reitzig, M., Henkel, J., & Heath, C. 2007. On sharks, trolls, and their patent prey: Unrealistic damage awards and firms' strategies of "being infringed." *Research Policy,* 36(1): 134–154.
15. www. hopkinsmedicine.org/webnotes/licensing/0306.cfm
16. Teece, D. 1986. Profiting from technological innovation. *Research Policy,* 15: 285–305; Arora, A. & Ceccagnoli, M. 2006. Patent protection, complementary assets, and firms' incentives for technology licensing. *Management Science,* 52(2): 293–308.
17. Consider, for example, a company attempting to demonstrate a novel technology that improves the efficiency of paper production. In theory, the company could build its own paper mill to compete with established players, but such an investment would likely run into the hundreds of millions of dollars. A far more likely scenario, in this situation, is that the company would choose to license the improvement to existing paper producers.

Recommended Readings

Etzkowitz, H. 2002. *MIT and the Rise of Entrepreneurial Science.* New York: Routledge.

Razgaitis, R. 2003. *Valuation and Pricing of Technology-Based Intellectual Property.* New York: Wiley.

Roberts, E. 1991. *Entrepreneurs in High Technology.* Oxford, UK: Oxford University Press.

Shane, S. 2004. *Academic Entrepreneurship: University Spinoffs and Wealth Creation.* Northampton, MA: Edward Elgar.

Wright, M., Clarysse, B., Mustar, P., & Lockett, A. 2007. *Academic Entrepreneurship in Europe.* Cheltenham, UK: Edward Elgar.

CHAPTER 5

LIFESTYLE BUSINESSES

OVERVIEW

The majority of academic research does not lead immediately to commercial products. Within the subset of innovations with near-term commercial potential, a further minority will present enough value creation potential to warrant a high-growth business requiring venture capital—the types of businesses that make headlines in *The Wall Street Journal*.

In this chapter, we're going to discuss a different type of commercial venture, one that generally does not receive significant fanfare. A lifestyle business is a viable option for opportunities that are not high-growth businesses with large markets. Though these businesses may be profitable, and in some cases more lucrative to the founder than a venture-backed growth business might be, the Lifestyle Entrepreneur option remains relatively unrecognized.

THE START-UP OPTION

According to a survey by the AUTM[1], Harvard's TTO created 7 start-ups between 2003–2005, compared with 20 by MIT, 19 by U of C, 3 by NYU and 3 by UNC. In other countries, start-ups are a more common outcome of university research. For example, Imperial College, London (United Kingdom) created 10 start-ups and filed 61 patents in 2006: roughly, a ratio of 1:6 compared with an estimate of 1:14 for MIT and 1:30 for the University of California.

At first glance, the number of high-potential university-based start-ups appears significantly lower than might be warranted from the hype or the expectations surrounding university technology transfer. Realistically, these numbers only account for start-ups in which the technology transfer office has been actively involved. These numbers significantly underrepresent the actual number of university-based start-ups. The gap is in how we document start-ups. For instance, technology transfer offices underestimate (1) faculty or student start-ups that do not have technology transfer office involvement, and (2) start-ups that are lifestyle businesses. Our discussions with faculty and TTOs suggest that new ventures linked to universities and university research but formed outside the formal TTO process far outnumber "official" start-ups spun-out via a formal technology licensing agreement.[2] Lifestyle businesses are those start-ups that cater to a niche market and offer modest opportunities for revenue growth. Consequently, the entrepreneurs who start such businesses often maintain full-time employment while managing the technology venture as a part-time effort. Some formal spin-outs and most of the informal ventures are lifestyle businesses. These lifestyle business opportunities should not be ignored by technology entrepreneurs—but a truly objective evaluation is required to ensure that the entrepreneur doesn't mistake a lifestyle business for something else (i.e., a high-potential business or vice versa).

Professor Fred Blattner (see Profile 5-1) has licensed university technologies for three businesses. The first, DNAStar, which he has owned (and at times managed) for 20 years, is an excellent example of a lifestyle business. His second opportunity, NimbleGen, was a venture-capital—funded growth company recently acquired by Roche. His commercialization instincts—and his interests and goals—clearly reflect the characteristics of the lifestyle entrepreneur. Blattner approaches commercialization by combining his love of research with practical business acumen:

> I am satisfied to spend money doing what's interesting. I haven't sacrificed the basic ability to live; I have a house and a mortgage. If this all collapsed, I would be out of money but I wouldn't be out on the street. This is a good hobby for me; I enjoy it. I've seen people get too involved with the science and lose sight of the fact that they're trying to make money in a business.

INVENTING ENTREPRENEUR PROFILE 5-1

Professor Fred Blattner

Fred Blattner brings confidence and enthusiasm to every endeavor, including his academic research and his commercial ventures. Blattner's successful university career parallels his venture experience. He's a founder or co-founder of three distinct businesses that have been spun-out of the University of Wisconsin. All are based on technology from his laboratory or from collaborative research. He evaluates commercial opportunities and his decisions to pursue commercial endeavors with a straightforward, practical, and unapologetically direct process.

For Blattner, commercialization as a logical extension to academic research goes back more than 20 years when his genetics research led to software for DNA sequence analysis. At the time, Blattner's lab had made the leap of putting the software on early desktop systems, obviating the need for mainframe computational power and extensive data storage. But the instigation for commercial efforts came from the business world.

> We were approached by City of Hope (a biomedical research facility in Southern California) about whether they could buy the system. That was my clue that we should think about selling them one. At about the same time, a program manager at NIH [National Institutes of Health] had learned about the new SBIR program and he said, "Why don't you start a company?" We thought about it, liked the idea and decided to do it. It was in my basement for a while. That developed into a very interesting saga, we never borrowed money or got any investors, we just sold software. Because personal computers were a rarity, we had to sell computers at the beginning so researchers could use the software.

DNASTAR was growing steadily and profitably, but Blattner's real focus was at the university: "I literally decided to devote my life to developing the Genome Center. This was a tremendous undertaking, and there was a need to devote full attention to this to get the space, people and funding necessary to establish a center up to the university's standards. Since I knew I could not devote full time to DNASTAR, the Genome Center and teaching, I hired someone to be DNASTAR's General Manager."

Blattner's next opportunity emerged a couple of years later as a result of his work at the Genome Center, utilizing microarray chips for genome assay hybridization. Microarray chips utilize thousands of small DNA segments attached to a slide to conduct a wide range of experiments. Current approaches were time consuming and expensive. Blattner had bought both spotted microarray and Affymetrix synthetic microarray machines for the center. Discussions on creating arrays for human c-DNA with Professor Mike Sussman (Genetics) and eventually Professor Franco Cerina (Physics) led to preliminary work on a novel gene chip array technology using miniature mirrors to create a "virtual mask" for DNA synthesis. (Please see Profile 13-1 on Mike Sussman and Franco Cerrina.) In theory, this "maskless" gene chip design would be dramatically more flexible and cheaper than standard gene chips. Blattner encouraged the team to establish and grow the venture (NimbleGen Systems) utilizing the same strategy he used to grow DNAStar. Instead, the team decided to seek venture capital to accelerate the opportunity—in part because they perceived that the opportunity could fit the high-growth venture-capital model.

> The three of us voted, and I was in favor of going it alone, and they voted to go with the [venture funder]. I was all right with that, because I had a hidden agenda of seeing how a venture-capital funded company really works…. I decided to shift into observer mode. I have made a few contributions…. One of the reasons I was a little dubious about NimbleGen was this was a pretty daunting situation. I wasn't sure whether a really careful venture capitalist would have taken this on.

In the end, NimbleGen would raise significant funds from venture-capital sources. In the spring of 2007, the company filed an S-1 document with the SEC to initiate an initial public offering (IPO). Before the IPO was executed, the company was bought by Roche for $272 million, a big success for the entire team.

In the last few years, Blattner's research has refocused on gene deletions, and he's formed another venture. Blattner originally led the scientific effort that first sequenced

(continues)

the complete E. coli genome, and much of his research has focused on that organism. Scarab Genomics, which Blattner started in 2002, has licensed technology related to genetic knockouts of E. coli:

> It's a platform company, similar to a software company. You're selling bacteria used to express proteins—it works like an operating system. The bacteria have a higher metabolic efficiency and offer emergent properties from getting rid of elements of the genome that confer genetic mobility. So the novel bacterial genome is much more stable and can express proteins more efficiently with less contamination.

Blattner's prior business experiences are especially valuable for this venture. He's aware of the many steps necessary to get a fledgling company running successfully. He recognizes that a start-up requires a significant investment of resources, including the time and energy of the founder. He's on a half-time leave of absence from the university so that he can be actively involved at Scarab. And he's always optimistic: "I think that always counts. I don't propose I've pursued every idea the companies have had, but I am always thinking that things are going to work."

Even for a relatively experienced entrepreneur like Blattner, however, the commercial process can bring unexpected twists. Recognizing opportunity and being able to quickly respond to it are important characteristics for the inventing entrepreneur.

> The eventual product was a big surprise to me. It turns out that it's injectible DNA. The insertion elements that hop around the genome, when we were able to create a string that had no mobile elements in it. This could be very helpful in a wide range of commercial applications including biopharmaceutical and biofuels production.

It can be difficult to assess what makes an entrepreneur successful. Sometimes the entrepreneur has more trouble than anyone isolating the skills or characteristics that have helped him/her achieve their goal. But Blattner has a particular view on what has helped him succeed.

> I think I have a high tolerance for what some people call chaos. I don't get upset when everything is going crazy. If I can see the pattern in it, it's good enough for me. That is difficult for a lot of people who prefer working more with knowns than unknowns.... I do a lot of mental projection of scenarios, but I have certain disciplines that I try to follow because they have worked for me in the past. Here's a rule: I never make an important decision until I've had a chance to sleep on it… it's not because I need more time, I think what happens during sleep seems to consolidate knowledge. You play out the scenarios of businesss decisions in your mind, and you might wake up in the morning and say, wait a minute, this guy knows that guy, and you might reconsider how to involve them to improve your decision options.

WHAT IS A LIFESTYLE BUSINESS?

Around the world, large corporations may generate greater revenues and dominate the airwaves, but small (and very small) companies comprise the numerical majority of business entities. Let us consider, for example, companies in the United Kingdom. There were 4.3 million businesses in the United Kingdom in 2005, of which 99.3% had fewer than 50 employees and another 0.6% (27,000) had between 50 and 250 employees. In fact, the significant majority (3.2 million, or 72.8%) of all businesses in the United Kingdom are sole proprietorships with no employees other than the owner himself. These sole-proprietor companies had a turnover of about £190 billion compared with companies that had employees (which had a turnover of £2,250 billion in 2005).[3] The United States presents similar data. According to the U.S. Census Bureau, there were 25.4 million firms in 2004 in the United States, of which 19.5 million had no employees,[4] 5.1 million had between 1 and 500 employees, and only 17,000 had more than 500 employees.[5] The patterns are similar across the world—small and medium-sized enterprises that can be classified as lifestyle businesses having a single owner and few employees are a sizable part of any economy, and these kinds of businesses are a viable option for technology entrepreneurs.

A "lifestyle business" is usually an organization with a niche product or a small market and does not grow into a large organization (whether because of structural limitations or because of the entrepreneur's preference). The Indiana Venture Center states: "A lifestyle business provides a very good living for the entrepreneurs involved; however, the business will never employ a significant number of people or create significant wealth for outside shareholders, employees, or the state."[6] We note that many lifestyle businesses involve the employment of the entrepreneur's family members or friends. Most businesses do not access significant external capital (i.e., via third-party investors), but are financed personally or with secured bank loans, or even through internal cash flow. Finally, exit options for lifestyle businesses are usually modest events, whether they involve dissolution, a planned transition within a family, or a modest third-party acquisition.[7]

Lifestyle businesses are distinct from technology-based growth businesses in the characteristics of their founders,[8] their strategies for growth,[9] and their aspirations.[10] These distinctions are important. If the entrepreneur wants to retain complete control of the technology and the commercialization process (entrepreneurial intent) or if the market opportunity is limited (value creation potential), then the lifestyle business may be the most appropriate avenue. The market opportunity is particularly critical; inventing entrepreneurs who misclassify a lifestyle business as a rapid-growth opportunity may suffer negative consequences when the business reaches limits to its growth. If the business has taken on private investors or debtors based on a presumption of growth, the entrepreneur could have unhappy stakeholders looking for a rapid exit. Basing the hiring of employees on growth that does not materialize can result in disgruntled employees and long-term human resource problems, including high turnover and a reputation for "overselling" candidates for key positions at the company. Like any other investor in an early-stage company, a technology transfer office that accepts licensing terms based on promises of rapid growth (thus becoming an investor in the new venture) may be displeased with a slow-growth business that generates limited royalties or equity returns.

The first stage in distinguishing lifestyle businesses from growth businesses is an opportunity analysis. Since many technology-based growth businesses require external capital, it would be easy to do this analysis using a traditional venture-capital rule of thumb—that a business able to be funded with venture capital must have a target market exceeding $500 million to $1 billion per year.[11] But any such stricture would be questionable, given that many technologies emerging from advanced research laboratories have no obvious discernible commercial market at all—or the market may be so novel that such an evaluation may fail to predict explosive growth.[12]

Better evaluations focus on a broader set of factors that will drive the commercialization potential for a given novel technology. Such factors include the following:

- Evaluating customers, including the size of the customer base, the value-added potential of the innovation, and customers' overall ability to adopt novel technologies
- Understanding the long-term geographic scope of the opportunity (i.e., is application of the technology limited to only a portion of the United States?)
- Calculating the long-term growth potential for the technology and product, based on adoption rates and trends in related industries
- Comparing exit potential based on industry averages and historical activity

Of these factors, we found that technology entrepreneurs usually had an excellent grasp of opportunity scope and growth potential, because they understood the extent of the technology's utilization to date. The weakness in their analyses usually results from a *failure to talk to actual customers about how they would utilize novel technology*. In addition, entrepreneurs sometimes use overly optimistic exit value multiples because they incorrectly compare their opportunity to significant successful ventures. This is especially common when an entrepreneur has a novel technology that offers a modest cost or quality improvement, but mistakenly believes that the technology will completely change the customer value proposition. Additional information about market analysis can be found in Chapters 9 and 10.

THE TTO AND LIFESTYLE BUSINESSES

Licensing niche technologies to start-ups presents special difficulties to the technology transfer office, because limited commercial potential challenges the investment-reward equation for the TTO. When a TTO licenses technology to a lifestyle business, the TTO may become a minority investor in a company with limited ability or incentive to generate investor returns. Lifestyle businesses, as a rule, provide income to employees rather than value growth to investors. In addition, most lifestyle businesses have exit scenarios that offer limited long-term upside potential for investors (see Chapter 14). As the TTO incurs significant expenses and overheads for a given patent or patent portfolio, the potential… may be questionable, the potential for achieving financial returns from such businesses may be questionable.

Unfortunately, this creates a dilemma for the technology entrepreneur, especially for one who is keen on initiating a commercialization process. An honest appraisal of the market opportunity could lead the TTO to either abandon the patenting process (to limit cost exposure) or demand strict or even prohibitive licensing terms (to attempt to capture appropriate returns on investment).

The sophisticated technology transfer office enables lifestyle businesses as part of a portfolio approach to technology licensing. Unfortunately, the resources to enable such an approach are not normally available to the average TTO. Ironically, the transition that is occurring nowadays from traditional technology transfer (licensing/selling technologies for cash to large well-resourced corporations) to equity-based technology transfer may be bypassing the lifestyle business option. The traditional model was somewhat analogous to a manufacturing company that sells a product. By contrast, promoting technology-based growth businesses places the TTO in a role roughly analogous to that of the venture capitalist, where high returns are necessary to offset the lost investments from failed ventures. The intermediate model of supporting faculty-based lifestyle businesses could be compared to that of a local lending institution. TTOs may have an opportunity to create lower-risk, moderate-reward "investments" by placing technologies into lifestyle businesses in which the technology entrepreneur and the TTO have a more equal risk-and-reward sharing arrangement.

CONSIDERATIONS FOR A LIFESTYLE BUSINESS

The decision to start a lifestyle business tends to be driven by two key factors: the desire to see a technology applied to a problem and the practical necessity of extracting the technology from the restricted environment of the academic research institution. It is important to emphasize that lifestyle businesses can be extremely successful and very lucrative for entrepreneurs. We conducted interviews with numerous entrepreneurs whose technology-based businesses are correctly categorized as highly successful lifestyle businesses. For example, John Devereux, the founder of Genetics Computer Group, gradually built the company until he sold it to Oxford Molecular and was able to retire comfortably. Professor Fred Blattner operates DNAStar with enough cash flow to fund an entirely separate technology-based company with a higher growth potential than DNAStar itself, because the new venture addresses more unsolved problems in the genomics space. This unusual situation, along with more details about Professor Blattner's entrepreneurial journey is described in Profile 5-1. In addition, lifestyle businesses usually offer the opportunity for the entrepreneur to retain significant (if not total) control over the disposition of the technology and the business. Combined with the intellectual enjoyment of working in one's chosen field every day, this often provides immense psychological satisfaction to the inventing entrepreneur.

In most lifestyle businesses, the technology innovator is one of the company managers, or perhaps the CEO. Sometimes the innovator enthusiastically embraces this leadership role, and sometimes the role is unavoidable because the venture can't bring in other managers with appropriate business experience.[13] The lifestyle entrepreneur should anticipate taking on responsibilities that have significant time requirements. Bootstrapping may be a reasonable option, but it can also limit growth rates if the start-up is constrained by a limited cash flow resulting from near-term sales of existing products or services.[14] The decision to start a lifestyle business begins with questions similar to those that relate to the licensing decision. In Table 5-1, we list questions related to the technology entrepreneur's purpose for starting a business.

TABLE 5-1 Considering a Lifestyle Business: A Personal Perspective	
Personal (Purpose)	*Questions/Factors to Consider*
Visualizing the ultimate goal	• Is it possible to effectively manage a small business without leaving my current job—or am I prepared to leave my current job? • Am I excited about the prospect of running a business? • Do I feel driven to bring this technology to the market to serve the needs of a niche customer set?
Grasping the significance of my technology	• Is my technology capable of solving business problems for a definable market segment? • Will the technology transfer office be willing to recoup patenting and other costs based on the long-term cash-driven success of a small business—or will the TTO require upfront cash from direct licensing to a large technology company? • Is the best commercialization path one that relies on expertise and innovation rather than distribution resources?
Understanding my personal affinity for the technology	• Am I driven to personally lead the commercialization of this technology? • Am I comfortable focusing on applying this technology to the market at the expense of new research and innovations? • Am I comfortable having my name and reputation closely associated with a small business venture that is bringing this technology to market?
Estimating the benefits associated with commercializing my technology	• Do the benefits of personally bringing this technology to market outweigh the benefits that might be gained from a third party's efforts instead (i.e., the innovator brings expertise, but an established player could have a distribution network in place)? • Should I be the primary beneficiary of the financial rewards that might result from the commercialization of the technology?
Setting boundaries for the need to control my technology	• Am I prepared to be primarily responsible for the success or failure of the technology in the marketplace? • Am I comfortable making the majority of the decisions at all levels of business operations?

TABLE 5-2 Considering a Lifestyle Business: A Commercial Perspective	
Commercialization (Opportunity)	*Questions/Factors to Consider*
Complementary assets	• Are the complementary assets associated with commercialization relatively limited?
Value creation	• Is the value creation from my technology dependent primarily on my own expertise and a self-contained technology solution?
Intellectual property	• Can my technology be marketed as a contained system that limits customers and competitors from quickly reengineering or copying value-creation characteristics?
	• Are the ongoing intellectual property costs associated with commercialization likely to be relatively small (including the probability of having to protect current and future patents)?

Responding "Yes" to a majority of these questions suggests that a lifestyle business may be the appropriate option for the technology entrepreneur. Our typology also requires an evaluation of the commercial opportunity. Table 5-2 identifies key questions related to the commercial aspect of a potential lifestyle business.

Considering the questions listed in Table 5-1 and Table 5-2 enables the technology entrepreneur to explore most of the broad issues that relate to making a decision about whether a lifestyle business is appropriate. If the answer to most of these questions is "Yes," then the opportunity presents the factors that could support a successful lifestyle business.

ENTREPRENEURIAL OPTIONS

By this point, we have already assumed that the inventing entrepreneur's technology does not belong in some file drawer. After considering some of the issues associated with licensing, however, the inventing entrepreneur may feel that licensing is not appropriate for the technology. Table 5-3 provides an overall summary of the information that we have presented concerning licensing entrepreneurs and lifestyle entrepreneurs and compares it with characteristics of the inventing entrepreneur.

As we prepare to talk about the inventing entrepreneur in the context of the technology-based growth company, it is useful to reflect on the challenges facing the technology researcher making the transition to corporate commercialization. Professor Franco Cerrina suggests why technologies are spun out of universities in the first place:

> When we're here (at the university) and we graduate students, our work comes to fruition in 5 to 10 years. Before you see something coming back, it takes a long time. The students have to go out and establish

TABLE 5-3	**Entrepreneurial Options**		
Issues	*Licensing Entrepreneur*	*Lifestyle Entrepreneur*	*Inventing Entrepreneur*
Ultimate goal	Scientist/faculty	Business manager	Faculty and/or business manager
	Focus on research	Focus on application	Focus on directed growth
Technology significance	Niche to significant	Niche application	Significant impact on broad markets
Technology affinity	Low to moderate	Very high	Moderate to very high
Commercialization benefits	Primarily benefits licensees, university, and faculty	Primarily benefits entrepreneur	Primarily benefits venture financiers and founders
Control requirements	Low	Very high	Moderate to very high

themselves–and you say, "Ah-ha! I did some good work on XYZ." In the case of novel technology commercialization—instead—there is a more immediate result with a company.

Another inventing entrepreneur at the University of Wisconsin-Madison, Professor Richard Burgess, whose venture we will discuss in detail later, has a slightly different view. Professor Burgess reminds us how difficult the process can be, and how important personal motivation and skills are.

Don't start a company unless you really want to start a company. If you're hesitant about it, it's not going to work. If the work you're doing needs a whole lot of basic research, then maybe you ought to consider doing that before you get too far into this process. The trouble is that you can't really do a lot of basic research in the company because you can't get funding to do that kind of research. You've got to see a pretty clear pathway; you can do research at the company but you can't take five years to do it.

Conclusions and Summary

Lifestyle businesses sometimes get a rap. The conventional image of the lifestyle business is the "mom and pop" store. The reality is that lifestyle businesses represent an empowering opportunity for researchers, scientists, and engineers to steer their innovations into commercial use and the public domain. The path may not appear as glamorous as hundred-million-dollar venture-funded deals, but lifestyle businesses may not require giving up as much control or tackling as many hurdles and obstacles. They can, in fact, be lucrative for the talented entrepreneur who utilizes creative financing and good cash management to retain ownership and grow the business organically.

The focus of this book will now transition to discussing the higher-profile *inventing entrepreneur* who is involved in industry changing opportunities. Before leaving this chapter, we would like to note that the media hype surrounding angel and venture capital has led many entrepreneurs to lose their objectivity when evaluating the long-term commercial potential of their innovations. The opportunity to develop many potentially successful lifestyle businesses has been missed in the drive to create high-growth externally funded companies that ultimately cannot be sustained. We hope that the technology innovator reading this book will carefully consider whether the lifestyle business is, after all, the correct commercial path.

Endnotes

1. U.S. Licensing Survey 2005. The Association of University Technology Managers (AUTM), www.autm.net/.
2. In addition, we note that circumstances do exist in which technology is "leaked" from universities, whether inadvertently or to purposefully circumvent the technology licensing procedure. We are not aware of statistics on such "unauthorized" technology entrepreneurship. We emphasize, however, that such activities may be unethical and possibly illegal.
3. Statistical press release dated 31 August 2006, URN 06/92. National Statistics. UK: Department of Trade and Industry.
4. "Non-employer statistics summarizes the number of establishments and sales or receipts of businesses without paid employees that are subject to federal income tax. Most non-employers are self-employed individuals operating very small unincorporated businesses, which may or may not be the owner's principal source of income." United States Bureau of the Census.
5. www.census.gov/epcd/www/smallbus.html
6. www.indianaventurecenter.org/faqs.asp#7
7. The value of any business, including small businesses and even sole proprietorships, is usually greater than its cash-flow generation capacity in a given year. Many a small business owner assumes that the *sole* value of the business is her own involvement, and that therefore, if she leaves, the business has no value. This is, in general, not the case. Business value may reside in customer lists, brand name, intellectual property codified into business practices, and trained employees. There are many examples of small business owners who exit a business *simply by closing up shop,* rather than by considering more remunerative options such as a third-party sale, acquisition by a supplier or vendor, or even sale to employees.
8. Aldrich, H. E. & Waldinger, R. 1990. Ethnicity and entrepreneurship. *Annual Review of Sociology,* 16: 111–135; O'Gorman, C., Bourke, S., & Murray, J. A. 2005. The nature of managerial work in small growth-oriented businesses. *Small Business Economics,* 25(1): 1–16; Kim, P. H., Aldrich, H. E., & Keister, L. A. 2006. Access (not) denied: The impact of financial, human, and cultural capital on entrepreneurial entry in the United States. *Small Business Economics,* 27(1): 5–22; Barringer, B., Jones, F., & Neubaum, D. 2005. A quantitative content analysis of the characteristics of rapid-growth firms and their founders. *Journal of Business Venturing,* 20(5): 663–687.

9. Delmar, F. & Shane, S. 2003. Does business planning facilitate the development of new ventures? *Strategic Management Journal,* 24(12): 1165–1185; George, G., Wiklund, J., & Zahra, S. A. 2005. Ownership and the internationalization of small firms. *Journal of Management,* 31(2): 210–233; Vohora, A., Wright, M., & Lockett, A. 2004. Critical junctures in the development of university high-tech spinout companies. *Research Policy,* 33(1): 147–175.

10. Wiklund, J. & Shepherd, D. 2005. Entrepreneurial orientation and small business performance: A configurational approach. *Journal of Business Venturing,* 20(1): 71–91; Stewart, W. H., Watson, W. E., Carland, J. C., & Carland, J. W. 1999. A proclivity for entrepreneurship: A comparison of entrepreneurs, small business owners, and corporate managers. *Journal of Business Venturing,* 14(2): 189–214.

11. To be clear, venture capitalists (VCs) often use this type of rule to help sift through the thousands of financing applications they receive annually—but we are also familiar with VCs that have regularly gone against this rule of thumb.

12. As one venture capitalist noted to us privately, "If you can identify the market for your innovation in a standard market research report, then you're already too late."

13. Often this is because the company can't afford to pay market rates for qualified executives, but sometimes competent managers are difficult to identify for a specific technology field, target market, or geographic area.

14. George, G. 2005. Slack resources and the performance of privately held firms. *Academy of Management Journal,* 48(4): 661–676; Penrose, E. G. 1959. *The Theory of the Growth of the Firm.* New York: Wiley; Baker, T. & Nelson, R. 2005. Creating something from nothing: Resource construction through entrepreneurial bricolage. *Administrative Science Quarterly,* 50: 329–366.

PART II

CULTIVATING AN ENTREPRENEURIAL IDENTITY

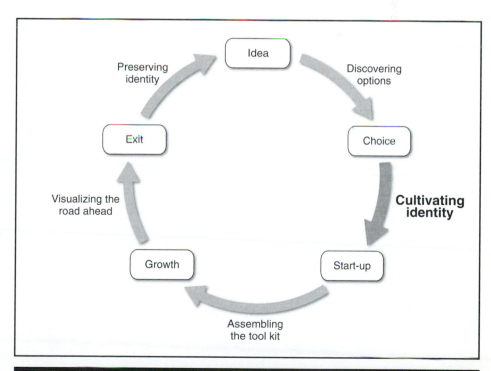

Stages in the Entrepreneurial Process

CHAPTER 6

THE ENTREPRENEURIAL ACADEMIC

OVERVIEW

Over the past 25 years, the roles of "entrepreneur" and "scholar" have converged in the inventing entrepreneur. This combination is especially fascinating in the case of the university faculty member who serves as an executive for one (or more) technology-driven businesses. Studies reveal that even as recently as the 1990s many professors perceived a stigma attached to faculty associated with start-up companies.[1] That stigma has been reduced or eliminated, whether formally or informally, as more research universities evolve policies to tolerate or even promote entrepreneurship within the faculty.[2,3] Some faculty even find themselves unexpectedly pressed to participate in venture creation.

It might seem odd to talk about University of Wisconsin–Madison Professor Jo Handelsman in this context, since she has never started a company to commercialize her technology or taken on an executive role in a commercial venture. She has, however, taken on a strong advocacy role to support commercialization efforts, after having carefully evaluated her own philosophical leanings:

> Almost all the company contacts have gone through me. I've heard some faculty say, "that's the way it is, we're the point people, we're the experts," and I've heard other people say they just turn it over to WARF [Wisconsin Alumni Research Foundation, University of Wisconsin's TTO] and work with their marketing. I've never went out and marketed, because people would see my talks and see the potential for [my research on plant pathology] and I would be contacted by people in industry.

Professor Handelsman's decision not to start a company reflects sophisticated analysis of her own goals and the requirements of such an endeavor. As we consider some of the challenges facing inventing entrepreneurs, it is useful to reflect on Handelsman's conclusions and opinions. While every innovator will need to reflect on his own unique talents, characteristics, and circumstances, Handelsman's analytical process presents an excellent model:

> I was never tempted at all by the idea of starting a company.... And now my recent inventions are much more commercially viable and have a larger market and potential, and so I feel even more strongly about it. The new work is largely pharmaceutical, and I can't even imagine starting a company in that arena. Success is so dependent on large-scale synthesis, fermentation and registration abilities. I thought the agricultural registrations were expensive; of course drugs are even more expensive.

WHO ARE ACADEMIC ENTREPRENEURS?

For some, like Professor George Church at Harvard, the entrepreneurial process has become well defined and orchestrated. Professor Church identifies himself as a tenured faculty first and an entrepreneur second. He took an active role in the creation of one of his most recent businesses, Codon Devices, which is commercializing a technology for designing and constructing synthetic genetic sequences. But Church states that he never considered leaving Harvard to serve as CEO—for a number of reasons. Although he was intrigued by the prospect of serving as a "go-between" for the lab and the commercial sector, he had always planned to stay at the university. In addition, Professor Church has always believed that inventing, rather than managing, is both his true strength and calling.

But for others, like Randy Cortwright of Virent Energy Systems, the opportunity to redirect and focus the research effort toward the development of a specific application (in this case, biomass-based hydrogen generation for energy applications) was the next logical step of a long-term research journey:

> I have a high risk tolerance. I am willing to fail at a lot of things. I love doing exploratory type of work, and that's where a lot of this came from. [My Ph.D. advisor] wants to do basic research, and I always thought: let's do something that's practical, let's get something out there. In Virent, I am still going to be working in a lab but I'll also be able to do what I wanted to do.

Paul Reckwerdt had a similar vision. When he founded Tomotherapy in 1997 with Professor Rock Mackie, Reckwerdt led the fledgling business while Mackie retained his medical physics faculty position. It would be hard to question that decision: Reckwerdt continuing leadership was instrumental in the company's success, including its initial public offering in the spring of 2007.

In some cases, it may be possible for faculty to retain a full-time (or nearly full-time) academic position while serving in executive management at a start-up. Hector DeLuca is the CEO of Deltanoid, but he brought in a chief operating officer (COO) to manage day-to-day operations so he could focus primarily on higher-level strategy, technology, and development issues. We do know faculty who found ways to balance a full-time faculty position with a full-time CEO position, but we believe that these situations are rare, and likely represent extraordinary circumstances. Our research suggests that such a role encompasses an enormous time commitment, with significant concurrent emotional and psychological stressors. Our investigations suggest that the most common leadership role for the faculty entrepreneur at a start-up company that is commercializing his own technology is that of chief science officer (CSO) or chief technology officer (CTO).

Regardless of the role the faculty entrepreneur adopts at the commercial entity, he will encounter a series of common challenges.

THE INTELLECTUAL CHALLENGE OF ENTREPRENEURSHIP

Nearly every inventing entrepreneur we spoke to mentioned the value of continuous learning and intellectual challenge. Some saw entrepreneurship as a stage of personal development, while others chose to retain their focus on academic research for intellectual fulfillment. We did not observe that clear patterns of personal characteristics were effective determinants of how research technology entrepreneurs would respond to the different kinds of opportunities for intellectual challenge. The decision to pursue the challenge within the business world rather than within the academic environment appears to be driven by factors of purpose and intent, in conjunction with resource-related factors (such as the availability of professional management and investment capital). Professor Richard Burgess provides an excellent summary of his own decision process:

> As background, I had been a researcher for 30 years at the university;
> I had founded the biotech center; I had been an angel investor in probably
> 10 companies; I had been active in economic development and
> technology transfer—but I had never been an entrepreneur. I had
> cheered my friends on from the sidelines and invested in their
> companies, but I had never done it myself. That was the appeal.

Some inventing entrepreneurs were even more specific about the types of intellectual challenge they sought and enjoyed. TRAC Micro CEO Virginia Deibel already had business experience when she made the decision to obtain a Ph.D. in microbiology. (Please see Profile 12-2 for her journey.) She knew the type of business she wanted to run, and decided that a Ph.D. was a necessary component of her strategy to gain credibility and improve innovation in her business. She actively sought the intellectual challenge of applying research directly to market issues:

> There's still that quest for information, but the thing that's different for
> me about the commercial setting is that it's not basic science, it is

applied science. I don't want to figure out fundamental gene promoter issues. But, if I can say that you can further activate that in this bacteria and make them very hardy, then you can use a smaller dose and still get the same effect, and that's a huge [cost] saving for customers.

One factor that appeared to contribute to a propensity for the intellectual challenge of commercial management was direct prior experience in a commercial setting, usually through research internships at large corporations or mentoring from other inventing entrepreneurs.

It is important to differentiate between the intellectual challenges found at an entrepreneurial firm versus the university research laboratory. Many of the entrepreneurs we interviewed described the excitement of moving a product toward the market and seeing it in use; others talked about the more facile nature of business operations, including such mundane tasks as equipment purchasing. No matter how "collegiate" the entrepreneurial environment can be, the rigors and focus of a start-up company will not mimic the learning and development-focused atmosphere of the university laboratory. Professor Church explains:

Particularly in an entrepreneurial environment, there's a laser-beam focus, there's a single fact of attention. There's usually something that is right now in the critical path that needs all your focus. In the academic world, you're on multiple fronts at the same time. You're teaching one day, you're working with your research group the next day, you probably have more than one research activity going. So you're bouncing between ideas; it's mentally very stimulating; you have this wonderful parade of students coming through to constantly renew things.

BUSINESS CHALLENGES

There is no shortage of business challenges facing the academic entrepreneur. The fundamental business challenge can be summarized as a bandwidth constraint. The academic scientist has developed sophisticated tools and skills to lead an active research program. It is unlikely that this individual has also researched the basics of business operations, much less actively managed a company. Experienced executives command high salaries because of demonstrated success in complex corporate environments. For the academic entrepreneur, learning the underlying skills to manage a successful company, especially in a high-technology field, is likely to be extraordinarily time consuming. This can be especially problematic if the entrepreneur retains an active university faculty position. Rather than focus on the business challenges facing every entrepreneur, we identify two key challenges associated with this problem of bandwidth: identifying competent mentors that can accelerate the business learning process and accessing basic knowledge on how a company functions.

ACCESS TO MENTORSHIP

Studies suggest that entrepreneurs consistently identify a trusted mentor as either a critical element of success or a desired resource. An experienced mentor is a valuable resource to the inventing entrepreneur.[4,5] The majority of mentors fall into one of two categories—either an other inventing entrepreneur with business experience (i.e., the mentor has at least one technology-based business that is ongoing or has been exited) or an experienced businessperson knowledgeable about business operations, preferably in the relevant technology sector. According to inventing entrepreneurs, mentors provide the following:

- Distilled business basics, including general advice on every aspect of business management from sales and marketing to bookkeeping
- Networking connections that range from recommendations on service providers to introductions to financiers
- Optimism and emotional support
- Honest and open criticism
- Open-ended evaluations of the business concept, often unhampered by a high affinity to the technology or to the market

Traditional entrepreneurs obtain value from mentors and advisors, but the value to the inventing entrepreneur may be proportionately greater. Mentors offer a shortcut to experience—the opportunity to sidestep a potentially lengthy learning process that would include time-consuming tangents and potentially significant mistakes and setbacks. The inventing entrepreneur's time may be the most precious commodity for a start-up venture. She may be balancing commercial efforts with her role in the academic environment (and perhaps family and social obligations as well), while the technology-driven market space may be moving faster than her ability to assimilate basic business skills and perform commercially focused analyses based on experiential learning.

The identification of a competent, enthusiastic mentor appears to be somewhat unpredictable. For the most part, the entrepreneurs we interviewed who sought such a resource have found one, though we didn't attempt to evaluate the competency of the mentors or the effectiveness of the relationship. While opportunistic by definition, the successful search for a qualified mentor likely hinges on networking—contacting as many relevant business connections as possible.

At the same time, many of our interviewees were explicit about the value of going through the learning process actively, and that includes making mistakes. Professor Farritor, one of the inventing entrepreneurs at Nebraska Surgical Solutions, a start-up company commercializing robotic surgical tools, comments:

> The only way to really learn is to go through the process. I tell students all the time you've got to do the homework; you've got to bang your head against the wall on the homework before you can try to get a decent grade on the exam.

ACCESS TO BASIC BUSINESS KNOWLEDGE

Many entrepreneurs commented on the difficulty in accumulating an effective set of basic business tools. Time constraints and lack of familiarity with business resources amplify this challenge. A few entrepreneurs had attended business seminars—often on raising private finance or on intellectual property—while most relied on their ability to learn on the job from service providers and partners.

In the course of our research, we did not uncover a simple solution to this problem. It is usually not feasible for the inventing entrepreneur to enroll in extensive business education classes (whether at a business school or at a related institution), and it appears difficult for those without any corporate experience to quickly adapt to both the functional business activities and the nuances of corporate behavior. Obviously, access to a mentor can help. Another option is to identify a competent Master of Business Administration (MBA)–level resource to serve in an operational and administrative role. In some cases, a recent MBA can help get the start-up venture off the ground by tackling administrative and operational issues. Our intent, however, is not to recommend specific roles or titles, because competencies, circumstances, and team building vary dramatically across early-stage ventures. Research faculty may be able to establish relatively quick connections to MBA-level resources through university channels, as compared with the potentially lengthy networking effort needed to find resources unaffiliated with the university. The entrepreneur can then rely to some degree on the basic business knowledge of that individual while simultaneously picking up general business skills.

PERSONAL CHALLENGES

Our research was, for the most part, cross-sectional or static. We utilized a snapshot approach, obtaining the narration and evaluation of the historical and/or ongoing processes engaged in by inventing entrepreneurs. Although we encouraged interviewees to compare current and past perspectives, such reflections are necessarily not confirmable. A longitudinal evaluation of the entrepreneurial challenges of inventing entrepreneurs would likely be revealing. Nevertheless, we feel certain trends are worth at least an anecdotal review.

PRIORITIZING GOALS

The single most common goal for commercializing novel technology identified by interviewees was the application of novel technology for broad use. The variety of responses, however, suggests that there are substantive nuances to this goal. We detected a general consensus that "application for broad use" involves making the innovation available to the public marketplace (as compared to purely academic or government use). In addition, we discovered that most (though not all) interviewees assumed that the ultimate measure of value for the innovation would be determined in the public marketplace (i.e, presumably in some form of financial success), rather than according to a more subjective measure of the "good of society."

Realistically, this vision of technology commercialization subsumes two factors. First, that the development of the technology application and subsequent market entry will be driven, in part, by the vision of the inventor. Second, that the rewards from market success will accrue, in part, to the investments and intellectual creativity of the inventors and the early commercialization participants because of the value of their intellectual creativity and long-term research investment. This may seem, at first glance, to merely reflect traditional capitalist theory, but it reflects a remarkable transformation in expectations and intentions. As recently as 20-25 years ago, the vast majority of academic researchers labored with little or no expectation of financial reward from the commercialization of their work.

Goal prioritization is also tightly linked to the question of affinity and conflict of interest. The technology transfer process tends to create complex and possibly conflicting incentives for dissemination of information. The academic inventor's goal of publishing results may conflict with the licensee's goal of preserving intellectual property rights.[6] Intellectual property prosecution has dramatically increased in complexity and perceived value, especially in the fields of biotechnology and software. Even within our limited sample, a significant number of inventing entrepreneurs commented on the potential conflict between academic publication and corporate intellectual property (or even trade secrets). We did not find that this issue of prioritization (i.e., prioritizing publication either above or below the need to maintain confidentiality regarding patent disclosures) was perceived differently by tenured versus untenured faculty.

REPERCUSSIONS WITHIN THE ACADEMIC ENVIRONMENT— CONFLICT OF INTEREST

We were somewhat surprised to note relatively few concerns about conflict of interest within the academic environment. Our observations, interviews, and direct personal experience with early-stage companies suggest that many academics do consider the potential conflicts of interest associated with participation in (or direct management of) a commercial entity that is marketing products or technologies originating from their own university laboratories. To a significant degree, however, our interviewees suggested that these issues were, for the most part, manageable. A few academics recommended early interaction with department chairs or departmental conflict-of-interest committees, whereas many simply failed to mention the issue at all. Professor Jo Handelsman provided the most thoughtful and introspective commentary on conflicts of interest. Her perspective appears to stem, in part, from her direct experience with managing conflicts of interest while she was a graduate student. Profile 6-1 describes her journey and perspective on technology transfer.

INVENTING ENTREPRENEUR PROFILE 6-1

Professor Jo Handelsman

Jo Handelsman isn't just a professor of plant pathology at the University of Wisconsin–Madison. Her activities include authoring books on controversies in science,[7] promoting women in science, and engaging in efforts to improve undergraduate education in biology. While it's perhaps uncommon for someone researching antibiotics to be cross-listed as a professor of industrial and systems engineering, it's all part of Handelsman's incredible breadth of experience and expertise. Unlike many of our interviewees, however, the one thing she's never wanted to do was start or run a company commercializing her own technology. For Handelsman, the issue of technology transfer goes back to her graduate school days, when she found herself at the center of the commercialization discussion:

> I thought a lot about the connection between industry and the university. As a graduate student I was asked to be on a panel that was about the interface between companies and university labs—and about when there are conflicts of interest and when there aren't. It was this large public forum with reporters, and I ended up very oddly being a focal point because my major professor was leaving the university to start a company. Everyone else seemed to assume that his departure had dire implications for me, but it hadn't had a negative impact on my career at all. However, these concerns weren't entirely unfounded—there were egregious stories of faculty who had turned their university research programs into companies. Some were even forbidding their own graduate students to talk about their work, but that was not my personal experience.

Professor Handelsman is not averse to the technology transfer process, but she's very explicit about the purposes of technology transfer:

> I think it's really important to spread the word to faculty that tech transfer is important—and not because we necessarily want to be entrepreneurs (although that's okay if that's what we want), and not necessarily because we want to get rich, and not because we want industry running the university, or whatever it is that people assume are the motivations for patenting and licensing the products of university research. Technology transfer benefits society and the university. The Bayh-Dole Act made it easy to say "this is your obligation, not just something you might like to do."

Handelsman's own work focuses on antibiotic production by bacteria, especially by species that haven't been successfully cultivated in the laboratory. And there have been numerous opportunities to consider commercial possibilities. A number of her technologies have been licensed to various corporations for use as biocontrol agents. But throughout this process, she has cultivated a sense of her own place within the academic community:

> You get to a stage in life where you kind of find out what you're good at. One of the things that make being a senior faculty member so much fun is that you can shed all the stuff that you don't do well. We all still have to do things that we don't enjoy, but at least we don't bother with the things we know we don't do well. I'm pretty good at teaching and leading an academic research group, so why would I go off and do something for which I have no apparent aptitude? If I had any belief I'd be great at it, perhaps I'd think I was depriving the world of some great talent, but I don't. There are lots of people out there who know business and can do a really

good job running companies and those are the people who should be commercializing university technology.

For Handelsman, there's also been a significant personal side to her research:

A number of years ago, my mother developed an immunological disease and ended up with multiple infections caused by antibiotic-resistant bacteria that ultimately caused her death after 17 years of miserable illness. I took care of her in her last few years—and became so frustrated watching the person I loved more than anybody in the world drowning in bacteria. I had spent my life studying bacteria and trying to find the agents to kill them, but there was just nothing I could do to help her fight the bacteria that were killing her. That has become a very private passion that fuels my research.

Handelsman is an example of an inventing entrepreneur functioning within the academic environment. She creates and leads programs across a wide variety of scientific and social topics. For Handelsman, entrepreneurship is about creating and building institutions that survive her; she views her contributions as based on the longer-term teaching and research models.

I think running a lab means being an entrepreneur. An entrepreneur is someone who builds something from nothing and that's pretty much what it is to build an academic science lab. You have an idea, you go out and convince other people it's a good idea to get money, you find smart people and you manage them and they produce things. In broad brush strokes—I think it's the same process in university research and business; it's the products that differ. But at a detailed level, there are important differences. To me, the biggest divide in day-to-day life in a company versus an academic lab is that the major product of an academic lab is education. I teach all day, whether I am in the classroom or in my lab. At a university, research serves education. And education can be inefficient. Sometimes educators need to nurture people through their own limitations, which is not always possible in start-up companies that have to [demonstrate results in a short time-frame.] Sometimes a professor needs to have faith in a student who isn't performing and help them find their way to being a fabulous scientist. Sometimes it's a long wait for that to happen and that wait is a luxury that industrial science simply can't afford.

We suspect that some of the perceived stigma and concern about conflict of interest has waned as universities have chosen to promote the commercialization activities of faculty. In addition, we suspect that many research universities have established appropriate mechanisms for managing conflict of interest—in order to avoid having to address such circumstances on an ad hoc basis.

Conclusions and Summary

Sometimes faculty make the conscious decision to be aware of commercialization opportunities and participate in the commercialization process without changing either their personal perspective or academic and research focus. George Church personifies this mode. Although he has had numerous opportunities to participate directly in commercialization, his long-term goals have always remained tied to the academic research laboratory. Other faculty members are entirely transformed by the process and choose to take on primarily commercial roles—whether they remain focused on research or on making a complete transition to organizational management. Reviewing these journeys and outcomes will be focus of the next two chapters.

The academic entrepreneur is an unpredicted evolutionary development in the world of traditional entrepreneurship. A variety of environmental forces have coalesced to encourage academic researchers, primarily focused on the development of long-term scientific discovery, to consider the value of active participation in the commercialization process. Changes in academic culture, including the perception of wealth accumulation, have played a significant role. The development of a sophisticated venture capital community—due in part, to the rapidly evolving nature of technology-driven competition—has made longer-term gestation periods possible for research-driven corporations. The evolving nature of technology transfer, empowered by both the Bayh-Dole Act and the precedent set by institutions (including Stanford, MIT, and the University of Wisconsin–Madison to name a few),[8] has created a niche in which technology experts can become commercialization catalysts. Anecdotally, the absolute number of successful academic entrepreneurs remains low. An institution such as UW–Madison, with more than 2,000 faculty members, has generated only a few dozen inventing entrepreneurs. But the number increases each year, and the success of only a few germinates the seeds of entrepreneurship in many more.

Endnotes

1. Bok, D. 2003. *Universities in the Marketplace: The Commercialization of Higher Education*. Princeton, NJ: Princeton University Press.
2. Murray, F. 2004. The role of academic inventors in entrepreneurial firms: Sharing the laboratory life. *Research Policy,* 33(4): 643–659.
3. Kenney, M. & Goe, W. R. 2004. The role of social embeddedness in professorial entrepreneurship: A comparison of electrical engineering and computer science at UC Berkeley and Stanford. *Research Policy,* 33(5): 691–707.
4. De Janasz, S. C. & Sullivan, S. E. 2004. Multiple mentoring in academe: Developing the professorial network. *Journal of Vocational Behavior,* 64(2): 263–283.
5. Duderstadt, J. J. 2001. Preparing future faculty for future universities. *Liberal Education,* 87(2): 24–31.
6. The disclosure of a novel technology via journal manuscript or scientific seminar may preclude the opportunity to file for intellectual property protection. For example, almost any type of public disclosure will restrict or eliminate the opportunity to file for patent protection in Europe.
7. Kleinman, D., Kinchy, A. & Handlesman, J. 2005. *Controversies in Science and Technology: From Maize to Menopause.* Madison, WI: University of Wisconsin Press.
8. Mowery, D. C., Nelson, R. R., Sampat, B. N., & Ziedonis, A. A. 2001. The growth of patenting and licensing by US universities: an assessment of the effects of the Bayh-Dole act of 1980. Research Policy, 30(1): 99–119.

CHAPTER 7

ENTREPRENEURIAL JOURNEY MODEL

OVERVIEW

Most academic researchers do not anticipate becoming inventing entrepreneurs. This is an important and powerful message for technology innovators considering technology propagation options. The transition does not happen overnight — the process is not complete when the technology license is signed. Inventors become entrepreneurs over time, accruing business experiences and skills. Each inventing entrepreneur travels an idiosyncratic path and discovers a unique, personal, entrepreneurial identity. There is no single or "right" form of inventing entrepreneur.

In this chapter, we offer a journey model to help innovators preview the entrepreneurial path. The model utilizes two pairs of contrasting factors. First, we distinguish between a research role and a commercial role. Second, we contrast a technology-based identity against a market-based identity.

A clear example of the tension between these factors can be presented through the eyes of Professor Michael Stonebraker, originally at UC–Berkeley but currently at MIT. His research on relational databases and other leading-edge data analysis tools has led to numerous start-up companies. But it all began with the realization that "impact" would depend on more than just innovation:

> We wrote an early relational database system. It was a very discontinuous storage technology from what was then the norm. We had it working very well at Berkeley, but there was a limit to the impact it could possibly have because it was an unsupported system. It was clear that [to have] any significant impact we had to commercialize the product.

From there, Professor Stonebraker made personal decisions about his own involvement that led to his active role as an inventing entrepreneur. As we explore entrepreneurial journey models, we will concurrently review the underlying factors that drive inventors' decisions to explore entrepreneurship.

ENTREPRENEURIAL IDENTITIES

A promising approach for exploring inventors' entrepreneurial decisions employs the concepts of role and identity from the social psychology literature. **Roles** are social positions that carry with them expectations for behavior and obligations to other actors.[1] **Identity** helps individuals orient themselves to their context, gives meaning to their experience, and provides guidelines for action.[2] The concept of **role identity** highlights the close linkage between the socially defined elements that underlie a role and an individual's own idiosyncratic interpretation of that role.[3,4] A role identity is the self-view or meaning attributed to oneself in relation to a specific role. As a role becomes closely tied to an individual's sense of self or identity, the individual tends to behave in accordance with this role identity.

For example, let's take the role of a professor. This role implies that people can reasonably expect a professor to engage in the teaching of students and in research to push the boundaries of knowledge. Identity, on the other hand, is the self-perception of the individual who is occupying this role. So the person who is a professor may believe that teaching is more central than research or vice versa. Consequently, a professor whose identity emphasizes only teaching is more likely to teach than do research. Therefore, role identity captures both the social expectations of the function as well as the individual's perception of what that function entails.

Role identities need not be contradictory. For example, while a person may be a scientist, she may also be a mother. These role identities do not necessarily contradict each other and can coexist comfortably. For an inventor who adopts the role identity of an entrepreneur this may not necessarily be the case. The social expectations for "academics" and "entrepreneurs" may incorporate distinct and even mutually exclusive elements; an inventor may find it a challenge to assume both roles. Consequently, managing these role identities is a critical process in the Entrepreneurial Journey Model. Identity changes are likely to accompany these transitions because new roles require new skills, behaviors, and patterns of interaction.[5,6] Individuals think about the decision to become involved in entrepreneurial activity in personal and career terms.[7,8,9] In subsequent chapters, we will discuss what these entrepreneurial activities include. It is sufficient now to note that entrepreneurial activities include those actions required for forming a new venture and facilitating operations (securing financing, hiring employees, and developing a product for consumers).

A key aspect of an individual's decision to embark on an entrepreneurial journey involves engaging in the evaluative process of comparing the role identity that one associates with entrepreneurial activity with that of a referent role[10] (for our purposes, the referent role is usually that of a scientist, a graduate student, or an undergraduate student). This evaluation entails an appraisal of the costs and benefits associated with the new entrepreneurial role—as well as an estimation of the transition magnitude involved in switching roles. Professor Stonebraker's journey, for example, is one that includes multiple roles and an evolving role identity (see Profile 7-1).

INVENTING ENTREPRENEUR PROFILE 7-1

Michael Stonebraker

Professor Stonebraker is one of the most prolific inventing entrepreneurs we interviewed. With four start-ups under his belt and a fifth start-up, Vertica, receiving $23.5 million in funds in two financing rounds, he's been through the process enough times to bring perspective and wisdom to the endeavor. He's served as CTO twice and CEO three times, somehow sandwiching all this between a full career at the University of California–Berkeley and a postretirement career at MIT. Stonebraker was one of the pioneers of relational database technology at UC–Berkeley, but at that time commercializing software from university research was a relatively novel concept. Fortunately, Stonebraker already had connections in the commercial realm, which helped move the concept forward:

> I happened to know the then vice president of sales for Cullinane Corporation[11]—we wrote a business plan for venture capital. At the time, the bulk of venture capital went to hardware companies, so the challenge was convincing them there were barriers to entry in the software business and something being a good idea didn't mean that Digital Equipment Corporation would come out with it next week.

The company they formed was Ingres Corporation, and Stonebraker served as CTO, but he makes no bones about his influence over the company:

> I found that being founder, CTO, and member of the Board of Directors, I had tremendous power over what the company did without having to deal with a lot of the bullshit . . . by the mid-1980s I was, in essence, the external technical spokesman for the company; I was well-enough known and it was my company—that if I resigned, the company would fail. I was essentially unfirable.

Although successful, the Ingres technology didn't compete effectively against Oracle, and the company was eventually sold to Computer Associates. Stonebraker's involvement had decreased in the later years, and he had retained his full-time position at UC–Berkeley. Within a few years, he was ready to spin out his second company, Illustra, based on significant improvements in the programmability of the system. Illustra was also eventually sold, this time to Informix. Stonebraker "inherited" the role of CTO of an $8 billion company. It wasn't possible to manage both the CTO job and his tenured position at Berkeley, so he took early retirement from the University of California system. From his CTO role at Informix, Stonebraker returned to academia, this time to MIT.

(continues)

Yet, in the midst of all these changes, he managed to start a third company. By this point, Stonebraker knew the process and the people:

> We'd written another prototype in the early 1990s that did federated databases and disparate locations and made them look like they were integrated. In 1996 I started a company to commercialize that. By then I could get venture capital funding. I recruited a VP of marketing whom I had known. That was the founding team of the company called Cohera. I was the CEO of that company.

Timing is everything—Cohera was a dot-com vintage business, and suffered from environmental issues:

> Cohera was the height of the dot-com bubble. At the VC's urging, we accepted vast amounts of money and expanded fast and did all the wrong things. In 2000, the market tanked. If we'd gone from 50 people back to 15, we might have survived. Like lots of other people we didn't do that, so we ended up running out of money. The company was sold to PeopleSoft, and the investors got most of their money back. That experience, loud and clear, convinced me that in a start-up you kiss every nickel, forever.

Since returning to MIT, Stonebraker has spun out two more businesses, including StreamBase, a system for dealing with high-bandwidth, low-latency data streams. Both deals were funded in Boston, demonstrating that track record and connections are transferable. Stonebraker is a bit of a contrarian, but is clearly energized by the start-up process. He strongly advocates tracking the pulse of the "real world" as a basis for performing research and developing technology solutions:

> My general feeling in computer science is that the overwhelming majority of research is worthless because no one is interested in the answer. If you want to have good research taste, you've got to spend time interacting with people with real problems—because solving real people's real problems is what constitutes, in my opinion, good research in my field. And to do that you've got to have one foot and both hands in the real world.

Stonebraker's experiences have given him broad perspective on starting companies in an extremely fast-moving and competitive field. It's perhaps no wonder that, unlike some of the academics we interviewed, Professor Stonebraker is focused primarily on execution:

> I have a slightly weird point of view, which is—in my 25-year-history of start-ups—it's rare that you have to compete early on against the elephants, because they're very slow moving. You have to prove it's a good idea to get their attention; they're not the competition. The number of people that can attract a first-rate technical team and execute quickly on a good idea is very limited. If the idea is transparent and obvious and there are low barriers to entry, then I'd be very concerned about spreading it around, but in my field that's not generally the case, so I'm much less concerned about who knows about it. The other characteristic is that, in all the companies I've been associated with, there have been other faculty members involved; the basic goal in academic life is to publish or perish—tell them they can't publish the ideas in the company and they won't participate, because they need to get tenure. So it pays not to worry about that particular aspect, because the value of really smart faculty people helping you solve downstream problems is far more valuable than the loss of secrecy involved. And the minute you get the product in the marketplace, everyone knows what you're doing. It's all about executing at lightning speed. That's the secret to start-ups: *spend no money and execute in zero time.*

Consider, for example, the role identity of a recent engineering Ph.D. with two immediate opportunities: an engineering position at a high-prestige company or the leadership role at a start-up company commercializing the research that was the basis for her graduate work. The responsibilities, activities, risks, and rewards of the two options are likely to be dramatically different; we expect that the role identity for the individual would be significantly different as well. Consequently, it becomes important to consider how "entrepreneurship" shapes the individual: *How does entrepreneurship fit with the inventor's role identity?*

THE ENTREPRENEURIAL JOURNEY MODEL

We developed a model to help map and interpret inventors' entrepreneurial journeys. The Entrepreneurial Journey Model captures the changes in an individual's role identity, especially as compared with the development of the venture or with other inventing entrepreneurs who may be associated with the same venture. Roles, as described earlier, are social positions that establish reasonably well-defined expectations on what or how the person should behave. There are two distinct sets of roles that emerge: research and commercial roles. *Research* roles include those social positions in which individuals are expected to engage in the pursuit of knowledge discovery (for example, scholars, professors, doctoral students, inventors, and scientists). *Commercial* roles include those social positions in which individuals are expected to engage in managing businesses (for example, executives, managers, analysts, and consultants, among others).

Identities are the reference points by which individuals internalize their social roles. Two such identities are pervasive among inventing entrepreneurs: technology- and market-based identities. An individual with a *technology-based* identity associates with the technology, the invention, or the application of science. An individual with a *market-based* identity focuses on the end users or customers who create demand for her inventions. Irrespective of the social roles that an inventing entrepreneur occupies, her orientation could either be toward the technology or the customer. When the research and commercial roles are juxtaposed with the technology and market identities in a matrix form, we have four distinct *role identities*.

Table 7-1 provides a set of questions and sample responses to help distinguish between research and commercial identities. Answering "A" for three or more of these questions suggests a role expectation that is primarily "research" oriented. Answering "B" for three or more of these questions suggests a role expectation that is primarily "commercially" oriented.

Similarly, we distinguish between a technology identity (Technology) and a market identity (Market) by emphasizing the individual's perception of what type of activities she would be most attracted to. The individual is asked to contrast between the processes of (1) improving the technical elements of an invention or product and (2) searching for a customer segment or industry niche that the invention is likely to target. Table 7-2 provides the relevant questions and sample responses for evaluating identity. Answering "A" to three or more questions

TABLE 7-1 Self-Evaluation for Research or Commercial Roles

Who Am I?	A	B
I am primarily expected to	Answer scientific questions or develop novel technologies	Create value from products and new technologies
I am expected to spend time	Guiding research projects	Meeting with customers
I see myself primarily as a	Scientist or researcher	Businessperson or salesperson
My strongest skills include	Managing long-term research projects and/or advancing basic science	Managing operations to achieve specific, focused results
When I'm done with this project, I will	Move on to the next scientific challenge, most likely in a closely related field	Move on to the next business opportunity, which could be in one of many industries or markets

suggests a "technology" focused identity; answering "B" to three or more questions suggests a "market" focused identity.

Combining the responses to Tables 7-1 and 7-2 places the individual in one of the quadrants of the journey model matrix. The matrix illustrates that every individual has an idiosyncratic starting point on an entrepreneurial journey. Given unique initial conditions and highly singular business-growth paths, no two entrepreneurial journeys will be quite the same. The matrix should be construed as a stylistic interpretation rather than a precise graph; marginal position changes cannot be tied to a *quantitative* change in identity characteristics or behavioral outcomes.

The matrix in Figure 7-1 shows example starting points for multiple entrepreneurial journeys. Although the concepts are segregated into quadrants, each axis should be treated as a spectrum. Placement in the far upper-left corner (circle "A") suggests a strong focus on long-term research on a specific technology. This researcher probably focuses on fundamental scientific areas such as understanding the gene sequence of a specific strain of bacteria or the underlying

TABLE 7-2 Self-Evaluation for Technology or Market Identity

Who Am I?	A	B
I would rather	Perfect my product	Search for new customers
I spend more of my time on	Technical efficiency	Understanding customer needs
It is easier for me to visualize	The next product	The next customer
My skills are best applied	When I can focus on getting the technology to do exactly what I want	When I can focus on getting the product into customers' hands
My work is done when	I've solved the technical problem	Customers pay for the product or service

FIGURE 7-1   The Entrepreneurial Journey Matrix

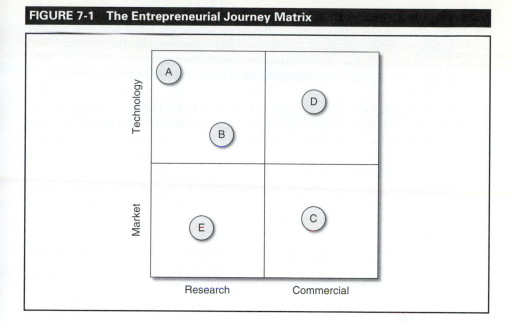

physics of atomic decay. A middle placement within the same quadrant (circle "B") would suggest a research focus on a specific technology but with some consideration or anticipation of possible applications. Perhaps this is a different molecular biologist working on a genetically modified bacterial strain for a novel disease research assay.

Circle "C" depicts a role identity focused on commercial applications to meet specific market needs. As an example, consider a doctor studying nosocomial infections.[12] Nosocomial infections are acquired during a hospital stay, and are not directly linked to the patient's primary pathology (disease). Roughly 5 percent of acute hospitalization patients develop nosocomial infections. To place the doctor firmly within the "C" quadrant, she would need to be effectively *indifferent* to the technology solution. She searches for any viable solution that addresses the patient (customer) need. Here, the hospital (institution) expects her to solve patient needs by inventing products or solutions that benefit the patient or the hospital without preference for the type of solution (i.e., pharmacological, diet-based, environmental, psychological, or physiological).

Circle "D" suggests a commercial role based on a specific technology embodiment. To contrast with the previous example, this might involve developing a specific antimicrobial treatment compound (i.e., perfecting a *product* rather than performing *research*) that effectively lyses cell membranes of infectious agents to reduce secondary nosocomial infections. Finally, circle "E" represents a research role designed to solve a customer problem (meet a market need) without as much focus on the specific technology. For example, the inventing entrepreneur could use commonly available research tools to understand the pathology of in-hospital infections. The research methodology is at work, but focused on outcome application rather than a specific technology innovation. These four quadrants help discern the inventing entrepreneur's role identity and its implications for the approach that she is likely to adopt to pursue an entrepreneurial opportunity.

Our interviews and reviews suggest that these role identities represent the basic spectrum of cognitive or mental models for inventing entrepreneurs. The purpose of the Entrepreneurial Journey Model is to create a visual "path" describing the idiosyncratic experience of the entrepreneur. The model is a tool for understanding the individual's role identity—the social expectations that are juxtaposed with the individual's own preferences. By clearly understanding where inventing entrepreneurs start, we can evaluate how individuals experience the entrepreneurial process, and whether changes (if any) in role identity at the end of the journey are permanent or temporary. We believe, even in cases where a researcher's role identity reverts to the starting point, that embarking on an entrepreneurial journey is a transformative process.

Later in the chapter we will discuss "types" of journeys that can be segmented based on path directions and outcomes. The innovator considering her commercialization options should consider the results of the self-evaluation of initial conditions mentioned earlier and note what role identity she currently enacts. Successful entrepreneurship can require dramatic changes in role identity, which can be subsequently mapped on the journey model diagram. Let us consider the example of one such entrepreneurial endeavor.

CASE STUDY: TOMOTHERAPY

As early as 1992, Professor Thomas Rockwell (Rock) Mackie was interested in developing software algorithms for managing the enormous quantities of data associated with medical imaging. One of the key members of his research team was Paul Reckwerdt, who had a mathematics background and exceptional software development skills. Their joint work with other colleagues led to the creation of Geometrics, a start-up that commercialized the Pinnacle software system for archiving medical images. The business was eventually sold to ADAC (Analytical Development Associates Corporation), which was subsequently acquired by Philips in 2000, and the Pinnacle software continues to be an industry standard.

Although Mackie and Reckwerdt were founders of Geometrics, they chose not to take active roles at the company. They had a different vision for a significant technology advance in radiotherapy. They believed they could combine advanced medical imaging with modulated, multidirectional radiation to target complex cancers while minimizing damage to surrounding tissue. This presented a dramatically different opportunity and journey than the technology-focused identity that led to Geometrics. Although Mackie and Reckwerdt anticipated some of the product development requirements (i.e., they presented some of the characteristics of a "technology-focused" mindset), they made the decision to focus on what they considered a more interesting and important clinical problem: cancer diagnosis and treatment (i.e., they were utilizing a more "market-focused" perspective).

Figure 7-2 shows the origination point of Mackie and Reckwerdt's journeys at the time of the formation of TomoTherapy in 1997.[13] Both faced a decision related to their future role identities. At the time Geometrics was formed outside of the university infrastructure, Mackie and Reckwerdt were in roughly similar positions—both were focused on technology research.[14] But the formation of TomoTherapy led to significant changes. Mackie retained his position at the university, supporting the company through applied research, broad strategic oversight, and academic reputation. Reckwerdt became the CEO of TomoTherapy (he would later become president when a CEO from the industry was brought in by their investors) and managed the commercial side of the venture. Their role identities diverged as they undertook the challenge of building TomoTherapy. This example illustrates the transformative power of entrepreneurship, in particular demonstrating how different initial conditions can lead to dramatically different endpoints for individuals involved in the same venture.

The journeys of the TomoTherapy founders illustrate that the role identities of the individuals and the demands placed on them by the venture change over time. In this example, two individuals who perceived themselves as scientists with a similar research focus experienced one journey similarly (Geometrics), but took

FIGURE 7-2 Mackie and Reckwerdt Journey Models

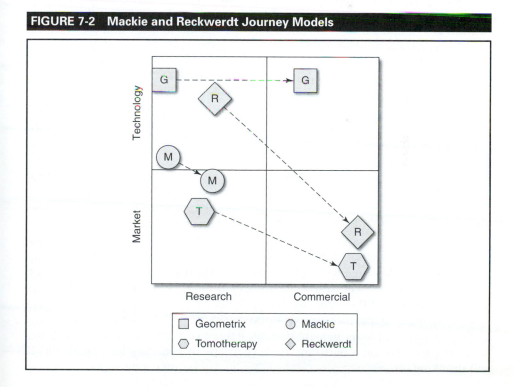

dramatically divergent paths for the second venture (TomoTherapy). Initially, both Mackie and Reckwerdt followed the path of the dedicated academic researcher, handing off the commercialization of the Geometrics/Pinnacle technology to external management. The development of the TomoTherapy technology, however, led Reckwerdt down the full commercialization path of the inventing entrepreneur.

APPLICATION OF THE JOURNEY MODEL

We have two goals for this journey model. First, we hope to provide an illustrative mechanism to qualitatively compare and contrast the experiences of inventing entrepreneurs. Second, we provide a simple heuristic to help nascent inventing entrepreneurs to compare resources, thought processes, and expectations. This thought experiment should be performed both in isolation (internal review and growth) as well as in contrast to a set of examples (external learning and benchmarking)—to allow for reflection on options and goals. It is important to note that the model **cannot predict** the inventing entrepreneur's journey based on starting conditions. But elucidating many of the factors that lead researchers to select one path or another should help nascent inventing entrepreneurs identify commonalities and incentives that help validate or reject options.

The journey model can be segregated into three obvious information sets: initial conditions, journey vectors, and final outcomes. The value of this categorization lies in comparing and contrasting the overall journey and the learning modalities that each entrepreneur experiences. Although the overall journey and the final outcome present fascinating stories, the initial conditions present the best learning opportunity for potential inventing entrepreneurs. Clearly, multiple circumstances affect both the journey and the outcome, which makes predictions and comparisons difficult—especially for novice inventing entrepreneurs unfamiliar with the world of technology ventures. But the initial conditions can be easily contrasted; nascent entrepreneurs can benefit from an objective review of starting circumstances.

Figure 7-3 illustrates a simple journey model. Consider the entrepreneurial journey of Professor A, who has been studying a biodiesel refinement process for many years. In the past five years, biodiesel has emerged into the political and cultural spheres as a potential mechanism for reducing dependence on foreign petroleum production. Professor A has been proposing such an option for many years, and has developed refinement processes that convert biomass to biodiesel with reduced waste and high energy efficiency. He is approached by entrepreneurs or existing energy firms to license his technology. He agrees to serve as interim chief technology officer of the company during the commercialization process. He remains a full-time faculty member but works closely with the corporation to develop a commercially viable refinement process. After two years, he arranges with the university to serve on a part-time basis (perhaps by reducing his teaching load and shrinking his research program) so that he can become a part-time employee

FIGURE 7-3   A Simple Journey

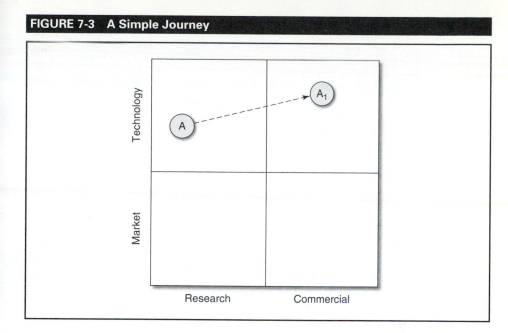

of the company. He adopts a commercially focused role and is keen to be identified with his technology, which the company will attempt to productize. His journey has taken him *across* the model space: from the "technology-research" quadrant into the "technology-commercial" quadrant. In this example, Professor A has not moved "down" into the "Market" space because he is serving primarily in a technology role (CTO) and presumably is not active in market need analysis. In our example, he remains focused on the development of a specific technology, rather than on the resolution of a specific market need.

The "journey" vectors refer to the transformational activities, processes, and events that affect the inventing entrepreneur. In our example, these would include the licensing event, his decision to sign on as CTO at the company and his subsequent experiences, the success or failure of the commercialization effort, and so on. These are dynamic factors, dramatically more complex and convoluted than can be easily represented.

A more "realistic" vector chart of Professor A's journey might look more like Figure 7-4, incorporating numerous reversals and directional changes. Professor A might spend time with a couple of the company's clients and consider market needs. He might investigate innovations that fail to pan out, requiring retrenching into technology research before a new solution leads to a commercially viable product. These events and the twists and turns associated with the pace of technology development and changes in market needs can influence the inventor's role identity as well.

In this example, the initial conditions represent the circumstances in which Professor A found himself (and his technology) at the time his innovation

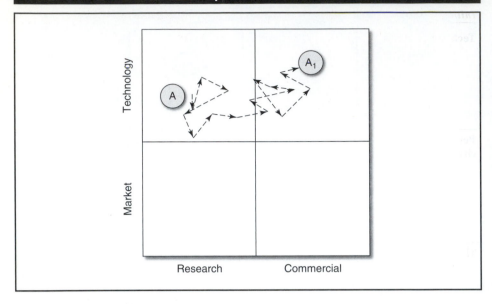

FIGURE 7-4 A "Realistic" Journey

appeared to have potential outside the laboratory. Of course, any given set of initial conditions is not a group of static variables. For convenience, we use "**initial conditions**" to refer to the set of external and internal factors at the time the inventing entrepreneur makes the primary decision to commercialize technology via a specific vehicle—whether that vehicle is licensing, creating a start-up, or something else. It should be evident that the same entrepreneur will experience different initial conditions for different technologies and/or ventures. The initial conditions can be broadly broken into three categories: (1) technology status, (2) personal circumstances, and (3) market conditions. In Table 7-3, we provide examples of these initial conditions and their implications for the timing required for embarking on an entrepreneurial journey.

Our interviews suggest that the critical factor determining the initial direction of the entrepreneur's journey is the innovator's technology affinity. Personal circumstances appear to play a secondary role, while market circumstances are the least critical. Some innovators value their ongoing research well above the pull of commercial forces or roles. For others, adopting a commercial role by running a start-up business is the next logical learning experience. Nevertheless, the initial conditions can significantly impact the inventor's role identity and the subsequent steps to be taken.

The "final outcome" is the position on the journey map showing the inventing entrepreneur's new role identity. In some cases, the inventing entrepreneur winds up back where she started, despite a long and meandering journey. Consider: A research scientist consults with a company that licenses her novel plant seed technology, ends up taking a two-year sabbatical to work at the company's R&D facility,

TABLE 7-3 Journey Model Initial Conditions		
Initial Conditions	*Examples*	*Implication of Timing*
Technology status	✓ Theory	Early
	✓ Testing	✓ Theory or proof of principle
	✓ Peer review	Prime
	✓ End-user tested	✓ Proof of concept or prototype
	✓ IP status	Late
	✓ Technology "awareness"	✓ Marketable product
Personal circumstances	✓ Tenure status	Early
	✓ Funding status	✓ Faculty seeking tenure
	✓ Size of research lab	Prime
	✓ Teaching/service requirements	✓ Tenured faculty
		Late
	✓ Family status	✓ Emeritus or retired faculty
	✓ Technology affinity	
Market conditions	✓ Consumer demand	Early
	✓ Industry lifecycle	✓ No quantifiable consumer need
	✓ Venture funds	Prime
	✓ Local management	✓ Consumers beginning to demand solutions
	✓ Availability of talent	
	✓ Local users	Late
		✓ Consumer need fulfilled by other products

participates in trade shows and even customer presentations and sales calls, and at the end returns to the university to take up her long-term research roles. It is quite possible that her role identity could have significantly changed: Perhaps her new role identity incorporates aspects of market identity in a commercial role. In this example, however, she has always retained her role as a researcher and her identification with technology-based solutions. She participated in commercial efforts purely to ensure that her technology would be utilized as she deemed appropriate. She resumes scientific research to leave the commercial roles behind.

Conclusions and Summary

In this chapter, we discussed the implications of a person's role identity and how it evolves during the entrepreneurial journey. Role identity is composed of distinct roles (societal expectations of a person who is occupying a job or function) as well as the individual's orientation and perception of what these roles entail (identity). The role identity perspective can be applied to individuals who occupy different roles (e.g., scientist, student) and have different identities (e.g., technical, consumer-oriented). Our model captures a common pattern seen among inventing entrepreneurs and can be formulated into a 2×2 matrix composed of research and commercial roles overlaid over technology and market identities.

The Entrepreneurial Journey Model reflects the individual's changes in role identity with exposure to entrepreneurial activities. Entrepreneurial journeys are not simple linear displacements of role identities. Often these changes in role identities are subtle and occur over time.

Exercise

- Write down the different roles that you currently occupy or perform. For each role, can you figure out if you adopt multiple identities?

- What is your interest in entrepreneurship? How do you think role identities could enable or come in conflict with your desire to be an entrepreneur? For example, are there aspects of specific roles (such as being a parent or an athlete) that would conflict with the role requirements of being a start-up entrepreneur? Are there elements of your current roles that would support or augment an entrepreneurial role?

Endnotes

1. Merton, R. K. 1957. Priorities in scientific discovery: A chapter in the sociology of science. *American Sociological Review,* 22: 635–659.
2. Gecas, V. 1982. The self-concept. *Annual Review of Sociology,* 8: 1–33.
3. Ibarra, H. 1999. Provisional selves: Experimenting with image and identity in professional adaptation. *Administrative Science Quarterly,* 44(4): 764–791.
4. McCall, G. J. & Simmons, J. L. 1978. *Identities and Interactions: An Examination of Human Associations in Everyday Life.* New York: Free Press.
5. Van Maanen, J. & Schein, E. H. 1979. Toward a theory of organizational socialization. In B. M. Staw (ed.), *Research in Organizational Behavior,* 1, pp. 209–264. Greenwich, CT: JAI Press.
6. Nicholson, N. 1984. A theory of work role transitions. *Administrative Science Quarterly,* 29: 172–191.
7. Burton, M. D. & Beckman, C. 2007. Leaving a legacy: Role imprints and successor turnover in young firms. *American Sociological Review,* 72(2): 239–266.
8. Ruef, M., Aldrich, H. E., & Carter, N. M. 2003. The structure of founding teams: Homophily, strong ties, and isolation among U.S. entrepreneurs. *American Sociological Review,* 68: 195–222.
9. Shane, S. & Khurana, R. 2003. Bringing individuals back in: The effects of career experience on new firm founding. *Industrial and Corporate Change,* 12: 519–543.
10. Samsom, K. 1990. *Scientists As Entrepreneurs: Organizational Performance in Scientist-Started New Ventures.* London: Kluwer.
11. Founded by John Cullinane, who purchased the IDMS (Integrated Database Management System) database system from General Electric. Cullinane Corporation was renamed Cullinet and sold to Computer Associates in 1989.
12. For more information, please see www.emedicine.com/ped/topic1619.htm.
13. For explicative purposes, we have included in the figure the Geometrics' journey from a research technology to commercial technology in order to contrast it with the TomoTherapy journey.
14. Professor Mackie, as faculty, was necessarily more focused on long-term research aspects. Even at this early stage, Reckwerdt was already more focused on market possibilities; thus, the qualitative difference between their initial locations on the matrix.

CHAPTER 8

SAMPLE JOURNEYS

OVERVIEW

In this chapter, we take a close look at entrepreneurial journeys as exemplars that highlight, rather than demonstrate, any particular technological or commercial achievement. Although every journey is unique, it is important to understand that some types of entrepreneurial journeys occur more frequently—whereas others are rare or idiosyncratic. We review six types of journeys to highlight the common role identity changes that occur among inventing entrepreneurs.

We believe that these journey types encompass a majority of inventing entrepreneur experiences. At the same time, technology entrepreneurs experience unique stresses and challenges, and thus each innovator has a highly personal experience. In fact, a number of these inventors will have multiple entrepreneurial experiences, and each experience adds to the journey that, cumulatively, forms and influences the individual's response and attitude toward entrepreneurial behavior. Consider Professor Hector DeLuca, who has participated in the process via at least three different models: Third-party traditional technology licensing, a hands-off role in a start-up, and as CEO of his own start-up. But his decision mode remains consistent, which is not uncommon for inventing entrepreneurs:

> The only reason I entered the business world—on the three or four
> occasions when I did—was because I wanted to see things happen that
> weren't happening with the organizations as they were. My primary
> interest is discovery; I'm excited about finding out something new. [A]
> lot of academicians want to leave it out there and go find out something
> new. [But] I'm not that way, I want to see it applied, and I want to see it
> used; that motivates me quite a bit.

Common goals, modes, and incentives across inventing entrepreneurs allow us to group journeys into recurring subtypes. We believe these groupings will help new inventing entrepreneurs better understand likely paths and outcomes.

JOURNEY 1: THE RESEARCH TRANSFER ENTREPRENEUR

A majority of the academic researchers developing innovative technologies that have commercial applications do not follow the commercialization path as the technology evolves into a product and enters the market. Professor George Church exemplifies this perspective; he has participated in the transfer of numerous technologies to corporations, but has remained a full-time researcher at the Department of Genetics at Harvard Medical School. He currently sits on more than a dozen scientific advisory boards that require various levels of involvement. Professor Church reflected on his personal philosophy regarding technology transfer and entrepreneurship:

> I was intrigued by the possibility of serving as a go-between for the research laboratory and private companies. I like to be able to invent freely on a variety of subjects. I've never wanted to serve as [executive management]. There's a different skill set to be a CEO, and the company depends on that CEO skill set. [Research scientists] shouldn't try to be everything . . . Be the technology expert and do what you're good at. Scientists who serve as CEOs are playing an inexperienced gambler's game.

It could be argued that the dedicated academic researcher's path is, from a technology transfer perspective, relatively static—and that graphing the path on our journey model would show no movement at all. We believe, however, that some movement is almost inevitable, especially in cases like Professor Church's. His role in advising start-ups has created intricate and extensive networks spanning both academic and industrial arenas. Although it is possible that the majority of Professor Church's research, at any given instant, is truly product- and technology-focused, we believe that his ongoing research portfolio actively reflects accumulated information about both market needs and commercialization characteristics.

In many cases, the journey of the research transfer entrepreneur remains in the upper-left quadrant of the journey model. For each technology or innovation, the scientist participates, albeit to a limited extent, in the transformation toward developing a product and identifying the market. Figure 8-1 shows some variants of role identity change (and reversion) along the product/commercial axes. The important element is that the scientist does not pursue the full commercialization journey, but instead returns to the primary role of researcher and innovator (usually) within the academic environment.

We found that most successful inventing entrepreneurs who retain their primary identity as academic researchers still move toward a greater awareness of market and commercialization factors. As Professor Church noted:

> It's a little hard for me to wrap my head around somebody who just wants to invent without any idea of putting it in the market. It is fun to

FIGURE 8-1   The Research Transfer Entrepreneur

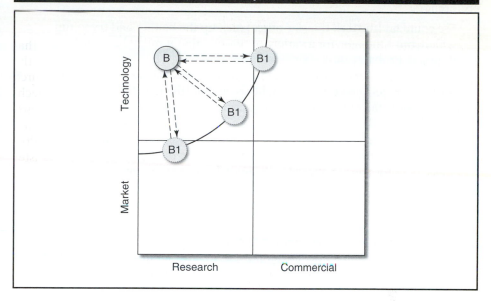

invent for its own sake. It's not a huge step, if you've got a good invention, to put it in the market. The whole cycle of feedback that you get—you try to bring something to market; you say, "that market was too small or not ready for it or full of competitors"—you get an intuitive feeling. Just like you get good at anything you practice a lot, you go through the cycle of going back to the drawing board and inventing again, this time with a more acute vision of what is actually needed.

JOURNEY 2: THE SABBATICAL ENTREPRENEUR

Another common entrepreneurial journey involves faculty that lead a start-up company while on a sabbatical (of usually 1–2 years). Professor Ron Raines used a sabbatical year to jump-start Quintessence, a therapeutics company commercializing biopolymers and novel ribonucleases. Ribonucleases (RNases) are ribonucleic enzymes that break down RNA. The company is developing RNases as therapeutic compounds that target certain cancers. During Raines' sabbatical year, he presented to venture capitalists, private investors, potential customers, and an extensive group of industry experts. This "idea pitching" process helped Professor Raines establish the level of market interest in his technology. He also assessed the financing environment, a critical issue facing most technology-based start-ups. At the end of the year, however, Professor Raines returned to his academic laboratory and turned over the leadership of the business to Ralph Kauten, a professional CEO with two successful start-ups already under his belt. Professor

Raines reflects on the process that led to the sabbatical, as well as on his personal preferences:

> We could let [the tech transfer office] pick up the banner and try to run with it, but I thought, for a variety of reasons, that it might be better to do it myself. Probably the major reason was that I was genuinely interested in doing that. In many ways it's more efficient because no one knows my research better than I do. You could argue that [the tech transfer offices] would know the other side of the equation—the business—better than I would, to be fair . . . The year this was all being done I was on sabbatical for the full year to avoid conflicts of interest. Though I enjoyed this experience—going to venture capitalists [to raise funds]—it's not what I want to do for a living. What I truly enjoy is my own research.

The Quintessence story is also illuminating because Professor Raines brought together a portfolio of technologies (including biopolymers developed by Professor Laura Kiessling, and ribonucleic enzymes and foldamers, or artificial molecules, that mimic the ability of proteins to form well-defined conformations). He assumed that the developing company could focus on whichever technology had the best commercial potential at any given juncture. Professor Raines demonstrates a mix of low-to-moderate technology affinity and control issues. He turned over the CEO role to a serial entrepreneur and understands that the commercial path may not be a straight line; but he also notes that he "still has control of the company."

A common model for the sabbatical entrepreneur is shown in Figure 8-2. The scientist, still primarily focused on the technology (rather than a product or

FIGURE 8-2 The Sabbatical Entrepreneur

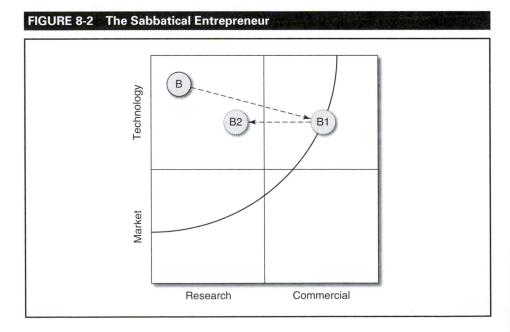

market), begins the process of commercialization by forming a company, seeking funding, and setting up the necessary infrastructure to perform research outside the university structure. As with Professor Raines, rather than taking a full-time role at the business, the sabbatical entrepreneur turns over most (or all) of the business management to others, and returns to a primary role at the university laboratory. But, unlike the research transfer entrepreneur, these scientists continue to focus on developing the specific technology transferred into the commercial venture and remain quite active in the business, retaining varying levels of control.

JOURNEY 3: THE RESEARCH-DRIVEN INVENTING ENTREPRENEUR

Not every inventor becomes an inventing entrepreneur. For some, however, the opportunity to actively commercialize a technology outweighs the lure of academic research. These inventing entrepreneurs experience some of the most transformative journeys. Paul Reckwerdt left his university position to be the interim CEO of TomoTherapy, and when venture capital investors brought in an industry CEO, he remained at the company as president, managing nearly all business operations. Another example is John Devereux, who completed his Ph.D. work while the commercial potential for his bioinformatics software was becoming evident. Devereux's software was one of the first systems targeting genomic analysis. John recalls the early development of the software and his enthusiasm for considering commercial applications of the technology:

> We made a set of [software] tools for [a professor] in the genetics department. They were really developed so Professor Oliver Smithies [who won the Nobel Prize in 2007] could write a major paper for the recombinant DNA literature. My career started off in professionalizing that work within Smithies research laboratory. When Reagan cut the budget in the early 1980s, obligations that the university had already made to people like me were going to be cut back. Smithies said that I would have to do one of two things with my career: I would have to learn to support myself through this work that I loved or I would have to start work on some of my core grants because he did not have enough money to pretend that I wasn't there. I was very excited about the work; it was the first thing that ever happened in my career where I'd been willing to put the amount of work in that was needed to succeed in a subject.

At that decision point, John chose to lead the commercialization of the technology rather than pursue a faculty position. He formed the corporation with one of his graduate students, negotiated the rights to the technology from the university, acquired physical space and equipment, and transferred the existing users (customers) to the business. The company grew to a multimillion dollar

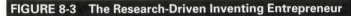

FIGURE 8-3 The Research-Driven Inventing Entrepreneur

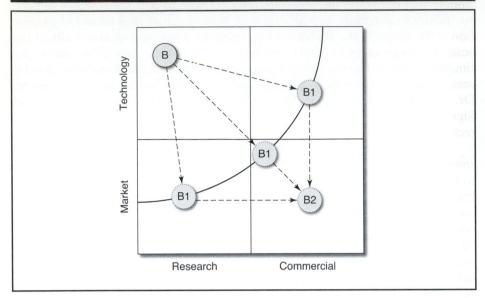

corporation under his leadership. He remained as CEO of Genetics Computer Group (GCG) until the sale of the company to Oxford Molecular, staying on through the transition for an additional three years. As John recounts, the situation wasn't exactly planned, but it allowed him to do the work he really enjoyed.

Figure 8-3 shows variants of the journey for the "research-driven inventing entrepreneur." Inventing entrepreneurs can adopt different role identities in commercialization—but the "research-driven" role identity may be the most intensive and transformative, because the inventing entrepreneur chooses to follow the journey to market commercialization, usually in a senior leadership role. In theory, ultimate success comes at "B2" in Figure 8-3, when the commercialization effort matches the market need. In reality, many technology start-ups do not reach this point. The company might fail or be acquired by another corporation. In addition, the diagram oversimplifies by suggesting that the journey is direct—as if there will be no detours or mistakes. It may take many years (or even decades) before technology start-ups achieve successful commercialization. Many struggle with failed development efforts, unexpected market shifts, resource constraints, and management changes.

The research-driven inventing entrepreneur faces significant challenges. In most cases, these individuals have limited business experience and are also unlikely to have extensive business networks. The infrastructure at a major research institution often shields researchers from many operational and administrative details (i.e., bookkeeping, regulatory compliance, other facilities management, and general human resource issues). At the same time, our research shows that many inventing entrepreneurs apply skills and knowledge developed within the research institution to the business environment. We found this application of skills and knowledge worthy of a detailed discussion—please see Chapter 10 for more information.

Not every research-driven technology entrepreneur enjoys a smooth transition when adopting a commercial/market-based role identity. The change from academic researcher to corporate manager can be difficult, frustrating, and sometimes unsuccessful. The success Dr. Devereux achieved at GCG can be linked to many underlying factors, including advantageous technology transfer terms, Dr. Devereux's leadership skills and vision, and excellent market timing. Significantly, the GCG technology was already in high demand at the time the technology was spun out of the university.

Professor Randy Cortwright's transition to the commercial space was not as smooth. Although his patent-pending hydrogen production technology appeared to have numerous commercial applications (from laptop batteries to megawatt-scale electricity generation), no prototype system had been developed, and the company needed additional funds to develop the technology beyond the proof of concept stage. While Dr. Cortwright envisioned a major shift to green-sourced energy, investors saw uncertainty and product risk, because the company was not certain which products would be marketed first. Early management issues also delayed the company's development. Eventually, Dr. Cortwright brought in a professional CEO, an individual with prior high-tech-growth company experience. The company obtained angel funding and a $2 million federal National Institutes of Science and Technology (NIST) Advanced Technology Program (ATP) grant, followed by venture capital. Unlike Professor Raines, however, Dr. Cortwright remains at Virent Energy Systems as chief technology officer.

JOURNEY 4: THE DUAL-ROLE INVENTING ENTREPRENEUR

The dual-role inventing entrepreneur adds another level of difficulty to the already challenging path previously described for the research-driven inventing entrepreneur. These individuals choose to remain part-time or even full-time faculty within a research insitution while also serving as management for a commercial venture. In some cases, this may only be limited to the early start-up activities (as with Professor Raines). But some inventing entrepreneurs deliberately choose to serve in multiple roles.

Professor Hector DeLuca's first commercialization activities involved licensing his technologies to large pharmaceutical companies. He was also involved in a commercial venture that enabled small-batch manufacturing of speciality pharmaceuticals. This commercial work did not involve licensing technology from his research program. Recently, however, DeLuca has become a dual-role entrepreneur.

Professor DeLuca is one of the most prolific chemistry researchers in the United States, with more than 75 patents and hundreds of peer-reviewed publications. His pioneering research on vitamin D has led to FDA-approved therapeutics (including Hectorol, now marketed by Genzyme). Prior to 2000, Professor

DeLuca had not taken an active role in the companies licensing his technologies (although he had served in various advisory capacities). In 2000, however, Professor DeLuca founded Deltanoid Pharmaceuticals, a corporation, developing and commercializing a specific set of vitamin D compounds developed originally in his university laboratory. DeLuca chose to be CEO of the company, with the intent of leading the company through significant growth. In Profile 8-1, we describe Professor DeLuca's journey.

INVENTING ENTREPRENEUR PROFILE 8-1

Hector DeLuca

Hector DeLuca is one of the world's foremost biochemists. More than half a dozen FDA-approved drugs originated from his university research. He has published more than 1,000 peer-reviewed academic papers. He was awarded the Roussel Prize of France in 1974, became a member of the National Academy of Sciences in 1979, and was placed on the National Task Force of the National Institutes of Health (NIH) Strategic Plan Committee in 1992. He served as chairman of the UW–Madison Department of Biochemistry for nearly 30 years. DeLuca's research on vitamin D compounds is recognized worldwide.

In the mid-1980s, responding to the need for small-batch specialized pharmaceutical production, DeLuca helped found Tetrionics, which provided outsourced specialty pharmaceutical manufacturing.[1] He was then approached by another Wisconsin entrepreneur academic about commercializing some of his vitamin D compounds:

> We were frustrated because big pharma had failed to develop any of our vitamin D compounds for osteoporosis in this country. [One company] had a license to our calcitriol and they just did a terrible job working on it, and so it never really got approved. Dick Mazess, who is also an academic entrepreneur, came to me and said we should have a vitamin D compound for osteoporosis, and he was willing to spend some of the money that he earned on the bone scanner (Lunar)—and so we started Bone Care International [BCI], and the purpose was to develop a vitamin D compound for osteoporosis. I helped start the company, got it going, hired a former post-doc of mine to run it.

Although there were some bumps in the road, the BCI story ended successfully. "It got going, but then they decided to develop a compound for treatment of kidney failure patients, which was a less expensive thing to do." In 2002, BCI had brought in a new CEO with extensive pharmaceutical experience to consider new options. The management team refocused BCI on renal disease and completed clinical trials in 2004, leading to a significant increase in sales. In June 2005, the company was acquired by Genzyme in a stock transaction valued at $700 million. Throughout this process, DeLuca had chosen to remain on the sidelines:

> No, I never thought of [taking a bigger role at Bone Care International], I knew I wouldn't be able to take charge of it—could not run it. It would deny my capability of further discovery of medicines.

By the late 1990s, however, a lot had changed. DeLuca felt that the overall environment for drug discovery start-ups was better. "I could start a company and still continue my discovery. That was very important to me. If I had to give up my discovery, I guess I wouldn't do it."

DeLuca had first-hand experience with Tetrionics and Bone Care International. Most importantly, he felt that there was a need for a new approach:

> [Pharma companies] want a lot more information than simply compounds. They begin to demand data on the safety of the compound: "does it work; prove it to me in an animal model." That's why Deltanoid came to be—to fill this niche of taking raw university inventions, doing what has to be done on them, and ultimately licensing them to the pharmaceutical industry for final development and marketing.

DeLuca felt the time had come to create a start-up company specifically focused on the stream of innovations in the vitamin D field coming from his laboratory. He formed Deltanoid in 1999 for that purpose. His credentials proved valuable for attracting venture capital, although DeLuca clearly had some concerns about matching VC interests with his own:

> We got our first outside money in 2001. We were financed at $4.2 million that was done by [local venture capitalists]. It was a long haul; I squabbled with VCs; their picture of a start-up is different from what I think it ought to be—they want to add value, sell the company, and get out. Anyone who wants to develop a true company—they're in conflict there. The VCs we work with are wonderful, but they have to work within the confines of their fund—in 10 years they have to get their money out some way. The concept of how VCs operate is contrary to really long-range development of industrial concerns.

In the end, however, DeLuca is philosophical about the possible outcomes for Deltanoid, and he considers the influence a business can exert beyond its own products and successes:

> I am interested in creating a high-value company, a company that doesn't have valuation by smoke and mirrors. It's a growing company and has a good product to offer, namely development of inventions, and has been successful at it and is sustainable on its own. Then you can't predict what happens, because I'm not always going to be in control anyway. The day I walk out it might be acquired. But my guess is that if the concept of what the company is all about is successful, even if it is acquired, the acquiring company might see the value in it, or someone else might say that was a valuable business and they want to start one to replace it.

The path of the dual-role entrepreneur is clearly one of the most taxing. This role identity combines all of the effort and stress of an academic research career with the challenge and fatigue of an entrepreneurial career. Often, dual-role entrepreneurs have to contend with suspicion or even outright criticism from both fellow researchers and corporate management for not being fully committed to their respective endeavors. Conflict-of-interest issues must be managed actively and conscientiously. Many inventing entrepreneurs we interviewed specifically warned against this route, strongly encouraging scientists to either "stick to what they know" or to take the risk of joining a commercial venture.

Figure 8-4 illustrates a simple version of the "split" that occurs when an inventing entrepreneur chooses to follow through on commercialization efforts for a specific innovation while maintaining a role within the university and, presumably,

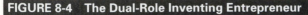

FIGURE 8-4 The Dual-Role Inventing Entrepreneur

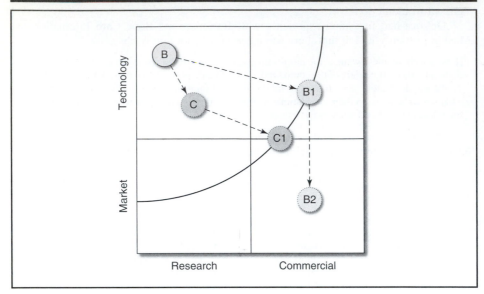

continuing novel research streams. From "B," where the initial innovation has been licensed to a corporation and is being prepared for market entry, the inventing entrepreneur begins moving towards "B1"—participating in the commercialization process associated with business operations and administration. Possibly at the same time, a new research or technology innovation stream is initiated at "C." We suggest that, in many cases, inventing academics with active commercial endeavors or prior commercial experience are likely to identify and pursue research activities that are more closely tied to markets (as shown by placing "C" below "B"). In this example, the innovation developed as a result of the new research is also being commercialized, shown as "C1." Clearly, this individual will be very busy, with the possibility of being involved in two independent major research programs as well as two commercial entities, in addition to typical faculty roles of service and education at universities. This journey creates the most challenges for the inventing entrepreneur, and may require maintaining a role identity that encompasses multiple roles.

In Chapter 5, we talked about Professor Blattner, who has been a founder of three start-up companies based on technologies developed at the University of Wisconsin–Madison. Figure 8-5 shows his Journey Model, which has required Professor Blattner to assume a unique role identity for each venture. In addition, Professor Blattner has retained his tenured faculty position, and oversees a significant, active research program. Professor Blattner's dual-role path has taken him through multiple commercialization processes. In the case of DNAStar, Professor Blattner started with a technology that was already in demand (please see Profile 5-1 for details). He successfully converted the technology into a product,

FIGURE 8-5   Blattner Journey Model

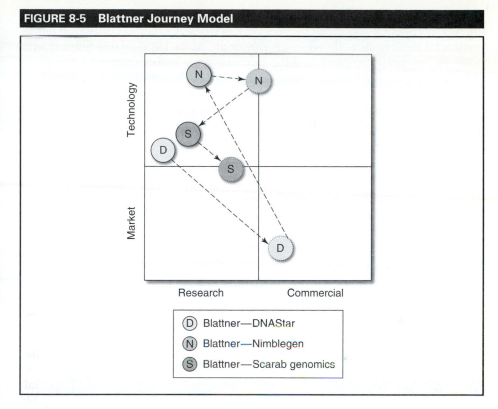

formed the commercial venture, and generated financial returns in the market-place. When Blattner helped initiate the Nimblegen venture, the technology was relatively undeveloped. Blattner's role was more limited, in part because the "product development" aspect of the commercialization effort was focused more on physics, computation, and engineering. As a co-founder of Scarab Genomics, however, Blattner is both funding and managing the business, and he is working to move it along a path similar to that of DNAStar.

JOURNEY 5: THE CORPORATE ENTREPRENEUR

Although we have focused primarily on academic researchers who participated in commercialization efforts, we want to briefly examine the journey of corporate technology entrepreneurs. Here we make a distinction between traditional corporate product development and commercialization that requires the innovator to intervene beyond his expected role (as a corporate scientist).[2] We use the term "corporate entrepreneur" to reflect both the initial focus on innovation (rather than commercialization) and the eventual commercialization activity.

Our first example is, Dr. Jeff Cernohaus, who was recruited by 3M to continue research on adhesives that he initiated as a doctoral student. Cernohaus's adhesive additive investigations led to novel polymer-combining technologies, but weren't directly applicable to 3M's core business. Cernohaus displayed entrepreneurial tendencies early on in his career at 3M by familiarizing himself with both the corporate structure and the key managers across functional groups in order to evaluate the leverage points for action. He believed that his technology was better suited to the research and product development occurring at Dyneon, a division of 3M that was focused on fluoropolymers. Cernohaus negotiated the transfer of his technology, and himself, to Dyneon.

> We figured out a way to make these materials,—a very economical way—using this process, where on the open market they might be thousands of dollars a pound [but] we could do it for five dollars a pound. I began lobbying [the director of another division] that these additives are interesting and we should bring them to the rest of the world. I basically had to lobby him for a year. Headcount is always an issue; it made business sense, and I finally went over on a sabbatical. The Tech Center fronted the cost of my salary for a year and gave the business unit a chance to look at my technology.

Figure 8-6 shows this corporate entrepreneurial journey. Cernohaus's experience at 3M and Dyneon taught him the value of identifying markets rather than simply inventing products. From his technology/commercial position he realized the necessity of understanding customer and market needs, and began spending

FIGURE 8-6 Cernohaus Journey Model

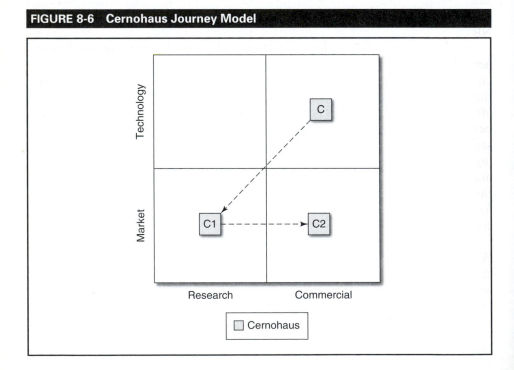

significant amounts of time with customers. He relied on his research training and skills to assess possible solutions to specific market needs, moving all the way into the research/market quadrant as he helped Dyneon commercialize a series of additive technology solutions. Eventually, however, his entrepreneurial skills and inclinations were no longer compatible with a corporate role, even at a firm like 3M, which is renowned for encouraging entrepreneurial thinking. He started his own firm, Interfacial Solutions, and began looking for market-driven technology opportunities. This final step moved him into the market/commercial quadrant. Of course, he anticipates identifying opportunities in the synthetic chemistry sector, which is focused on adhesives. Regardless, Cernohaus applies a different heuristic to opportunity identification than most academic researchers—he assesses potential market options before focusing on specific product formulations.

Mike Fouche presents a different story, but his journey might be reflective of the classic "corporate entrepreneur" example. After working for Ford Aerospace (originally Loral) on neural network technologies for satellites, Fouche went to Boeing to work on space systems projects. He continued his focus on neural networks for flight guidance systems, eventually focusing on helicopters. Convinced that Boeing's interests in autonomous helicopter guidance systems wouldn't match his own, he left Boeing to work on the technology himself.

Over the next few years, he struggled to obtain funds, and even took a project-based job at Northrop-Grumman briefly to make ends meet. In 2001 he officially formed Neural Robotics Inc. (NRI), working out of his garage to develop small, fully autonomous helicopters for surveillance and limited payload (<50 kg) delivery. The next year, on the basis of early indications of customer interest for NRI's products, he quit his job at Grumman to focus solely on NRI.

Initially Fouche was convinced that the target customers were television news stations that wanted visual traffic reports. Since then, he discovered a different, more enthusiastic customer segment—gas pipeline and energy companies that need to monitor infrastructure. These customers need aerial surveillance to effectively monitor their key assets; traditional airplane-based sensing is too expensive. Remote controlled or autonomous helicopters equipped with traditional sensing equipment (usually video and/or infrared) can provide rapid-response, high-accuracy feedback, whether across a significant geographical area or for high-specificity locations. NRI has grown to seven full-time employees and has raised more than two million dollars in external capital. The company has focused on developing an autonomous helicopter that has more payload than competitor products.

Figure 8-7 shows this version of the corporate entrepreneurial journey. Fouche began in a commercial environment working on a technology without a clear market application. Although he was convinced there was a viable market, he knew that the technology couldn't be developed in a cost-feasible way within the large aerospace corporations. So he had to leave the commercial field to do classic "garage" research (shown in the Figure 8.7 as "F1"). When the market application emerged and customers showed interest, the full commercialization effort ensued.

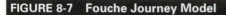

FIGURE 8-7   Fouche Journey Model

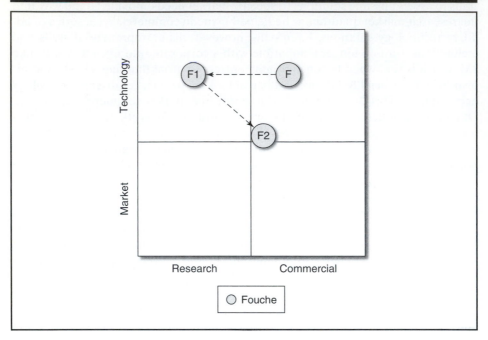

The concept of the corporate entrepreneur is not new—the story of the disgruntled employee who starts a company to compete with a former employer in a niche opportunity is well-established. The role identity dynamics, however, can be much more complex than for the academic researcher who wants to commercialize technology. In most cases, the corporate entrepreneur *must* leave the originating environment; there are relatively few corporations with active technology transfer programs that outlicense non-core technologies. The commercial nature of the corporate environment may, at first, appear to be advantageous to the corporate entrepreneur's transition, but our limited research suggests that the research role played within the corporate environment retains dramatic differences from the entrepreneurial role required for venture creation—and corporate entrepreneurs may not be better prepared, from either a logistical or role identity perspective, than academic entrepreneurs are.

JOURNEY 6: THE BUSINESS-FOCUSED INVENTING ENTREPRENEUR

Much of our discussion has focused on researchers based in academia who license their own (or related) technology from academic institutions. But we did interview and study entrepreneurs who rely on academic knowledge and research to start ventures unrelated to the institution. These "business-focused"

FIGURE 8-8   The Business-Focused Entrepreneur

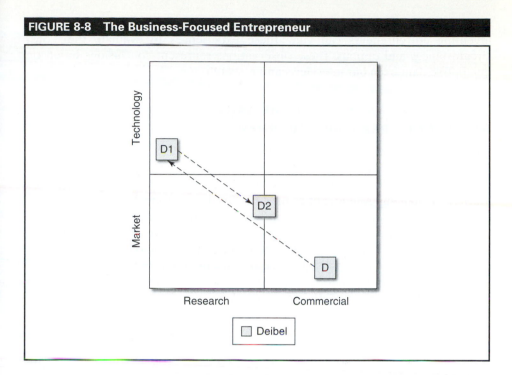

inventing entrepreneurs bring a business mindset to the laboratory by commercializing technological concepts rather than patented technologies.

Virginia Deibel, for example, sought a doctorate in pathology primarily to establish her credentials for providing food pathology consulting services to clients. As the CEO of TRAC Microbiology, Deibel believes that the analytical tools and research output from her studies help her manage the business of tracking down pathogens and contamination problems for food industry clients. As her company has grown, she's become more interested in establishing an in-house research program to develop new investigative tools. Her academic and research experience have changed her goals for the business—she wants to engender a work environment that thrives on scientific and personal challenge as much as on commercial success.

Figure 8-8 shows this unusual path. From a strictly commercial/market perspective, the entrepreneur gains technology and research skills and expertise. In her return to the commercial realm, we see that Deibel retains some of the research/technology focus, as exemplified by her interest in establishing more in-house research capacity.

LESSONS FROM THE JOURNEY MODEL

Stepping back from the common types of journey models as well as from the examples of individual journeys, it is important to ask whether there are broad lessons that can be integrated and learned from these observations. We make a number of observations about the output of the journey model and how nascent inventing entrepreneurs can view these experiences to evaluate their own circumstances and options. These observations represent conclusions based on qualitative data from our interviews and research.

THE VENTURE PATH IS NOT THE SAME AS THE ENTREPRENEUR'S JOURNEY

One of the most powerful lessons of the journey model is the distinction to be made between the inventing entrepreneur's journey and the commercialization path of the technology or the business venture. In some cases, the entrepreneur's journey in changing role identities may be closely tied to the commercialization effort. The entrepreneur may develop business skills; acquire knowledge of industries, markets, and customers; and even absorb market-based concepts for solving customer needs that are independent of her technology-focus. In such cases, we would not be surprised to see the inventing entrepreneur significantly involved in the commercialization process, which might include taking on a senior management role. We anticipate that many entrepreneurs elect to remain in the commercial world and to adopt an entirely different role identity.

But such parallel development does NOT guarantee that the entrepreneur's personal journey will *synchronize* with the operational journey of the commercial venture. We'll talk about exits in Chapter 14, but even assuming that the inventing entrepreneur's exit coincides with some form of corporate exit, she could still choose to revert back to her original role identity as a researcher within an academic environment.[3] Even during the time that the inventing entrpreneur is actively involved in commercialization, there are many scenarios in which her personal path diverges from the commercial work. As an example, the company may be focused on near-term product development, while she works on long-term research unrelated to the current product offerings. Alternatively, the company could choose to focus on a technology stream unrelated to her original research. In some cases, the company identifies target markets that are dramatically different from the researcher's original expectations. This can be especially difficult for the inventing entrepreneur originally motivated to address a specific problem (such as an unusual disease). The personal experience, or transformation, that the inventing entrepreneur experiences may have little or no relation to the commercialization process. For example, as the company becomes more and more market-focused, the researcher may become more engrossed in underlying technological or scientific issues. Finally, many innovators have no involvement with the commercial process, and many more help initiate commercialization but retain their primary role identity as an academic researcher.

EVERY JOURNEY IS UNIQUE AND PERSONAL

Because every inventing entrepreneur starts from idiosyncratic initial conditions, personal characteristics, and role identity, and because no two commercialization efforts follow the same path, every inventing entrepreneur's journey is unique. Nearly all our interviewees commented on the transformation process, noting the dramatic impact each experienced either during or after the entrepreneurial experience. This effect was not dependent on initial conditions, the entrepreneur's level of involvement in the commercial venture, or the outcomes of the commercialization efforts. The entrepreneurial process has a profound effect upon the entrepreneur. Because inventing entrepreneurs tend to be highly driven, analytical, and self-reflective individuals (whether by nature or by training), the journey has transformative effects on the psyche and identity of these individuals.

IS THERE AN OPTIMAL PATH?

After reviewing the common paths of both the inventing entrepreneur and the commercialization effort, we might assume that there is an optimal path for a given effort that moves from upper left (technology/research) to lower right (market/commercial). This is accurate at the most simplistic level, because commercial success demands that technologies must be converted into products and positioned for the right market opportunity. This conclusion, however, reflects the simplification necessary in the Entrepreneurial Journey Model. The Model only has two extremely broad characteristic dimensions, and this simplification hides nearly all of the operational, logistical, and administrative complexity inherent in most technology commercialization efforts. Plotting a "linear" path to market/commercial success presumes that nearly every element of business planning can be predicted in advance (market need, product form, competitive response, operational development) and that no unexpected challenges arise or that no mistakes are made. Our opinion is that the optimal path is conceivable, but nearly impossible to accurately predict or implement in practice. Showing the linear path in the Entrepreneurial Journey Model is a shortcut necessitated by the simplicity of the model.

Nimblegen provides a clear example. The development of Nimblegen's intellectual property (IP) portfolio (especially patent protection) occurred in the shadow of IP work already established by Affymetrix. Although Nimblegen's technology fundamentally differed from Affymetrix's products, the applications were similar enough that Nimblegen was unable to secure the right to manufacture and sell competing products in markets where Affymetrix had patent protection. From this point in the journey, Nimblegen (and the inventing entrepreneurs who started it) had many path options leading in dramatically different directions. One option could have been to revert back to the "research" role and attempt to engineer around the Affymetrix patents. In fact, however, Nimblegen eventually settled on a geography-based solution that completely changed the nature of the business. The company set up operations in Iceland, where Affymetrix had failed to establish patent protection, and began offering the technology solution as a service, rather than as a product. Customers don't buy Nimblegen chips—they ship their test articles to Iceland where Nimblegen performs the assay work and ships back results and data.

In other words, the "optimal" path one could take along the diagonal in the Entrepreneurial Journey Model was not available to Nimblegen because of exogenous factors. This highlights the fact that the Entrepreneurial Journey Model is, fundamentally, a retrospective or introspective tool, rather than a heuristic for evaluating opportunities based on external factors.

While the Entrepreneurial Journey Model can show the theoretical or actual path that a commercial venture travels, our focus is on the inventing entrepreneur. For the venture, there are many potential exogenous measures of success, including financial rewards, market acceptance, or the eradication of a serious problem (such as a disease). Commercial venture growth and success can ultimately be measured by returns to shareholders and market share. Inventing entrepreneurs may have similar goals, including financial success. Though "success" can be fairly measured across commercial ventures, each inventing entrepreneur has his own definition of success, both for himself and his technology. There is no generalized "optimal" path through the Journey Matrix for an inventing entrepreneur.

CAPITAL INTENSITY AND THE VIABILITY OF ADOPTING MULTIPLE ROLE IDENTITIES

The Entrepreneurial Journey Model does not address the question of capital intensity for a given technology or innovation. Capital intensity is the amount of capital required to develop or produce a given good or service. For example, the oil refining business is extremely capital intensive because of the costs associated with building and maintaining oil drilling rigs and with transporting the product. Another example is the pharmaceutical industry, where the high cost of clinical trials is an essential factor.

An inventing entrepreneur should attempt to evaluate the relative capital intensity of her technology. Unfortunately, an accurate estimate of capital intensity may require making assumptions about product incarnations that may not be obvious. The Nimblegen example is again useful—the founders probably couldn't have predicted the service model in Iceland (as opposed to a traditional production and sales model). At the same time, some useful assumptions can be made on the basis of readily available industry information. A novel biodiesel refinement technology could be extremely capital intensive, especially if it requires completely new refining facilities or significant retrofitting of existing facilities. In general, software innovations are not as capital intensive, although many software entrepreneurs (whether academic or commercial) underestimate the likely investment in customer support.

Significant variation in capital intensity can exist for a given opportunity on the basis of strategic and exit planning. For example, a company anticipating bringing a novel cancer therapeutic to market must anticipate raising hundreds of millions of dollars for extensive animal and human testing. A company hoping to develop a series of lead targets to be sold to the pharmaceutical industry would expect to spend tens of millions of dollars before generating revenue. But a company that provides a novel tool to improve the pharmaceutical industry's process of testing lead targets might generate revenue much more quickly.

Capital intensity requires careful consideration, because the institutional capital markets, unlike the academic research markets, are highly concentrated. Of the $25.5 billion in venture capital invested in 2006, more than 67% was invested in California and the New York City/Boston regions.[4,5] Although venture capital funds do invest outside of their regions, venture capital is not always available close to universities and other research institutions that are not proximate to large cities. Inventing entrepreneurs must be aware of the relative capital intensity required for commercialization as well as the relative availability of capital financing.

The impact on role identity stems from the innovator's technology affinity and need for control. The greater the capital intensity, the greater are the funding and infrastructure requirements to reach successful commercialization. These factors increase the complexity of the venture and the probability that the market outcome could differ from the initial vision. Inventing entrepreneurs unwilling to transfer authority and responsibility to management may want to consider long-term, high-intensity commitments to the commercialization process, and base such commitments on the degree of capital intensity required by the particular commercialization effort.

The Bone Care International example is useful here. The company's efforts to commercialize Professor DeLuca's vitamin D hormones for osteoporosis were not successful, due to a combination of business and technology factors. The decision was made to target a new market: end-stage renal care. If DeLuca had chosen to be more actively involved from the start, and if his technology affinity had been so entrenched that he was unwilling to change markets (and management), it's possible the company might have failed instead of being acquired by Genzyme at nearly $700 million. In this case, DeLuca's retention of his primary role identity supported the necessary changes being made at a highly capital-intensive company.

THE JOURNEY TRANSFORMS THE INVENTOR

Professor Hennessy of Stanford University described his experience as transformative. This is indicative of the evaluative comments we heard from most of our interviewees. In some cases, inventing entrepreneurs struggled to put into words the effect of their particular experience. Yet nearly all interviewees referred to it as a seminal period that impacted their long-term goals and aspirations. In some cases, of course, the experience reinforced their core beliefs. While Professor Handelsmann states that she is comfortable with the world of licensing and start-ups, she clearly retains her original research/technology role identity.

For most inventing entrepreneurs, the experience represented the start of a completely new way of thinking, and usually gave rise to a new perspective on their own research streams and processes. As we have noted, not every inventor becomes an inventing entrepreneur. Those who do, however, can expect a transforming experience, one that may dramatically impact every aspect of their lives, including their academic career, family and friends, and personal growth and development.

Conclusions and Summary

In this chapter, we introduced a model for describing the inventing entrepreneur's personal experience. The Entrepeneurial Journey Model identifies the inventing entrepreneur's mindset along two axes: a Technology-Market axis and a Research-Commercial axis. An inventing entrepreneur should be able to identify which of the four resulting quadrants best matches his current perspective on his role in the technology development and commercialization process. That role may change over time; the path which the inventor pursues is the entrepreneurial journey.

To assist with this exercise, we identified a number of common journeys based on our observations of inventing entrepreneurs. These "templates" may help the novice inventing entrepreneur examine his own goals as well as prepare for likely outcomes. We encourage aspiring entrepreneurs to consider that the commercialization path of the venture or technology is not necessarily the same as the entrepreneur's journey.

Each entrepreneurial journey is idiosyncratic: every inventing entrepreneur brings unique characteristics to the journey, each starts in unique circumstances (initial conditions), and each journey comprises unique situations and events. Undoubtedly, there can be similarities between inventing entrepreneurs' experiences and journeys, but we have been struck by the dramatic differences in perspectives, outcomes, and growth across the spectrum of journeys, even between examples with strong similarities across many variables.

Entrepreneurial journeys are transforming experiences. Inventing entrepreneurs may experience significant changes in their role identities: how they see their own roles (functions, jobs) and what other stakeholders (students, customers, family, university administrators) expect of them. Regardless of whether inventing entrepreneurs return to their original role identity, they almost always acknowledge dramatic shifts in their thinking, based on perspective shifts, acquired knowledge, and powerful ordeals.

Exercise

- What are your role identities? How would you characterize your role identities right now?
- How do you think your role identity would change if you participated in commercializing your technology?
- Which of the six journeys described in this chapter will likely resemble your potential journey?
- What are some contingencies that may influence your journey? How might your journey change? What can make it change?

Endnotes

1. Tetrionics was acquired by Sigma-Aldrich in January 2006.
2. Burgelman, R A. 1983. A process model of internal corporate venturing in the diversified major firm. *Administrative Science Quarterly,* 28(2): 223–244; Campbell, A., Birkinshaw, J., Morrison, A., & Batenburg, R. 2003. The future of corporate venturing. *MIT Sloan Management Review,* 45: 30–37; Dushnitsky, G. & Lenox, M. J. 2005. When do firms undertake R&D by investing in new ventures? *Strategic Management Journal,* 26(10): 947–965; Zahra, S. A., Neubaum, D. O., & Huse, M. 2000. Entrepreneurship in medium-sized companies: Exploring the effects of owner-ship and governance systems. *Journal of Management,* 26(5): 947–976; Ireland, R. D., Hitt, M. A., & Sirmon, D. G. 2003. A model of strategic entrepreneurship: The construct and its dimensions. *Journal of Management,* 29(6): 963–989.
3. Presumably, the commercial venture would continue to be an ongoing concern.
4. www.pwcmoneytree.com/exhibits/MoneyTree_4Q2006_Final.pdf.
5. See National Venture Capital Association for the latest figures: http://www.nvca.org.

PART

ASSEMBLING THE ENTREPRENEURIAL TOOL KIT

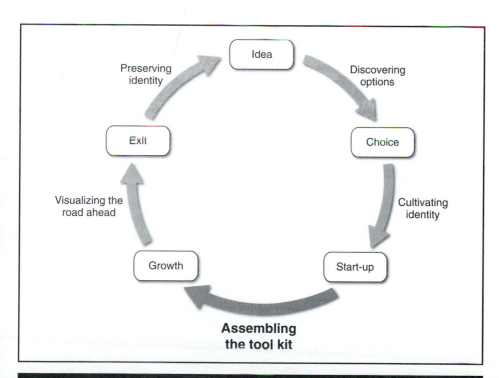

Preserving identity

Idea

Discovering options

Choice

Cultivating identity

Exit

Start-up

Visualizing the road ahead

Growth

Assembling the tool kit

Stages in the Entrepreneurial Process

CHAPTER 9

UNDERSTANDING INDUSTRY CONTEXT

OVERVIEW

Of all the strategic issues associated with starting a venture, understanding the industry context and the market opportunity may present the greatest challenges for the inventing entrepreneur. Numerous tools exist to enable analysis, but even the most widely recognized business tools may be unfamiliar or even disconcerting to the scientist. There is no shortage of books, articles, consulting heuristics, or general advice on how to evaluate industry attractiveness and market size. In this chapter, we discuss an important set of tools that enable a quick, relatively clear analysis of the industry and the opportunity. We will explain the difference between an industry and a market for the technology and discuss the broad implications for the potential success of a venture based on a given technology. This chapter helps the inventing entrepreneur appreciate key industry factors and market dynamics that influence the growth potential of every new venture.

For many inventing entrepreneurs, evaluating the industry and the market marks a transition to unfamiliar territory. Early activities in the technology transfer process include technology testing, intellectual property prosecution, and team building. Many inventing entrepreneurs quickly adapt to these functions using their existing skills and experiences.

The success of the venture, however, will require operational and market-focused skills. As the Entrepreneurial Journey Model shows, inventing entrepreneurs that take an active role in commercialization must begin developing and utilizing skills associated with business operations as well as customer and market analysis.

Typically, the inventor may appreciate the specific applications of a given technology without possessing a sophisticated understanding of the commercialization process or the product. Professor Stephen Rao of the Cleveland Clinic represents an excellent example of the inventor who develops market sophistication primarily to aid the commercialization process. In 2003, Professor Rao was at the forefront of functional magnetic resonance imaging (fMRI) technology. At the time, Professor Rao was at the Medical College of Wisconsin, one of the three research facilities (along with the University of Minnesota and Harvard/ Massachusetts General Hospital) where fMRI was first invented and demonstrated. He knew the technology could be used to evaluate how pharmaceuticals impact brain functionality, but he hadn't considered specifically what product or service can be created. He acknowledges his own inexperience, as well as the difficulty of guessing where to initially target the technology:

> I'm not a businessperson. I'm learning, but I wouldn't say I have any expertise in business. Some of the big challenges were in finding out what customers need and knowing how to get this to market. I think we thought initially that a lot of the work we were doing in neurogenerative diseases would come online a lot faster, but I recognize now that's going to be a slower process. We had to switch gears in the middle to go into presurgical mapping, which wasn't our original intention.

As this example illustrates, data gathering, heuristics, and analysis can't guarantee that a technology targets the right customer demographic. Our goal, therefore, is to give the inventing entrepreneur basic tools to evaluate products and markets as well as some common sense advice about preparing for the unexpected. We'll clarify some of the common terminology associated with industry analysis. We believe that a rational *process* can be utilized—one that eliminates egregious errors and that helps attune the inventing entrepreneur to a market-based mindset. The inventing entrepreneur that utilizes rational and reasonable evaluative tools for industry and market assessment is better prepared for the challenges of commercialization. We hope these tools will help inventors respond more effectively to the inevitable course corrections required at a growth technology venture.

INDUSTRIES AND MARKETS

Broadly, an **industry** is defined as the set of suppliers or producers of a particular product or service, whereas a **market** is the set of buyers or consumers of the product or service. Consequently, when we consider industry factors, we are concerned about competition and the availability of resources to produce a technology-based product. When we consider markets, we evaluate trends underlying customer needs. Typically, the starting point for evaluating technological opportunities is to clearly understand the market by answering basic questions: Who will buy the product? What benefit does it have for that end user? How big is the market? The purpose of this process is not to analyze the broadest possible data set, but to ensure that obvious market and customer trends aren't missed in the rush to bring an innovation to commercial light.

TABLE 9-1 Evaluating Broad Market Trends		
Trend	*Questions*	*Possible Data Sources*
Demographic	• Do the sociodemographic trends in the target consumer groups support the assumption that there will be an increased need for the innovative product or technology?	Statistical Abstract of the United States (U.S. Census Bureau), literature reviews, Market Intelligence (Mintel), Databases
Political	• Will the political environment for the foreseeable future affect the diffusion of the technology in the marketplace? • Is there a tax or a regulatory incentive for technology adoption?	Recent legislation, history of lobbying action within the industry, broad literature reviews
Natural	• Are natural resources available to support large-scale commercial production of the technology? • Will changes in the availability of natural resources influence the positioning (e.g., cost, availability) of the technology or competitive technologies?	Statistical abstracts, raw materials production data, literature reviews
Economic	• Do the economic trends of the target market support the assumption that there will be a customer need or ability to purchase the proposed technology?	Statistical abstracts, stock market and other financial data, literature reviews
Sociocultural	• Do the sociocultural trends support the assumption that there will be a need or desire for the proposed product? • Are those trends limited in scope (i.e., fads)?	High-level review of cultural trends, discussions with potential customers
Technological	• How rapid is technological innovation in your industry? • How rapidly is innovative technology diffused within your target market? Are the target customers quick adopters of new technologies?	Review of industry trade publications, history of R&D spending within industry, history of capital investment within target segment

Entrepreneurs and managers typically scan the environment for six important trends: demographic, sociocultural, natural, economic, regulatory, and technological.[1,2] The sample analysis in Table 9-1 illustrates some of the questions that might be asked about market trends.

This exercise provides a backdrop for the topic of market trends—a broad canvas upon which market options and possibilities can be explored. It can identify high-level issues (for example—that significant changes in health care reimbursement could impact efforts to market high-end products having marginal, though real, value to patients). Or it could provide a mechanism for considering geographic factors in long-term market entry planning. It is not, however, a crystal ball for predicting the success of a given technology. When reviewing market trends, the key questions to ask pertain to the macro trends in the target market and how these trends favor the introduction of a novel technology.

INDUSTRY ATTRACTIVENESS AND THE VALUE CHAIN

We now turn our attention to how the industry structure influences the new venture. The most commonly used framework for understanding industry structure is Porter's "Five Forces" model.[3] Developed nearly 30 years ago, it's arguably still the best introductory tool for quickly and effectively evaluating *industry attractiveness,* a qualitative measure of the capacity of firms within an industry to sustain profitability. The Five Forces include Existing Rivalry (degree of competition), Threat of Entry (degree of difficulty of entering an industry), Supplier Power (bargaining power of suppliers to increase input material prices), Buyer Power (bargaining power of buyers to demand lower prices), and Substitutes (alternate product categories that can satisfy customer needs). Each of these five factors impacts the profit margins of firms operating within an industry. In Figure 9-2, we illustrate how these forces influence industry profitability.

FIGURE 9-2 Influence of the Five Forces on Industry Profitability

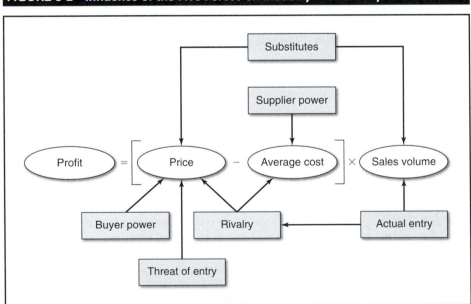

As can be seen in Figure 9-2, buyer power and new entrants exert downward pressure on the selling price of the product. Rivalry influences both the selling price and the average cost of manufacturing the products competition within an industry lower selling prices and, in some cases, decrease the average production cost of the product as more suppliers of the components emerge—thereby decreasing the cost of the input materials. Often, however, greater rivalry forces a company to increase the cost of the product by bundling in new features and services to differentiate its product.

For a new venture based on novel technology, early analysis of broad industry structure and profit-sustaining capacity can be very useful. While quantitative data is almost always available and beneficial, one of the strengths of the Five Forces analysis is that it lends itself to "common sense" analysis. In Table 9-2, we provide additional details about the Five Forces and describe the preferred outcome of the analysis from the nascent venture perspective.

Once the Five Forces are evaluated (and, usually, given a rating such as "low, medium, high"), the overall attractiveness of the industry is assessed. Industries that receive preferred assessments across many or all of the Forces demonstrate the potential for higher average profitability. Presumably, a new

TABLE 9-2   Five Forces Analysis

Industry Force	Explanation	Preferred Assessment
Rivalry	Exit barriers, industry concentration, fixed costs, industry growth, intermittent overcapacity, product differences, switching costs, brand identity, diversity of rivals	**Low rivalry** (i.e., limited competition within the sector)
Barriers to entry	Absolute cost advantages, learning curve, access to inputs, governmental policy, economies of scale, capital requirements, brand identity, switching costs, access to distribution, expected retaliation, proprietary products	**High barriers to entry** (i.e., it is difficult for new firms to enter)[4]
Supplier power	Supplier concentration, importance of volume to supplier, differentiation of inputs, impact of inputs on cost or differentiation, presence of substitute inputs, threat of forward integration, cost relative to total purchases in industry	**Low supplier power** (i.e., suppliers are unable to extract value from the new venture)
Buyer power	Bargaining leverage, buyer volume, buyer information, brand identity, price sensitivity, threat of backward integration, buyer concentration, availability of substitutes, buyers' incentives	**Low buyer power** (i.e., buyers are unable to drive the venture's prices down or easily switch to competitors)
Substitutes	Switching costs, buyer inclination to substitute, price/performance, tradeoff of substitutes	**Limited substitutes** (i.e., customers have few other options)

venture would prefer to compete in an attractive industry where the average profitability is high. Many start-up companies (or even pre-start-up teams) do a good job of identifying where the highest value opportunities exist. We were involved with a university spin-out that was commercializing a novel synthetic wet adhesive technology developed at a Big 10 university in the United States. As the success of 3M shows, adhesives represent a broad product base across thousands of market applications. A start-up, however, has to pick target opportunities carefully, because limited resources must be applied with discretion. In this case, the team determined that scaling up production for industrial applications would require significant investments in infrastructure. In addition, the compound tested well against other medical adhesives, which are limited by biocompatibility concerns, but not as well against industrial adhesives, which are held to less stringent standards for safety. Medical applications would require minuscule quantities but could generate dramatically higher profit potential per unit. While being no guarantee of ultimate success, the Five Forces assessment helped the team focus on specific applications that had a more attractive market potential.

Performing this assessment objectively may pose challenges for inventing entrepreneurs, especially for those with high technology affinity. Too often, we have seen entrepreneurs use this type of model as the *justification* for an opportunity, rather than as an honest analysis of the attractiveness of a given market space. Throughout this book, we have tried to stress the importance of dispassionate appraisal of business opportunities. Our experience with dozens of early-stage firms suggests that market assessment remains prone to subjective reasoning rather than objective analysis. It is relatively easy for an inventing entrepreneur to *assume* that a market is attractive because he has been performing scientific research aimed at solving specific types of problems in that market. After all, his research is funded, he's regularly contacted by industry leaders and experts, and he can see how a developing innovation could represent an improvement on existing technology.

In general, we have seen two major types of errors in this assessment process. The first type of error is misunderstanding the problems that need to be solved in the market space. One of the inventing entrepreneurs profiled in this book, Professor Shane Farritor, had initially developed a miniaturized mobile tool for improving visualization during laparoscopic surgery. The device was, as numerous investors concurred, exciting, and it generated a lot of positive press for the university. But, when pressed to explain exactly why surgeons would use it, Professor Farritor and his colleagues realized that they couldn't come up with a rational explanation for why surgeons, hospitals, and insurance companies would pay for that embodiment of technology to be used on an everyday basis.

There is no question that the market for novel, minimally invasive surgical tools is attractive: Average net income as a percentage of sales for the top 20 biomedical companies in 2006 was 11%. There was only one company with negative net income (Boston Scientific); if that firm is removed from the sample then the average jumps to 15%.[5] But Farritor's team hadn't worked out exactly which problems needed to be solved in the market or how the innovative technology would improve or change existing surgical procedures. For example, if the device were used in standard laparoscopic surgery, then the market was relatively unattractive, because the existing substitute (laparoscope) is well proven, easy to use, and meets the current needs. In addition, competition is relatively intense in that space, which has many established players. In this case, the high barrier to entry (FDA regulatory clearance and a national sales and support team), works *against* the start-up, because the marginal value added by the product won't be attractive to venture capitalists.

On the other hand, once the team identified alternative technology embodiments that could be used in a developing market segment, the evaluation looked very different. Farritor's second- and third-generation technologies could be used for natural orifice transluminal endoscopic surgery (NOTES). Currently these surgeries aren't performed in the United States,[6] but because they may offer a way to perform surgical procedures without external incisions, the concept has generated optimistic speculation.[7] Farritor's start-up company, Nebraska Surgical, hopes to drive this market by providing miniaturized tools that directly address currently unsolved issues for natural orifice procedures. From a Five-Forces perspective, the substitute is the existing set of traditional laparoscopic and endoscopic tools. But these may not be a viable substitute if natural orifice surgery delivers on its promise of "scarless" procedures resulting in dramatically reduced patient recovery time. Buyer power will be low, as patients demand the less painful procedure and surgeons and hospitals would have to update their skills and infrastructure to accommodate the demand. Competition will likely be among nascent participants, with the more established medical device companies acting as acquirers. The bottom line: The nascent market for tools for natural orifice surgery, though speculative, is likely to be significantly more attractive than the mature market for laparoscopic tools.

The second type of market assessment error is much harder to address. It represents the fundamental flaw of making a market evaluation based on circumstances driven by "nonmarket" factors or even by the influence of a few key individuals or organizations for which information may be hard to confirm. An excellent, though disappointing example of this was in the field of transgenic technologies for pharmaceutical applications in the late 1990s and early 2000s. A number of promising transgenic technologies were in development, including one that we were directly familiar with. An opportunity existed to genetically modify certain domesticated animal and plant species to enable production of high-value proteins. For example, a drug like Herceptin™ is currently produced via protein expression from Chinese hamster ovary (CHO) cells in production facilities that cost hundreds of millions of dollars to build and maintain. A single facility can often produce only a kilogram of purified protein in a year.

On the other hand, a single transgenically modified cow could theoretically express the same amount of protein in its milk in a year. And some experiments have suggested that the genetically modified animal might pass on the genetic modification to successive generations. The implications for low-cost drug production could be enormous, potentially reducing the fully-loaded manufacturing cost by a factor of 1000 or more. And, in fact, in 2006 Genzyme Transgenics brought to market in Europe a protein produced in goats' milk.

For the past 10 years, however, the transgenic technology issues have been trumped by an entirely different problem, one that is not yet fully resolved. The United States Food and Drug Administration (FDA) determined that it did not have enough information about the safety of the genetic modification process—or about the consistency and safety of the product—to begin approving drugs produced via this method. Arguments that the drugs were molecularly identical to those produced in standard pharmaceutical manufacturing processes were not persuasive, for a variety of reasons. To date, the FDA has not clarified standards for evaluating transgenically produced pharmaceuticals,[8] although a couple of products are undergoing the regulatory approval process.[9]

But for a number of companies, including the one we were directly involved with, the FDA's stance represented an enormous hurdle, though not directly associated with market "attractiveness." Genzyme Transgenics had the resources to survive for 15 years without an approved product, but many smaller firms were forced out of the business or were acquired for relatively low prices because of the uncertain regulatory process. In theory, a high barrier to entry is, all else being equal, indicative of an attractive market. But in this case, the barrier was the regulatory hurdle for the customers of the manufacturing process (i.e., the drug companies attempting to get regulatory approval for human use of a pharmaceutical product produced via transgenic animals), and that hurdle turned out to be insurmountable.

Is it possible that careful evaluation of the industry and the market would have turned up this possibility? At the time, everyone we spoke to stated that change at the FDA was "right around the corner," and that the FDA couldn't ignore the growing body of scientific evidence that appeared to support the safety of transgenically produced pharmaceuticals. The FDA, however, did not change its position; the company we knew, along with dozens of others, didn't survive.

Notwithstanding the difficulty of correctly assessing such eventualities, every inventing entrepreneur should make the attempt to evaluate market attractiveness. To that end, we'll perform a simplified version of the process.

Let us take an example of hydrogen fuel cell technology with specific application for the mobile telephony market.[10] The market for mobile telephones is growing globally because of inexpensive calling plans and infrastructure investments by large players. To better understand industry attractiveness, we provide a description of the direct competitors that are developing fuel cell technologies. As can be seen in Figure 9-3, the competitive rivalry is significant with a high number of substitutes and substantial threats of new entry. Given that buyers are limited in number (in this case, the cell phone manufacturers who also face price pressures from the mobile service providers), they are likely to require lower prices. These industry dynamics suggest that unless the technology solution is far superior, the industry sector is likely to face significant price pressure and the venture will face stiff competition.

Evaluating industry attractiveness can also provide insight into target markets. It's not usually necessary to perform a full analysis of the attractiveness of the

FIGURE 9-3   Fuel Cell for Mobile Telephony Industry Analysis

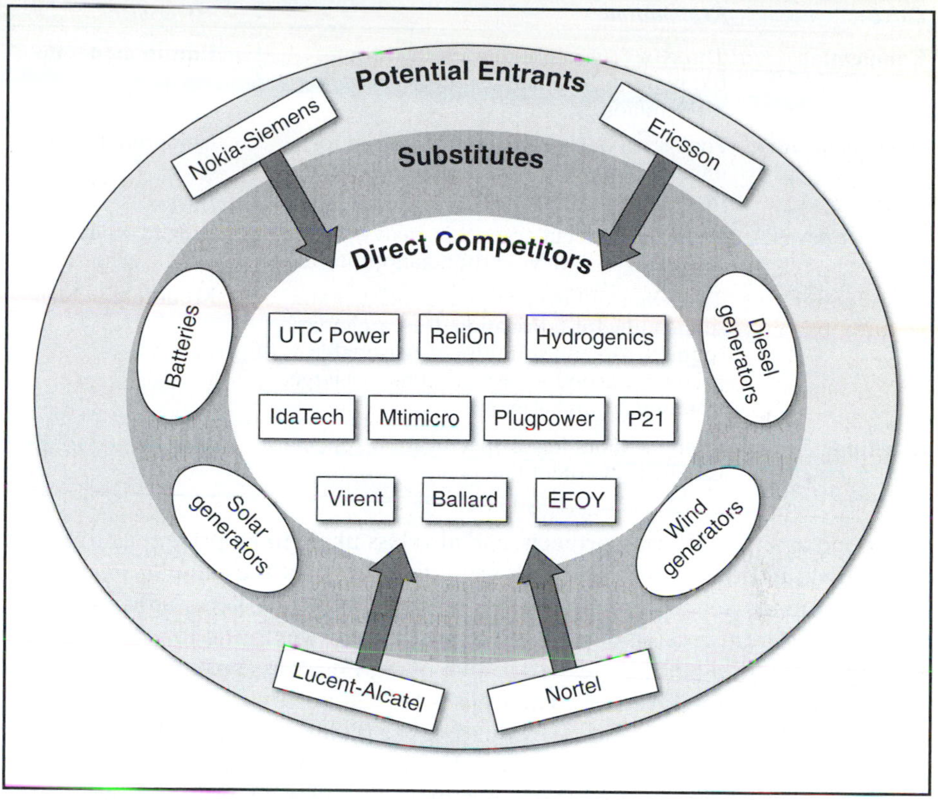

customer market to generate high-value insight. Consider Mike Fouche's comments about customer types for his company's autonomous helicopter technology:

> Originally, I thought the market would be television stations [using the autonomous helicopters for traffic monitoring], but there are a lot of them that have very thin margins. And when you combine thin margins with being risk averse, it is not a favorable context. We had two TV stations that signed on and then backed off. We're not even going after the TV market anymore; it's more pipelines and utility companies.

If we reflect on the economics and the business model of these customers for a moment, we can develop relatively straightforward conclusions about market attractiveness. For instance, the TV stations get limited marginal value from the technology, especially since the link between the use of the technology and additional revenues (generated via an increased viewership that results in high advertising fees) is likely to be tenuous. But pipeline companies and utilities need rapid-response mechanisms to assess problems and evaluate mission-critical assets. In addition, utilities are likely to have significantly more cash available for

TABLE 9-3	Summary Five-Forces Analysis for Nanopositioning Systems	
Force	*Explanation*	*Assessment*
Competition	Three or four major players worldwide, but none with annual revenues exceeding $500 million.	**Low to moderate**
Barriers to entry	High level of sophistication required for engineering work; limited qualified scientists or engineers available.	**Moderate to high**
Supplier power	Sophisticated, but accessible, materials and technologies (AFM, carbon nanotubes, etc.).	**Low to moderate**
Buyer power	Two levels of buyers: research market and semiconductor fabrication. Research market requires top-end solutions at reasonable prices; semiconductor market makes large, infrequent purchases.	**Moderate to high**
Substitutes	Going without lower-specification systems usually is unacceptable.	**Low**

safety and asset-monitoring projects, and also less likely to be price sensitive than TV stations. In other words, although we're talking about the same *business* (selling autonomous helicopters), evaluating various target markets might yield dramatically different assessments of the opportunity. Attempting to sell to the TV stations yields an inherently less attractive overall business concept, because the "Buyer" factor in the Five Forces analysis is far less positive.

Table 9-3 shows a Five Forces evaluation of a highly specialized field (nanopositioning systems) in which we see new technologies being developed. An academic innovator in this specific field might complete a similar analysis to consider the overall attractiveness of the target industry.[11] Though buyer power is high, the presence of few substitutes and competitors augurs well for a new entrant into this business. This industry sector is structurally attractive for a new venture.

At the same time, we expect that early-stage companies in this field will face two major problems: first, the ability to attract and retain key people having specialized expertise; second, the fact that customers can exert significant power in their purchasing process, limiting economic gains and making market entry for a start-up with constrained funds very difficult. In theory, once a company reaches some minimum or critical scale, it should achieve cost economies of scale and even command price premiums from customers because of the limited number of available product options. A start-up, however, may find itself at a significant disadvantage to industry stalwarts. Breaking into this industry will require a highly differentiated product and significant financial resources for funding long-term R&D and sales activities.

The evaluation of the target market may challenge inventing entrepreneurs and experienced businesspeople alike. Consider again Professor Rao and Neurognostics. The application of fMRI technology for diagnostic and long-term therapeutic purposes appeared to be highly attractive, with few viable substitutes and limited buyer power. But as the company began talking to hospitals, drug companies, and insurance companies, it became clear that a better near-term target would be augmenting clinical trials of therapeutics for neurodegenerative disorders. While the buyers (pharmaceutical companies) have more substitutes, they also have more resources (cash) as well as the clear need to find tools to accelerate their own production process (drug discovery). It is generally accepted that each day's delay in bringing a new drug to market costs the manufacturer millions of dollars.[12] If fMRI improves the clinical trial process for blockbuster neurological drugs, the pharmaceutical companies should be very attentive. Professor Rao's story is provided in detail in Profile 9-1.

INVENTING ENTREPRENEUR PROFILE 9-1

Professor Stephen Rao

Dr. Stephen Rao never intended to start a high-tech company. It wasn't even his idea. "The dean called me and said, 'I really think there may be potential for spin-out companies in the technology you folks have developed.'" The technology is functional Magnetic Resonance Imaging, or fMRI, a technique that uses fast-pulse MRI on a patient performing cognitive tasks—in order to identify brain function by observing changes in blood flow. Dr. Rao, now at the Cleveland Clinic, was a clinical neuropsychologist at the Medical College of Wisconsin (MCW) when fMRI was developed, and he began using the technology to evaluate the effect of certain drugs on patients with neurological disorders like attention deficit hyperactivity disorder (ADHD) and multiple sclerosis.

The Functional Imaging Research Center at MCW has conducted more than $40 million of research on fMRI. Dr. Rao was the director of the Center, overseeing eight post-docs, more than 25 graduate students, and a staff of 10—as well as working with more than 30 faculty from 10 separate departments at MCW. His name wasn't on any of the patents being filed by MCW, and although the center was already contracting with pharmaceutical companies for targeted research, he'd never thought about a commercial venture. But the world of technology transfer has evolved in the last 30 years, and some university administrators have begun acting like venture capitalists, walking the halls of their own research buildings looking for novel technologies with commercial potential. Bill Hendee, the dean of the Graduate School of Biomedical Sciences at MCW, knew that fMRI was one of the school's strengths. In addition, Hendee was serving on the board of directors of a new organization in Milwaukee called "TechStar," a technology incubator:

> I was already starting to do work getting funding to look at things like MS, ADHD, early Alzheimer's, Parkinson's, and Atkinson's disease—and we were also doing studies looking at the effects of different types of drugs. We were looking at drugs that were already approved; for example, how Ritalin affects healthy individuals and individuals with ADHD. The Dean said, "I'd like to have somebody talk to you about a thing called TechStar, an incubator involved in trying to help scientists develop their own company. Could you assemble your regular monthly meeting and talk to them?" And I said, "Sure, but I'm not really interested."

(continues)

The staff at TechStar felt MCW's fMRI know-how and expertise had significant commercial value. But could that value be captured? Dr. Rao met with TechStar staff, and was eventually introduced to angel investors. The technology appeared to have significant potential—it could determine the mode of action for potential drug compounds, which could help pharmaceutical companies accelerate the regulatory process by demonstrating safety and efficacy. But the system developed by Dr. Rao and others at MCW had another use—measuring changes in brain function to predict neurological disorders years before the onset of physical symptoms:

> The idea was to use fMRI to look more objectively at drug response that might be useful for pharmaceutical companies. We also started thinking about a software company, where some of the things we were using could be used as a [neurological disease] diagnostic tool in the hospital setting.

With the help of TechStar, Dr. Rao founded Neurognostics. The company has raised more than $3 million from private investors and has received regulatory clearance[13] from the FDA to market a turnkey system that allows facilities with an MRI machine to perform fMRI scans. The company has initiated service work on clinical trials for pharmaceutical companies, and is looking long-term toward a software solution for disease diagnosis. For Dr. Rao, working at the interface between research and commercialization has been an extraordinary learning experience:

> I really knew very little about business. My father's an insurance salesman. We didn't have any private businesses, and I never saw myself in that. Everything was new to me—developing a business plan and the financing. I think I've learned a tremendous amount, but I wouldn't by any stretch of the imagination consider myself as an expert in any of these areas. The company brought in a CEO from the medical imaging field, a move that I welcomed.

He also reflects on the relationship he formed with the CEO, and how bringing in that individual created a more tenable role for his own continuing participation:

> Before we hired a CEO, I felt like I was doing a lot of things to hold the company together. We had just decided to move from downtown out to the [research] park, and a lot of decisions were being made about routine things—where we should buy our staples and phones. The last thing I wanted to do was get involved in day-to-day management. It was a blessing to have a CEO involved in hiring and day-to-day responsibilities; to me that was fantastic. We hired a CEO I relate with very well. We both respect each other's opinions. He seeks out mine, I seek out his, and we work closely together.

Dr. Rao recently accepted a new position as director of the Schey Center for Cognitive Neuroimaging at the prestigious Cleveland Clinic, though he maintains a relatively active role at Neurognostics. He acknowledges the uncertainty associated with commercial ventures, but overall he appears to be cautiously optimistic about the company's potential:

> I've always felt when it comes to research grants that I had some degree of control. My feeling is you work harder and you can do it. With the business it's really different; you don't always know. [The CEO] and I have some soul-searching moments where we can't decide whether the company is on the path at just the right time and the right place, or whether it's too late. Timing is everything in business; you hope you're in the right place at the right time, and I think we are, but it's hard to tell.

We recommend the Five Forces Model for evaluating profit sustainability in given industries as a measure of industry attractiveness. For innovations that transform industry structure or drastically shift customer buying criteria, this heuristic may be more difficult to apply. Such transformational businesses may arise from disruptive technologies, which we'll discuss next.

DISRUPTIVE TECHNOLOGIES

Romanelli and Tushman describe a theory of industry evolution called "punctuated equilibrium," in which competition tends towards a stable environment.[14] "Sustaining" innovations that support the current market value proposition are the norm because these innovations foster improved product performance within the accepted product paradigm. Once in a while, however, the stability is punctuated by upheavals caused by significant technological innovations—where the entire industry is reconfigured to take advantage of the new innovation. Disruptive technologies create entirely new value propositions for customers, often creating entirely new customer sets. Products based on disruptive technologies are typically cheaper, simpler, smaller and frequently, more convenient to use. Christensen further developed this concept by observing (among a number of industries) the disk-drive industry between 1970 and 1995.[15] Christensen defines disruptive technologies as innovations that:

- Involve (usually) novel configurations of existing components and technologies,
- Emerge via new industry entrants, and
- Serve market sectors that are not developed (or don't even exist) when the innovation comes online.

Christensen's book, *The Innovator's Dilemma,* has had a significant impact on business thinking, especially in the high-technology sectors.[16] The book's terminology is being used in business practice, military analysis, and law.[17,18,19] It is important to realize that "disruptive" is not the same as "novel," a distinction that is often missed both by entrepreneurs and financiers.[20] These innovations target a customer segment that may not exist, sometimes offering a value proposition unattractive to current customers. Assessing whether an innovation is disruptive is not necessarily intuitive. In fact, although the inventing entrepreneurs described in this book have generated hundreds of novel innovations and technologies, very few of those innovations would qualify as truly disruptive technologies. For example, Tomotherapy is not a disruptive technology, though the application of collimators and optimizing software represented a significant leap forward in radiation modulation. Fundamentally, however, the market sector (cancer patients) was fully developed well before Tomotherapy brought its first products to market, and the same patient set was already being treated with less advanced systems.

Alternatively, Virent may be a disruptive technology. Although the catalytic process for biofuel production is a technological advance, the underlying engineering, physics, and chemistry are well understood. Cortwright and the Virent team changed enough variables in previously analyzed catalytic reactions to optimize hydrogen production at a variety of scale efficiencies. The hydrogen production process offers a novel method for producing a fuel source not currently cost-competitive, because current applications run effectively on established battery and internal combustion systems. The customers buying "efficient energy" cells don't need to resort to hydrogen at this time, because the performance characteristics of their own products are already being met. But as petroleum costs increase and the performance requirements for applications change (such as the requirements for cell phones, laptops, and eventually automobiles), the new price-performance curve could favor hydrogen fuel cells or battery systems powered through hydrogen production. Clearly the market isn't fully developed—even the phrase "The Hydrogen Economy" remains a visionary statement about the possibility of reducing dependence on fossil fuels.

Christensen notes that start-up companies have inherent advantages for bringing these types of technologies to market, because large companies suffer from myopia and often see only their current technological or customer needs and high infrastructure costs of change, among other factors.[21,22,23] Randy Cortright describes this uncertainty as something that would be nearly impossible to tolerate in a larger firm: "We're crawling, and then walking, and then when we finally see the market, that's when we'll go for the financing that we'd need." It's interesting to note, however, that in June 2006, Virent raised $7.5 million in private financing that was led by two very large corporations: Honda and Cargill.

Another possible disruptive technology is Nebraska Surgical's miniaturized surgical robots. These devices are not, in and of themselves, technological innovations—they utilize miniaturized versions of off-the-shelf components in specially designed housings. The innovation is philosophical—the idea that miniaturizing surgical tools for remote control led use inside the body may offer surgeons the opportunity to perform minimally invasive procedures faster and with less pain and recovery time for patients. The devices meet most of Christensen's characteristics—they are simpler, cheaper, and currently offer fewer features than standard laparoscopic tools. If the company can successfully engender a market for surgical procedures that require fewer incisions and decrease tool costs, it might disrupt the entire field of minimally invasive surgery.

START-UP LOCATION CHOICES AND THEIR IMPLICATIONS

The world may be shrinking, thanks to the Internet and to nearly ubiquitous telecommunications systems, but the impact on a start-up's location choice will likely be limited. Anecdotal evidence clearly points to the success of certain technology clusters—Silicon Valley, Route 128 (Boston), the Research Triangle (Raleigh–Durham, North Carolina), and so on. Audretsch and Feldman (among others) have rigorously documented these clusters (or "geographically mediated knowledge spillovers").[24] Some regions have developed a unique identity that, in turn, attracts new ventures in a particular industry sector (e.g., San Diego and its biotechnology companies).[25] While this represents a fascinating area of research, our discussion will be limited to how this issue relates to the inventing entrepreneur's options and decisions to start a new venture.

A start-up company founded on university technology is likely faced with limited geographical options. In theory, companies can be formed anywhere (and, in the United States, do not need to be located in the same state in which they are incorporated), but our experience, in agreement with the general research results, suggests that both real and perceived factors lead most start-ups to choose one of two locations: either the local environment or an established area with a cluster of companies and organizations in similar and related fields. We believe this choice is specifically driven by the following factors: availability of capital, availability of human resources, proximity to customers, and ease of access for key personnel.

Most university spin-outs require the continued input of the inventing entrepreneur, at least in an advisory role. This immediately encourages the location of the company within driving distance (or at worst, within a reasonable distance by flight) from the founding academic laboratory. A significant number of these spin-outs hire employees from the founding institution, often directly out of the founders' own research program. Again, local facilities simplify this process.

On the other hand, one of the most common factors for choosing an alternative location involves private capital sourcing. Venture capital within the high-technology sectors is highly consolidated. For example, in the second quarter of 2006, 36% of the $6.7 billion of venture capital invested came from the Bay Area. Together, the Bay Area and Boston accounted for nearly 50 percent of all venture capital investments in the United States.[26] Similarly, the Cambridge and Southeast regional clusters represent the majority of the United Kingdom's venture capital investments.

It's an axiom that venture capitalists don't like to take connecting flights. While our own investigations found no shortage of VC partners involved in deals in non-airline-hub locations, we also found numerous spin-outs with stories of VCs willing to invest if the company could be relocated to Silicon Valley or Boston. In general, it appears that the "remote" VC investment model works only if there is a trusted local partner who can actively oversee the investment and work with the new venture. The "clustering" of venture capital and technologically innovative businesses (and their customers, manufacturing facilities, and top-tier institutions) provides advantages to nascent firms that may include lower-cost components, the availability of specialized labor, and knowledge spillovers that could potentially benefit the venture.[27,28]

These positive benefits are not limited to university-based start-ups and inventing entrepreneurs alone. A recent example of a relocated business is Confederate Motorcycles. When the company abandoned its New Orleans facility in the wake of Hurricane Katrina, CEO Matthew Chambers moved the organization to Birmingham, Alabama, where it inhabits a facility adjacent to the Barber Motorsports Park, home of the world's most renowned motorcycle museum.

Sometimes inventing entrepreneurs bring their own strong preferences to the geographical selection process. Professor Ron Raines, one of the founders of Quintessence, states clearly that in a perfect world he'd keep company operations local:

> I really want to create value in Madison (Wisconsin). I think Madison is poised for this because of the strength of the university in the life sciences. I think it would be much more fun for me. I have a friend at Yale who started a company in California; he flies out there once a week to spend time with his company, and it's just a horrendous lifestyle.

Many inventing entrepreneurs find ways to keep their start-ups local by mobilizing the necessary resources within the local region. Most founders acknowledge that advantages could be found to placing a start-up in a geographical environment that had already attained a "critical mass" of resources. It seems likely that location can impact long-term growth options for a high-technology firm; the availability of funds and skilled human resources are likely to be the most critical factors.

COST AND DIFFERENTIATION STRATEGIES

Although early-stage investors inevitably focus on the strength of the management team, they also consistently seek opportunities that can generate a long-term sustainable competitive advantage. Porter narrowed sustainable competitive advantage to two primary strategies: low cost and differentiation strategies. In conjunction with target market breadth, Porter's model is a simple two-by-two chart (see Figure 9-4). Porter states that successful, profitable companies will either be low-cost or differentiated companies, serving either a niche market or a broad-based market. There are rare situations in which successful companies are both low cost and differentiated—Toyota is often proposed as one of the most well-known examples—but these exceptions prove the rule, because they occur due to extraordinary circumstances or exceptional capabilities.

FIGURE 9-4   Strategies for Competitive Advantage

	Broad	Mass market/cost-focused	Mass market/value-added
Market	**Niche**	Narrow market/cost-focused	Narrow market/value-added
		Low cost	**Differentiated**
		Strategy	

Our experience and observations suggest this is true for entrepreneurial ventures as well. Some early-stage ventures provide superior functions or services at a lower price point than existing technologies and competitors. But Porter's point is that such advantages are hard to maintain in the long run; entrepreneurial ventures rarely have the resources to focus on multiple long-term advantages, especially when competing with well-resourced and established organizations.

The logic for this proposition is relatively simple. A company that attempts to be both low-cost and differentiated won't be able to effectively compete with companies that focus on one strategy or the other. Low-cost-focused companies should achieve greater economies of scale (i.e., operate at a lower cost through dealing in increased volume and learning to operate with fewer errors), whereas differentiation-focused companies should be able to spend more on R&D and product development to further differentiate their products and generate higher unit margins (by charging higher prices). Toyota was able to maintain advantages across both axes on the basis of aggressive cost-management and quality-assurance techniques that reduced manufacturing errors. The company was able to use cost savings to invest in longer-term research and development ahead of the general automotive industry. Early-stage ventures are unlikely to be able to make similar commitments. And such advantages are truly hard to maintain over time—Toyota eventually formed Lexus to go after the most differentiated market (luxury automobiles)—while focusing primarily on reliability and moderate pricing for the Toyota brand. And while Toyota's continued success (compared with recent problems at GM, for example) is a testament to their cost and quality programs,[29] independent reviewers have noted that the quality gap between Toyota and many other carmakers has closed somewhat, even as certain American car manufacturers compete directly with Toyota on price.[30]

For the inventing entrepreneur, this model provides one of the most useful, basic tools for evaluating competitive positioning. It asks the innovator to answer the fundamental question of how the *company and its products* (not the technology innovation) provide value to customers. That answer must match market dynamics and customer purchasing behavior.

As an example, consider a novel pathogen detection technology targeting the processed foods market. Given the thousands of illnesses in the United States attributed to foodborne pathogens every year, there appears to be a need for more effective testing.[31] So the founders of our hypothetical company evaluate the competitive environment and determine that their innovative test is roughly 100 times more sensitive than industry-standard assays. Their first instinct is, therefore, to charge more for the test, because it provides a value-added service not currently available. While this conclusion seems to fit the basis of Porter's model, it misses the underlying issues within the target market. If we consider the long-term perspective, food processors do want their food to be high quality and safe (i.e., pathogen free). But the business reality is more subtle.

At some level, plant managers don't want to use a more sensitive test than necessary. Nearly every food sample will have some level of pathogens—and the human system is capable of resisting surprising numbers and types of foodborne pathogens. A zero-tolerance policy on pathogens is effectively impossible. Realistically, food processing plant managers are balancing the risk of pathogen outbreak (and the possibility of bad press and lawsuits) against the relatively high cost of testing. Most governments provide standards and testing protocols for food quality management, usually in the form of guidelines rather than mandates, and plant managers can use these standards as a basis for establishing testing systems. Significantly increasing the sensitivity of pathogen testing is, in some ways, counterproductive to the plant manager, because it will certainly lead to more detection events which result in higher costs, but no additional revenue. If the tests are costly, then the start-up is asking a manager to pay more in exchange for apparently unnecessary improvements in safety. The value proposition to the end consumer may seem clear, but the value proposition to the processor may not be as straightforward. A common response to this example is to suggest that the processor consider a branding strategy based on quality assurance and better testing. Our discussions with processors turned up a different reality—the meat packagers and distributors don't want to mention safety at all, for fear of attracting attention to the issue of foodborne illnesses in the first place. The concern is that the topic is so negative that a branding strategy would actually result in lower sales—because consumers would, consciously or not, associate that brand with the potential for foodborne illnesses.

Many technology innovations from university research endeavors will fall into the "differentiated" rather than "low-cost" strategy area. Novel therapeutics for untreated diseases, improved diagnostics and treatment modalities, and more sophisticated data analysis algorithms all provide added functionality or quality to the final product concept. But sometimes the "low-cost" strategy is hidden in the fine print of the technological innovation. The entire Virent business model was driven by the need to produce hydrogen cost-effectively to compete with fossil-fuel options. Neural Robotics' unmanned helicopters are a low-cost alternative to full-sized helicopters for aerial surveillance. The Nimblegen technology offers genomics analysis at a fraction of the cost of an Affymetrix chip.

We have sometimes found a slight bias among inventing entrepreneurs—a preference for "differentiated" products, as if a low-cost strategy (i.e., meeting customers' minimum purchasing criteria at the lowest possible price) was just slightly distasteful. This disposition likely reflects the high affinity most inventing entrepreneurs retain for their innovations.

Providing a low-cost product or service is *not* synonymous with low quality. Consider Vertica, Profesor Stonebraker's current venture. The innovation is novel and sophisticated, but the long-term business model is based on data analysis that is low cost on a per-transaction basis:

> The basic idea is that database systems are really good at processing [static] data. But if you look at Wall Street feeds, streaming data is coming at you like a fire hose. Streaming data is very badly served by current software, so we wrote an engine that was very good at

processing fire hoses of data with low latency, and we're currently selling that on Wall Street. The long-term vision is that the microsensor technology revolution is going to cause everything on the planet that is worth anything to be tagged to report its state or location in real time, and that will generate just torrents and torrents of real-time data [that need to be processed efficiently].

THE NEW BUSINESS ROAD TEST

Thus far, we've reviewed some basic business analytical tools for evaluating opportunities. Inventing entrepreneurs should consider creating a "feasibility plan," as described by John Mullins in *The New Business Road Test*[32], to test whether or not the innovation in question can form the basis for a successful business. Mullins recommends various assessments designed to analyze the opportunity and the company's ability to serve that market.

This exercise should result in a document that feeds almost directly into a complete business plan, and the work associated is rarely wasted. It is especially useful for inventing entrepreneurs (and those without prior start-up or business experience) because it focuses on the areas which we believe are not usually the strengths of inventing entrepreneurs:

- Determination of the near-term strategic goal for the *type* of venture to be formed (e.g., a small, sustainable service business, an R&D company that can be sold to an established competitor, or a fast-growth business with high near-term capital needs and high long-term profitability)
- An objective, systematic assessment of customer needs (customer research)
- An objective, rational evaluation of the opportunity (market analysis)
- Careful consideration of the resources necessary for creating a sustainable business (including capital and expertise)

Mullins describes the "seven domains" of opportunity attractiveness shown in Figure 9-5. It should be immediately evident that some of the domains require evaluating the external environment ("market attractiveness," "industry attractiveness," "target segment attractiveness"), which can be accomplished with tools we've already described. On the other hand, evaluating the team involves turning an eye to the key people in the venture (whether the "team" is just the inventing entrepreneur or encompasses a broader group of employees, advisors, and supporters). We'll talk more about the importance of management in later chapters, but for now the following quote from Paul Reckwerdt of Tomotherapy to highlight the analysis that Mullins describes:

Hire the expertise you don't have. Most successful businesspeople understand their skills and their good points and their weaknesses. If you're really a scientist, get a CEO, get a CFO [chief financial officer], get a COO, and get them to run the day-to-day business. We couldn't

FIGURE 9-5   The Seven Domains Framework

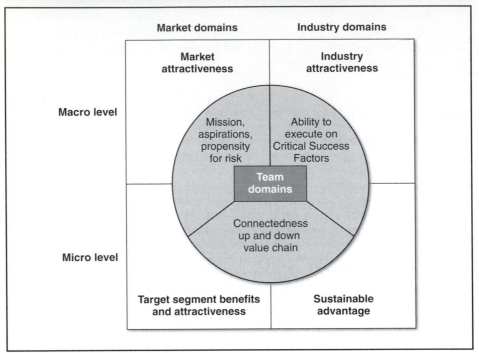

afford those people, so we stepped in, but we made mistakes that might have been prevented if someone had been there with more experience.

Rather than dissect the feasibility plan in detail (readers are directed to *The New Business Road Test*) we provide in Table 9-4 a simple outline of the feasibility plan's sections, together with some sample questions that should be considered. We encourage inventing entrepreneurs to review the results of this exercise with trusted advisors to identify additional factors (and/or strengths and weaknesses) that would not be obvious to the new businessperson. Starting a business, especially a technology-based growth business, is a learning experience. *The New Business Road Test* provides an excellent mechanism to summarize information in a relatively easily, communicable form that helps "translate" the technology opportunity for a business audience.

CHECKING THE BASIC PREMISE

In this chapter, we discussed the details of industry context and market analysis in reasonable depth. However, the fundamental premise of the start-up as the mechanism by which inventing entrepreneurs commercialize their inventions

TABLE 9-4 Feasibility Plan[33]	
Executive Summary	• What is the purpose of the venture? • What broad advantages will the venture leverage to succeed? • Why is the venture needed?
Micro-level Market	• What is the target market? • What target market problems can your technology address? • Can you demonstrate that customers will pay to have this problem solved? • How large is the target market? • Is it an attractive marketplace in which to compete? Is it growing?
Macro-level Market	• What is the total market size? • Is it an attractive marketplace in which to compete? • What is the overall growth opportunity? What other trends are evident in the broader market?
Macro-level Industry	• How attractive is the industry? (Five Forces model) • How will your entry into the industry change structure or participant interactions?
Micro-level Industry	• What are your sources of competitive advantage? • What functional areas will drive your ability to create value for your customers while generating profit margins? • What general strategy will you use to create advantage (low cost/differentiated)? • What capabilities or resources will your organization utilize that competitors may not be able to copy? • What are the business metrics for your operations (sales, costs, margins, production cycles, financing required)?
Team Characteristics	• Describe the team's mission and goals. How much risk is the team prepared to take? • Does the team have a specific time horizon for success?
Team Execution of Critical Success Factors (CSFs)	• What are the CSFs for your business? • Does the team have the experience and knowledge to execute these CSFs? • Are there "fatal flaws" that must be addressed?
Team Connectedness	• Does the team have the connections and knowledge to be able to execute functions throughout the value chain? • Are there "holes" in the team's areas of expertise?
Summary and Conclusions	• How attractive is this opportunity? • Can any of these assumptions be proven/disproven quickly and easily?

needs a brief cross-check now that we know more about industry and market dynamics. In Chapter 4, we introduced the concept of "complementary assets" as a basis for comparing two licensing options: either to an established organization with commercialization infrastructure or to a start-up venture. At this stage, we assume that a venture is already in place (or in process), and that the issues facing the entrepreneur (and management) are about prioritization and resource allocation. Our anecdotal evidence suggests that most inventing entrepreneurs have a baseline expectation of "going it alone" on their commercialization work. We suspect this stems from the experience of pursuing highly individualized research.

Innovative, technology-driven businesses are likely to generate novel technologies both within and outside the core technology focus. In some cases, the outliers may turn out to be the truly valuable commodities, but it is rare that a start-up commercializes every technology that emerges from the R&D laboratory. To this end, the inventing entrepreneur should have basic decision models for when to pursue commercialization on a solo basis, when to ally with other organizations, and when to license or abandon technologies. In Table 9-5, we show simple decision heuristics that are based on barriers to entry and the competitive environment. Our experience suggests that inventing entrepreneurs often make two judgement errors. First, they tend to overstate how difficult it will be for competitors to imitate or re-engineer the technology. Second, entrepreneurs tend to understate the magnitude of the assets required to bring the technology to market. Such assets usually include physical infrastructure (such as access to large-scale raw materials and manufacturing facilities), but can also include human resources, financing, and even sales and distribution infrastructure.

Note that some of these decisions can be separated out into individual "make or buy" decisions. For example, a start-up medical device company would likely be wise to outsource premarket subscale manufacturing (because of the costs of infrastructure and regulatory documentation), but could attempt to ramp up early sales and marketing without a distribution partner. The decision to "go it alone" almost

---

TABLE 9-5 Complementary Assets and Technology Commercialization Options

Commercialization Options	Does the Inventing Entrepreneur Have the Required Complementary Assets?	Barriers to Imitation or Entry in the Industry	Number of Capable Competitors
Start-up option (going it alone)	Yes	High	Few/None
Alliance option (seeking out a partner)	No	Moderate/High	Few/Some
Licensing option (sell the technology)	No	Low	Many

always entails additional risks—and presumably additional rewards. For each "go it alone" decision, the company evaluates the implications against its own opportunity cost—the cost of financing and the cost of not pursuing other projects.

Conclusions and Summary

This chapter has provided the entrepreneur with critical tools for evaluating the context of the business opportunity. We would be disingenuous to suggest that in these few pages a person new to business could develop a robust understanding of corporate strategy. Inventing entrepreneurs may at first feel overwhelmed with the breadth of concepts and information underlying strategy and industry context. We have, however, found many scientists and engineers who quickly embrace the strategic models and put them to work.

In part, we want to give inventing entrepreneurs a sense that the world of business, and specifically business strategy and decision making, can be approached as an *analytical exercise,* similar to laboratory problem solving. Unfortunately, despite an endless array of business models and systems, the gap between "business analysis" and "business success" remains wide. We have all heard stories about (or known personally) individuals with no business experience or even educational success who became leaders of business empires. And there is no shortage of stories about the best business analysis leading to appallingly poor business decisions. Perhaps this is not so different from the laboratory, where even the best theories sometimes fall prey to experimental error, and serendipity can still play a major role in discovery and innovation. Regardless, we encourage the inventing entrepreneur to consider playing an active role in the business and strategy planning processes. Utilizing these (and other) tools is an educational challenge in itself, and will certainly help the innovator better understand the path toward commercial success.

Endnotes

1. Aguilar, F. J. 1967. *Scanning the Business Environment.* New York: Wiley.
2. Hambrick, D. C. 1982. Environmental scanning and organizational strategy. *Strategic Management Journal,* 3: 159–174.
3. Porter, M. 1985. *Competitive Advantage.* Free Press, New York.
4. We state that "high barriers to entry" is preferred, because it is generally indicative of opportunities in the technology sector in which intellectual property, scientific and engineering expertise, and/or capital intensity prevent less technologically advanced firms from competing effectively. In most cases, however, this same effect creates a high hurdle for a new venture, because the cost of entering the market may be very high, requiring venture capital or strategic partnerships. Our presumption, for the sake of argument, is that sufficiently innovative and value-creating technologies can achieve such funding, and therefore, that the high barriers to entry are advantageous for sustaining long-term profitability.
5. Summary data compiled from Google Finance (http://finance.google.com/finance?catid=57164583), July 2007.

6. The first "natural orifice" surgery in the United States was performed at Columbia University on March 21, 2007. See Denise Grady. "Doctors Try New Surgery for Gallbladder Removal," *New York Times,* April 20, 2007.

7. Stephen Jeffrey. "Turning Surgery Inside Out," *The Economist,* June 7, 2007.

8. www.pharmacytimes.com/Article.cfm?Menu=1&ID=4116.

9. www.the-scientist.com/news/display/24247/.

10. Many thanks to Gianluca Bisceglie for providing this example.

11. Readers are referred to *Competitive Advantage* by Michael Porter. A good summary can be found online at www.quickmba.com/strategy/porter.shtml.

12. Noffke, T. 2007. No Time to Delay *Supplement to the Pharmaceutical Executive,* 7: 22–23.

13. In this case, the company obtained a "510(k)" clearance from the FDA, which means that the product was shown to be "substantially equivalent" to another previously approved product.

14. Romanelli, E. & Tushman, M. 1994. Organizational transformation as punctuated equilibrium—An empirical test. *Academy of Management Journal,* 37: 1144–1161.

15. Christensen, C. 1997. *The Innovator's Dilemma.* Boston: Harvard Business School Press.

16. As an example of how widely this terminology and heuristic have spread, *InformationWeek* and Credit Suisse have created the Disruptive Technology Portfolio "to track the emergence of companies that are changing the world. Included in this portfolio are companies that are leaders in emerging markets such as wireless, on-demand services, the Internet, and Linux." (See www.informationweek.com/disruptive/.) We have not evaluated whether the inclusion of any given company in the portfolio means it is commercializing truly "disruptive" technologies.

17. A recent presentation by John Doerr of Kleiner Perkins, one of the true fathers of venture capital, was summarized as follows: "Doerr gives his list of what he feels are important new disruptive technologies. His first choice is wireless and his second is services for enterprises." http://edcorner.stanford.edu/authorMaterialInfo.html?mid=1277.

18. Meth, Sheldon Z. "Disruptive High-Energy Laser Technology," DARPATech 2005, April 9–11, pp. 191–193.

19. The terminology has even been used by the Supreme Court: "When Congress has been concerned about disruptive technologies such as this, it has demonstrated the will to regulate. . . ." *Metro-Goldwyn-Mayer Studios, Inc. v. Grokster, Ltd.* (04-480) 545 U.S. 913 (2005).

20. In numerous discussions with venture capital groups, we've repeatedly perceived a specific interest in identifying "disruptive" technologies. Frankly, we aren't convinced that most financiers want to back a "disruptive" technology, so much as they want to find an innovation that creates a competitive advantage that can be protected.

21. Levinthal, D. & March, J. 1993. The myopia of learning. *Strategic Management Journal,* 14: 95–112.

22. Rosenkopf, L. & Nerkar, A. 2001. Beyond local search: Boundary-spanning, exploration, and impact in the optical disk industry. *Strategic Management Journal,* 22: 287–306.

23. Katila, R. & Ahuja, G. 2002. Something old, something new: A longitudinal study of search behavior and new product development. *Academy of Management Journal,* 45: 1183–1194.

24. Audretsch, D. B. & Feldman, M. P. 1996. Innovative clusters and the industry life-cycle. *Review of Industrial Organization,* 11: 253–273. See also Feldman, M. P. 1999. The new economics of innovation, spillovers, and agglomeration: A review of empirical studies. *Economics of Innovation and New Technology,* 8: 5–25.

25. Romanelli, E. & Khessina, O. 2005. Regional industrial identity: Cluster configurations and economic development. *Organization Science,* 16: 344–358.

26. Dow Jones *VentureOne* Press Release, July 24, 2006: "U.S. Venture Capital Investing Reaches $6.7 Billion, Highest Quarterly Investment Level Since 2001."

27. Sorenson, O. & Stuart, T. 2001. Syndication networks and the spatial distribution of venture capital investments. *American Journal of Sociology.* 106(6): 1546–1588.

28. Cohen, W. & Levinthal, D. 1990. Absorptive capacity: A new perspective on learning and innovation. *Administrative Science Quarterly,* 35: 128–152.

29. Consumer Reports Brand Report Card, Jan 2007: "Toyota dominated the study, earning the top position in more than half of the six brand-attribute categories. Thirty-seven percent of interviewees named it as the best in at least one category. That performance provides insight into how Toyota has evolved into such a universal powerhouse . . . *Consumer Reports'* first Brand Report Card survey shows that consumers hold Toyota in the highest regard for most key categories, and their interest in Toyota products could fuel even greater sales in the years ahead."

30. "Ford Beats Toyota in Quality Ratings," Associated Press, June 6, 2007.

31. "We estimate that foodborne diseases cause approximately 76 million illnesses, 325,000 hospitalizations, and 5,000 deaths in the United States each year." Mead, P. S., Slutsker, L., Dietz, V., McCaig, L. F., Bresee, J. S., Shapiro, C., Griffin, P. M., & Tauxe, R. V. 1999. "Food-related illness and death in the United States." *Emerging Infectious Diseases,* 5(5). Centers for Disease Control and Prevention, Atlanta, Georgia.

32. Mullins, J. (2004). *The New Business Road Test,* Prentice-Hall/Financial Times.

33. Adapted from Mullins, J. (2004). *The New Business Road Test,* London: FT Prentice Hall.

Recommended Readings

Christensen, C. 1997. *The Innovator's Dilemma.* Boston: Harvard Business School Press.

Mullins, J. 2006. *The New Business Road Test,* 2nd ed. London: FT Prentice Hall.

Porter, M. 1985. *Competitive Advantage.* New York: Free Press.

CHAPTER 10

ACCUMULATING
BUSINESS SKILLS
AND KNOWLEDGE

OVERVIEW

An endless variety of how-to books catalog the steps necessary to form and operate a start-up business. Our goal, therefore, is not to attempt to provide instruction on all of the mechanics of such activities, but to make the process relevant (and, if possible, clearer) to the inventing entrepreneur planning to commercialize technology via a start-up company.

The role taken by the inventing entrepreneur will determine how many of the practical details she will have to assimilate and implement. Inventing entrepreneurs, however, should not mistake the administrative activities of a start-up for the core commercialization effort. For example, Professor Handelsman never formed a start-up, but she effectively marketed her innovations to corporations, whether formally via direct contacts or indirectly through research seminars. She effectively supported the commercialization work without ever dealing with the administration technicalities of a start-up company. But many inventing entrepreneurs get a lot more involved in corporate organization and administration, whether by choice, chance, or necessity.

Mike Fouche is a good example. Fouche worked as a research engineer at numerous large aeronautics corporations, but his research on neural networks for autonomous aviation led him to eventually start his own company, Neural Robotics. Fouche comments that the funding processes aren't that different from academia or even a start-up: "I learned that as long as I kept showing results I kept getting more money. And so I did reports—progress reports. I don't know where I learned this but I would do technical reports to show I wasn't just playing in a sandbox." Fouche formed the corporation and led the organizational activities, serving initially as the CEO. This is nearly the opposite end of the spectrum from Handelsman, and requires dramatically more time, effort, and learning.

Assimilating business skills requires more than just understanding the legal and administrative aspects of how companies function. In the end, it's about leveraging that knowledge and combining it with technological savvy and market insight. We teach business school students that once the information is gathered and the analysis completed, the time comes for decision making. In situations where the inventing entrepreneur serves in an executive role (such as CTO or especially CEO), she will find herself making decisions that can make or break the business. Fouche describes one such early situation, which not only drove the direction of the company but also his personal career:

> The only way I could get the valuation up was to demonstrate that there was a market. How do you demonstrate there's a market? Well the best thing I could think of was to have some customers on board, and that's pretty tough, especially when you don't have a product. That's when I decided that would be my strategy for the summer. I would take a small amount of angel money at a lower valuation and try to show there's a market, and if that was successful I could go for the big money. And that's when I knew it was time to quit my day job.

FORMING THE BUSINESS

The formation of a legal entity (presumably for the purpose of licensing and commercializing a technology) may seem complex and daunting. Anecdotal discussion suggests that inventing entrepreneurs who contract with competent corporate legal counsel (and delegate the business formation activities to them) avoid significant concerns and stress. The reality is that most states in the United States provide relatively simple mechanisms for venture formation, setting initial fees below $500. It should be noted that appropriate organizational documentation for an operating venture (i.e., bylaws or an operating agreement) represents more significant documentation and cost. The creation of a venture *designed* to support external financing, fast growth, distributed ownership, and external management (as opposed to owner-managers) should utilize expert legal services because long-term financing and control issues will hinge on proper organizational parameters. While the amount of proper legal documentation compiled by competent attorneys for venture creation can be significant, most experienced firms will review the business potential of such ventures and offer deferred and/or reduced billing to high-potential clients.

TIMING: WHEN DO YOU FORM A START-UP?

A question that often emerges is the timing of the legal formation of a company.[1] Although there are no obvious trends or recommendations regarding the optimal timing for the formation of the venture entity, we make the following broad observations:

- There are no strategic disadvantages to forming the legal entity relatively early. Entrepreneurs should keep in mind that entity formation will generate legal bills that must be paid. In addition, once the legal entity is established, some minimum administrative documentation will likely be necessary on an ongoing basis, which will require either the entpreneur's time, additional legal costs, or both. For example, in most of the United States, limited liability company (LLC) owners must file annual reports to the state of incorporation; these reports provide basic administrative information about the entity, and all corporations must file quarterly reports regarding employee count to the state's Department of Workforce Development.

- In our experience, most U.S. technology transfer offices are prepared to participate in licensing negotiations on a conceptual level prior to the legal formation of the entity. Once the negotiations reach a stage where documents are being produced and reviewed (i.e., terms for royalties or equity ownership), most TTOs will prefer to establish formal interaction with the entity (even if the entity is wholly owned by the inventing entrepreneur).

- Some venture investors (angel and VC) are prepared to review opportunities prior to the formation of the venture entity, and certainly prior to the completion of financing documentation (e.g., a private placement memorandum). The creation of the entity (presumably accomplished with some founder investments) and the licensing of the relevant technology are, of course, necessary precursors to the successful solicitation of external financing.

The decision of when to form the start-up may be deliberate and planned. In some cases, however, external factors may drive the process. Professor Shane Farritor at the University of Nebraska-Lincoln had been preparing to start a venture to commercialize miniaturized robotic surgical tools he developed with Dr. Dmitry Oleynikov of the university of Nebraska Medical Center. They had delayed forming the venture while developing the intellectual property portfolio and the technology status within the university structure. The university had already been touting the technology, and it became clear that additional delays might result in longer-term problems. They made the decision to take the plunge. Professor Farritor's story is told in Profile 10-1.

CHOICE OF LEGAL ENTITY

The selection of corporate entity, while limited, is not trivial. First-time entrepreneurs are encouraged to review the literature on entity selection as well as to seek trustworthy, experienced legal counsel. Technology-based companies may present additional complications—for any of the following reasons:

- The company will own or have rights to intellectual property that may represent a significant portion of the total enterprise value of the venture.

- The entity may solicit third-party investors who may have specific preferences for entity type.
- Various elements of control may be at issue, including ownership, management, and technology disposition.
- Different entity types have different short-term and long-term tax implications for owners and investors.
- The entity may accept third-party investments where control and tax treatment issues may be salient.
- The entity may need to be positioned for specific types of exit events.

INVENTING ENTREPRENEUR PROFILE 10-1

Professor Shane Farritor

Many researchers we interviewed have traveled relatively far down the commercialization path, either leading the corporate effort or supporting it from within the academic environment. Professor Shane Farritor, at the University of Nebraska, is just getting started. Dr. Farritor's robotics and mechatronics expertise has taken his work all the way to Mars as part of the NASA Pathfinder project. But his recent work is more terrestrial and more human. Working with Dr. Dmitry Oleynikov at the University of Nebraska Medical Center, Professor Farritor has developed a series of microrobots for minimally invasive surgery. The robots are placed entirely inside the patient during the procedure and controlled remotely by the surgeon.

Not every innovation comes directly from ongoing research. Farritor is the first person to note that the original idea wasn't even his:

> I met Dr. Dmitry Oleynikov, and he told me of his history of using medical robots and specifically using laparoscopic robots, and to my surprise he had some technical knowledge of issues in robotics and he thought we should try to collaborate.... Dmitry sent me a list of five things he'd like to work on. Immediately I locked on to the miniature in vivo robots.

The process of bringing a novel technology from the idea stage to the benchtop and then to actual use is always a challenge. Farritor notes that Dr. Oleynikov's participation was essential for keeping the focus on the eventual use of the technology:

> It took us a couple years before we got something that would function—it's a very difficult problem, much more difficult than we thought originally.... Dmitry has always pushed toward the clinical activity that could be done with these robots.

In fact, neither Farritor nor Oleynikov were actively considering the logistics of commercialization. In this case, an active process within the university sparked consideration of a technology transfer process:

> I was living this naïve dream of being a happy professor sitting in the lab helping graduate students build these cool robots—being happy to have these great applications and this surgeon to work with ... we were making technical progress so fast I wasn't thinking about anything long-term in implementation. Finally, I got a call from our dean's office: "The dean would like you to present to this advisory committee." So I said "Sure," and he introduced me to members of the advisory committee. And I made the presentation and left that day and thought nothing

of it. Then I got another call asking me to come make another presentation.... They'd like to know more.... Really it was at that meeting that I learned that this group was seeking to create start-up companies from technology in the university, and I'd survived the first-round hazing, or whatever it is. And they were talking about my interest in starting a business around this idea, and I said, "Sounds like fun," and that gets me where I am today.

In February 2006, Professor Farritor and Dr. Oleynikov formed a corporation with Steve Platt, PhD, a third collaborator from the engineering department, and negotiated for the technology rights with the University of Nebraska Medical Center. They hired an interim CEO and raised funds from angel investors. Over the course of the following year, the company experienced successes and challenges as the team pushed toward a product design that could be manufactured and used in actual surgeries. In April 2007, a survivable pig surgery was performed using a visualization device finalized and manufactured by Nebraska Surgical Solutions. The cholecystectomy (gall bladder removal) was successful, representing a significant milestone for the business.

Farritor knows there's a lot of work still to be done. He is standing at the technology transfer interface between the academic environment and the business world, and the process is already impacting his mindset and ideas:

> I think I want to be a professor, because there are aspects that are tremendous; you get good students; it's like having smart kids. Also the freedom is unbeatable, and you have security.... But I wouldn't mind having my hand in three, two, or even one [company]. It is likely that one's failed by then and I'm starting a new one and one's still limping along. The companies that are playing this game are trying to get hardcore technology into the hands of users.... The ultimate way to find out if it succeeded is if people are willing to give you money for what you have, which is a different measure for me.

Our experience suggests that the primary entity types are the C corporation and the limited liability corporation. In some cases, founders have organized a C corporation with an "S"-subchapter status, which allows the company to pass profits and losses on to the owners rather than pay corporate taxes (or accrue tax losses)—so long as the entity meets certain ownership requirements (usually involving a maximum number of owners, for example). In general, we have observed that the majority of technology-based companies, especially those anticipating rapid growth, have selected the C corporation.

The following list represents the most common explanations for this trend:

- The C corporation reflects the most established case law regarding control and disposition issues, providing the best basis for legal documentation.

- Private investors focused on high-growth businesses are less interested in pass-through losses (or gains) than in a downstream exit event to generate returns.[2]

- A general perception exists that it is easier for large firms to manage the administration and accounting associated with acquiring a C corporation than it is to do the same with an LLC.

- A general perception exists that LLC law is more varied among the states than C-corporation law.

Inventing entrepreneurs should not, however, simply jump to the C corporation. There are many examples of business types that are clearly more appropriate for an LLC, especially businesses that will generate real cash returns—and businesses that do not anticipate near-term exits via acquisition or IPO.

ALLOCATION OF OWNERSHIP

Academics often approach the allocation of ownership with certain misconceptions. In most cases, these misconceptions simply reflect ignorance about ownership, control, and financing. As we have stated, the entrepreneurial journey usually presents formidable learning challenges. Because these issues will be relevant throughout the life of the venture, special attention should be paid toward getting them "right." Table 10-1 lists some of the common misconceptions.

TABLE 10-1 Misconceptions about Ownership and Control	
Misconception	*Reality*
Graduate students and other research staff who participated in the development of the technology should receive founder shares.	While this may represent a sense of "fairness," it is inherently problematic. It is unlikely that any individual could appropriately allocate ownership based on contribution, especially since such research contribution might extend back 5 or 10 years.
	Founder shares should reflect contribution, but also commitment—it is relatively unlikely that all the contributors to the technology will continue to support the development and commercialization of that technology for the next 5 to 10 years.
	Requiring individuals to sign confidentiality and noncompete agreements would likely hinder their academic and/or corporate employment options. In the worst case scenario, an individual who receives founder shares (as a graduate student, for example) may end up working on related/competitive technology in another environment, but still retain the rights associated with founder ownership.
The majority of the value creation associated with the technology took place prior to the licensing event.	Clearly, the development of the technology prior to licensing created value; if the technology has been licensed for cash and a royalty stream then a value can be directly assigned.
	When the technology is licensed into a start-up company, then the value creation is projected based on equity ownership and the execution of the commercialization plan. In this case, it is anticipated that the majority of the value creation will take place after the licensing event.
	For example, a patent might be licensed to a start-up company in exchange for 10% equity ownership (plus certain royalty fees). When the company raises $1 million in funding for a one-third stake in the company, that 10% ownership is effectively worth about $200,000. If the company successfully

brings products to market and is acquired for $50 million a few years later—and assuming (for example) that 50% dilution occurred through additional financing—then the license value is now $1.67 million, an increase of 735%.

I will be able to maintain control of the business until the exit event.	Although such an outcome is possible, it does not usually represent the situation when outside financing is obtained.
I should get as high a valuation as I can to make sure I maintain as much equity (control) as possible.	As a general business concept, the seller has the right to charge what the market will bear. There are instances of majority owners demanding and receiving unusually high valuations for investments on the basis of reputation and long-term potential. At the same time, such thinking can be shortsighted: Some investors bring significant talent, knowledge, experience, and connections to their investments and expect to obtain higher returns. Also, it is possible to overvalue a business in a financing round, which may make future financing events difficult.
Employees, advisors, and founders should have more equity than investors, since we are supplying time and expertise—whereas the investors are only providing money.	Again, some companies are successful at retaining a majority equity component. In the case of companies that achieve an initial public offering (IPO), the majority ownership is almost always in the hands of the financiers. Companies without significant financing needs may be more able to retain majority ownership within the nonfinancial stakeholders.

SELECTING OFFICERS AND DIRECTORS

Researchers usually have extensive experience with peer review and critical oversight. Inventing entrepreneurs may choose to serve as an officer or director, roles that may leverage relevant skills and experience. At the least, the entrepreneur will likely interact closely with officers and directors. It is useful to note the differing functions of corporate officers and corporate directors and make observations on their selection. A corporate officer is an individual serving as an executive of a company who shares legal liability for his or her company's actions. A director is an individual elected by a corporation's shareholders to establish company policies, including selection of operating officers and the distribution of dividends. We could paraphrase this by stating that officers run the company while the directors oversee the officers to the benefit of the shareholders. The role of director also involves significant legal compliance issues (often referred to as fiduciary duty) in regard to which the director must put the interests of the shareholders ahead of her own.[3]

Corporate officers should be selected based on their ability to build the business; directors should be selected for corporate oversight experience. In the case of early-stage technology businesses, the selection of directors often involves a number of other factors. For example, a director can bring industry connections, links to financiers, and credibility to a small business with a limited operating history. It is common to see the board of directors of early-stage technology companies composed of (1) the inventing entrepreneur(s), (2) a representative of an invested venture financier, and (3) an industry executive (or former executive) with direct market experience in the target sectors.

Managing director selection (and the size of the board) isn't necessarily simple. In the absence of the types of people described above, inventing entrepreneurs often select directors (and sometimes officers) who are closely linked to the entrepreneur—colleagues, friends, and even family. While not necessarily problematic, we believe these are, in general, suboptimal selections, especially in the case of directors. The role of the director requires the broadest perspective for serving the shareholders, and inexperienced boards could end up focusing on the success of the technology and the continuation of marginal status-quo results at the expense of long-term shareholder value creation.

SERVICE PROVIDERS

The selection of service providers will have a long-term impact on any venture. We encourage inventing entrepreneurs to pursue such selections diligently. We have often seen inventing entrepreneurs hiring the first attorney, accountant, and banker that they interview. While such decisions can be successful, we recommend a more thorough approach.

The first important advisors in technology companies tend to be the corporate and intellectual property counsel. In Table 10-2, we suggest a set of minimum criteria needed for the selection of legal counsel.

The dichotomy between these two types of criteria highlights both the distinction in services and the differences in required outcomes. Fundamentally, corporate counsel serves the company by supporting the business of the organization—finance, contracts (with customers, partners, suppliers), and human resources being the most common areas. Intellectual property (IP) counsel, on the other hand, serves one highly specific primary role: championing the company's IP portfolio to the appropriate patent offices (such as the United States Patent and Trademark Office or "USPTO") and other patenting organizations. Missing a single filing deadline, a competitive patent citation, or even critical word nuances within a filing document can have significant, hard-to-fix consequences. As such, the entrepreneur's selection criteria for corporate counsel should focus on a combination of demonstrated competence in general business and affinity with the entrepreneur; selection of IP counsel should focus almost primarily on technical expertise—especially relevant technology knowledge and a history of successful patenting work.

Founders should be aware that setting up the necessary documentation and support will likely exceed $10,000 in corporate legal bills.[4] In one recent example, we are familiar with the founder had prior start-up experience and had negotiated to defer all corporate legal bills until after the seed funding round was closed.

TABLE 10-2 Selecting Counsel		
	Minimum Criteria	*Value-Add Criteria*
Corporate Counsel	• Experience with early-stage firms • Willingness to reduce and/or defer fees • High affinity between entrepreneur and counsel • Experience with early-stage, private financing • Attention to detail, organization, and planning	• Experience in target industry/sector • Connections to financiers, customers, and suppliers • Senior counsel provides services (instead of junior attorneys)
Intellectual Property (IP) Counsel	• Extensive experience in the technology field • Extensive history of successful patent prosecutions • Attention to detail, organization, and planning • Senior counsel provides services (instead of junior attorneys)	• Willingness to reduce and/or defer fees • High affinity between entrepreneur and counsel • Experience with early-stage firms • Connections to financiers, customers, and suppliers

Corporate legal billing at that time (including start-up, consulting contracts, the financing round, and various other issues) totaled $17,500.

It is much more difficult to estimate IP fees. The company just described exceeded $40,000 in IP-related legal costs in the first year, because the company had to refile patents previously prosecuted by a university technology transfer office as well as initiate significant new patent filings. Even this number may be low for rapid growth start-ups: One experienced Boston CEO commented that he generally expected to spend more than $250,000 in IP-related costs in the first year of a medical device start-up. In general, founders might expect to pay between $10,000 and $20,000 per patent filing, depending on industry and complexity, and on whether IP counsel will bill for getting up to speed on the technology field and the specific invention. Inventing entrepreneurs should have a careful conversation with IP counsel about billing. Inventing entrepreneurs should be prepared to pay for expertise in this area. Paying $400 per hour for an expert in the relevant technological field may be more cost-effective than paying $200 per hour for an attorney who will need to become educated about the technology (at client expense), and who many be unfamiliar with the relevant patent office's history with the technology field.

The next key service provider is the accountant. Accounting services are often missed by new entrepreneurs, simply because the functional outcomes don't seem mission critical when the company is started. Conforming to accounting standards and providing standardized financial reports and asset management does not have the urgency of IP protection, product development, or sales efforts. At the same time, accounting services are relatively inexpensive, usually straightforward, and can save significant rework in the long run. Technology-based ventures can have some peculiar accounting issues, especially with regard to technology assets (especially intellectual property), grant funding, equity and stock options. In addition, correctly establishing accounting books and filing appropriate tax documentation will prevent red flags and expensive revisions from occurring prior to external financing events. In most cases, start-up firms can combine limited accounting support with standardized software (Quickbooks® and PeachTree appear to be the most common in the United States) to create a minimal system that will meet the company's needs for a few years. The expense should be less than $5,000 in the first year (we've seen total billings below $1,000 in the first year).

Every start-up business should have banking facilities. A start-up technology business is no different. The selection of a bank in the early stages of a growth business may not be a particularly critical decision, especially since most banks won't be actively involved in cash management simply because there are relatively few differentiated services that can be provided at that stage. Inventing entrepreneurs should note the following:

- The same bank that provides excellent personal banking services may not provide comparable services for a small business.
- Bankers that tout their ability to help small businesses grow may not, in fact, have much to offer the technology company that will have no revenues.
- Some banks do offer low-fee banking facilities for small businesses, but charge other fees to compensate (for example, a bank may have no monthly fee but charges a per check fee).
- Changing banks is relatively easy and cheap, and making a poor selection now can usually be remedied relatively easily at a later time.

Finally, most start-up companies have an extended network incorporating advisors and consultants that add expertise, knowledge, wisdom, and connections to the company's resource base. One of the most prevalent comments from inventing entrepreneurs was the desire for an expert mentor, usually on the business side, who could help navigate unfamiliar territory. We encourage inventing entrepreneurs to seek competent advisors. But the selection of any consultant or advisor can be complicated for the following reasons:

1. The entrepreneur is often seeking expertise in a sophisticated technology field—and it may be difficult to separate the experts from individuals who mean well but don't have the necessary depth of knowledge in either the technology field or the business field.

2. It may be challenging to match the incentives of the consultant and the company—the company may need to conserve cash while the consultant (primarily) needs to generate income.

3. Stock options can be an effective incentive for consultants and advisors (note that some will not accept stock options), but placing a value on a stock option package can be nontrivial.

We would hope that the strongest consultants and advisors have the best interests of the company at heart, and we note that industry retirees with a personal interest in the business may provide expert assistance for fun rather than remuneration. In one example, we are familiar with a retired *Fortune* 50 senior executive agreed to provide help as needed, with no stated limit on the number of hours (including connections to his network) for $1,000 a month and a small stock-option package, all of which would be deferred until 12 months had passed. His rationale: He liked the business concept and the founders, but hadn't convinced himself whether it was a good investment or not. He didn't really need to make more money, and preferred to work on something fun rather than accept significant responsibility. He was willing to invest his time to see if the company had significant growth potential.

At a minimum, inventing entrepreneurs should do the following prior to hiring important consultants and advisors:

1. Request and contact two to three references, especially other industry experts and/or former clients, to discuss the individual's qualifications, credibility, and integrity.

2. Ask a business expert to review any compensation agreement.

3. Establish a working agreement that ensures that the company rewards success (for example, project-driven compensation) and allows the company to terminate the agreement in the event that success is not forthcoming.

4. Ensure that confidentiality and noncompete clauses are in place to protect the company.

WRITING AND USING THE BUSINESS PLAN

There is a plethora of books that help entrepreneurs write effective business plans. In general, these books provide helpful information alongside irrelevant advice. Every business plan should be unique—especially technology-driven growth business plans; any detailed "recipe" will have hits and misses. Our goal is to help the inventing entrepreneur develop an understanding of the elements of a high-quality business plan and to highlight common errors. Arguably, the single most useful preparation for writing your business plan would be to read other business plans (both successful and unsuccessful). Consider contacting various people and organizations (attorneys and accountants, other entrepreneurs, local financiers, business colleagues, etc.) to see if they have nonconfidential business plans they can share.

The value of writing a business plan extends beyond the document's usefulness for raising funds or evaluating opportunities. For many inventing entrepreneurs, writing the business plan combines both a learning process and the critical requirement of fully justifying the technology's market value creation. Professor Farritor commented:

> I'm still that naïve guy, but I've learned a few things. I know more about the business world just from the act of writing a business plan.

PURPOSE OF THE BUSINESS PLAN

The business plan has become *de rigueur*. Writing a quality business plan, however, is a significant undertaking and thus should be justified by intended use. The most obvious application is to raise external financing, usually from angels or other venture financing sources.[5] Another application is to communicate the mission of the business (and the near-term plan) to potential employees, current employees, grant organizations, service providers, and so on.[6] Some founders test new opportunities against the business plan—if the new opportunity doesn't match the plan, either the opportunity shouldn't be targeted or the plan is wrong. And, sometimes, it's helpful to write a business plan simply to codify information and ideas that have yet to be committed to paper (and scrutiny). Our assumption will be that the plan is being written primarily to:

1. Clarify the business concept, near-term goals, and proposed strategy,
2. Ensure that the entire team (including new/potential members) shares the same goals, and/or to
3. Seek external financing.

PREPARING TO WRITE THE FULL BUSINESS PLAN

The creation of a high-quality business plan is significantly more complicated, time consuming, and *reflective* than most resources suggest. In one example, the business plan for a start-up technology company in the medical device sector began with six months of background research (including customer, competitor, and market research), and went through three versions that were provided to prospective angels for feedback before the final document was produced for distribution. This example is particularly instructive because the customer research showed that potential customers in the target market (companies producing cardiac intervention devices) didn't want a novel solution to a problem they felt was already solved. On the other hand, customers in an alternative, initially low-priority sector (orthopedics) were ready to pay for shared product development because the innovative technology presented a long-term opportunity to treat a condition lacking an effective treatment (small bone fractures). This enabled the start-up to provide anecdotal data in the business plan regarding potential customer interest.

In general, we have found a simple expansion and review process useful for the development of the complete business plan. In most cases, start-up companies (especially in the technology sector, and especially when seeking external financing) will need to have multiple document-based "introductions" to the company: a 1- to 2-page "teaser" or elevator pitch, a 3- to 5-page executive summary, a 10- to 25-page business plan, and a 10- to 25-slide presentation.

Figure 10-1 shows the business plan writing process. Each document reflects a different focus and usually progresses from the broadest analysis of the opportunity to a contextual message incorporating analysis and tactical planning. As documents are developed, each should be reviewed for clarity and consistency

FIGURE 10-1 Business Plan Development Process

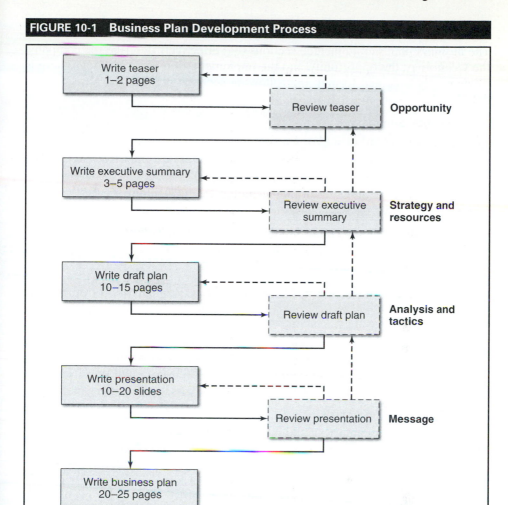

against prior documentation. If the message of the presentation doesn't match the executive summary, then one or the other is flawed or incorrect. In some cases, the process may have to proceed backwards (either rewriting a document after review or returning to a previous document) to ensure that all output reflects the current analysis of business opportunities and goals. If possible, inventing entrepreneurs should seek a critical review from two independent sources. The preferred external reviewers are a potential financier (angel, VC, etc.) and either a potential customer or an industry expert. These represent the business's critical customer groups (investors purchase the company's stock, customers purchase the company's products), and should provide the best critique of the document's validity effectiveness.

THE NUTS AND BOLTS OF BUSINESS PLANS

The business plan should include sections that effectively describe the company, the technology, the opportunity, and the implementation plan. Although there is no generally accepted format, the following sections provide the basis for addressing these issues:

1. Executive Summary
2. Opportunity, Market, and/or Customer Analysis
3. Competitor, Competitive Environment, and/or Competitive Advantage Analysis
4. Management/Team Description (Including Team Capability Gaps)
5. Product/Service Description
6. Underlying Technology and Intellectual Property (IP) Portfolio Description
7. Sales, Marketing, and Distribution Analysis
8. Financial Information

We'll review each section now, providing a basic explanation of purpose as well as some "Do's and Don'ts" as guidance to the novice business plan writer. We cannot emphasize enough that every business plan is unique. Telling the "story" (i.e., describing the novelty and value of the innovation in conjunction with the passion of the team to commercialize it) is critical; writing the plan from scratch is the only way to assure that the team's enthusiasm and the strength of the opportunity are communicated.

1. EXECUTIVE SUMMARY

The executive summary should recapitulate the basic information appearing in most of the other sections of the business plan; the tone of the executive summary may be more enthusiastic than the rest of the plan. The executive summary is probably the first or second section a financier will examine (the other likely target being the management team). Great executive summaries capture the reader's interest by quickly explaining the company's purpose and advantage; poor summaries fail to explain what the company will accomplish (i.e., the business will solve an unmet problem or take advantage of an opportunity) and why the company will be successful (i.e., the unique resources of the business will create a competitive advantage).

2. OPPORTUNITY, MARKET, AND CUSTOMER ANALYSIS

The most common mistake made in this analysis is identifying a broad market opportunity without drilling down to the specific product that customers purchase. In one hyperbolic (but true) example, we reviewed a plan that described a novel software technology for adapting advanced computer-aided design (CAD) systems to the design of commercial construction infrastructure (fire detection and sprinkler systems). The technology was quite interesting and the team was enthusiastic, but the market analysis in the business plan stated that the target market was the entire U.S. construction industry (shown at $3 trillion per year).

The real market, of course, is the demand for fire safety design software (likely less than $100 million per year). Such a gross error has no impact on the actual business potential of the technology, but reflects poorly on the competence of the team.

At the simplest level, this section must accomplish the following:

- *Explain what problem or unmet need the company will address.* "Improving warehouse pallet tracking" is not as clear as "Enabling warehousing and logistics providers to reduce costs by 25% by improving pallet tracking accuracy to 99.9% with embedded radio frequency identification (RFID) transmitters and a novel database architecture using automated error identification and notification." Obviously, clarity and brevity are valuable, but our experience is that financiers prefer specifics to pithiness.

- *Demonstrate that an appropriate target market exists.* Statements about the size of the warehousing industry are not sufficient. Appropriate metrics in this example might include the cost of inventory management for warehouses, how much these businesses spend on information systems, the impact of cost savings on the businesses' profitability, and the relative value-add created compared with the cost of the product and implementation.

- *Demonstrate that actual customers are likely to purchase the product/service.* A surprising number of business plans don't reference any contact with potential customers. Without direct feedback, the business plan has a limited basis for claiming that the product or service meets customer needs. It may not be necessary to name specific companies, but the strength of the plan is closely tied to the strength of the assertion that customers are prepared to pay.

- *Establish some basis for sales projections.* In most cases, the business plan should suggest revenue potential. This may be based on careful financial projections, competitor analysis, or even information from potential customers. Accuracy is more important than specificity—financiers and other outside readers are usually looking for order of magnitude rather than hard and fast dollar figures.

3. Competitor, Competitive Environment, and/or Competitive Advantage Analysis

The competitive section of the business plan represents the opportunity to demonstrate how the venture will differentiate itself from existing solutions and compete for business. In cases where numerous competitors and products exist, simple tables can often provide effective comparisons of product and technology features. Such analyses must be objective, however, and include accurate assessments of the company's technological and operational strengths and weaknesses. Otherwise, a brief précis on key competitors or competitive technologies is the best starting point.

The most common mistakes made in this section are: (1) claiming that because the technology or product is novel there is no competition, (2) failing to identify large competitors that could improve products or reengineer innovations in order to compete, (3) failing to identify other early-stage competitors, and (4) failing to acknowledge that customers could choose to live without the innovation at all. We have, unfortunately, seen many business plans that boldly state: "There are no competitors for this product." Usually a single Google search for the product or for technology key words proves the statement wrong. Some errors may be difficult to avoid—information on other start-ups can be scarce or nonexistent, and even searches of patent application databases and government grant approval records may generate limited results. The inventing entrepreneur's allies in this search may include: the technology transfer office and local/regional venture capitalists. In many cases, the tech transfer personnel may have detailed research on the relevant technology sector—and this may include useful information on start-up activities. A venture capital fund with expertise in the relevant technology sector will almost certainly know about recent start-up activity and may be able to share limited, nonconfidential information.

In general, the competitive section should accomplish the following:

- Establish the competitive environment by 1) identifying companies currently competing in the field, 2) identifying potential new entrants, and 3) evaluating the intensity of competition.[7]

- Demonstrate the competence and knowledge of the management team by showing how the competitive positioning of the new product or technology will fit into the market landscape. There are two challenges here. First, the plan must show how the company will effectively compete against the option of "going without", i.e., potential customers who choose not to address the unmet need with any solution because they believe that the cost of technology adoption outweighs its benefits. Second, the plan must show how the company will compete against entrenched competitors with established products.

- Elucidate the most critical characteristics of the opportunity to create near-term (and, if possible, sustainable) competitive advantage (this was discussed in Chapter 9).

4. MANAGEMENT/TEAM DESCRIPTION (INCLUDING TEAM CAPABILITY GAPS)

Many financiers tell us that they read this section of the plan first. Research consistently shows that both angel investors and professional venture capitalists believe that the management team is the first critical criterion for an investment decision. This section should accomplish the following:

- Identify the senior managers and key advisors; a brief synopsis of relevant credentials and experience should be included. In many cases, it is appropriate to include one- to two-page resumes in the appendices.

- Identify current "holes" or "capability gaps" in the management team. This analysis should include information on whether the company expects to hire staff to address these weaknesses.

- Identify the members of the board of directors (if the company has one) and provide relevant background for those individuals..
- Identify key advisors who are actively supporting the company's efforts.

For most inventing entrepreneurs, this section "writes itself," because the team includes the founder(s), an advisor or two, and sometimes the first employees. While there is nothing inherently wrong with this, a few comments are appropriate. The desirable attributes for a senior management team of a technology-based start-up are (1) prior (preferably successful) entrepreneurial experience, (2) full-time commitment to the venture, and (3) sector-specific experience in dealing with the market and/or customers.

Many business plans offer up bios of key personnel that disguise prior employers. We've never understood this practice, as such information should be made available. Leaving out key information or choosing to hint at it can send up a red flag to a financier that there is information the company would prefer not to disclose.[8]

5. PRODUCT/SERVICE DESCRIPTION

The entire plan should be written to convey a clear and effective description of the venture's product or service. This section should provide detailed product/service characteristics, pricing (including value-add analysis, if appropriate), and possibly a detailed explanation of the projected product development process, including anticipated improvements. It may be appropriate to include related information such as the results of various product tests (i.e., pre-clinical-trial data for therapeutics, stress-test data for electromechanical inventions, or other performance testing outcomes). Although photos, schematics, and product/process diagrams can be very helpful, we have also seen business plans that focus on such drawings and descriptors, resulting in a product section that is 10–20 pages long by itself. Some documentation may be appropriate for an appendix, but entrepreneurs should be wary of creating a business plan that exceeds 25 pages, especially at the start-up stage.

Academic entrepreneurs often assume that the product and technology should be the first and longest section of the plan. While this is really a subjective issue, a detailed, prominent product section might be relevant for potential employees, internal goal management, and/or business partners. For investors, however, the details of product characteristics and performance often play a secondary role to the evaluation of the management team, the market opportunity, and the competitive environment. This may be counterintuitive to inventing entrepreneurs, who assume that investors want to evaluate the technology and product above all else.

There's no doubt that professional investors want to invest in a product or technology that offers the potential to change a market. But surveys have shown that both venture capital funds and angel investors believe that the strength of the management team and the market opportunity are the two most important investment criteria.[9] This isn't to suggest that product characteristics aren't important to potential investors; within the context of the business plan, however, potential investors are examining a complex interplay of variables. Sometimes it's easier to *eliminate* a deal because of obvious problems with the management team or the market opportunity, even before work goes into evaluating the technology. Investors seem to believe that the management team, market opportunity, and competitive positioning are indicators that can be more quickly evaluated than specific product features.

6. UNDERLYING TECHNOLOGY AND INTELLECTUAL PROPERTY (IP) PORTFOLIO DESCRIPTION

For many technology-based start-ups (especially those spun out of university research programs), intellectual property represents a significant perceived source of value. The following contributing factors should be noted:

- In many cases, and especially for new entrepreneurs, the IP represents the only obviously *verifiable* asset.

- The team may have little or no prior entrepreneurial or corporate management experience.

- The true target market may be extremely small—precisely because the technology represents a novel opportunity.

- Competition may be surmised on the basis of current competitors and other academic research projects, but may not be clearly assessable because of the potential change in market dynamics if the technology achieves adoptions.

Intellectual property often serves as a measurable test case for potential investors. Investors may request IP documentation from the entrepreneur both to evaluate the company's IP position as well as to test how the entrepreneur performs under pressure. How does she respond to requests for information? Does the IP development to date reflect a careful, skilled process or does it appear chaotic? Can the entrepreneur clearly explain complex science to laypersons? Does the entrepreneur understand the nuances of the patenting process and the active applications? Unlike market data and product comparisons (which often represent the entrepreneur's interpretation of limited available information), the Intellectual Property portfolio represents a concrete series of documents (in particular, a discrete set of "claims" regarding what technology, processes, and applications the inventor is trying to protect from imitation and competition) that can be scrutinized and evaluated. This process may help an investor form a sense of whether he will be able to establish a strong working relationship with the entrepreneur.

An important note should be made here about confidentiality. The majority of business plans usually have "Confidential" prominently stamped on them; many include statements of assumed confidentiality on the part of the reader. The reality is that such "proactive" assertions of confidentiality are probably unenforceable without a separate non-disclosure agreement (NDA). And the reality is that most professional investors (including every VC we've ever dealt with) will not sign a CDA prior to seeing the business plan. We caution entrepreneurs about putting truly confidential information into documents for general distribution, especially in the IP section. If significant advances in research and development cannot be discussed in the business plan, entrepreneurs can note this fact and state that detailed information can be made available separately.

This often represents one of the challenges of early discussions with professional investors. The company would like to discuss recent innovations that haven't been "protected" yet, but the potential investors won't *legally* agree to keep the information confidential. An investor may assure the entrepreneur of his intent to keep information confidential, but entrepreneurs disclose truly critical information at their own risk.[10] The vast majority of professional investors are scrupulous individuals of the highest integrity, but we have heard stories about less pleasant individuals who have obtained confidential information and used it for their own ends.

7. Sales, Marketing, and Distribution Analysis

Academic researchers often find this section to be the most challenging section of the plan to prepare, because the concepts and issues are likely the most foreign. The purpose of the section is to describe the mechanisms the business anticipates utilizing to promote products and services to the marketplace, ensure that customers have the necessary information about and access to products and services, and close actual sales. The questions listed in Table 10-3 may help ensure that your business plan provides the minimum (and appropriate) information required.

8. Financial Information

Entrepreneurs often spend the most time on the financial section of the business plan; detailed (sometimes extremely detailed) financial projections are often included in this section. Realistically, nearly all prospective investors (and, usually, the entrepreneur herself) will acknowledge that the projections are speculative at best, and nonsense at worst. We recently chatted with an individual who has served as the CEO of more than a half-dozen growth technology firms in the United States and Europe. He's about to take on a very early-stage deal in the United States, and he commented that there was simply no way to predict long-term revenues because the market for the novel technology won't exist for at least two more years.

The financial section is, for most investors, purely a sanity check. It is a rare entrepreneur that develops a financial section using reasonable *sales goals* based on customer interviews and pre-sales feedback. The majority of seed-stage, technology-based business plans create financial projections purely to demonstrate that the business is "investor-friendly"—it has the theoretical potential to generate greater than a tenfold return for investors. As an example, a relatively

TABLE 10-3 Minimum Information Required for Sales, Marketing, and Distribution Section of the Business Plan

Subsection	Questions to Answer	Additional Comments
Sales Cycle	• How long is the sales cycle? • Are there specific stages within the sales cycle? • Can critical decision makers be identified as customers?	Entrepreneurs often underestimate the length of the sales cycle. Data should be based on actual sales, or on information from customers or competitors.
Marketing Channels	• What marketing channels are used by competitors and accessed by customers? • How will the start-up utilize those channels? • If the start-up anticipates alternate or novel channels, what are the likely costs and delays?	In rare cases, start-ups can "hire experienced salespeople" to generate sales (especially when each sale is large). Even so, customers expect to hear about new products and technologies through standard mechanisms. The best source of information is, again, customers.
Distribution	• How will the product be made available to customers? • What is the distribution cycle (from order to production to delivery)? • If relevant, how will returns be managed?	It is not surprising that entrepreneurs don't address this issue—it's hardly relevant when a product is two to four years from completion. In such cases, limited discussion of industry standards should be sufficient. In cases where product sales and shipments are imminent, the business plan should demonstrate that the team has appropriately anticipated operational needs and costs.

simple internal rate-of-return (IRR) analysis (using reasonable assumptions about exit valuations and VC success rates) suggests that VCs are looking for investment opportunities that can grow to $50 million in annual revenues within four to six years. It shouldn't be surprising, then, to discover that a significant number of business plans show $50 million to $100 million in revenues by the fifth year of operation.

Any financial projection must be based on a significant number of assumptions, both internal and external to the business. And without an operating history (specifically—past sales), it's generally safe to assume that the margin of error associated with those assumptions dramatically overshadows the accuracy of the projections. Business plan writing books (and books on start-ups in general) state that three- to five-year projections must be provided—together with a not-insignificant level of detail. This is true for any business with an operating history and/or historical financials. For seed-stage technology-based start-ups and early-stage growth-phase companies, we recommend slightly different approaches.

Seed-stage technology-based start-ups.   When a start-up with a technology license and some initial ideas seeks funding, most investors do not need, nor value, financial projections showing income statements three years away. Our experience suggests that the most important financial factors are (1) the budget (and burn rate) needed for the business to reach two to three critical milestones (usually within the first 8–16 months) and (2) the longer-term revenue potential if the business is successful. These data address the key questions for seed investors: How much money is needed to ensure the company survives long enough to generate value? How big a reward is possible for the risk being taken?

In one start-up, we worked with, it was appropriate to develop a 14-month *budget* (rather than an *income statement*) that would enable the company to accomplish three goals: outsource high-quality manufacturing of the first prototype, complete product testing of the prototype (and an additional pre-prototype product), and initiate discussions with potential partners and customers to confirm key product characteristics, price points, and likely demand. The start-up informed potential investors there would likely be no revenue in years one or two, but provided high-level analyses showing the longer-term revenue potential if the company successfully introduced products into the market (an analysis made on the basis of related product revenues, statements from customers about demand, and end-user market statistics). No pro forma income statements were provided. The goal of the seed financing round was to demonstrate that the product could be produced at scale and that customers saw a need for the product. We believe that most early-stage investors do not want to aggressively evaluate complex Excel spreadsheets; rather they want to evaluate the risk-reward equation at a high level.

Early-growth-stage companies.   Let's assume that the business is currently generating limited revenues (whether grants or product sales) and the company needs to expand operations across a variety of functions (such as R&D, manufacturing, and sales). Pro forma financial projections should be developed, but with an eye toward function and milestones rather than specificity. We've been fascinated by pro forma projections that are dramatically more sophisticated and complex than the financial recording and reporting systems used by the company to manage operations. Certainly, some sophistication may be valuable for attempting to predict sales, but few investors at this stage will review 50 pages of detailed projections.

In most cases, developing a relatively simple spreadsheet model can help management consider the key factors driving sales and costs. Three-year pro forma projections likely represent the far end of what can reasonably be anticipated; forecasting beyond 24–36 months will probably be as misleading as revealing. Detailed budgets may be significantly more valuable than pro forma projections, because they will likely reveal the true cash needs of the business (which, for R&D-stage companies, should be milestone driven)—as opposed to the profitability of the business (which may be optimistic at best). Cash flow projections can be helpful, but for most early-stage companies cash flow is not significantly different than budget. Cash flow analysis can be problematic because it usually reflects fluctuations in the cash cycle (driven by sales and operations) rather than fluctuations in the development cycle (driven by R&D and operations). Cash flow analysis also tends to understate likely cash needs, because entrepreneurs often manage to both underestimate costs and overestimate likely revenues.

EXIT EVENTS

The "exit" event generally refers to a corporate transaction involving a significant change in ownership. Examples include the sale of the business, a merger with another firm, an initial public offering (in which the company's stock become available for trade on a major market such as the NASDAQ), or some other type of refinancing event in which owners and investors have the opportunity to cash out some or all of their investment. There is probably an endless set of permutations for possible exit events, including negative exits. Our goal is to focus on this topic in the context of the business plan. Chapter 15 will focus on operational aspects of exits and their impact on the inventing entrepreneur.

Investors and advisors usually check to see whether the entrepreneur has considered exit possibilities. It is important, however, to dispel two myths about venture financiers and business plans.

Myth #1: Venture financiers expect entrepreneurs to have an exit already planned out.

Myth #2: Venture financiers expect that whatever exit is described in the business plan will actually take place.

Venture financiers are almost always both intelligent and practical. They are aware that information in the business plan tends to be speculative, and perhaps the only item more speculative than the financials is the exit strategy. Why, then, do financiers demand to see the entrepreneurs' perspective on exit?

The exit strategy is as much a psychological indicator as it is a planning or preparation tool. One of the key purposes of the business plan, after all, is simply to ensure that all the key assumptions have been identified, agreed on, and most importantly, *written down*. The exit strategy does not represent a crystal ball prediction. It represents (1) an understanding about potential mechanisms for generating returns, (2) a demonstration that the entrepreneurs have at least a limited working knowledge of the financial markets, and (3) a written commitment on behalf of the entrepreneurs that they are prepared to relinquish control[11] at the appropriate time. Information in the business plan about exit strategies, especially for an extremely early-stage business, should be directed toward demonstrating thoughtfulness and flexibility rather than prognostication. Venture financiers expect a positive acquisition or IPO for an exit event. The vast majority of successful exits for angels and venture capitalists occur by acquisition, as the IPO is, on the whole, a relatively rare event.

For most early ventures, the most useful statements in this section would cover the likely time frame for exit and identify the *type* of potential acquirers. For example, a medical device start-up could anticipate an acquisition exit occurring in as little as three years—on the basis of bringing a product to market immediately following a 510K regulatory clearance. Alternatively, the company could suggest a longer time frame on the basis of achieving more significant sales and distribution. A start-up pharmaceutical company can usually only consider early exits on the basis of successful preclinical or Phase-I clinical studies. Bringing a novel therapeutic all the way to market suggests an exit strategy that is at least six to eight years away.

Identifying the time frame sends clear signals about the entrepreneur's goals and vision, because it suggests what must be accomplished before the entrepreneur is prepared to relinquish control. Finally, it also may send signals about the entrepreneur's market savvy. In the late 1990s, start-up pharmaceutical companies could sell lead targets with limited preclinical data. In the mid-2000s, big pharmaceutical companies attempted to reduce their risk exposure by demanding Phase-I and even Phase-II data prior to acquisition. Savvy entrepreneurs should be aware of current market conditions, despite the fact that any likely exit will take place years down the road—when conditions could be very different. Table 10-4 identifies some basic "Do's and Don'ts" in considering what information to include in the busines plan regarding exits.

TABLE 10-4   Exit Information Do's and Don'ts

Do	*Don't*
• Mention different possible exit options (acquisition, merger, IPO) to the extent that each is realistic.	• Propose a specific exit option unless circumstances warrant (e.g. if the company already has an acquisition offer, then it is appropriate to provide details).
• Discuss realistic selling price to earnings (P/E) ratios for your industry and type of business (for example, service businesses generally obtain a lower price–earnings ratio than product businesses).	• Suggest that IPO is the primary exit option unless your industry sector and geographic region have a clear history of successful IPOs.
• Discuss realistic milestones that could trigger an exit event, such as a product launch or a revenue target.	• Predict that you will be able to sell the company on the basis of internal milestones that are not clearly linked to market value, unless the industry has a history of such acquisitions.
• Emphasize relevant team experience with mergers, acquisitions, and IPOs.	• Identify a specific time frame for exit, unless it's tightly tied to specific milestones.
• Mention possible (target) acquirers, especially if those firms have strong cash reserves, a vested interest in protecting their market position, and a history of acquisitions.	• List the biggest companies in your industry without explaining why they would want to buy your firm.

GETTING HELP

Some inventing entrepreneurs write a business plan unaided, either because of unusual expertise or because of the determination to learn a new skill. Some outsource the entire effort, either via the assistance of an investment group actively participating in strategic development or simply by paying a consultant with expertise in business plan preparation. A vast array of organizations and individuals can help the innovator prepare a business plan. Technology transfer offices may have deep expertise in market analysis and technology valuation, and some work closely with graduate schools of business to identify and access appropriate resources. The United States Small Business Administration's "Small Business Development Centers" comprise facilities, services, and expertise across the country.[12] Many have specific courses on writing business plans. Numerous not-for-profit agencies, including the Service Corps of Retired Executives (SCORE),[13] offer free counseling for new entrepreneurs. As is often the case with free services, quality will vary and is based heavily on the individual(s) providing assistance.

Additional resources to consider in business-plan development include business mentors, including respected associates, former (or current) entrepreneurs, or business school professors. Trusted contacts developed in the business community represent excellent sounding boards for business-plan drafts. Many inventing entrepreneurs turn to family members and friends, with or without business expertise, to review early business-plan documents. We encourage inventing entrepreneurs to seek out impartial, expert advice, and to carefully depersonalize any critiquing of the business plan.

APPENDICES, DOCUMENTATION, AND OTHER ISSUES

A clear, well-written plan can usually provide critical information to both internal and external audiences. The strength of a new venture founded by an inventing entrepreneur rests on the technology more than any other factor; yet it can be difficult and sometimes inappropriate to describe the technology in adequate detail in the body of the business plan, because the most up-to-date information on technology development may be complex or even confidential. For this and other reasons, detailed appendices for technology-driven start-up companies have become more common. If external reviewers consistently ask for certain information (e.g., details on patent filings, full resumes for the management team, more detailed financial projections, additional details on the technology and/or recent experimental data), appendices covering specific topics may be warranted. As a rule, we suggest that the appendices shouldn't exceed 10 to 15 pages. After all, additional information can always be provided separately. When it comes to business plans, brevity is invaluable, since financiers may read hundreds or even thousands each year. Table 10-5 provides some additional "Do's and Don'ts" for business plan appendices.

Finally, it's generally a good idea to keep both electronic and hard copies of all the various documents and resources you utilize to build the business plan.

TABLE 10-5 Business-Plan Appendices Do's and Don'ts	
Do	*Don't*
• Follow the same formatting conventions for the appendices as you did for the rest of the business plan.	• Treat the appendices as a dumping ground for trying to answer every question you think an investor might ask.
• Provide summary financial information in the main body of the plan, and more detailed financial projections, if appropriate, in the appendix.	• Provide three to five pages maximum for additional financial documentation (unless unusual circumstances make such disclosure necessary).
• Provide one-page resumes for the senior management team if you have only provided short bios in the business-plan body.	• Provide an entire curriculum vitae.
• Consider including a more sophisticated explanation of the technology, especially if your venture is a true start-up.	• Simply copy the first few pages of an academic grant proposal or a recent academic research paper.
• Consider adding a few selected quotes or copies of popular press articles that focus on market feasibility or milestone achievements.	• Provide copious popular press clippings that do not address specific issues but simply provide good public relations copy.
• Have two versions of the business plan (whether electronic or hard copy)—one with the appendix and one without.	• Provide original documentation, because it may not be returned.
	• Provide sourcing materials without confidence that such materials are truly representative of available data.

Although most investors will perform some amount of due diligence on their own, you may be asked if you have supporting documentation for your market or competitor analysis. If you can be organized enough to produce a binder (or zip file) with all the articles, market studies, and other sources that you analyzed for your plan, you may signal your organizational skills and the depth of your knowledge.

REALISTIC ANALYSES

It is critical to convey a sense of professionalism and realism in the business plan. Realistic analysis isn't just for the business plan, it's the basis of the company's understanding about customer behavior and market evolution. It's important to note the difference between accuracy and specificity in this context, and to provide a reality check.

We've read thousands of business plans; most provided some amount of customer and market research. Many, however, seemed focused on providing *specific* numbers rather than *accurate* numbers. Explicating customer behaviors and market projections should be an exercise in *accuracy*—that is, providing relevant, appropriate, well-researched information that gives stakeholders (including management and potential investors) an accurate sense of what to expect in the market. Providing market information with a high level of *specificity* often seems useful—projecting market size out 10 years based on speculative growth figures can demonstrate just how big the opportunity will be. But any apparent specificity is an illusion. We believe it's better to utilize rounded figures with high confidence than exact numbers that are unlikely to be correct.

Market projections should be premised on current information about the target market. The reality, of course, is that many (if not most) early stage technology companies eventually target markets that are completely different from those described in the first business plan. (See Profile 10-2 for Mike Fouche's story and a good example of the process of changing target markets.) But it's important to put down the best information available, knowing that circumstances could change. If there is a lot of uncertainty about the target market, then entrepreneurs should probably be explicit about this uncertainty. This is one of the reasons that savvy investors prefer to invest in proven teams. A strong team will identify the right product for the right market, regardless of what was written down in the business plan.

INVENTING ENTREPRENEUR PROFILE 10-2

Mike Fouche

Mike Fouche's entrepreneurial journey took many years and covered numerous jobs. Fouche is an engineer who chooses to start his own venture when he realizes that the technology he's been working on won't be commercialized by his employer. Fouche had been at Ford Aerospace (sold to Loral in 1990) working on unmanned aerial vehicles (UAVs)—specifically, unmanned helicopters. The physics of helicopter flight is, in many ways, dramatically more complex than that of fixed-wing aircraft. The U.S. military has had autonomous airplanes for decades, but autonomous helicopters have been a bigger challenge. When Fouche transferred to Boeing, he had high hopes that the advent of neural networking technology would dramatically advance the science of autonomous flight. He'd learned about neural networking on his own after hearing about its use for other applications.

In the end, Fouche realized that he just wasn't happy at Boeing. He left to move back to Huntsville, and took consecutive jobs with three other aerospace companies, including Grumman, trying to find a balance between the work he needed to do to support his family, and the work he wanted to do on autonomous helicopters. He'd been advancing his own helicopter technology for a couple years, borrowing working space from one of his employer's clients, when opportunity knocked:

> I had my helicopter in the shop [of the company where I was doing subcontractor work], and one day an angel investor came into the shop and said, "Hey, what's this," and the manager said, "Oh, that's some guy doing this helicopter project...." And I learned about private investing through that guy.... That was my introduction to private investing.... I had no idea you could go out and sell stock and get a start-up going.

As with many technology-driven start-ups, there were lots of surprises along the way. Fouche discovered that the conventional wisdom about the market for autonomous helicopters was wrong:

> If you do a Google search on autonomous helicopters, anybody who's doing these kind of projects will talk about applications—and invariably at the top of the list is television stations and news stations.... We're being driven by the market [to the pipeline companies] in the sense that we think there's more money there.... There's pipelines in populated areas, they have deep pockets, and once they buy the technology they'll probably buy many of them.... The Russians are a good example: They came to visit us for five days, and they are waiting for us to hit a technical milestone. It wasn't top of the list, but we got more and more customers inquiring. We had one pipeline customer—it kind of surprised us—bought a machine eight months ago. About the same time they bought, the people at GazProm contacted us.

Fouche has also struggled with management challenges. He'd never really intended to serve in a CEO-type role. In fact, he served as CEO of the company for a while, then brought in an outside manager—a decision that didn't work out. But he always saw himself as the engineer, the technology expert—rather than the corporate leader:

> I've always been the engineer, very good at solving problems at the companies I went to—not because I was brilliant but because I was very dogged in pursuit of what the problem was. Other engineers would give up and I would keep going at it. I only learned the business side because it was a necessary evil. I had to understand the business because if I didn't then nothing else was going to work—because then I wasn't going to get to do the engineering.

But this and many other experiences have expanded Fouche's understanding about how businesses function. He'd managed subordinates in many of his technical positions for large aerospace companies, but hadn't had to drive a broader mission. Running a small start-up business has dramatically increased Fouche's appreciation for the value of key human resources:

> People are really important. I understand why people like being in business, because business is about people. That's probably one of the biggest things I've learned: that it's all about relationships.... I have made more friends, and a few enemies—more friends in starting this company in the last three years, than I have in the last 20 years.... Business just isn't transactions; it's people. The more you understand that, the more you're going to be successful.

Ultimately, Fouche is convinced that he couldn't have done this work within a big corporation. There are many possible reasons for this: The technology may not be critical to the corporation's core interests, management may simply not be aware of or interested in the opportunity, or resources may not be available to support the necessary development work. In the case of autonomous helicopters at Boeing, it's quite possible that the target market wasn't attractive enough to warrant the necessary investment, especially given the infrastructure and administrative costs associated with any long-term research project:

> This could have been done at a big company, but there's no way they would sell it. They couldn't afford to sell it for what we sell it for. It wouldn't fit in the product line. This would have ended up as an internal research project. You see this in the government—Unmanned Autonomous Vehicle (UAV) projects that go on for years and years.... But for us, doing this as a start-up is ideal, because you can charge the least for it, and you're hungry.

(continues)

The future of Neural Robotics, Inc. is still uncertain. In the summer of 2005 Fouche was talking about the coming 12 months being a "make-or-break" time frame. And now, though the company has made some sales and improved its products, they're still a long way from significant success. But Fouche has no doubts about his decisions, and he's clear that his own life has been transformed by his entrepreneurial experience:

> It's a life-changing experience. You learn a lot about yourself. Because your flaws are exposed in a big way—and unless you just want to blame everyone else, you're going to figure out where your weaknesses are because you're going to want to try to patch them up, strengthen them up. You learn a lot about yourself; you learn a lot about other people.... It's like a roller-coaster ride for people; it puts everything else in perspective; you go through some very intense emotions, and some of the things you worried about before suddenly don't seem so important anymore. I remember when I worked at Boeing I suddenly got concerned that I might run out of money in a year, and now a year seems like forever. The experience is so intense it changes how you view life after that.

REALISTIC CUSTOMER ANALYSIS

When we review business plans, we are struck by how few rely on explicit information from potential customers. There's no shame in a business that doesn't have customers yet. But there is something worrisome about a company that has never sought direct feedback from potential customers (whether they are end users, distributors, intermediaries, etc.). This process is often confused with "market research," which is really the effort to determine how large the market might be. Customer research or customer analysis is the effort to determine what customer needs really are and whether the proposed product or service could fulfill those needs. When asked how his newest start-up, Scarab Genomics, identified its first product offering, Fred Blattner replied:

> We stumbled into it. But the reason we did manage to get the knowledge was that I really went around to a lot of companies and made contacts and talked to people. And I didn't ask, "What do you want," I asked, "what are you doing?" And that's really important; you don't ask what they want, because if they knew what I know, they wouldn't be doing what they're doing. Find out what they are trying to do, not what they are doing.

The role of the university professor affords special latitude in talking to potential customers. Most corporations understand that technology developed at universities may be destined for the commercial world, but our experience suggests that businesspeople are generally willing to talk openly about product potential and applications with academics when they might otherwise be tight-lipped. We recently arranged for an inventing entrepreneur to meet with a potential customer in the railroad sector. Getting the meeting was relatively easy, and once the technology had been effectively presented, the railroad staff was eager to suggest applications on their system. The professor left the meeting with a completely new model for how customers might use the technology—a model that was based on the needs of a customer set he hadn't previously considered.

We recommend that inventing entrepreneurs talk with *at least* 10 potential customers (or individuals/organizations between the venture and the end-user) to establish credibility and provide a basis for a speculative revenue model. Obviously, this number varies with the industry (some industries would require fewer and some would require more—especially when the industry is fragmented). In most cases 10 potential customers provides a qualitative basis for understanding how customers might (or might not) use the technology. Inventing entrepreneurs should share the technology (taking into account any confidentiality issues[14]) and ask many questions. Good questions to ask potential customers include the following:

- What are the biggest unsolved problems in producing your product or service?
- Are there limitations to the technology that you currently use?
- If you had technology like "X," how would you likely use it?
- What technology advances are valuable enough to your business that you'd be willing to pay for them?

REALISTIC MARKET ANALYSIS

Market analysis for a truly novel, market-changing product ranges from challenging to impossible. The inherent gap between the entrepreneur (who often believes fervently in an unproven market) and the investor (who believes just as fervently that entrepreneurs overestimate everything) can be enormous. Part of the problem is that there is no "accepted" standard for market-analysis reliability. A skeptical investor may never get comfortable with market projections regardless of how much detail is provided. An enthusiastic investor may be prepared to take market evolution on faith. A realistic market analysis probably will not answer every question about the target market size. It should, however, provide order-of-magnitude estimates at an appropriate level of detail to help investors self-select in or out of the process.

Market survey information and Google searches will often provide a rapid, order-of-magnitude estimate for the total market. For example, we find that industry statistics can often be quickly estimated by "Googling" the appropriate key words along with "billion." For example, Googling *dialysis billion* retrieves stats (in the first 10 hits from reliable sources) on end-stage renal disease (ESRD) costs in the United States that range from $18 billion to $23 billion per year. In other cases, industry experts, associations, or newsletters will often provide convenient, accessible top-line market-size information. But these may not reflect the true target market, which is usually a subset of the overall market space.[15]

Savvy entrepreneurs know that the real data is with customers and industry participants. One inventing entrepreneur's company struggled to size a market for a novel therapeutic application that had the potential to revolutionize certain trauma treatments. The novelty was the problem—the trauma incidence numbers were readily available, but the data on what subset of those traumas would be candidates for the treatment simply didn't exist. The solution arrived when a potential industry partner shared their own analysis—they'd been trying unsuccessfully to develop a similar solution and had put the resources of a *Fortune* 1000 firm behind the effort, which was something the entrepreneur simply couldn't do.

In discussions with industry participants and customers about the true target market, focus on the characteristics of the target market: Which applications does the technology really address, and what value could it create for users? Depending on the customer set, information from a few data points can be extrapolated to estimate the broader market. For example, speaking with a handful of representative hospitals about expenditures on Picture Archival and Communications Systems (PACS) should provide a preliminary snapshot of the entire market. In many cases, such results can be cross-referenced to high-level market summaries. For example, the medical imaging market is $8 billion to $10 billion per year in the United States, but the PACS submarket is in the range of $1 billion to $2 billion per year. If the true target were middle-tier PACS customers in the United States, then the likely market size is probably around $500 million per year. Comparing the data from customer discussions will be the key to understanding whether that number is closer to $100 million or $1 billion.

REALISTIC COMPETITOR ANALYSIS

Inventing entrepreneurs are sometimes flustered or annoyed by the competitor analysis process. On the one hand, current competitors may not be able to compete with the new technology, and on the other hand, the real competitors probably cannot be identified because they're also working in stealth mode. The business plan should identify both active competitors (even if the underlying technology appears to be outmoded) and potential competitors (including companies in related fields and high-profile research labs or identified start-ups). A process for quickly identifying these organizations includes the following:

- Google or other Internet searches for product/service keywords
- USPTO (or appropriate country) patent searches (including patent application searches), followed by Internet searches for relevant inventors and assignees
- Discussions with informed industry experts

In most cases, the competitive section of a start-up company business plan *can't* thoroughly predict and evaluate the likely competitors. Resource and information constraints limit such idealistic goals. But the plan should send three signals—first, that the entrepreneur and the company have performed a reasonable search for competitive products and technologies; second, that the search will be ongoing, with results relayed as appropriate; and third, that competitive threats and developments will be taken seriously. This perspective is only sensible—both for the entrepreneur (who shouldn't pursue the endeavor in the face of insurmountable competition) and for the potential investor (who knows that information is imperfect but appreciates being reassured that the entrepreneur is making the appropriate effort to evaluate the competitive environment).

REALISTIC BUDGETING

Preparing a budget should be one of the more straightforward tasks for the inventing entrepreneur. In 1999, 2000, and 2001 we saw many plans with revenue projections but no budgets. Entrepreneurs often asked investors to trust management's ability to spend money as needed to go after "fast-moving" opportunities. We believe the business plan for an early-stage technology business should include a relatively detailed budget designed to show the anticipated expenses needed for reaching logical milestones. For example, imagine a novel medical device developed in a mechanical engineering department. The technology is spun out into a start-up company founded by the inventing entrepreneur. The business plan calls for $500,000 to produce 25 units of the prototype for animal safety testing. The budget should clearly show how the funds will be used to meet that milestone. If the funds will be expended in six months, then a six- to nine-month budget is appropriate. The plan probably should include some estimate of fund requirements for the next milestones (scale manufacturing, FDA regulatory process, etc.), but explicit budgets should not be necessary.

On the other hand, the early commercialization of a novel software product for mapping social networks might need a more flexible budget. Imagine that this particular company will also need $500,000, but the milestones involve completion of alpha testing at a single site, final development of the automated data-entry system, and beta testing at three as-yet-unidentified sites. Compared with the previous example, where a significant portion of the costs will go towards outsourced manufacturing and animal safety testing, a greater percentage of the software company's budget will be driven by human resource utilization. Thus, it is appropriate to show a budget that extends beyond the anticipated milestone date. This helps the entrepreneur and potential investors understand (and prepare for) the cost of missed milestones.

In general, we've found that budgets of 25–50 line items provide excellent detail without overwhelming the reviewer. It's not generally necessary to separate out things like "postage" or "faxing costs." Any line item less than 1 percent of the total budget may represent too much detail. Depending on the circumstances, we do recommend the use of "contingency" line items to provide budget flexibility and reduce clutter and unnecessary complexity.

REALISTIC REVENUE PROJECTIONS

No single item in the business plan will come under more scrutiny than the revenue projections. Out of all the guesswork that goes into a start-up, the revenue projections usually have the least basis in fact. The most common quantification method we see is the "top-down" approach, in which various market surveys are quoted and arbitrary market penetrations are selected as being "reasonable." Here is an example: "The total market for end-stage renal disease in the United States was $22.8 billion, according to the NIH. If we can capture only 5% of that market with our new technology, we'll have $1.14 billion in annual revenues."

This type of analysis suffers from at least two flaws. First, it ignores any pricing issues associated with bringing novel technology to market. If the success of the venture is based on being able to offer products or services at significantly lower prices than current options, the total available market could shrink. Alternatively, if the system is dramatically better than current systems, the company should have the option of charging a premium. Second, it sidesteps the real issue, which is how customer purchase decisions are made. Why will 5 percent (or 10% or 50 percent) of customers switch to the new technology? We often read business plans that state that because the technology is so much better than anything available, the company should easily reach 10 percent market share. If the claim is true, why shouldn't the company dominate the market with a 50 percent, or even 75 percent share? The reality is that such approaches usually have no basis in how new technologies are adopted or how customers in the target market make decisions.

A less common, but arguably more effective process involves a "bottom-up" approach for estimating demand. This often starts by identifying specific customers likely to acquire novel technology—so-called "early adopters." In some cases, it's possible to suggest a price range and customer target numbers that result in near-term market estimates. For example, novel surgical robots are more likely to be adopted at research hospitals and high-end clinics where surgeons have more flexibility about tool choices and research budgets. A reasonable estimate of the subset of organizations and/or facilities likely to adopt the technology can be developed, along with pricing based either on available products or insurance reimbursement policies. Here again, customer research (not market research) is the telling point for quality information. Revenue projections that are based on anecdotal information from potential customers carry significantly more weight than "market-based" analyses. Knowing how customers buy the products is the best first step toward rational revenue projections.

As a side note, anticipated funds from federal or other reviewed grants (such as Small Business Innovation Research [SBIR] or Advanced Technology Program [ATP] grants) should be noted *separately* from product sales and revenues. Although such grants do provide cash to the organization (and are usually classified in the "Revenue" category), they do not represent sustainable, profit-generating sales associated with long-term value creation. Mislabeling such proceeds is simply inappropriate.[16]

INTRODUCTION TO START-UP FINANCING

For technology-based growth companies, especially ones with long-term development timelines prior to market entry, the topic of finance presents special challenges. We'll introduce the topic here, and then devote all of Chapter 11 to a more detailed discussion of finance. Our interviews with inventing entrepreneurs and direct experience working with them suggest that many scientifically trained entrepreneurs would benefit significantly from increased exposure to information about early-stage financing.

Nearly all non-service businesses require some amount of external financing—whether limited funds for obtaining inventory or significant funds for extensive research and development.[17]

The types and amounts of funds available to technology ventures vary, primarily by the stage and type of the business. At founding, the most traditional sources of capital are the founders' own funds (credit-card debt, second mortgage, savings, guaranteed bank loan) and loans (or investments) from family and friends. Business experts suggest that more than 95 percent of businesses (and perhaps in excess of 99% of businesses) start with this type of funding. In most cases, founder and friends and family capital is used for the first $50,000 to $100,000 of external financing. Obviously, some individuals and families have access to significantly more capital, but these are the exceptions.

The most simple transactions are loans: An individual (a founder or friend) or organization (such as a bank) provides cash and the business agrees to repay that cash, along with interest. An equity investment occurs when the business agrees to sell partial ownership in the company for investment capital. In the most simple version of an equity investment, the investor owns some portion of the company and has the right to pro rata profits generated by the company whether from ongoing operations or from the sale of assets (including the sale of the entire company).[18]

There are other sources of start-up capital. Technology-based companies in the United States can apply for Small Business Innovation Research (SBIR) grants, which start at about $100,000 for Phase-I grants but can exceed $1 million in Phase II. Advanced Technology Program (ATP) grants are larger (usually $2 million) and are designed for longer-term research projects. Most U.S. states have various grant programs for new companies, ranging from funds to support business-plan writing to multimillion dollar technology and workforce development programs. Alternatively, some start-up companies out-license noncore technologies (or core technology in noncore fields) to other companies to generate cash.

The need for external capital can pose a special challenge to inventing entrepreneurs. One of the common threads in early-stage financing is the investor's desire for proof of commitment. For a bank, such commitment comes in the form of hard assets or a personal guarantee. For an equity investor, commitment could be a minimal cash and/or effort investment by the founder—and/or the founder taking a full-time role at the company for a below-market salary.

Whether or not the inventor has accumulated wealth, we observed that many academic researchers find it difficult to invest personal cash or put personal assets at stake to start a business. When inventing entrepreneurs emerge from the R&D group of a large corporation, instead of an academic research lab, they are generally more prepared to spend savings and guarantee loans to get their businesses started. This may simply reflect the disparity in situations. Academic researchers may perceive significantly more risk associated with the venture because they compare it to their academic position; corporate-based entrepreneurs are more likely to have already chosen to leave employment and see the venture as their best path forward.

After the business has seed funding in place, it's possible the company will need to consider additional rounds of financing. A good starting guide to understanding the full financing process for high-technology growth companies is *High-Tech Start-Up* by John Nesheim. Nesheim's book is specifically focused on institutional venture-capital funding but provides a good high-level picture of the growth of start-up firms and likely financing needs. An excellent complement to this title is *Angel Investing* by Robinson and Van Osnabrugge, which provides the most comprehensive analysis of private angel investing in high-technology companies.

Our own experience leads us to a number of thoughts and recommendations for inventing entrepreneurs.

- *Consider the likely long-term funding needs of the business.* Perhaps the best way to do this is to identify companies that have commercialized comparable technologies and determine how much external financing was required. We often see inventing entrepreneurs misled by their own financial projections, painting a rosy picture of profitability that is based on immediate success. While such circumstances are possible, considering comparables often provides a more realistic picture.[19] Many inventing entrepreneurs often don't consider downstream financing needs while raising seed or angel capital. The most savvy managers effectively project long-term financial needs and incorporate those expectations into their financing plan.

  Often, we are asked by entrepreneurs (not just inventing entrepreneurs): "Why shouldn't I just raise money at the highest valuation I can get?" This is an excellent question, and shouldn't be answered blithely. If the entrepreneur is focused on maximizing her own stock value (and nothing else), then such a strategy is viable. After all, if investors buy overvalued stock, they may be punished in future financings while the entrepreneur will be better off than if she had sold stock at a fair value. This will continue to be true, even if the company experiences future down rounds. Clearly, however, issues of trust between the founder and the investors may develop, and the entrepreneur may find investors pressing for harder bargains in later rounds. Investors tend to have long memories and tight networks—and if the entrepreneur raises funds for another start-up, she might discover that previous deals emerge as negative data during bargaining. There can be many other implications: Stock options granted at the inflated stock price may be worthless to employees, reducing their incentive to perform. Financing valuation and negotiation is a wonderful, specialized, and surprisingly complex topic that merits careful consideration by entrepreneurs (with guidance from experts). Our simplest advice: Focus on long-term value creation, not short-term paper profits.

- *Raise money to meet measurable, value-building milestones.* Aphorisms about financing are ubiquitous, including "Raise money when you can, not when you need it" and "Raise as much money as you can—no company ever failed for having too much cash." Our own experience and observations suggest that raising money is often seen as an end, rather than as a means to an end. *A company raises money to create value through operations*, presumably significantly more value than the investment amount. *Raising funds in and of itself, does not increase the value of the underlying business.* To that end, the company should be raising funds to meet *specific, measurable, value-building milestones*. In some instances, the milestones are obvious: signing a product development contract with a market leader, completing preclinical trials, or hiring a competent, experienced CEO. In other cases, milestones can seem clear while still requiring interpretation. For example, a software company might state that the milestone is completing version 0.9 of the product; but who defines when v0.9 is complete? A better milestone might be completion of a one-month beta test at five client sites. At the completion of each milestone, risk should be reduced from the company's long-term plan. When risk has been reduced, the expected value of the venture should be increased. Thus the set of milestones should be closely tied to the long-term financing plan—defining how much money the company must raise, what will be accomplished with those funds, and how much value will be created.

- *Understand the financing process, including information requirements, documentation, and timing.* Many entrepreneurs are surprised at how much information investors want to see, how much documentation has to be reviewed, and how long the entire financing process can take.[20] It's important to remember that formal private investments generally require a minimum amount of investigation and documentation *regardless of the financing amount*. Most attorneys will recommend creating a private placement memorandum (PPM)—a document that establishes a set of information on which the investment decision is based, and which usually includes a detailed list of risks associated with the investment.[21] Investors will often request detailed information about every aspect of the company's operations, and may perform extensive additional research on the company, the technology, the management team, and the market.[22] This entire process can take significantly longer than entrepreneurs expect, regardless of the financing amount. In 2002, an angel group we worked with made a $1.3 million investment in one company after four months of diligence, but took eight months to complete a $350,000 investment in another start-up. Early-stage companies must plan ahead for financing: We've seen companies run out of cash while waiting for an investment to close.

- *Get qualified help.* There's no question that financing is a critical, complex process. In many cases the inventing entrepreneur will play a key role, including participating in presentations to potential investors. Sophisticated managers know when to delegate responsibilities to experts, including corporate counsel and financial advisors. When the inventing entrepreneur and key managers must keep the company moving forward, the time they spend raising funds is time *not* spent developing technology, products, and customers. An experienced mentor can be one of the most valuable resources in the financing process.

  The set of norms, legalities, and intricacies of seed and growth financing can be particularly confusing to inventing entrepreneurs. It is unlikely (and probably inefficient for) the inventing entrepreneur to become an expert on small-business finance. A minimum level of competency definitely empowers early-stage decision making, but we strongly encourage inventing entrepreneurs to identify individuals and organizations that can help sort through the details of early-stage financing. There are lots of ways to raise and spend money to create value, but there are only so many hours in a day.

- *When possible, partner with "smart money."* When individuals and organizations invest in an early-stage technology business, they become partners in the venture. Some entrepreneurs and managers do not take advantage of this partnership. Many early-stage investors have experience, connections, and other resources beneficial to growing businesses. Some investors can add significantly more value to a business than by just providing working capital. If nothing else, investors are often a link to more investors downstream. Long-range financial planning should consider whether certain investors would bring more value to the table. The right financier can make connections to customers and partners, and can share the accumulated wisdom of other businesses and investments. Such qualified partners may come with a price tag—if the investor believes that he brings value to the business, he may demand a better deal.

Conclusions and Summary

In this chapter, we introduced the inventing entrepreneur to information and critical business skills that may be unfamiliar to the professional researcher. We assume, for example, that the researcher does not need lessons in leading either short- or long-term research projects, and that the general management skills associated with lab management, operations, and administration will transfer reasonably well to business operations. Business-plan writing and private financing, however, are often unfamiliar "art forms" to the novice entrepreneur. Inventing entrepreneurs should plan to immerse themselves in these topics, but also to find trusted advisors and experienced businesspeople to help navigate these critical aspects of technology-based growth companies.

Endnotes

1. Carter, N., Gartner, W., & Reynolds, P. 1996. Exploring startup sequences. *Journal of Business Venturing,* 11(3): 151–166.
2. Specifically, venture capital funds structured as limited partnerships may have significant accounting issues associated with an investment in an LLC that generates pass-through losses or gains.
3. Daily, C. A., McDougall, P. P., Covin, J. G., & Dalton, D. R. 2002. Governance and strategic leadership in entrepreneurial firms. *Journal of Management,* 28(3): 387–412.
4. In his blog, Guy Kawasaki comments that he spent $4,800 on legal bills associated with the following: a trademark filing, general discussion of various IP issues, preparation of the incorporation documents including bylaws, and stock purchase agreements. He comments: "You could do less legal work and do it cheaper, but if you ever want to raise venture capital—much less go public or get acquired for more than scrap value—this is not the place to save a few thousand bucks" (http://blog.guykawasaki.com/2007/06/482413_for_lega.html). In another example, *Mlive.com* reports: "Miller Canfield lawyers will prepare and file the legal papers needed to form a company, which can cost about $7,500 in legal fees" (www.mlive.com/weblogs/print.ssf?/mtlogs/mlive_latest/archives/print230775.html). We note that the Mlive.com reference does not clarify whether this includes appropriate documents for a seed financing round or not. *AskTheVC.com* suggests that it should be possible to get the incorporation and set-up documents, along with legal assistance and documentation for an angel round of financing, for about $10K total (www.askthevc.com/2007/06/what_are_standard_legal_fee_ar.php). Our experience suggests that inventing entrepreneurs should be prepared for $10K as a minimum, because the inventing entrepreneur may require significant discussion with and expertise from the attorneys. If the entrepreneur doesn't fully understand what is going on, the spectre of significant additional legal expenses down the road will surely appear. Kawasaki probably knew exactly what he needed and asked for it. As the *AskTheVC* site suggests, negotiating for set fees is an excellent idea.
5. Eckhardt, J. T., Shane, S., & Delmar, F. 2006. Multistage selection and the financing of new ventures. *Management Science,* 52(2): 220–232.
6. Bhide, A. 2000. *The Origin and Evolution of New Businesses.* New York: Oxford University Press.
7. Competitive intensity may be correlated to the stage of market/industry development; growth markets tend to be less competitive, because there are many new potential customers, while mature markets tend to be aggressively competitive, because every company is fighting to maintain or grow market share by stealing customers from other companies.
8. Disguising prior employers is suspect because there are few valid reasons for not disclosing the information. One valid reason would be that the individual has not officially left the employer. This could represent a significant problem; investors are naturally suspicious of entrepreneurs still earning full-time paychecks. Another valid reason would be that the prior employer is a likely competitor of the new start-up, which represents a completely different set of potential problems. In some cases, individuals disguise prior employer information out of the misguided sense that "A *Fortune* 100 telecommunications company" sounds better than "AT&T."

9. Van Osnabrugge, M., and Robinson, R. *Angel Investing*. 2000. Josey-Bass. San Francisco, CA.

10. One of the key values of establishing relationships with industry experts and respected businesspeople is the additional weight this brings to the discussion with professional investors. Reputation is critical in the professional investing field, and unscrupulous professional investors are less likely to use confidential information improperly if there are established players on the other side of the table.

11. This could mean control of the company, the technology, or the commercialization vision.

12. www.sba.gov/aboutsba/sbaprograms/sbdc/index.html.

13. www.score.org/.

14. In general, it is unlikely that inventing entrepreneurs will use a non-disclosure agreement in this process, so it may be necessary to limit information provided.

15. For example, novel software for helping doctors track dialysis patients' health stats and for predicting the onset of dialysis-related complications does NOT have a market of $18 billion to $23 billion.

16. In most cases, such funds are restricted to technology development and testing. The fact that these funds are generally not supposed to be used for marketing or sales activities highlights why they should be separated from true sales.

17. If the technology enables fee-based consulting services that will generate immediate revenue, outside funding may not be necessary to get the business started. We note, however, that attempting to convert a "consulting" business into a "product" business is dramatically more challenging than it may appear, because the revenue and cost models are usually different enough to create internal conflicts with regard to resource allocation. The decision to organically grow a business via service revenues should be carefully weighed against the difficulty of transitioning down the road to a product sales model.

18. "Equity transactions" can be extremely complex. We simply can't go into the detail that this topic warrants; please see the "Recommended Reading" section for more information on this subject. Competent advisors and legal counsel should be consulted regarding either equity or loan transactions.

19. Professor Farritor of Nebraska Surgical has reviewed the history of Intuitive Surgical, arguably the only historical comparable for his company in the robotic surgical field. Intuitive Surgical raised $150 million in private financing prior to its IPO. Significant funds were required for FDA clearance of the daVinci™ robot, and Intuitive Surgical chose to develop a fully integrated national sales and distribution effort.

20. The process of reviewing information in preparation for an investment is generally referred to as "due diligence."

21. Inventing entrepreneurs may be surprised to learn that such a document is usually designed to protect the company (and the founders) from investor lawsuits in the event of failure. The PPM requires that investors acknowledge that they have received information that is adequate for making their decision, and that they are qualified to make this type of high-risk investment.

22. In one case, a group of angel investors got permission to share a start-up business plan with the former CEO of the start-up's biggest competitor and industry leader. It may have seemed like a risky proposition, but when the former CEO verified that the start-up company's technology outdated the market leader's technology, the angel group made the investment.

Recommended Readings

Baird, M. & Swanson J., 2003. *Engineering Your Start-Up*. Belmont, CA: Professional Publications, Inc.

Barringer, B. 2008. *Effective Business Plans*. New York: Prentice Hall.

Dorf, R and Byers, T. 2005. *Technology Ventures: From Ideas to Enterprise*. New York: McGraw-Hill.

Nesheim, J. 2000. *High-Tech Start-Up*. New York: Simon & Schuster.

Sahlman, W. 1997. How to write a great business plan. *Harvard Business Review*, July-August, 98–108.

Timmons, J., Zacharakis, A., & Spinelli, M. 2004. *Business Plans That Work*. New York: McGraw-Hill.

Van Osnabbrugge, M. & Robinson, R. 2000. *Angel Investing*. San Francisco, CA: Jossey-Bass.

11

PRIMER ON FINANCING THE TECHNOLOGY-BASED GROWTH COMPANY

OVERVIEW

No matter the technology, the team, or the market, every company must have cash to operate. Start-up companies and growth companies often need cash that they can't generate from profits (usually because there are no profits or the profits must be reinvested in research and development[1]). Growth financing, as we refer to it in this book, deals with how companies fund activities that can't be supported by internally generated cash flow. For most start-up technology companies, including the vast majority of companies founded by inventing entrepreneurs, raising funds from external sources is an absolute necessity.

The scope of this book does not allow us to cover all the nuances of private financing. In this chapter, we will discuss the key concepts associated with funding a technology-based, growth business. We'll identify the differences between angels and venture capitalists. We'll also highlight the requirements for completing early-stage private financing. Our goal is to help the inventing entrepreneur jump onto the learning curve of this relatively esoteric topic, thereby increasing her comfort with regard to a presumably unfamiliar subject.

We have extensive experience working with, advising, and observing inventing entrepreneurs. Despite the necessarily critical nature of the financing process, the success of the entrepreneur's venture is unlikely to be directly tied to the sophistication of the entrepreneur's financing expertise. We've seen entrepreneurs turn over the entire financing process to financial advisors and hired executives, and we've also seen entrepreneurs learn the necessary skills and work to raise the funds on their own. There is no question that financing is an essential aspect of the success, and arguably even the *existence,* of the technology-based growth company. Successful financial management, however, can be accomplished either by inventing entrepreneurs who develop sophisticated knowledge of corporate financing or by established professionals brought in for that purpose.

GROWTH FINANCING

Of all the organizational issues that the inventing entrepreneur must address, financing—and specifically *fundraising*—appears to be, universally, the most mysterious. This might seem odd, since most inventing entrepreneurs tend to have more than just a passing knowledge of general finance, whether through managing a research laboratory or from participating in the internal workings of a corporate budget. In fact, many academic researchers are particularly adept at raising research funds, whether through internal university mechanisms, competitive grant-writing or direct solicitation of donations. Our focus, however, is on financing events in which the funders explicitly anticipate monetary returns for their investment. This element creates the dramatic distinction between general finance, or general financial management, and financing (or fund-raising).

Fundraising is often a necessity for technology-based growth companies for two reasons. First, most of these companies, especially when they are based on technology spun out of an academic research lab, will need to fund research and development activities for some time period before producing a viable product. This funding could come from research grants such as the Small Business Innovative Research (SBIR) program. There is divided opinion on whether grant-based funding for start-up ventures is the most effective path to success,[2] but some institutional funders are comfortable cooperating with the nascent company to devise a strategy for product development and commercialization that may include grant-based funding.[3]

Second, a significant portion of technology businesses (including software companies) require extensive working capital for expansion (after completing R&D and bringing a product to market) in order to reach a break-even point.[4] This is an essential concept to understand, because companies may fail due to of capital constraints,[5,6] even if the technology has been proven and products are generating sales. The simplest way to explain this may be with the chart shown in Figure 11-1.

The data for this chart, which is purely fictional, is provided in Table 11-1. It is clear that the company initially has R&D and other expenditures associated with proving the technology and developing a sellable product. But by Year 3, the company is generating revenues—so why does it still have negative yearly cash flow? The costs of expansion are high, and expenses are usually incurred before revenues are generated, especially in growth situations. Let us consider two examples to explain this.

A small light manufacturing company near Philadelphia is operating at a reasonable profit. The Company has the opportunity to serve new clients in

FIGURE 11-1 Understanding the Fundraising Needs of a Growth Company

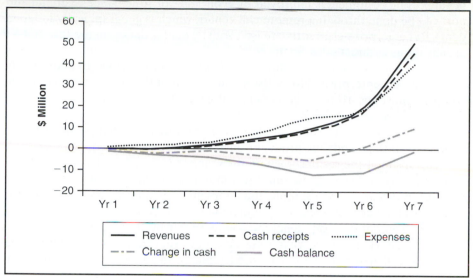

Alabama, but will have to open a new facility there to provide rapid turnaround times on orders. Unless the clients are willing to make payments in advance (which is unlikely), the company must make an investment to build a facility, obtain supplies, hire staff, and initiate manufacturing before any new sales will be generated. These same factors can be applied even if the company is considering growth within the existing facility: Increasing output will generate additional costs (staff, supplies, overhead) well before cash is generated from incremental sales. Most companies pay for supplies when those supplies are ordered; most companies pay employees on a continuous basis regardless of the work completed. But sales aren't usually billed until the finished product is sold, and sometimes actual cash from sales isn't received for weeks or even months.

Consider an additional example: An enterprise-class software company started in Chicago begins selling product in the Chicago area. The entrepreneurs and investors want to see a rapid national expansion, because the per-unit cost of

TABLE 11-1 Hypothetical Growth Company Cash Need Projection

(Millions)	*Yr 1*	*Yr 2*	*Yr 3*	*Yr 4*	*Yr 5*	*Yr 6*	*Yr 7*
Revenues	$-	$-	$2	$5	$10	$20	$50
Cash receipts	-	-	2	4	9	18	45
Expenses	1	2	3	8	15	19	40
Change in cash	(1)	(2)	(1)	(3)	(5)	1	10
Cash balance	(1)	(3)	(4)	(7)	(12)	(11)	(1)

The numbers in parentheses represent negative numbers.

supplying product is small compared to development costs, and the per-unit cost of supporting customers is improved by economies of scale (since customer support can be done through a remote call center, which is geographically independent). But enterprise-class software isn't sold by mail order or on the Internet—it usually requires direct sales. So the company hires direct salespeople, who may be earning six-figure salaries in addition to significant commissions. In addition, the sales cycle on enterprise-class software may be months, or even years. So the company must absorb those costs *before* it generates revenues. And, even when the sale is recorded, in some cases there may be delays between the actual sale and the receipt of cash—for example, a client may demand that payment be distributed over time while the product is installed and tested.

The upshot is the result shown on the graph in Figure 11-1: Even as the company expands and sales grow rapidly, it may need significant infusions of cash just to stay afloat. In the example, the company is generating solid revenues by years 4 and 5, but is still spending more than it is receiving in cash. In fact, the company generates a positive net income in Year 6, but is still operating at a net negative cash balance until Year 7. Based on this set of calculations, this company would anticipate needing at least $12 million in financing, and most likely more, even as the company begins generating profits. And this example is probably optimistic about expansion costs, since it shows revenues (and even cash receipts) exceeding expenses during rapid expansion in year 7. Many companies experience rapid expansion at a time of significant cash needs.

Most early-stage technology-based companies must raise external funds to get off the ground and move towards commercialization. The standard mechanism is private financing—usually from angels and/or venture capitalists.

But fundraising for early-stage technology companies is not an especially well-defined practice, even within the venture-capital industry. Part of the problem is that growth-company financing is, in and of itself, at least as much art as science. Consider as an example the chart shown in Figure 11-2, which depicts national-average information on the valuation of seed-round investments by institutional financiers in the United States during the "Internet bubble" years.

Does the *average* value of tech-based growth companies really vary this much quarter to quarter? Obviously, the quantitative answer is "yes." We should note that the sample we are considering is only a few hundred firms each quarter, and that there is significant variation in what technology sectors are "hot" at a given time. At the same time, at least one longitudinal trend should be obvious—that of the increasing perceived value of early-stage firms during the final years of the 1990s, which was followed by the abrupt decline in perceived value of early-stage technology firms during the stock market decline of 2000 and 2001 when the "dot.com bubble" burst. Inventing entrepreneurs need to acknowledge that, average valuations follow broader economic trends. The price investors are willing to pay depends on their perceived long-term returns from the investment as well as their opportunity cost, both of which are influenced by current market factors. Company valuations don't exist in a vacuum. The biotech company worth $5 million could be worth half as much (or twice as much) in another year, based on purely exogenous factors.

FIGURE 11-2   Median Venture-Financing Valuations 1998–2001

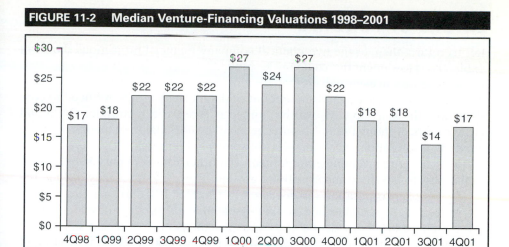

Source: "The State of Venture Capital" Powerpoint Presentation, John Gabbert, VentureOne Corporation, March 2, 2002.

In addition, even the definition of "seed state" financing is, at best, fuzzy. It could refer to the first financing event for a start-up company that has just licensed a technology from a university, or it could refer to the financing event for an established business seeking sales expansion funds, if that happens to be the first time the company seeks external capital.

From there, the analysis becomes even less clear. The data in the graph undoubtedly includes investments in companies with little or no operating history, which means that the "valuation" is based on speculative projections of future value creation, rather than objective analysis of operating history and growth. Put bluntly, there is no generally agreed-on method for calculating the exact value of an early-stage technology company. There are many techniques and many rules of thumb. So while a group of financiers would likely come to some agreement about the valuation *range*, and—given time—would certainly find some middle ground with regard to closing a deal, it's relatively unlikely that there would be a single set of defensible calculations that would lead inevitably to the final number.

Every financing round for a technology-based growth company is idiosyncratic. The management teams vary dramatically, the markets are strikingly different, and each technology is, by definition, innovative and often untested. The commercialization paths are often long and complex, and involve risks that are demonstrably not assessable. Venture funders anticipate that a significant number of the technology-based growth firms they fund will fail, despite the best efforts of everyone involved. Most of these companies present uncertain market potential, non-quantifiable risks, diffuse timelines, and no operating history to benchmark. It's not surprising, after all, that financing events are heavily negotiated events that incorporate valuations based on factors as diverse as the anticipated product market opportunity 10 years down the road as well as the current state of the equity markets.

LAYERS OF FUNDING

Let us return, then, to the hypothetical company financial projections shown in Table 11-1. How might this company be funded?

Before we can even address that, we must note that the yearly financial information shown hides a significant amount of detail. Realistically, we need to consider how the start-up costs will be funded before we can consider R&D and growth costs. Although some ventures receive institutional investments from the moment of formation, such examples are somewhat unusual.[7]

Typically, the inventing entrepreneur and other founders must supply some capital just to get the company off the ground. These expenses may include the legal costs of incorporation (as discussed in Chapter 10), early salaries for key employees, early customer and market research, early product development or prototyping, and other essential activities.[8] As an example, a recent start-up we observed in the medical-device space spent roughly $80,000 getting to a point where the team could raise funds from local angel investors. About $30,000 of that was paid out in cash, while the remainder was effectively "borrowed" from creditors (by delaying payments) and employees (in the form of deferred salaries). This process of spending funds the company doesn't have is sometimes referred to as "bootstrap finance,"[9] in homage to the concept of pulling oneself up by one's bootstraps (without visible means of support).

So it is likely that our hypothetical company is going to need some money from founders. In some cases, founders can augment their up-front investment with money from family members and close friends.[10] In more traditional businesses (such as restaurants, service firms, and even light manufacturing), these funds are often brought in as debt. But for early-stage technology firms, equity investments are more common, even for the very first funding rounds. Table 11-2 shows the primary difference between debt and equity investments. Debt represents funds loaned to a business which must be repaid, usually with interest.

TABLE 11-2 The Difference between Debt and Equity Investments

	Debt	*Equity*
Instrument	Loan	Stock purchase
Interest	Usually pays interest	May pay dividends, which are often deferred in the case of very early-stage companies
Principal Repayment	May have specific repayment period	Usually does not have repayment period
Profit Sharing	Does not share in profits	Confers ownership and share of profits
Payout Preference	Supercedes equity holders for any salvage value payments in the case of failure/bankruptcy	Paid out after debts and liabilities in the case of failure/bankruptcy

Debt is usually "secured" to the assets of the firm—if the company fails, debtholders will be first in line to receive proceeds if the assets of the company are liquidated. On the other hand, debtholders have no intrinsic right to the profits generated by the business—the business can usually pay off the debt at any time. An equity investment occurs when an investor purchases stock in a company, thus becoming a partial owner. Because equity investors are owners, they have a right to the profits (or losses) of a business. In the event the company fails, however, equity-holders ("shareholders" or "stockholders") will only have rights to the asset value of the firm after the debtholders have been paid.

Because many early-stage technology growth firms may not generate profits (or even revenues) for years, debt investments may not be viable because the firm cannot make interest or principal payments. In addition, because of the high risk of failure, most investors prefer to have the opportunity to share in the profits of the business as an owner.[11] Debt investments do not usually carry that upside reward, and thus aren't attractive to investors who know that most high-tech start-ups fail.

The hypothetical start-up company described above has many options for fundraising. The company could attempt to raise all the money in one large financing round—upwards of $12 million. Alternatively, the company could raise funds in smaller amounts over time. The advantage of raising all the money at once should be evident: It would reduce the risk associated with missed milestones and an inability to raise funds later, and it would decrease the costs that result from key management spending time raising money over the seven-year period rather than focusing on the business.

Nevertheless, there's a very good reason to consider raising smaller amounts in the short term: valuation. At the start, the company has a relatively low valuation. A common rule of thumb is that a company with a technology license from an academic institution (and not much else) is probably worth no more than $1 million.[12] Let's return to the enterprise-class software company, and imagine that the venture has attracted a reasonably strong management team (including industry professionals), and already has an alpha prototype completed. We might argue arbitrarily (but not unrealistically) that the company is worth $2 million. Assume that the company raises $12 million; the theoretical valuation of the company after raising the money is $14 million.[13] And the corollary to that conclusion is that the investors who provide the $12 million will own more than 86 percent of the company.[14]

Now consider that the company raises $1 million instead. The valuation after the round is $3 million ($2 million in value plus $1 million in cash),[15] and the investors own 33 percent. The company spends a year developing a beta prototype and installing it at a few customer sites. Looking ahead, the company needs to raise $3 million more for the next two years of operations. But because the company has hit some key milestones, the valuation of the company has increased.[16] Let's assume that the value of the company has increased to $6 million on the basis of achieving those milestones. In raising the next $3 million, the new investors get 33 percent ownership (postinvestment valuation of $9 million = $6 million value plus $3 million cash). The original owners (i.e., the owners before the first financing round), who had 67 percent after the first round, now own 45 percent.

Let us take this analysis one final step. The company continues to make progress, and at the end of Year 3 has met the financial projections and is generating revenue. Imagine that the value of the company has been doubled and doubled again—up to $36 million. Raising the final $8 million will confer 18 percent ownership on the new investors. Our founders have retained almost 37 percent ownership. This compares very favorably with the 14 percent ownership they would have retained if they had raised all $12 million up front. Obviously, staging the financing this way is more complex, more risky, and likely more time consuming. Not having the extra cash reserves means that unexpected problems or setbacks could be difficult to navigate and that the cost of missing a milestone could be very high—even potentially fatal to the business.[17]

MILESTONE-BASED FINANCING

This tension between risks and returns represents one of the most difficult challenges for inventing entrepreneurs, because the stakes are qualitatively different than those experienced in the research laboratory. Funding streams for academic research labs are multidimensional—and can sometimes be applied across programs and projects. And, of course, at the very core of the laboratory funding system are faculty salaries, which don't have to be obtained from private financiers each year.

For any business, available cash is the lifeblood of the organization. For early-stage technology firms, that lifeblood is scarce, often difficult to raise, and all too easily spent. Fundamentally, inventing entrepreneurs must make critical decisions about when to raise capital and for what specific purpose.

In nearly all situations, we encourage "milestone-based financing" for early-stage technology firms. The rationale is straightforward—funds are raised so the company can strive to complete a milestone that clearly demonstrates increased value. This should enable the company to raise more funds if needed. This appears quite intuitive, but selecting appropriate milestones is often a tremendous challenge. For many early-stage companies with truly novel technologies in the medical device and pharmaceutical sectors, there is no viable way to generate revenues within the first years of operations. Expensive regulatory hurdles must be cleared prior to marketing and sales activities. For these firms, establishing clear measures of "value creation" is especially important, because potential investors must be convinced of progress despite the lack of market validation.

Let us consider a novel medical device technology being developed for a significant application, such as heart-valve repair. The company may have performed mechanical testing or even limited animal testing, but at the current stage human testing is at least a year or two away. In the meantime, the industry is moving quickly, and both small and large firms are working on alternative solutions. The inventing entrepreneur's instinct may be to perfect the device to ensure that additional tests most accurately reflect the technology's potential. This is one option, but we cautiously suggest that there may be other paths that have a higher probability of success. By focusing on "perfecting" the product, the inventing entrepreneur may be attempting to achieve a level of theoretical functionality that doesn't match surgical utilization practice or the market need. In this scenario, the company may expend its resources on seemingly fruitful R&D that will actually lead nowhere. The company may fail entirely rather than hit a milestone that would have generated additional funding.

Imagine instead that the company chooses to freeze the design and perform specific animal tests to demonstrate functionality and safety, as well as initiating discussions with medical practitioners to establish current baseline usage trends. Doing so will create immediate feedback on usefulness, likely generating a list of both critical as well as "nice-to-have" product features. In addition, this strategy provides shorter-term milestones that can be presented for additional financing.

The inventing entrepreneur faces another dilemma: The fact that "demonstrated value" means dramatically different things to different people. For example, a venture-financing group may be focused on positive safety and efficacy results in animals and/or humans. But an organization looking at acquiring the technology (as opposed to investing in it) may be focused on the strength of the intellectual property portfolio, especially in relation to its own or competitors' patent positions. Maintaining and expanding the IP portfolio is likely critical to the long-term exit strategy, but may be perceived as less important to the entrepreneurs in the short term because of the difficulty of demonstrating milestone-based value to potential investors.

Early-stage technology-based companies must make difficult choices to prioritize milestones. Inventing entrepreneurs usually have good instincts about technology development, but investors often focus on market-based measures. The accomplishments of comparable companies in similar fields may provide a template for milestone planning. Experienced entrepreneurs, managers, and financiers will know what creates value in the appropriate industry space. This is one situation where early contact with financiers can make a big difference. It's not uncommon for an inventing entrepreneur to hear the same progress-related question over and over again from different financiers: "Have you completed an animal trial?" or "How many beta sites do you have operating?" When the same milestone crops up repeatedly in these discussions, inventing entrepreneurs should take notice.

OBTAINING PRIVATE FINANCING

"Raise money when you can, not when you need it." Most inventing entrepreneurs will appreciate this truism the moment they initiate private financing efforts. A company initiating its first financing activities is effectively desperate for cash. But the lack of assets and successes to date limits any demonstration of credibility. Financing is rarely easy, but the first funding event can be especially challenging.

Raising private funds often appears glamorous. Press releases touting financings of $20 million and reports describing quarterly venture-capital investments belie the realities of the private-capital industry. General statistics suggest that venture-capital firms fund less than 5 percent of the deals they consider, and the numbers are probably not significantly different for angel networks. Some venture-capital firms receive one hundred business plans every *week*. And angel investors can be hard to find and even tougher to pitch.[18]

Obtaining private financing for a high-tech start-up requires identifying qualified, interested investors; negotiating an appropriate valuation and deal structure; agreeing on uses of funds; and executing the deal. This process can take anywhere from a week to more than a year. Every deal is idiosyncratic; lessons learned from any one deal may have no application to another, even in the same technology field.

Assuming that an inventing entrepreneur has developed a business plan and confirmed financial projections, she can then rationally propose how much much should be raised. Then she can consider the risk-reward profile of the opportunity and make preliminary decisions on the type of financing and target investor. There are still, however, many factors to be considered: the strength of the management team, how much funding needs to be raised, the time frame for market entry, the likely exit mechanisms, and so on. Reviewing the difference between angels and venture capitalists is a good starting point for determining which route to pursue (see Table 11-3).

TABLE 11-3 Comparing Angels with Venture Capitalists

	Angels	*Venture Capitalists*
Investing Entity	Usually individuals or a special-purpose entity that funnels individual investments	Institutional fund that makes multiple investments
Entity Oversight	Limited or no management	Professional management
Underlying Investors	Usually only private investors	Private and institutional investors
Decision-Making Process	Individual decisions, often fully decentralized	Investment committee, centralized decisions
Entity Liability	Individual responsibility	Responsible to shareholders
Entity Participation	A managed angel network may participate in potential profits, otherwise none	Management participates in upside via profit sharing
Philosophy	Angel investing is primarily a participatory activity	VC can be seen as an investment instrument for passive investors
Investing Amounts	$10,000–$1,000,000 per investor; $100,000–$5,000,000 for a network	$250,000–$40,000,000 for a specific VC, $500,000–$100,000,000 for a syndicated investment
Follow-On Investments	Follow-on investment potential is usually limited	Follow-on investments can be anticipated if the company meets milestones

There are a few rules of thumb that may help inventing entrepreneurs consider whether angels (or an angel network) or a venture capitalist is the right funding target. First, how much control will the team accede to the investors? Angels, on the whole, tend to offer more hands-off oversight. Although both angels and VCs normally take board seats, venture capitalists are more likely to have activist board members, and even to demand deal clauses that give the investors control of the board in the event that key milestones are not met. Second, what is the time frame for a potential exit? Although both angels and VCs are considered "long-term" investors, angels tend to be more patient. The VC has a "vintage" fund with a set time frame for generating returns to investors; angels want to see returns as well, but they tend to be more emotionally involved in investments, often giving management the benefit of the doubt in difficult circumstances. Third, how early in the development stage is the technology or company? Although some VCs do actively seek out very early-stage opportunities (and some inventing entrepreneurs and early-stage teams have so much experience that they can obtain VC funding immediately), angels generally are prepared to invest in true seed-stage opportunities, while VCs prefer to see some risks resolved.

Despite these general rules, inventing entrepreneurs may discover that the realities of fundraising, especially early in the process, tend to direct the team toward angels, even if a VC investment would be preferable.[19] For example, VC funds are heavily concentrated in limited geographies—especially the Bay Area and Boston. When Professor Shane Farritor considered funding options for Nebraska Surgical, he learned that there was only one venture-capital firm in all of Nebraska, and that firm only invested in information-technology (IT) deals. In theory, Nebraska Surgical could have made a focused effort to obtain seed-stage funding from a VC (and the company did talk to one VC in California), but it quickly became apparent that an angel round was more viable.

One more key factor should be noted. There is a general axiom about start-ups and funding—that "good companies get funded." In general, we agree, but we would probably add some caveats. A more accurate statement might be "good companies with strong, well-connected management teams get funded." Our experience is that successful funding events often pivot on the strength of the management team and the connections that team has to angels and venture-capital groups. Nebraska Surgical is an excellent example—more than 80 percent of the company's seed-investment round came from individuals who knew the founders personally before the company was started.

The fundraising process can be straightforward, but it can also be slow and stressful. And many companies will go right to the brink of bankruptcy waiting for funds to arrive. Tomotherapy reached that point relatively early on, and salvation came from advance payments on their first product sales rather than an emergency financing event. For Conjugon, Professor Burgess's start-up commercializing a novel bacteriological technology for pharmaceutical development, a lengthy fundraising process with venture-capital firms was eventually jump-started by bringing in additional angel capital from prior investors. That story, and Professor Burgess's entrepreneurial journey is described in Profile 11-1.

Professor Richard Burgess

Professor Richard Burgess has researched oncology and genetics for more than 40 years. He sees himself as a mentor to many students as well as faculty. He has made angel investments in high-tech companies and has provided advice and direction to faculty members who started companies to commercialize novel technologies. Burgess's identity is primarily tied to a broader vision of knowledge creation and community development:

> I do a lot of what I do to learn more and to be more effective and to do community building—so that's not a selfish motive. I have to be careful not to talk about my idealistic and altruistic motives to investors, because they don't want you to do things for those reasons; they want you to be very hungry. But the fact is, I get a lot of satisfaction out of these activities independent of profit motive.

Looking back on his career and opportunities, it becomes somewhat clear that Burgess found his true calling relatively early and, more importantly, understood the strength of his affinity for that calling. He recalls an opportunity he had in the mid-1980s to leave the university to work for a West Coast biotechnology company, and his realization that he'd already found his niche:

> I almost left to become their research director. It was in Seattle, which is where my family lived—they offered me three times my university salary, but I decided that I really identified with being a scientist and a professor more than with being an executive in a biotech company.

Almost 15 years later, Professor Marcin Filutowicz approached Burgess with the concept for a revolutionary technology based on bacterial conjugation as a platform for combating antibiotic-resistant bacteria. Burgess had a relatively lengthy history of advising other researchers on technology commercialization, and he brought a more reflective approach to the technology transfer decision:

> Marcin came to me one day, probably in 2000, and said, "I have an idea and would like to bounce it off you and see what you think about whether it could be the basis for a company." And people have come to me in the past and still come to me, and to some of them I respond, "Well, I don't think that's the basis of a company, but that's an interesting technology that you should take to [a company] that's already doing that kind of stuff and license it to them." If it's a single product idea, I would say license it to someone who is in a position to develop that product and market it. But if it's a platform technology that could generate many products then I would consider telling them to go for it…. We went through a period of close to six months to a year where we brainstormed about what we could do with this idea. That was one of the most exciting times of the project—we would go sit out on Henry Mall and talk about what we could do with this—what applications we could have.

It was during that reflective process that Burgess developed a clear perspective on what the primary driver should be for inventing entrepreneurs starting their own companies:

> The other thing I did was to go to talk to some people I knew like Winston Brill who had started Agricetus … in Brill's case, the big take-home message was: "Don't do this unless you have a

fire in your belly—unless you have a passion and you really want to do this—because it isn't easy. Don't start a company unless you really want to start a company. If you're hesitant about it, it's not going to work."

This time, Burgess chose to start his own company, and found himself on the other side of the table seeking angel funding.

Throughout the process, Burgess never really wavered in his identity as a scientist and professor. He leveraged his connections around the community—from the business school to the investment community—to help get the company off the ground and to identify individuals who would form the business team. He hired a recent MBA to lead the general administrative and operational activities of the fledgling company, and once funding was secured the company began interviewing CEO candidates:

Neither one of us ever thought about going to work for the company full-time. We knew that was not our strength. We had no particular training in it. We both did and still do identify ourselves as being research scientists rather than business executives. Not all scientists feel that way; some feel they can do everything—but usually those are the ones you want to avoid, because they don't know when to let go.

One of the most fascinating aspects of Burgess's primary identity as a scientist is that, despite his own successful angel-investing activities, he clearly prefers the mindset of the investigative researcher to that of the market-driven developer:

The worst feeling I had in this whole thing was that as soon as very many people got involved as investors, they started pushing on the timeline: "You've got to get to Phase I by such and such a time"—and the image came into my mind of a ski-jumper. You can play with your bindings and adjust your skis while you're up at the top, but once you start down the ramp, if something goes wrong, you're screwed—and that's sort of the way I was feeling. You don't have enough money; if you decide to go a certain way, and it doesn't work, you probably don't have enough money to go back and change things and make it work. It's a feeling of "you're not in control." You really don't have the luxury of making course corrections—significant course corrections. I wish there was a way that the pressure wasn't on the young company quite so much … you wish that people would ignore you for about a year, and let you do logical, rational research.

In 2006, Conjugon reached a financing crisis. The company had shown good animal results for the development of a novel bacteria-based antibiotic that was intended to be effective against bacteria shown to be resistant to current antibiotics. But institutional financiers were concerned about the process of bringing a bacteria-based therapeutic through the FDA. The science and the test results seemed positive, but a lot would hinge on how risk-averse the FDA would be.

The company had raised nearly $3 million from private investors and various technology grants. But additional testing and clinical work would cost millions more. By the summer of 2006, everything seemed to hinge on a couple of venture-capital firms still evaluating the opportunity, even as the company began to cut back on expenses to conserve cash. In the fall, the company went back to its investor base of angels to raise $900,000 in bridge capital. The move paid off, and in December the company closed a $3.3 million financing that was led by Rosetta Partners of Illinois.

A lot of hard work has gone into Conjugon, and the company has had successes and failures. Burgess is optimistic, noting that the technology has developed better than

(*continues*)

he imagined was possible. But he also acknowledges that the success in such high-risk ventures can't always be predicted in advance:

> I was fortunate, the technology seems to have worked, the people we've hired have been extremely good, and generally speaking we've made the right decisions when we need to make them—but there's a lot of luck in that.

Raising private funds requires specific investment documentation, often referred to as a private placement memorandum (PPM). The use of this type of documentation represents a legal requirement to abide by government regulations regarding the sale of unregistered (i.e., not publicly traded) securities.[20] This is a relatively esoteric area of securities law, and well beyond the scope of this book. Inventing entrepreneurs who anticipate raising funds must obtain competent legal counsel to assist with this process. For example, the United States' SEC regulations are designed to protect unsophisticated investors from losing money to fraudulent opportunities.[21] A PPM or other investment documentation may protect the company (and, by extension, the founders and principals) from unwarranted lawsuits in the event that the investors are unhappy with their returns.

Most investors will expect to see a relatively robust business plan. Many investors, whether angels or VCs, will request significant additional documentation—ranging from unpublished patent filings to detailed backgrounds of the management team or summary customer/market research information. Most angel groups and VCs will not initially sign a confidentiality agreement. Although "professional confidentiality" can usually be relied on, inventing entrepreneurs are again encouraged to demonstrate some levels of caution. Stories circulate about unscrupulous private investors who obtain confidential information from technology-based start-ups under the pretext of an investment interest, but utilize the information for their own purposes.[22] The inventing entrepreneur and her team should have an agreed-upon understanding (that includes the input of counsel) regarding what information can be distributed freely and what requires a confidentiality agreement. Most angels and VCs will sign a limited confidentiality agreement if they become very serious about a potential investment.

As the information exchange continues, one side or the other will likely draft a *term sheet* that outlines the primary terms for the potential deal. In a term sheet document, key aspects of the deal will be spelled out, including valuation, total funds to be raised, board representation, investing instrument (type of equity), and milestones. The team must be prepared to negotiate this document, and eventually to negotiate a full investment agreement.[23] Inventing entrepreneurs should note that, generally speaking, venture-capital investments will require more documentation and more complex terms than angel investments. Retaining competent corporate counsel with prior experience in negotiating private equity investments is essential.

Some investments may be **tranched,** or staged. A large funding round might be split into smaller funding events over time. A company that needs $20 million might agree to $5 million now with $15 million to follow, assuming that certain specific milestones are met. In some cases, the terms for the follow-on investment will be specified in advance. A biomedical technology company we are familiar with agreed to a staged seed round of financing. Although $450,000 was invested, the company could only access the first $50,000 until the management team interacted with 10 medical device companies to confirm that a potential market existed for at least one embodiment of the company's underlying technology. The investors retained the right to reclaim the rest of the capital in the event that the market research process was unsuccessful. The management team agreed to these terms because the technology was in an extremely early stage, and because they had already had contact with some of the firms in question. This type of investment mechanism can be helpful to both management and investors, because it can create relatively clear milestones that reassure investors while keeping management focused on company-building activities rather than continuous financing efforts.

BEYOND SEED-STAGE FINANCING

There is a significant difference between financing early-stage R&D and financing growth and expansion. Successful inventing entrepreneurs who reach this latter stage should already have access to the necessary expertise and advice (corporate counsel, other members of the management team, other entrepreneurs, directors, etc.); therefore, a detailed review of this exciting and challenging stage in company development is not appropriate for this book.

One key point is relevant, however, if only to highlight prior comments about early-stage financing. A technology-based growth company looking for expansion capital has many advantages over true start-ups that are trying to raise capital: Milestones have been met, products developed, and (presumably) the IP portfolio expanded. Perhaps the two most important factors, however, are customer responses (or sales growth) and the satisfaction (and expected future participation) of previous investors. Sales growth should be self-evident, but the experience of previous investors merits some additional discussion.

In nearly all cases, new financing rounds *dilute* current investors. Earlier in this chapter this was shown mathematically by comparing the founder stakes based on whether required financing is obtained in one event or staged over time. Ownership dilution occurs when new investments decrease the ownership fraction of previous investors. In an oversimplified example, a company founder owns all 10 shares of stock in his business: He owns 100 percent of the company. He authorizes the company to sell 10 shares of stock to his partner for $10. Now each individual owns 50 percent. The share price is $1, and the total value of the business is $20. The dilution in that financing round for the founder was 50 percent.[24]

It is important to distinguish between *ownership dilution* and *value dilution*. **Ownership dilution** represents the impact on shareholder control of the organization. **Value dilution** occurs if the financing event actually decreases the total value of the previous investors' ownership stakes. Imagine, first, that in our example the original founder paid $5 for his shares of stock, and spent that money creating the business. Although the financing event (authorizing the company to sell the second share of stock) dilutes his ownership by 50 percent, the value of his own shares rises from $.50 per share to $1 share. No value dilution has occurred—to the contrary, his total ownership value has increased by 100 percent (from $5 to $10). Unless ownership control is at stake, a private investor should be willing to accept ownership dilution so long as total ownership value increases. For example, an angel investor who owns 3 percent of a start-up company valued at $1 million should be happy to see his stake drop to 2 percent if the new company valuation is $5 million. His ownership value has increased from $30,000 to $100,000.

Value dilution takes place in "down rounds," situations where the value placed on the company in the new investment round is lower than previously established. This type of event usually occurs for one or more of the following reasons:

- The company has failed to meet milestones,
- The company is facing new, unexpected challenges, and/or
- The company was overvalued in a previous financing round.

The first two factors represent implementation or environmental issues. Either can effectively increase the perceived risk of an investment in the company, or suggest that the timeframe to success will be longer than originally anticipated. The third factor, over-valuation, means that the company sold stock to investors at a price that was artificially high. In most cases, this happens because the management team was overly optimistic about the status of the company while the investors did not apply enough skepticism to the negotiating process.

Current investors usually have an acute interest in the terms of anticipated financing rounds. And their decision to reinvest or not may be a key indicator of their true perception of the progress made to date and of the company's potential for success. Let's examine this by building on our simple two-person example. The partners now want to bring in an investor, who likes the founders and believes in their technology. The partners want to raise $20 to expand the business. They would like the investor to buy 10 shares of stock for $2 each. At the end of this transaction, there would be 30 shares outstanding, for a total company value of $60. The partners' stakes would each be worth $20, and each person would own one-third of the company. While our example may seem trivial, imagine multiplying each of the share numbers by 1,000,000 to see what this might look like in a real financing situation.

In the negotiating process, however, the potential investor demands that each of the founders participate in the funding event as well. After all, she reasons, if they really believe this is a good investment opportunity, they should be willing to invest as well. She suggests that she buy seven shares, the first founder one share, and the partner two shares. If the founder and partner believe in the opportunity and have the financial resources to make the investment, the decision may be relatively simple. But from a risk-reward perspective, the founder and the partner may prefer not to invest. The founder, after all, paid $5 for 10 shares, but will pay $2 more to have a total of 11 shares. His *averaged* share purchase price has just gone from $0.50 per share to $0.64 per share. His partner's averaged share purchase price rises from $1 to $1.20. Assuming that the company is successful, they will both presumably benefit, but in participating in this new round, they effectively decrease their over-all rate of return, no matter how successful the company is.

The partner's perspective is especially important. His ownership stake will decrease from 50 percent to 40 percent, but his ownership value will increase from $10 to $24. Without the coinvestment, his ownership stake drops to 33.3 percent but his total ownership value goes from $10 to $20. By demanding that the partner rein-vest, the new investor hopes to ascertain whether the marginal difference (6.7% ownership for $4) is attractive to the partner who previously invested at $1 per share. She wants to make sure that the founder and partner believe that the current share price is still a great investment opportunity. If the founder and partner balk at reinvesting (presuming they have the financial resources to co-invest), then the new investor may suspect that she's not being offered a great investment opportunity.

Inventing entrepreneurs should take two lessons from this example. First, that some investors will want to see founders investing both effort *and cash* into the company—commonly referred to as having "skin in the game" and "sweat equity." Second, new investors want to see previous investors continue to invest in new rounds of financing, which demonstrates that current shareholders are happy with progress to date and optimistic for the future. Therefore founders and management must keep their investors constantly apprised of progress, even neg-ative progress. We often talk to entrepreneurs about developing a true partner-ship with their investors. Establishing a relationship of trust will be critical for negotiating new financing rounds and asking investors to reinvest. This is espe-cially important because current shareholders face a dilemma when negotiating new financing rounds in which they anticipate reinvesting. If the new share price is relatively low, they enjoy a "bargain" on the new investment, but experience more dilution on their previous investment. If the new share price is relatively high, they experience less dilution on their previous investment, but less of a bar-gain on the new purchase. The psychological value of previous investors' commit-ment to new financing rounds should not be underestimated.

Conclusions and Summary

Although many inventing entrepreneurs are familiar with budgets, projections, and even cost analyses, the topic of private financing is likely to be an unfamiliar and nonintuitive subject area. Terminology, practices, and expectations are, unfor-tunately, not even always consistent within the field of early-stage financing, mak-ing the learning challenge that much greater. We believe that a basic understanding of early-stage financing is essential to the inventing entrepreneur, but strongly encourage her to identify competent, experienced financial experts to guide or lead the financing process.

Endnotes

1. Realistically, most start-up ventures that license technology from an academic research facility will have no near-term revenues from which to generate profits.

2. Although competitive research grants may be described as "free money" for start-ups, there are significant drawbacks. First, each application represents a significant time investment. Second, the process cycle is lengthy—funding for approved grants may not become available until nine months or more after the original application. Finally, grants funds usually carry restrictions; at the least, U.S. federal grant funds cannot be used for sales and marketing activities. Thus some observers argue that appropriate venture funding is more efficient than grant funding.

3. Hsu, D. H. 2006. Venture capitalists and cooperative start-up commercialization strategy. *Management Science,* 52(2): 204–219.

4. The point at which the company is self-sustaining by generating enough cash from sales to cover expenses.

5. Holtz-Eakin, D., Joulfaian, D., & Rosen, H. S. 1994. Sticking it out: Entrepreneurial survival and liquidity constraints. *Journal of Political Economy,* 102(1): 53–75.

6. Van Praag, M., De Wit, G., & Bosma, N. 2005. Initial capital constraints hinder entrepreneurial venture performance. *Journal of Private Equity,* 9(1): 36–44.

7. In such cases, the inventing entrepreneur has already had successful ventures, and can count on an extremely positive reception from specific venture-capital firms. For example, Professor Stonebraker described his strong relationship with a number of venture-capital firms; that relationship-based investing can be seen in recent financings for his companies. Stonebraker's company Streambase (founded in 2003) raised $11 million in 2005 from investors that included Highland Capital Partners and Bessemer Venture Partners. His next venture, Vertica (founded in 2005), has raised $23.5 million, including money from both Highland and Bessemer.

8. Bhide, A. 1992. Bootstrap finance: The art of start-ups. *Harvard Business Review,* 70(6) 109–118.

9. Ibid.

10. Bates, T. 1997. Financing small business creation: The case of Chinese and Korean immigrant entrepreneurs. *Journal of Business Venturing,* 12(2): 109–124.

11. This is the underlying concept of "risk and reward." Venture capitalists take a significant risk when investing in an early stage technology company; they expect a commensurate reward, usually through an exit event. Banks loan money to businesses based on the expectation that interest and principal payments will be made, or that the loan can be recouped by selling of the firm's assets in the event the company fails.

12. This is an extremely unsophisticated rule of thumb, and should be used with caution. Some faculty might be thrilled to believe the technology or venture is worth this much, while others will undoubtedly be offended. And it's even more difficult to predict the expectations of the technology transfer office with regard to any given technology.

13. Valuation starts out as simple arithmetic: Preinvestment valuation + Investment = Postinvestment valuation.

14. Ownership = Investment/Postinvestment valuation.

15. Pre-money valuation + cash invested = post-money valuation.

16. Venture investors often use a rubric of doubling the value of the investment each year. This represents a 100 percent annual rate of return, which may seem incredible. Remember, however, that the venture investor anticipates that some investments

will return nothing at all. The venture investing model is based on achieving returns exceeding 20 percent per year over a portfolio of investments. If the model assumes one big success for every three complete failures, then that one success must generate 75 percent annualized returns to provide a portfolio return of 33 percent over 5 years.

17. This returns to the "risk–reward" concept. If the founders and management team are willing to take the additional risk, they may obtain higher rewards. If they fail, they may get nothing at all.

18. Keep in mind that most angel networks and venture capital groups don't even review many of the unsolicited business plans they receive. At one angel network in the midwestern United States, that we worked with 1500 business plans were submitted over four years. Of those, less than 1000 were actually reviewed, and only 50 were brought to the attention of the individual angels. In the end, only 8 investments were made.

19. VC funding may be preferable if significant follow-on investments will be required. In addition, rapid growth start-ups can benefit from the industry connections and team-building capabilities of an institutional financier.

20. In the United States, these are Securities and Exchange Commission (SEC) regulations.

21. The United States Securities Act of 1933 establishes federal information requirements to protect investors when purchasing stock that is not publicly traded. It's interesting to note that the Securities and Exchange Commission (SEC) was officially formed the following year via the Securities Act of 1934.

22. Such as to better inform an existing portfolio company or to forward the VC's own research on a separate investment opportunity.

23. A term sheet is often a few pages long. The full investment document could be significantly longer, and could include extensive supporting documentation and side agreements.

24. In that his ownership stake decreased to 50 percent of its former level.

Recommended Reading

Camp, J. 2002. *Venture Capital Due Diligence*. New York: Wiley.

Gompers, P. & Lerner, J. 1999. *The Venture Capital Cycle*. Cambridge, MA: MIT Press.

Nesheim, J. 2000. *High-Tech Start-Up*. New York: Free Press.

Van Osnabrugge, M. & Robinson, R. 2000. *Angel Investing: Matching Startup Funds with Startup Companies*. San Francisco: Jossey Bass.

PART IV

VISUALIZING THE ROAD AHEAD

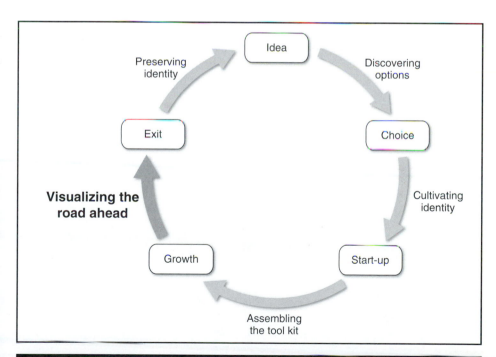

Visualizing the road ahead

Idea

Preserving identity

Discovering options

Exit

Choice

Cultivating identity

Growth

Start-up

Assembling the tool kit

Stages in the Entrepreneurial Process

CHAPTER 12

THE MANAGERIAL CHALLENGE

OVERVIEW

To grow a technology-based start-up company, the inventing entrepreneur must interact with, and potentially manage, a team of talented individuals. This chapter focuses on the relationship between the innovator and the management team— in other words, the inherent challenges faced by the innovator who serves in a role of significant responsibility at the company.[1] Our goal is to help the inventing entrepreneur carefully consider her options for identifying *who* will lead the commercialization effort and in what capacities.

Randy Cortwright understands this issue as well as anyone. He formed Virent in 2002 on the basis of his biofuels engineering work at the University of Wisconsin. At the time, a significant aspect of Virent's operational plan had been to leverage the expertise of a professional management team. The connection seemed perfect—the fuel cell division of a large energy firm was being ramped down by corporate headquarters, and a group of qualified, experienced managers were excited and enthusiastic about transitioning to Cortwright's high-potential start-up. But the "perfect match" didn't work out, because the culture and experience of a start-up differs dramatically from the world of large corporations, and corporate managers often find that transition challenging or impossible. Cortwright reflects on how this changed his perspective on human resources in the high-tech start-up world:

> People can tell you how they think you should do it, but really you've got to go and talk to someone who has done it. I am starting to differentiate people when they come to me and say they want to be involved. I find out what their background is—why would they be value-add? That's where we faced a stumbling block. We brought in

people who hadn't done it before — they thought they knew how to do it, but they had blind spots; they didn't know what they didn't know, and that hurt us in the beginning. That's what I would do differently now — to bring in someone with experience.

In this chapter, we'll discuss why management is critical for the high-technology start-up company, and why the inventing entrepreneur needs to carefully consider managerial issues early on in the process. We'll focus on possible roles for the inventing entrepreneur, as well as how she can effectively interact with "professional management."

WHY MANAGEMENT IS IMPORTANT

The importance of skilled management for a start-up can't be overstated. Endless real-life situations have been documented in books, case studies, and coursework. We teach MBA students that most investors will read the "Management" section of a business plan immediately after the executive summary — and some will read it *before* the executive summary. When Nebraska Surgical prepared to present to a premier Boston venture capital firm, they were encouraged to put the management bios on the first page of the PowerPoint presentation, even before the product or business description.

Expert practitioners and investors suggest that management is the primary element of a successful start-up: "Though a good market is critical also, without an exceptional management team even the most ideal market cannot be fully exploited."[2] In effect, management is the one fully mutable variable in the start-up equation. Each management team will bring a unique set of skills (and flaws) to the commercialization process. The team will determine every remaining aspect of the business: location, target market, financing plan, product development and roll-out, and customer management. No two management teams will function exactly alike. Most managers will make decisions based, in part, on their decision-making experiences in the past. In the case of Virent, the management team transplanted from a large corporation was unable to make effective decisions that required "start-up" thinking.

One inventing entrepreneur, considering the possibility that he would ultimately own less than 10% of his company in the long-run, expressed dismay: "I've spent almost 10 years working on this technology," he stated. "Why won't I be rewarded for that?"[3] The stark answer is that while the market values the underlying technology, the market places the majority of value on the adoption of the technology in the marketplace.

Most inventing entrepreneurs reap the rewards of technological achievement within their established market (i.e., the academic and/or scientific market) on the basis of the work they have done discovering or developing innovative science and technology. Such rewards are usually measured in the following areas: tenure and other leadership positions, journal publications, citations, academic awards, and, in some cases, monetary awards. But to generate the financial rewards that are the primary measure of market success, the technology must achieve significant market adoption. Statistics show that inventors and technology transfer offices rarely own more than 10% of stock in ventures at the time the company reaches IPO; it is relatively safe to presume that commercialization execution probably represents 90 percent or more of the technology's value creation in the market.

Consider the following examples. In the case of most novel human therapeutics, more than $100 million will be spent to bring a drug to market (the industry average cost of development, including the cost of drugs that fail to reach market, is close to $1 billion per new drug). This almost certainly dwarfs the relevant development expenditures within the research institution *prior* to licensing. For a novel software technology, the "to market" costs can be considerably lower than for a therapeutic, especially in the world of Internet-based software downloads. This is because the upfront costs for software start-ups tend to be relatively low, consisting primarily of programmer time; full execution of a software sales model, however, usually requires significant customer support expense. Again, we consistently see that commercialization costs dramatically exceed the costs of early development within academic structures. Common sense suggests that larger investments demand larger shares of returns. Whether or not, at some philosophical level, there exists some measure of true value for the relevant contributions (i.e., whether the early discovery is in some way, inherently more valuable than the ability to sell products to customers), in the end, the market mechanisms place the majority of rewards with the commercialization process.

As noted, extensive anecdotal evidence suggests that venture capitalists and angel investors consider management the most important aspect of the business in their investment decision. Randy Cortwright would agree (see Profile 12-1). Professor Farritor emphasizes the same issue: "I believe in the mantra of 'people, people, people.' I'm starting to recognize that's really the most important aspect of the whole process."

INVENTING ENTREPRENEUR PROFILE 12-1

Randy Cortwright

Decades of research and development on "clean" fuels has generated relatively modest progress, especially in terms of market adoption. Marginal improvements in solar and wind power have not led to a revolution in energy generation systems. Novel methods for biomass and other waste-product conversion technologies have yet to significantly impact oil and gas dependence. For Randy Cortwright, a chemical engineer, what started as an energy production research project funded by Cargill changed into a venture-capital funded start-up (Virent Energy Systems, Inc.) trying to jump-start the hydrogen economy. Of course, Cortwright recalls, it didn't start that way: "I wanted to get my Ph.D and go and be a college professor someplace. But [during] my first year I met my future wife, and she was starting at the medical school…. She wasn't going to leave Wisconsin. So I rearranged my plans."

(continues)

Virent provides an excellent example of the potential travails of a start-up. At first, everything came together beautifully. Cortwright formed a corporate entity and obtained the license to the technology from UW-Madison. He learned that the local subsidiary of a national fuel research company was being wound down, and the local managers were enthusiastic about working with Cortwright to build Virent. Virent obtained state and federal grant funding to set up shop in a local incubator. Cortwright built a subscale demonstration model that produced hydrogen efficiently at low temperatures from biomass. And the United States Patent Office was responding favorably to the company's broad claims about novel methods and processes. Cortwright explains:

> We started talking about it in fall 2001, and then got more serious in spring 2002. [We] incorporated on the first of June, 2002. Initially [my partner] was working part time at Enable Fuel Cell Corporation (Enable); I was part time at the university. We started out being a virtual corporation—we started out writing a number of proposals to the federal government. We had numerous opportunities for funding from SBIRs and ATP programs, Department of Defense, the U.S. Department of Agriculture, the National Science Foundation, and the Department of Energy. In addition we had support from the state of Wisconsin. We didn't have a facility until fall of 2002. Just a small room, reasonable rent, that sort of stuff. And by that time [my partner] had brought in a number of other people—Enable had actually gone under, so we had people with business development and business experience. We got our first SBIR started January 2003—and then [got] funding from the state as well.

But the road wasn't as smooth as it looked. Virent needed private capital, and the team began seeking angel funding. The process exposed the company's unanticipated weakness—the outside managers:

> Virent had two lives—one was the start-up part. It turned out that the people we hired as management were not experienced entrepreneurs. They had all come from other larger companies—well-financed businesses—that's what they were used to working with. So when we went to start doing a funding round, ... we weren't getting much traction as far as financing was concerned. Then I began talking to the angel investors; the feedback was that we had intriguing technology, very early-stage, but our management team wasn't going to get us there. Essentially, we let go of the management team that had come over from Enable.

This type of situation is never easy. To Cortwright's credit, he identified the problem and addressed it directly. His scientific training may have made the necessary transition a little easier:

> We originally brought that group in because we believed they were experienced with business, and then we found out we weren't financeable because of them. Initially you throw all your trust onto them, and if you find out they're not doing their job, then you have to fix it. That's the part about being a scientist: Okay, mistake made, we have to fix it and move on from there.

The resurrection of Virent was relatively swift. The management team was released, and Cortwright identified a qualified start-up entrepreneur to serve as interim CEO. The combination of Cortwright's passion and technical expertise and the CEO's professional experience and knowledge began to pay off:

> We were able to make presentations that people could get excited about, because we had technology that could be world changing. Not only can we generate hydrogen, but we can generate fuel gas from renewable resources that will have the potential in the future to provide power around the world—that's not using oil, and that's not producing net CO_2 content. That's when it started getting exciting. We could go to investors; we could sell them that story; they could say, "Yes you have an intriguing technology, you have the people there"—mainly they were looking at [the new CEO]—"that could make this go."

Cortwright learned two critical lessons—understand the market and identify key leaders. When asked about how he would advise a new inventing entrepreneur, his response focused on the importance of talking to customers as early as possible:

> Do your homework. You've got the technology—start talking to your potential customers. They're the ones that are going to buy it. You may think you know what the technology is good for, but no one may want to buy that. Go out and get [invited to give scientific] talks; start learning their problems: Could your technology solve their problems? That's the problem that we had as a company—it's a neat idea, in the future, renewable energy—but there wasn't anybody out there; there wasn't a marketplace.

The reward for bringing about the transition in management teams has been obvious. In June 2006, Cargill, Honda, and venture-capital firms invested $7.5 million in the company. In 2007 the company received an additional $2 million grant from the USDA and DOE, adding to the more than $4.5 million already received in federal grants. In the end, however, Randy is philosophical about the progress of the company to date and his own rationale for taking the plunge:

> Congratulate me in five years. If we make it through five years, it means there was something there with the technology. If we're still around with the company then I'll feel we accomplished something. I'd be really mad if I hadn't tried to do this, and somebody else did and they hit the market. If I don't do it, someone else will do it. Why not me? I'm the one that knows the most about it. Let's do it. That's how we got started.

VISION AND IMPLEMENTATION

When asked about strategy and prioritization, the CEO of one high-tech start-up told us, "First I deal with the things that can kill the company today. Then I deal with the things that can kill the company tomorrow. After that, I work on stuff that's merely urgent." The reality of high-tech start-up management can consist of an almost endless series of firefights. Large organizations often have resources to support emergency management: rapid data collection and analysis, historical precedent and knowledge, a cadre of experienced managers, and cash for accessing ad hoc expertise and raw manpower. A start-up may only have the time and skills of the management team and the expertise of a limited set of part-time or ad hoc advisors. We often find that the strategic vision and implementation at a technology start-up (including planned execution and firefighting) are concentrated in the judgment and abilities of a few individuals—sometimes only one. The capabilities of that individual or small group will drive the success or failure of the endeavor.

No amount of strategic vision can guarantee faultless ramp-up of a high-tech start-up company. Implementation skills alone aren't sufficient for driving rapid growth, because high-tech start-ups must be flexible enough to adapt to changing conditions, humble enough to admit judgment errors, and visionary enough to see beyond mistakes to new opportunities. The successful high-tech start-up CEO will have the vision to chart a path from the company's current situation to the long-term goal as well as the implementation skills to move the organization nimbly and cost-effectively down that path.

MANAGEMENT CHARACTERISTICS AND EXTERNAL PERCEPTION

We have yet to see a completely satisfactory explanation of the management skill set necessary to lead a growth business, especially in the high-tech sector. In addition it is difficult to suggest ways for inventing entrepreneurs to effectively test for those skills, either in themselves or other potential managers.

One possible starting point is to consider how outside investors will evaluate the management team. Some studies suggest that top management teams serve as a proxy for lack of information about the future of the venture; in other words, good teams signal good opportunities and consequently good value for money.[4–6] Empirical research confirm our conversations with venture financiers, suggesting that the criteria of highest perceived value are the following:

- Prior experience in managing successful growth-oriented start-ups
- Prior experience in managing a company in a related or similar industry or sector
- Prior experience in bringing a product to market

While successful entrepreneurial executives are most preferred, financiers often favor someone who has experienced failure as a technology entrepreneur to someone who hasn't been through the process at all. This "tolerance for failure" may seem counterintuitive, but it makes particular sense in the context of technology ventures. First, running a technology start-up is difficult—not necessarily because it involves higher mathematics or advanced logic skills—but because it is complicated and fast-moving. Leading a technology venture requires knowledge across numerous functional and market areas as well as the ability to prioritize a seemingly endless array of activities and issues.

Second, technology start-ups are particularly sensitive to human resource issues. Within the small start-up team, every player may be critical. Incentives, oversight, feedback, and direct management in this type of situation appears to be dramatically different (and usually more stressful) than human resources management at almost any other type of firm. Venture capitalists often state that people are the single biggest headache associated with successfully building technology-driven companies. Failed entrpreneurs have direct experience with the worst situation: managing a team in a technology venture that is going under. Presuming that the collapse isn't completely attributable to that manager's poor decisions, it's likely that he will know how to respond under fire in another opportunity. Nesheim explains: "Prior bankruptcy experience is valuable; failure has its rewards. Mature investors have seen six out of ten of their children go under. They know that it was not all the fault of every employee; the big breaks account for a lot of the outcome. Therefore . . . top managers from defunct companies are actively recruited to new startups."[7]

Finally, managing a high-tech start-up appears to be physically, emotionally, and psychologically demanding. The individuals who choose to repeatedly tackle such missions probably enjoy the challenge and feel driven to succeed under those conditions. Thus, it is advantageous to the portfolio investor to prefer a manager (even a failed manager) with previous experience over a high-potential but inexperienced manager because the experienced manager (1) will have a head start on the specialized knowledge required to grow a start-up, (2) will already have many of the necessary relationships in place and presumably can build more, and (3) apparently enjoys the work enough to do it more than once.

Financiers may not reject an investment opportunity purely on the basis of management's lack of direct experience. At the same time, the savvy inventing entrepreneur will carefully review the necessary skills and experiences when considering her own role at the company and when identifying and recruiting outside managers. Perhaps the most colorful explanation of a necessary management characteristic for an entrepreneur comes from Wilson Harrell, who over the course of his lifetime started over 100 companies:

> My own belief is that the ability to handle terror, to live with it, is the single most important—and, yes, necessary—ingredient of entrepreneurial success. I also believe that it is the lonely entrepreneur living with his or her personal terror who breathed life into an otherwise dull and mundane world.[8]

RISK REDUCTION

When reviewing the literature and talking to entrepreneurs and investors, we are sometimes surprised at the lack of emphasis on management's role in risk reduction. We suspect two reasons for this common omission. First, most of us implicitly incorporate risk management within specific business functions (such as technology development or financial planning). Second, technology start-ups are so inherently risky that the concept of explicit "risk reduction" as a strategic planning element may seem like hubris. Randy Komisar says the words that no one wants to hear:

> If you're brilliant, 15% to 20% of the risk is removed. If you work 24 hours a day, another 15% to 20% of the risk is removed. The remaining 60% to 70% of business risk will be completely out of your control.[9]

Commercializing technology engenders personal risks (personal liability, professional reputation, etc.) as well as more general organizational and technological risks (poor execution damns the technology to irrelevance, poor financial planning limits the organization's ability to grow, etc.). Management selection and function can mitigate or exacerbate any and all of these risks.

For example, some inventing entrepreneurs clearly value their professional reputation above everything else. Others are prepared to do anything to ensure that a novel technology achieves utilization. Few inventing entrepreneurs, however, actively consider the potential risks associated with personal liability or the impact of such risks on family and lifestyle. It is generally not possible to quantify either the probability function of these risks or the entrepreneur's risk preferences, but our observations suggest that most inventing entrepreneurs can identify a specific issue or goal which trumps all other considerations (few inventing entrepreneurs will sacrifice professional reputation at almost any price, for example). This issue is the flip side of the goal identification discussed previously (please see Chapter 2, in particular the five Foundations of Entrepreneurial Purpose), and should primarily be used as a "sanity check." If the inventing entrepreneur's greatest perceived risk is her academic reputation, then the decision to serve as CEO of a start-up while still serving as full-time faculty may warrant revisiting.[10] As a corollary, the inventing entrepreneur may want to consider how to balance the risk of the failure of the growth business against the potential success of a smaller, bootstrapped company. The commercialization of a novel technology creates inherent risks; rapid growth generates additional inherent risks. Randy Komisar suggests that the majority of the risks associated with a new enterprise are out of the control of the entrepreneur, but the early decisions about growth strategy and management can significantly change the risk profile of the venture.

MANAGEMENT MODELS

The three most common management models we identified in our interviews and research are the following:

- **The Inventor as Recruiter**—a model in which the inventing entrepreneur identifies an external group (whether a venture capitalist, incubator, or other mechanism) to form a new entity to license the technology

- **The Inventor as Advisor**—a model in which the inventing entrepreneur participates in the formation of a new entity to license the technology but serves primarily in an advisory role (possibly as a part-time CTO/CSO or Advisory Board member and, in some cases, as one of the company founders)

- **The Inventor as Manager**—a model in which the inventing entrepreneur serves as a senior manager of the entity that will initiate commercialization.

We interviewed many inventing entrepreneurs who have been (or are) CEOs of the entity commercializing their technology. Some were reluctant and some were enthusiastic about leading the venture. None felt they had been well-prepared for the role, and all described difficulties with regard to prioritization and time management. Many noted the sacrifices necessary to lead a commercial entity, as well as the unexpected responsibilities associated with it. In Table 12-1, we note some of the advantages and disadvantages of each management model, along with some of the most significant issues the inventing entrepreneur will likely face.

Obviously, no one model is preferable or optimal across all contexts, but a rational review might suggest one model over the others. The inventing entrepreneur should carefully evaluate her personal circumstances and technology affinity, as well as the likely difficulty of commercialization.

TABLE 12-1	Management Models for Inventing Entrepreneurs		
	Recruiter Role	*Advisor Role*	*Manager Role*
Advantages	• Least time involvement (once team is assembled) • Retain current position	• Active involvement in technology development and positioning • Retain current position	• Active involvement in company strategy and execution • Potential for additional financial rewards • Opportunities for learning and challenge
Disadvantages	• Least control • Financial rewards may be limited by license agreement • Possibility for discontent with licensee activities or direction	• Time commitment will likely be higher than anticipated, especially at the start • Sense of control may be illusory	• Will probably be necessary to leave academic/corporate position • Significant time commitment • Potential for negative long-term financial and career implications • Unanticipated conflicts and stresses
Questions to Ask	• Will I be happy turning over the technology to others? • How important is my current position and research stream? • What other obligations do I have (family, etc.) that will be influenced by this decision? • Can I honestly say that I understand the change in lifestyle that may be required?		

It is critical to note the difference between "management" and "control." Some inventing entrepreneurs are very focused on maintaining control of their technologies (and the commercialization vehicle and process). The reality is that "managing" commercialization is not synonymous with "controlling" it. Professor Church's comments are particularly valuable, especially in the context of technologies that will require venture capital:

I don't think [inventing entrepreneurs] should have delusions about any kind of control. They should expect to lose control almost immediately. If they are control freaks it will be wrested from them even faster. I would definitely try to reduce their expectations in that regard. Clearly, you want leadership, you want to make decisions without waffling, but you don't want necessarily to expect that everything is going to go your way. It's a lot of consensus building—finding middle ground. Being CEO is less about what *you* think than about making a decision that's somewhere in the middle of everybody—and if they think that if they are CEO they are going to be some kind of dictator, they should get over it.

INTERACTING WITH PROFESSIONAL MANAGEMENT

In discussing this topic, we aren't suggesting that inventing entrepreneurs should expect more or less general interpersonal conflict with business managers than would be expected in any commercial environment. Inventing entrepreneurs, however, bring two specific issues to the corporate management environment that don't factor into most traditional management interactions. First, the inventing entrepreneur may have a personal stake (affinity) in the innovation or novel technology. Second, the inventing entrepreneur may have a larger ownership stake than most (or all) of the other employees.

The reality is that most inventors who participate in commercial propagation of their technology do not stay with the corporate entity for more than a few years.[11] Within the general business context this may not be unusual or unexpected—management change at corporations is a regular, accepted process. The media, however, has highlighted counterexamples such as Michael Dell, Bill Gates, and Larry Page and Sergei Brin, which may lead novice inventing entrepreneurs to perceive these individuals as "normal" instead of exceptions. In addition, the inventing entrepreneur may assume that since she discovered or developed the underlying innovation, she will forever retain the ability to influence or even drive the commercialization process. Such an outcome is, in fact, unlikely. There are many examples of inventing entrepreneurs who work closely, comfortably, and successfully with businesspeople and professional managers for extended periods of time. More commonly, however, the inventing entrepreneur's involvement in commercialization ends well before corporate exit event occurs, and circumstances of minor or significant conflict with management are unfortunately common. We delve into this topic to provide insights and suggestions that may improve the inventing entrepreneur's commercialization experience. Given the importance of management to the success of the venture, it is incumbent upon the inventing entrepreneur to have appropriate expectations for interacting with or participating on the management team.

NATURAL CONFLICTS BETWEEN FOUNDERS AND PROFESSIONAL MANAGEMENT

Regardless of the management model implemented, most inventing entrepreneurs find themselves in conflict with senior management at one time or another. One reason is that technology commercialization differs from technology research. Sal Braico, the CEO of ConjuGon commented:

> The scientists (at the university lab) are constantly coming up with new ideas: new ways to use the technology and novel theoretical ideas on

how to improve the technology. They constantly ask us, "Can you work on that?" And the answer is "No," because we've got to stay focused on the key product and target. We've only got so many resources, and if we don't get that product and target right, there may not be a second product. There are too many things that can go wrong at a tech start-up; we can't be going off in all directions like a research lab.

Some inventing entrepreneurs see a start-up as a natural extension of the academic research laboratory. Like the research lab, it has income (grants and sales), scientific staff (often "graduated" from the academic lab), and multiple projects. Some start-ups are effectively hamstrung by inventing entrepreneurs who cannot separate the company from their labs. In effect, the company becomes another concept testing site and grant-writing base instead of the launch pad for market-ready products. This can be a natural source of conflict when professional management has been brought in to focus on market commercialization.

Equity ownership may generate conflict focused on dilution effects and fundraising. As discussed in Chapter 11, entrepreneurs often misunderstand the implications of ownership dilution in early-stage financing. Whether appropriately or not, inventing entrepreneurs may perceive dilution more negatively than management, and may balk at financing opportunities management would otherwise accept.

Hiring and firing may also become flash points for conflict. The highly creative researcher who excelled in the lab may not have a clear role in the business; the inventing entrepreneur may struggle to develop strong relationships with business staff hired into the firm. The inventing entrpreneur may disagree with management about which skills and talents are most critical in new hires, or even about which active employees are adding the most value to the business.

The last potential area of notable conflict is culture. Culture conflicts encompass a broad range of issues (including, arguably, the previously mentioned points as well), but usually center on the following issues: perks and expense policies, treatment of junior staff, and organizational purpose. Obvious differences between research laboratories and corporate environments can create friction. While academic settings may offer certain perks uncommon at a start-up company (flexible hours, extensive infrastructural support, status, generous sick leave and vacation policies, etc.) the corporate environment sometimes yields other types of bonuses (better travel accommodations, more lenient expense reimbursement policies, and so on) that can seem extravagant or unnecessary. While a collegial environment may be the norm within the lab, the corporate office may be a no-nonsense, fast-moving setting. As Professor Handelsman noted, within the academic research lab she has the freedom to train a student researcher over a four-year time frame. Corporate management probably will not be willing to make that type of investment in a new research scientist, and high-potential employees who don't perform within a one- to two-year period (or less) may be asked to leave.

Finally, for many inventing entrepreneurs, the technology being commercialized may be only one development effort within a broad academic research stream established to generate scientific knowledge over the long-term. The company commercializing the technology, however, will likely focus on that technology or a few applications of that technology, specifically for the purpose of generating financial rewards relatively quickly. Our observations suggest that, this conflict may be so obvious that it is not discussed.

CREATING MUTUAL INCENTIVES FOR SUCCESS

The responsibility for aligning goals and incentives falls to both the inventing entrepreneur and corporate management. Our direct experience and observations strongly suggest that corporate management believes that the venture's long-term goals (profitability and exit)—along with the appropriate incentives (financial rewards and the added value of reputation and pride)—are self-evident. As noted previously, most inventing entrepreneurs feel that technology adoption is the primary long-term commercialization goal, with financial rewards an important but secondary outcome.

When the inventing entrepreneur chooses to serve as management, *she implicitly accepts the corporate goals and incentives structure of the company, especially if she becomes a significant equity shareholder, officer, or member of the Board of Directors*. In the event that she arranges for external financing, she is *explicitly* accepting those goals and incentives—unless she strikes an unusual deal with highly altruistic investors. On the other hand, if she chooses the "advisor" or "recruiter" model described earlier in this chapter, she has effectively approved those goals and incentives for the team and the technology, without implicitly or explicitly affirming her own allegiance to them. She may wield a significant amount of influence over the effort and intend to benefit from the financial success of the endeavor (via equity, stock options, and/or consulting fees), but she may be able to retain the "academic" perspective on long-term purpose (adoption vs. financial returns). She may also bear little fiduciary responsibility to shareholders.[12]

The only viable process for aligning goals and incentives is discussion and negotiation. Inventing entrepreneurs can initiate this process within the context of early strategic and financial planning.[13] In the best cases, the financial incentives that drive management can be closely linked to adoption goals that motivate the inventing entrepreneur. For example, management compensation can be closely linked to revenue generation (or in a more extreme example, simply to customer utilization patterns). Conflict associated with incentives will probably emerge around two issues: first, the fact that customer adoption is a necessary but not sufficient condition for maximizing long-term financial rewards, and second, the company's strategy for how it would react in financial straits. The first issue is relatively straightforward. Consider the following example: If the inventing entrepreneur's primary goal is broad utilization, then she might advocate establishing a low price point that encourages adoption by every potential customer. Management, on the other hand, may believe that the company has a temporary monopoly opportunity, and may choose to price the product significantly higher, generating larger profits from fewer customers.

The second issue (how the company will respond to financial difficulties) requires more careful thought. Most high-tech start-ups will struggle, and many will fail. Although no entrepreneurs start a venture expecting it to fail, some "Plan B" thinking may be valuable, whether early on or as the venture develops. And even if the venture is successful, it's very likely that detours and difficulties will slow or even stop the development path at one time or another. "Just-in-time" (JIT) manufacturing clearly has its place, but "just-in-time" strategic and financial planning may be a different story. JIT is sometimes described as "lowering the water level to see the rocks" in order to identify bottlenecks and manufacturing inefficiencies. This same process applied to strategic and financial planning may reveal fundamental differences in goals and motivation at a time when the company needs relatively quick action. If the company experiences financial difficulties—whether due to delays in development or production, or simply because of unexpectedly slow adoption rates—management may need to make rapid decisions about resource allocation (expenditures) and resource access (financing). Depending on the circumstances, the inventing entrepreneur and corporate management may have dramatically different perspectives on raising additional funds and on how to spend those funds.

For example, the inventing entrepreneur might prefer to raise as little money as possible to protect her ownership stake, while management prefers to raise as much money as possible to ensure the greatest chance of hitting milestones and bringing a product to market. Alternatively, management might prefer to bring a suboptimal product to market as early as possible to begin generating revenues while the inventing entrepreneur would prefer to perfect the product (since her affinity to the technology affects her willingness to have a suboptimal product associated with her research or name). In another circumstance, she might prefer to retrench the company in research and development while management is prepared to terminate key R&D resources to conserve cash. Resolving these types of situations as they occur is the most common outcome; some conflict could be avoided with early discussions about strategy and goals.

Separating Personal Issues from Business Issues

Our final note on interaction with management involves separating "personal" issues from "business" issues. Our discussions with academic innovators tend to reveal deep affinities for their research, their institution, and their technological achievements. We believe that most of these affinities spill over into a venture formed to commercialize those technological achievements. In contrast, we note that professional management brought in to execute the commercialization effort must, by definition, have a significantly lower affinity for such technological achievements: It is likely they will not have worked with the same technology in the past, may be new to the community, and may not even personally identify with the market need.

While corporate management may clearly see the business operations as "personal" (in that they are tied to operations by responsibilities and potential rewards), we anticipate that corporate management will not, for the most part, feel as strong a personal tie to the underlying technology. In this scenario, it's possible the inventing entrepreneur will take certain setbacks personally, while the management team will not. Alternatively, management may be anxious to establish corporate partnerships, raise capital, and disperse decision-making authority; the inventing entrepreneur with high affinity may have difficulty "letting go" of the reins. These distinct responses can prove divisive: The inventing entrepreneur may not feel that management takes such transitions seriously enough, while the management team may see evidence of "founder's syndrome."

It would be easy to suggest that the management team's perspective is more appropriate; they are functioning within a set of established rules. And the inventing entrepreneur does bear responsibility for acknowledging the change in norms once a technology enters the commercial setting. This reasoning ignores the human reality of personal attachment and the value of the passion and commitment that is usually necessary to drive market change. Randy Komisar notes:

> As I tell the MBA classes I sometimes address, it's the romance, not the finance, that makes business worth pursuing. You need something . . . that by itself will inspire you, and others with you, to prevail, no matter what adversity arises. In my experience, the promise or hope of money by itself won't do.[14]

Regardless of the management model utilized, however, the primary responsibility for separating business and personal issues on a day-to-day basis falls to the inventing entrepreneur, because the inventing entrepreneur has signed off on the commercialization process. We simply note that, without that individual's passion and drive, it is unlikely the business would exist at all.

THE INVENTOR AS MANAGER

The inventing entrepreneur who decides to serve as a senior manager will encounter additional challenges. Three key issues we identified are (1) conflict of interest, (2) development of managerial skills, and (3) time management.

CONFLICT OF INTEREST

As technology transfer offices have become sophisticated with regard to start-ups, they have also become adept at handling conflict-of-interest issues. Inventing entrepreneurs who commercialized technologies 20–30 years ago often found themselves immersed in ad hoc, highly contentious conflict-of-interest discussions with colleagues, university administration, and sometimes even non-university organizations. Most universities had not established clear oversight mechanisms to manage conflict of interest. These ad hoc discussions could become heated if professional colleagues felt that the concept of financial reward was inherently repugnant to the "pure scientist." Although similar sentiments may still surface, most institutions now have conflict-of-interest committees in place with well-defined procedures for managing everything from corporate contributions to research to the appropriate utilization of student and staff resources on subsidized or contracted activities. "Top-down" pronouncements from university administrators have often set a tone supporting commercialization activities and the appropriateness of financial rewards both for the researchers and the institution.

Our advice to nascent inventing entrepreneurs within academic institutions is straightforward. As soon as they determine that they will participate in technology commercialization (in whatever role: advisor, CTO, CEO, or other), they must inform the appropriate individuals within the institution (most likely the department head). If inventors consider the start-up option following invention disclosure to the technology transfer office, the inventor should inform the department chair or unit head. In most cases, managing conflicts of interest involves written statements and plans to separate commercial work from academic research. In one example, a researcher was simply required to state that he would not allow a commercial entity to access university resources (such as scientists, students, or technicians). Most universities also have policies that define how much time faculty members can spend on non-university activities. Inventing entrepreneurs should make certain they understand these regulations.

AUGMENTING THE MANAGERIAL SKILL SET

Most inventing entrepreneurs who choose to participate in managing a business will discover gaps in their knowledge and skill sets. These are especially common in administrative areas involving government filings and regulations, organizational documents, human resource administration, and general accounting and finance. For the most part, the management tools necessary can be outsourced or learned from books or instruction. Service providers, advisors, consultants, Small Business Development Centers, mentors, and sometimes government offices can be tapped to educate the inexperienced business manager.

We believe, however, that leading a commercial entity differs significantly from leading a research laboratory. Accessing the necessary skill set, however, is not as simple as outsourcing human resource administration. One suggestion would be to participate in a subsidiary role before taking on a senior management role. Professor Stonebraker notes that after serving in technology leadership roles for his first two start-up ventures, he was prepared to take on a senior operational management role if necessary:

> It's difficult to recruit a president at the very beginning; presidents are notoriously risk averse, so you get going with whatever team you can assemble, and worry about the rest of the team over time. For start-ups

3 and 4 I was acting president for the first year. In the Ingres days, I didn't know anything. By the time I founded Illustra, I was perfectly competent at being VP of engineering, and during the first year of any company that's the job position of key experience: Keep expenses down; set the tone and culture of the company . . . so I'm perfectly capable of doing that. The place where I'm not very good is that I don't know how to run a sales organization.

There are other mechanisms for developing leadership skills. Small Business Development Centers and most business schools (and executive education programs) offer leadership classes, sometimes in conjunction with project management training courses. Securing a mentor's assistance and advice for oversight and feedback can be an effective learning process. As previously noted, entrepreneurs consistently note the importance of mentoring as well as the challenge of finding an appropriate mentor. We suspect, however, that in many cases this lack of mentoring is due primarily to a failure to initiate and implement a comprehensive search for help. In discussions with business leaders and former entrepreneurs, we have generally observed interest in helping new entrepreneurs, and we've seen countless examples of active and former executives mentoring inexperienced entrepreneurs. This may suggest how important extensive networking is—both to new entrepreneurs and to a developing technology community in general.

PRIORITIZATION AND TIME CONSTRAINTS

In *High-Tech Start-Up,* John Nesheim provides some information suggesting that technology entrepreneurs, on average, do not work more hours than *Fortune 500* managers. He does note, however, that there may be additional stresses on entrepreneurs—the same stresses described by Wilson Harrell as "The Terror." Nesheim's commentary on the impact of technology entrepreneurship on family relationships and general mental health should be read by every technology entrepreneur. We did not attempt to quantify work hours, nor did we attempt to obtain qualitative measures of either stress or "terror" on inventing entrepreneurs. We do, however, want to note a few additional aspects of technology entrepreneurship that may help prepare the academic researcher considering the entrepreneurial route.

Our own anecdotal experience and observations offer a slightly different calibration from Nesheim's. We have seen that the start-up executive often cannot cleanly separate his start-up company from the rest of his life. The start-up entrepreneur may work the same number of hours (at the office, on-site) as the *Fortune 500* executive, but we suggest that the start-up manager rarely gets mental respite from the concerns of his business. As University of Wisconsin–Madison entrepreneurship professor Bob Pricer once said, "When you run an early-stage business, it's the first thing you'll think about when you wake up in the morning, and the last thing on your mind when you fall asleep at night." Virginia Deibel, CEO of TRAC Microbiology adds:

> The responsibility for 17 employees surprises me. When I wake up at
> 3 A.M. and think, "Am I going to make payroll next week? Can I build
> this company into something that will be fulfilling and challenging to all
> of those people?" That's a new experience I didn't expect. I love the
> work, but those 3 A.M. sessions are exhausting.

Realistically, the *Fortune 500* executive likely gets many more perks than the entrepreneurial manager to offset the stresses of the job. These might include flying first class, staying at comfortable hotels, and not worrying about expense account reimbursement. In addition, the *Fortune 500* executive will have extensive support staff to assist with some of the more tedious administrative tasks; when meeting schedules change, the entrepreneurial manager may deal with re-routing and coordination on her own.

We also suggest that the physical, emotional, and psychological stress of running a small company may not be well measured simply by the number of hours spent working. First, we suspect that a not-insignificant amount of "personal" time is spent by the entrepreneur considering business issues or worrying about business situations—time that isn't counted as "work hours." Stress-induced wake-ups at 3 A.M., family mealtimes that turn into discussions about problem employees, driving time spent pondering the next day's critical sales call, and other "nonwork time" incidentally committed to business planning all contribute to the total psychological tension experienced by the entrepreneur, in spite of the fact that these activities are not considered "work."

Next, the element of responsibility may carry a significantly higher emotional toll for the entrepreneur. The entrepreneur may have fewer employees than does a *Fortune 500* manager, but the *Fortune 500* executive manager knows that the organization will continue without her. For the inventing entrepreneur serving as CEO, no such mitigation is likely. In addition, the entrepreneurial CEO probably knows (and likely hired) every single person at the firm; many of those individuals may be close friends or even family. Finally, we note again the issue of the inventing entrepreneur's deep affinity to her technology: It is likely that the technology entrepreneur is emotionally attached to a specific technology commercialization path—and to the organization traveling that path.

Time management and responsibility prioritization can be extremely difficult. The inventing entrepreneur who leaves an academic post to lead a company will likely experience a combination of increased hours and worktime variability.[15] The inventing entrepreneur may realize significant disruptions in family time, physical fitness, and free time. It is likely that the start-up company will not provide the regularity of an academic schedule, and inventing entrepreneurs may find it extremely difficult to plan vacations or even free weekends. These issues should be discussed early with family and friends.

We have observed academic researchers who, in unusual cases, serve as CEOs of new ventures without leaving their academic posts. One individual accomplished this by obtaining significant venture funding relatively early and recruiting enough managerial talent to oversee all operational functions at the company. This enabled him to serve as a "virtual CEO"—participating primarily in high-level strategic decisions without having to engage in day-to-day management. In another example, an individual was widely regarded as being unusually dedicated and driven—having previously founded two other companies. In this case, we note that the individual was also heavily focused on organic growth for the firm, rather than venture-funded growth, which did reduce some of the complexity and strains. Regardless, we believe that these are exceptions to the rule, and our general recommendation would be that inventing entrepreneurs investigate the option of serving in that "dual-role" with extreme caution.

Our observations and cautions aren't intended to scare off the inventing entrepreneur. Some inventing entrepreneurs, like Wilson Harrell predicts, seem to thrive on stress and terror. Virginia Deibel may be one of them. She's one of the "outlier" inventing entrepreneurs we interviewed: She obtained her PhD in pathology specifically to enable her activities as a business manager. Rather than focus on a specific underlying technology or innovation, Deibel is focused on a specific market application: food safety and food-borne illness pathology. She brings a research mentality to an entrepreneurial journey based on business rather than academic research. Her story is told in Profile 12-2.

INVENTING ENTREPRENEUR PROFILE 12-2

Virginia Deibel

Virginia Deibel represents a different type of academic entrepreneur. Rather than form a company based on academic research, she pursued academic research because she had already planned to start a business. She had worked in her family's business while getting a master's degree in pathology, but decided she needed the PhD as well:

> I had finished my master's degree. As I began working more, my family and I started discussing succession planning in the business. I decided that in order to be adequate in the view of both our customers and employees, I needed to further my education. I didn't want people to feel like I was taking over just because I was the owner's daughter, so I decided to get my Ph.D. That took eight years, because I continued to work full time while I got the Ph.D.

In the end, taking over the family business wasn't Deibel's best option, and she decided to go into business for herself, forming TRAC Microbiology, Inc. ("TRAC" stands for "Testing, Research, Auditing, Consulting"):

> In January 2001 I opened the doors to my own laboratory. I wrote a business plan, and with the plan obtained $400,000 in financing from a bank. I rented a space, remodeled the space for three times more than I thought it would cost, hired employees, and opened a business. Technically, I still had a year and half of graduate school left. If you were to ask me what I did wrong, I would say, "Everything."

The first few years at TRAC weren't easy. Despite her prior business experience and extensive time within the university, Deibel found that running a company posed significant challenges:

When you have a new technology, the first thing somebody says to you is "First of all, what can it do?" And the second question is "How much is it?" And for scientists, that's a really hard question. People ask, "How much do you charge a day? How much are these services? How much is this research?" You have to go back and say, "What are my expenses? How much was my equipment?" You have to go back and do your cost analysis, and my question was: "What's a cost analysis?" My accountant kept saying, "Cash flow, Virginia, cash flow." And I said, "But we have cash flow," and he said, "Yes, but it's cash flow out. We need cash flow in." The financial part of a business is overwhelming for a scientist because we never ever thought about it.... Business is hard; if you don't make money, you're done. It is about the bottom line.... It's the first thing you have to learn; it's about making money: Can this provide what I need it to provide? I need it to cover overhead, insurance, payroll, and still generate profit after that.

Deibel had to make many changes to keep the business functioning. She changed the original name of the business from "Brain Wave Technologies" to "TRAC Microbiology." She began participating more actively in all aspects of hiring. And she eventually accepted the apparently fundamental distinction between scientists who want to do sales and salespeople who understand science:

If I had to tell anybody when they start a business what to do first, [I would tell them,] "before you even have an inkling of where you're going to be, start looking for a salesperson, because they talk the language." I went through a number of scientists who wanted to do sales—and they couldn't do it—because they didn't get it. Because sales is a whole different animal.

There's no question that Deibel loves what she does and appreciates the value her academic career and research contribute to her management role. When asked about her company's mission, she inevitably talks about creating a place for scientists (not businesspeople) where they will be challenged to learn, grow, and solve problems. But management remains a significant challenge, even after many years in business:

Management is also hard as a scientist. When I was doing my graduate work, my colleagues were so bright and so motivated—and they would be there at all hours and we would have the most amazing discussions about "What if." In the business world it's not like that at all—you have to motivate them, you have to give them a reason, you have to manage them because if you don't they're going to make mistakes—and frankly, a lot of times they just don't care. It's a sea change from the academic environment.

For Deibel, the skills developed in the academic research environment have proven effective time and time again. She especially appreciates the ability to analyze and evaluate problems and come up with detailed plans for solving them. At the same time, she's learned to approach management and research from a more focused, business perspective, and, when necessary, to improvise:

What it's shown me—every day—is what I'm made of. It has presented me with incredible problems to solve, and I love that problem solving. Even if I have no idea how to approach this problem I'm just going to throw mud against the wall and see what sticks, and I have to sling mud against the wall every single day.

(continues)

In the end, Deibel has found a very different niche for herself than most of the academic entrepreneurs we've profiled. She seems to have significantly more tolerance for the day-to-day risk inherent in small business management and ownership; she relishes the freedom and randomness that the business environment adds to the scientific problem-solving process. And she has no doubt in her mind that she belongs in the faster-paced business world. When asked whether she has ever considered returning to the academic research structure, she responds:

> Not even for a nanosecond. The downside of university research is that you do research for research's sake, not for an applied outcome…. Many times within the academic lab we'd be encouraged to go off on these tangents—"That's an interesting premise; go test it out,"—but then it would turn out not to have any applicability. I believe in making my own way. I believe I get measured for being better this year than last year by getting more knowledge this year than last year…. And [the academic world is too] slow for me. I really like the energy [of the business world]; I love that every day I go into the lab and I have no idea what I'm going to face: "All right, come get me."

Conclusions and Summary

The inventing entrepreneur's decisions regarding management (especially decisions relating to her own level of involvement and authority), may be the most far-reaching and difficult decisions she makes. In the majority of cases we considered, inventing entrepreneurs chose one of two basic options. Many inventors chose to retain academic researcher status and farmed out the primary management and authority to an external agency (while retaining some level of involvement ranging from purely advisory to active). Others determined that their unique qualifications required direct involvement in commercialization.

The finance community (specifically venture capitalists) clearly prefers the first outcome. We found no clear qualitative differences regarding satisfaction or self-actualization between entrepreneurs who chose one path or the other. At the same time, inventing entrepreneurs who assumed leadership roles in a commercialization venture consistently admitted the following:

1. They experienced a steep learning curve in the course of acclimating to the business and commercialization environment.
2. The venture was significantly more time consuming than they had anticipated.
3. They would have benefited from more access to support, mentoring, and knowledge.
4. They would definitely choose to do it again, but would do many things very differently.

Inventing entrepreneurs who retained a primary research role commonly expressed the concern that the technology might not be commercialized. It is useful to note, however, that this sentiment was less prevalent among researchers who took active advisory roles with the companies commercializing the technology. It appears that active participation may alleviate this concern, whether because the probability of commercialization is increased by the participation of the researcher, or because involvement augments the perception that reasonable commercialization efforts are being made.

We strongly encourage inventing entrepreneurs to carefully consider their options with regard to managerial involvement in technology commercialization. The decision will impact their lives far beyond the confines of the research lab and the commercialization venue. Advice from current and former inventing entrepreneurs tends to parallel individual experiences. Entrepreneurs who led ventures encourage risk-taking and skill extension (i.e., taking a leadership role in the commercialization effort). Researchers who remained in the academic lab recommend focusing on existing strengths and proven expertise (i.e., staying at the university and recruiting professional managers to lead commercialization). At this time, we are unaware of reliable qualitative or quantitative data to suggest which strategy is ultimately more likely to achieve commercial success or financial rewards. Until such data are available, the inventing entrepreneur's response to the managerial challenge must be a personal one—based primarily on her own goals and beliefs.

Endnotes

1. In general, we refer to the "management team" as the set of individuals serving in executive, officer, and/or leadership roles. In a start-up, it might be only one or two people. Even if the inventing entrpereneur does not serve in an executive capacity at a start-up commercializing his technology, as the original innovator (and perhaps a significant stockholder), he may still have a leadership role. The issues discussed in this chapter are likely to be relevant, unless the inventing entrepreneur completely disengages from the commercialization process.
2. Swanson, J., & Baird, M. 2003. *Engineering Your Start-Up: A Guide for the High-Tech Entrepreneur,* 2nd ed., Belmont, CA: Professional Publications, Inc.
3. Some inventing entrepreneurs, for example, comment that without their original scientific contribution, the opportunity to commercialize the new technology would not exist; they note that research expertise is probably more unique than operational or sales expertise.
4. Cohen, B. D. & Dean, T. J. 2005. Information asymmetry and investor valuation of IPOs: Top management team legitimacy as a capital market signal. *Strategic Management Journal,* 26(7): 683–690.
5. Cooper, A. C., Gimenogascon, F. J., & Woo, C. Y. 1994. Initial human and financial capital as predictors of new venture performance. *Journal of Business Venturing,* 9(5): 371–395.
6. Westhead, P., Ucbasaran, D., Wright, M., & Binks, M. 2005. Novice, serial and portfolio entrepreneur behaviour and contributions. *Small Business Economics,* 25(2): 109–132.
7. Nesheim, J. 1992. *High-Tech Start-Up* (p. 92). Saratoga, CA: Electronic Trend Publications.
8. Originally from Harrell, W. "Entrepreneurial Terror." *Inc. Magazine,* February 1987, as quoted by Nesheim, J. 1992. *High-Tech Start-Up* (p. 149). Saratoga, CA: Electronic Trend Publications.
9. Komisar, R. 2000. *The Monk and the Riddle* (p. 152). Cambridge, MA: Harvard Business School Press.

10. We have observed that serving as management (especially CEO) of a start-up company may generate concerns about conflicts of interest or financial motivations, creating friction within the academic environment.
11. Burton, D., Sorensen, J., & Beckman, C. 2003. Coming from good stock: Career histories and new venture formation. In M. Lounsbury & M. Ventresca (eds.), *Research in the Sociology of Organizations* (pp. 229–262).
12. Unless her ownership stake is so significant that she is effectively helping make corporate decisions.
13. We anticipate that professional management is unlikely to initiate such a discussion; as noted, management tends to assume that standard corporate goals have already been implicitly accepted.
14. Komisar, *Monk and the Riddle* (p. 93).
15. Technology start-ups are notorious for defying effective family time and vacation planning because of the unpredictable nature of project activities and resource needs.

CHAPTER

PREPARING FOR GROWTH

OVERVIEW

For novice inventing entrepreneurs, preparing for growth may seem presumptuous, given the challenges the start-up must overcome long before the growth phase. At the early stage of the process, for example, the focus on technology licensing and business-plan development takes precedence. We believe, however, that inventing entrepreneurs, no matter how early in the process, can benefit from understanding the implications and complications of operating a high-growth business. While no amount of preparation can ensure success, we hope this brief overview provides inventing entrepreneurs with a sense of the challenges and opportunities that emerge once the business begins to take off.

Growth management presents special challenges.[1,2] As with business-plan writing, there is no lack of literature on managing growing businesses. Unfortunately, while business strategy theory (designed primarily for medium-to-large firms), has been anchored by methodologies and heuristics that have proven useful over time, a limited consensus has developed on exactly what goes into both successfully growing a small business and building value in a fast-growth company. Most entrepreneurs and business experts will note that many of the same resources, skills, and advantages that serve larger businesses will also serve smaller ones. In previous chapters, in fact, we have utilized and recommended various tools and frameworks developed originally for analyzing large businesses (especially industry analysis in Chapter 9). But the inherent risks associated with commercializing leading-edge technology, combined with the constraints and strains associated with growing a business, adds to the complexity and uncertainty of analytical frameworks and tool-based planning.

Our goal, therefore, is to suggest helpful thought models and tools, based on our own experiences and anecdotal observations. We're primarily focused at the strategic level for three reasons. First, we believe that helping inventing entrepreneurs consider some of the strategic issues they will face a few years down the road may provide insight and motivation to evaluate near-term decisions (such as level of personal involvement or the preliminary selection of a business model). Second, the operational and logistical details and challenges facing a growth firm require discussions far beyond the scope of this book. Business schools devote entire courses to growth activities, and consultants base entire practices on helping firms navigate rapid growth. Finally, we don't want to overburden the inventing entrepreneur with technical and financial details that may not be useful in the near-term.

As an excellent starting point for self-evaluation, we recommend Professor Amar Bhide's three questions for entrepreneurs:

- What are my goals?
- Do I have the right strategy?
- Can I execute the strategy?[3]

Professor Bhide developed these based on his observations of several hundred start-up ventures over eight years. We hope inventing entrepreneurs will return to these questions at the end of the chapter or the end of the book to establish priorities among the vast array of opportunities and problems they face.

No matter how much planning and preparation goes into the start-up and growth process, inventing entrepreneurs will often find themselves attempting to direct a business that has taken on a life of its own. This is especially likely if the technology is truly compelling. Professor Michael Sussman, who cofounded NimbleGen with Professors Franco Cerrina and Fred Blattner, briefly describes this dilemma:

> We were going to get SBIRs (federal grants), the usual way. And then things were heating up. Other people were going to be getting into this area. We got worried about the [how quickly the company would have to grow and change just to] keep up.

Understanding the growth process may seem premature to the inventing entrepreneur still making decisions about technology licensing. But considering these issues early may inform licensing and other early-stage processes,[4] and will certainly enable more sophisticated discussions about business financing and strategy.

UNDERSTANDING THE GROWTH STRATEGY OR GROWTH TYPE OF THE BUSINESS

A useful exercise for the inventing entrepreneur will include tacitly identifying the *type* of growth business envisioned. Will the business experience rapid growth or modest growth? Is the underlying technology truly revolutionary or does it represent incremental improvements over existing technologies and products? Though many inventing entrepreneurs tend to see their technologies as "revolutionary" and anticipated products as "market changing," more careful scrutiny is warranted. The market reality (especially how customers see novel technologies) often surprises first-time inventing entrepreneurs, both in terms of complexity and adoption pattern. Let's consider an example, and then walk through a simple process for understanding different types of growth businesses as well as the resulting implications for inventing entrepreneurs and professional managers.

When Rock Mackie and Paul Reckwerdt developed the Tomotherapy concept (radiation-based cancer treatment), they combined novel imaging theory with an innovative treatment implementation system. The Tomotherapy technology (including imaging, software, hardware, and radiation delivery) represents cutting-edge innovation—no other organization has attempted to commercialize a similar treatment system. The radiation beam can be moved 360 degrees around the patient and simultaneously modulated for intensity and cross-sectional profile, allowing for optimized treatments that target complex shapes while minimizing adjacent tissue damage. In sum, the Tomotherapy system can treat more complex, more advanced cancer cases than any other radiation treatment system. From a purely *market-based* business perspective, however, the product is *evolutionary,* not *revolutionary*. It uses existing, well-understood technologies (a linear accelerator, beam collimators, extensive optimization software) to treat a relatively well-understood market need. The extremely sophisticated system improves and combines existing technologies to create a significant market advantage. The software and hardware innovations were nonobvious and technically very challenging—significant research and development were required to achieve success. But these do not qualify the firm as "revolutionary." The market already existed, and the physical infrastructure to support radiation therapy has been in place for a long time (hospitals, oncologists, onsite radiation therapists). For purposes of classifying strategies and growth businesses, a revolutionary technology or firm completely changes how customers use technology or creates entirely new customers. Tomotherapy has succeeded as a growth business by employing an evolutionary strategy—displacing less sophisticated applications in a well-established field.

Truly revolutionary technologies and businesses are rare. Genentech was one, because recombinant DNA changed broad industry sectors, including pharmaceuticals. Start-up companies like Akamai and Cisco revolutionized Internet traffic (and, by extension, the use of the Internet) by putting revolutionary technology and products into both new and existing markets. George Church's genomic sequencing technology was revolutionary because it changed the science of genetics (and continues to impact numerous scientific fields today).

Inventing entrepreneurs should understand, however, that revolutionary technology does not equate to easier commercialization efforts. Inventing entrepreneurs sometimes seem to see the "revolutionary" designation as a badge of honor and a guarantee of fundraising success. While we have no objective method for determining whether certain types of innovations (e.g., revolutionary vs. evolutionary) are fundamentally "better" than others, we can state for certain that truly revolutionary technologies (and companies that rely on revolutionary products) must surmount some of the highest hurdles to achieve commercialization success. Capital costs are likely to be high, along with ongoing R&D expenses. The company may bear significant costs associated with market adoption and with attracting and retaining talent. The cost of mistakes may be very high and the path to a fully functional product lengthy and complex.

By comparison, the evolutionary model is simpler, more predictable, and less costly. Paul Reckwerdt has put countless hours and emotional investment into Tomotherapy—but consider how much more difficult the process would have been if the company's products were based on a previously unknown technology (instead of radiation). In addition to every other challenge, Tomotherapy would also have had to convince regulatory agencies and customers (including hospitals, doctors, and patients) that the new modality was both as safe as and more effective than radiation therapy.

Imagine, for a moment, an inventing entrepreneur has developed a way to teleport people using some form of previously unknown cosmic energy. It might seem this would be immensely easy to market, but consider the following: How much testing will people want to see before they are convinced it is safe? Will the government regulate it? Will everyone buy one for home use or will there be centralized systems? Who will control traffic? What will pricing look like? Will insurance companies be willing to insure its use? Will insurers be willing to provide product liability insurance to the company? Businesses commercializing truly revolutionary technology pose special growth challenges, because such businesses bundle technology risks along with commercial- and market-acceptance risks.

"Revolutionary" and "evolutionary" are only two of numerous types of growth business strategies. Many growth businesses operate on the basis of "hustle,"[5] relying on operational ingenuity, marketing and sales creativity, and old-fashioned elbow grease to anticipate market needs quickly and simply outsell competitors. Some inventing entrepreneurs presume that patents (or even just patent applications) obviate the need for this type of strategy. Realistically, however, many patent applications fail, some issued patents are challenged in court or engineered around, and sometimes patents turn out to be irrelevant because other technologies emerge that meet similar market needs. Hustle-based businesses rely on superior execution of the company strategy—they rely on "how well" it's done rather than the uniqueness of "how" it's done.

This is a useful lesson for inventing entrepreneurs, because very few companies utilize the characteristic elements of one strategy to the exclusion of all others. A revolutionary company that also employs hustle skills, or a propagator company that utilizes niche company strengths, may obtain additional advantages over competitors. Some caution is appropriate, however: It is unlikely that a company can *equally* employ multiple strategies. A company can't easily be both a speculator and a niche company: The necessary investment in uncertain resources, for example, isn't conducive to targeting small market segments with incrementally differentiated products.

TABLE 13-1   Business Types and Resource Implications

Growth Type	Description	Example	Resource Implications
Hustle	Advantage based on superior execution, especially in sales and marketing	Jefferson Wells (outsourced corporate finance, bookkeeping, and other services)	Retaining motivated employees is critical. Company must utilize novel processes or market new products to stay ahead.
Revolutionary	Paradigm shift with regard to meeting customer needs (or creation of entirely new customer needs)	Amazon (online/ virtual retail)	Significant investment in R&D and infrastructure is needed to bring product to market. Significant investment in sales/marketing is needed to change market behavior and dynamics.
Evolutionary	Incremental improvements in technology or applications that augment customer benefits	Tomotherapy (radiation-based cancer treatment)	Active research and development process is needed to stay ahead of competition. Strong execution is needed to capitalize on advantages.
Propagator	Leverage of existing products, technologies, or markets in order to deliver value to new or developing markets	Any iPod accessory	Must meet minimum criteria for quality or functionality to enter market; must manage development and marketing against a broad competitive field.
Speculator	Investment in limited resources, contrarian approach to opportunities	Oil field development	Requires very significant up-front investments in uncertain resources.
Enabler	Underlying technology that supports or improves existing or developing products or markets	Vertica (novel database technology)	Requires a potentially large investment in research and development. Strong business partnering skills may also be required.
Niche	Innovation targeted at smaller, specific market	Confederate Motors (motorcycles)	Requires focused, specialized R&D and competent market targeting.

If an appropriate growth strategy can be identified, then it's possible to align the various functions and resources around that strategy. A hustle-based business requires exceptional sales and marketing staff (and probably strong customer service as well). Revolutionary technologies and products usually require investing extensive resources to demonstrate how and why the technology should be utilized (especially to potential customers, who may not even be aware they need the technology).

Another common model in high-technology sectors is an "enabler" model, where the inventing entrepreneur's research has resulted in novel mechanisms for improving existing products, services, and systems. Vertica's software, developed by Professor Stonebraker, could be used to track the location and statistics on every vehicle traversing a broad expanse of freeways and surface streets. The underlying algorithms may be revolutionary (i.e., truly novel processes for managing exceptionally large, changing data sets), and the ultimate services may be evolutionary (i.e., improved mechanisms for customers to monitor location and other relevant information), but a company founded on this type of technology might choose to *enable* other companies to offer novel services and solutions, rather than to offer the value-add services directly to end-users. For example, if the company licenses this technology (i.e., selling the software) to traffic systems integrators, those integrators could help municipalities better manage rush-hour traffic patterns. Alternatively, the technology could be combined with a system like Google Maps to enable travelers to receive information (and advertisements) about nearby businesses and services. In that example, Google is the end-user service provider, not the software company with the data management system.

An enabling business will likely need business development professionals who can sort through partnership options and establish corporate relationships that create value for both entities. It will also need competent scientists and engineers that can mold the company's products and services to link seamlessly into existing (and novel) products and solutions. We differentiate this from a "niche" model because the scope of an enabling business can be enormous. We also differentiate it from a "revolutionary" model because the company may have the ability to enter and dominate a market without making massive R&D and infrastructure investments or having to dramatically change customer and market behaviors.

It's important to remember that a (proposed) business may or may not perfectly match one of the business types that we've described. Even if it does, the inventing entrepreneur will likely find that certain nuances must be adapted to the specific market sector or competitive environment.

TRANSITIONING FROM PROJECT MANAGEMENT TO BUSINESS ADMINISTRATION

As we reviewed our interviews and case studies, we noticed that each of the new ventures described passed through a crucial transition. Most early ventures look like *projects*—in fact, most look like extensions of the research projects that generated the original innovation. Over time, however (usually within 12–24 months), administrative functions develop around the project. The original project will change, and new projects will be started. Specific commercialization activities will emerge from development projects. Whether planned or unplanned, this process marks the transition from *project management* to *business administration*.

This is a natural and necessary transition. Technology companies that fail to undergo this metamorphosis either remain stuck in the R&D phase or fail to match their products to market needs; those companies usually do not grow or succeed. The transformation itself can be very gradual as both philosophy and motivation evolve. At the same time, discontinuous changes in a limited number of functional elements usually signal the transition. By identifying both the high-level mindset and some of these functional elements, we hope to help the inventing entrepreneur 1) identify the changes that must take place, 2) identify the changes that are occurring (or have already occurred), 3) prepare for some of those changes, and 4) understand that the processes and tools to manage these changes are relatively well established and do not need to be reinvented from scratch. Table 13-2 identifies key elements that differentiate between project management and business administration.

While this transition from project management to business administration may be accelerated or eased by the hiring of professional managers, the transition must occur for the company to grow, regardless of who is actively running the company. Competent service providers, professional managers, and advisors can help the inventing entrepreneur handle this transition efficiently.

Inventing entrepreneurs may find the transition to be especially challenging because many business functions may appear to be either nonessential or non-value-adding. As an example, most academic environments provide exceptional human resources support, which severely reduces the amount of paperwork associated with hiring, firing, payroll, and general human resources administration. The

TABLE 13-2   Elements of the Transition from Project Management to Business Administration

	Project Management	*Business Administration*
Perceptual Shifts		
Strategic Focus is ...	Prove concept and complete product	Meet customer needs
Venture team composed of ...	Scientists, engineers, technicians	Management, scientific, production, customer staff
Value Creation through ...	Innovation	Sales
Functional changes		
Finance	Managing expenses	Managing total budget
Administration	Ground–up (self-directed)	Top–down (policy-directed)
Human Resources	As needed to complete projects	Based on administrative planning

amount of paperwork associated with these activities, and the number of relevant business regulations, may be a significant surprise to inventing entrepreneurs.[6] Some inventing entrepreneurs end up short-cutting human resource management. We believe this is a potentially significant mistake for two reasons. First, as we've emphasized repeatedly in this book, human resources represent the most critical element of a technology venture. Failing to provide appropriate oversight and administration increases the potential for downstream problems. Second, while government oversight rarely targets early stage firms, a run-in with a government agency, either early in the process or in the long-run, would likely generate disproportionate costs to the firm (both in time and money).[7]

The transition from research focus to business focus presents both challenges and learning opportunities for every inventing entrepreneur. Numerous times in this book we've mentioned NimbleGen. We've profiled one of the founders, Professor Fred Blattner, and talked about NimbleGen's technology and path to eventual success. In Profile 13-1, we complete the story with the entrepreneurial journeys of the other two academic founders, Professors Michael Sussman and Franco Cerina. We chose to tell their stories separately from Professor Blattner, because he had prior entrepreneurial experience when NimbleGen was founded. For Sussman and Cerina, NimbleGen was a completely new experience, and their changing roles help highlight the implications of growth at a start-up technology firm.

INVENTING ENTREPRENEUR PROFILE 13-1

Professor Michael Sussman and Professor Franco Cerina

The NimbleGen story is the result of a true collaboration. The development of the company's novel gene chip technology required Sussman's understanding of the need for rapid, inexpensive analysis; Professor Fred Blattner's creativity; and Cerina's physics and engineering expertise. After making the initial disclosures to the technology transfer office, the three inventors decided to start a company. Professor Cerina describes the decision process:

> We said, "Okay, let's start a company," because it was clear from the beginning that we wanted to do that. I liked the idea.... It is nice to see your ideas come to fruition and be made into something useful.... In the early stages, we wanted to go on our own....Professor Blattner had already started one company, so [we were] hopeful we'd be able to move quickly. The reality was something else.

The technology transfer office had arranged a meeting with a group of investors who were also prepared to help manage the company. The team had turned the offer down initially; they had plans for building the business themselves. But incorporating a business and operating it are two totally different processes. It became clear that the three founders were struggling to jump start operations. Professor Sussman described his frustration over just trying to get everyone in one place at one time:

> Weeks and months go by; [I said] let's have a meeting. Fred organized the meeting for 12:00 noon at a Chinese restaurant, so I get out there at 10 to 12:00. Fred didn't remember that the

meeting was on, and Franco was always late—I didn't know that, I was still getting used to that
.... So I left, and I get back to my office and Fred calls me and says, "Hey, we have a meeting."
And I said, "I was already there," and Fred says, "Yeah, but Franco's here now, come on." And
I said, "No, I don't go down there twice a day." So, I realized that, my God, we can't even get a
meeting together—so I called [the investors] up and said, "We'll give you half the company;
run with it."

In the end, the team did play an integral role in commercializing the technology,
but professional management was brought in to run the business. NimbleGen was a
relatively complex business to operate, and it had to overcome numerous hurdles to
succeed. For Professor Sussman, the focus was always on getting the technology into
broad use:

I'm a biologist; I want to use these [gene] chips to cure cancer. I want to use these chips. I want
these things in my lab solving solid biological problems.... If I'm excited about something scientifically, I don't think about anything else.... Reputation I don't think about—I probably should
... but I have tenure ... and this is too cool. I want to get those machines out there; I [couldn't]
do that in my lab; there [had] to be a company.

Professor Sussman and his colleagues did have a lot of lessons to learn about business, especially venture-funded business. Sussman jokingly noted that the investors valued their cash investment over his brainpower, which necessarily meant there had to be
negotiation about ownership and control. For Professor Cerina, there were other issues
and conflicts. Unlike Blattner and Sussman, he took on a formal role at the business as
VP of Engineering. At first, he found it liberating to be able to direct purchases and
activities without the bureaucracy of university administration. But with that freedom
came responsibility for the commercialization program, which is very different from a
research process. Cerina described that tension explicitly:

NimbleGen has always been very application based, and rightly so. Rather than saying, "We
have a cool technology—let's develop it more," [we said] "The machine is working, don't fix
it," which is the way it should be, even if I [didn't] like it.... You have these great ideas [for
research that the company could address], but that's not really possible. Most start-ups [aren't
so much fun] because the funding may be there, but [there aren't enough] people to do the
research. You have to make it into the market and start establishing yourself. So everyone has
to be very market focused. So there was a bit of frustration from my point of view, but that's to
be expected.

Eventually, Professor Cerina left NimbleGen and a full-time engineer was brought
in to manage final product development and implementation. But the founders experienced other changes as well. As the company focused on marketing and distribution
issues, engineering and design innovation became relatively less critical. Eventually, all
three founders were informed that their consulting and advisory services were no
longer needed. Professor Sussman commented wryly: "It's really something to be fired
by your own company."

At the same time, Sussman learned that being familiar with a process doesn't necessarily make it simple. When asked whether the second company has been easier to
start and run, he responded: "Not exactly, actually.... I was a little more familiar with
the process, [but] it's still nerve-wracking; we're still learning."

Interestingly, Dr. Sussman's new venture has chosen to pursue a slower commercialization route. The company has relied more heavily on grant funding than venture

(continues)

funding, and is putting more ownership controls in place much earlier than Nimble-Gen. But the underlying goal is the same: to bring innovative biotechnology tools and systems to mainstream markets. At the time of these interviews,[8] NimbleGen's growth process had hit some bumps in the road, so we asked Sussman and Cerina about their goals and expectations for success. Sussman's comments reflect a strong research focus:

> I don't live and breathe money; I wouldn't know what to do with a lot of money.... I don't want to worry about the money.... I'm excited that the technology helped a lot of people. I think that's fine.

And Cerrina's comment reflects a certain pragmatism as well as engineering humor: "There is a non-zero probability of doing a lot of work for nothing."

As previously noted, NimbleGen was acquired by Roche for $272 million in June 2007 while NimbleGen was in the process of preparing for an IPO. There may have been tough times and doubts, but the NimbleGen innovation played out successfully, growing from three founders struggling to meet at a Chinesse restaurant into an international business generating tens of millions of dollars in revenues each year.

CROSSING MOORE'S CHASM

The traditional industry lifecycle model suggests that companies have succeeded with new technologies when they begin selling product to "early adopters." These customers are leading-edge users that demand top performance and will pay high prices to stay at the forefront of their own industries. In *Crossing the Chasm*[9], however, Geoffrey Moore revises the traditional technology adoption lifecycle by placing a gap between "early adopters" and the "early majority." He suggests that although a novel product can be sold to enthusiasts and visionaries solely on the basis of the product's novelty and purported advantages (regardless of the benefit/cost proposition), early-majority buyers represent a more difficult sell. They want a clear cost/benefit proposition, preferably backed up with references from other early-majority buyers. Consequently, growing a new venture entails gearing the company to shift its focus from a small group of customers to a mass-market strategy. Figure 13-1 shows Moore's "chasm," placed between the early adopters and the early majority. The traditional lifecycle graphic places those submarkets directly adjacent to each other, as if the transition between selling to one group and the other were relatively seemless. Moore argues this is fundamentally incorrect. Here is how he describes the thinking of the early majority:

> The early majority want to buy a productivity improvement for existing operations. They are looking to minimize the discontinuity with the old ways. They want evolution, not revolution. They want technology to enhance, not overthrow, the established ways of doing business. And above all, they do not want to debug somebody else's product.... The only suitable reference for an early-majority customer, it turns out, is another member of the early majority.[10]

FIGURE 13-1   Moore's "Chasm"[11]

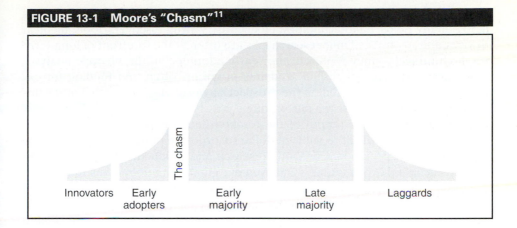

The chasm

Innovators | Early adopters | Early majority | Late majority | Laggards

Inventing entrepreneurs need to consider shifting selling strategy from "innovation focused" to "value-creation focused" as early as possible for two key reasons. First, the inventing entrepreneur's high affinity to her technology often obscures the need to establish a proven value proposition to majority customers. Second, these same entrepreneurs often have the greatest experiential and knowledge limitations with regard to understanding broad industry marketing and sales. Consider an example in the broad field of proteomics. Imagine a specific advance in structural proteomics, such as the use of high-throughput methods for evaluating three-dimensional protein structures. Understanding protein physical structure is important because protein structure directly affects the protein's interaction with the genome and the cell environment. Our hypothetical innovators have adapted nuclear magnetic resonance (NMR) spectroscopy to improve the level of structural detail generated evaluating certain types of protein branching sequences. They publish a well-received paper and are contacted by a forward-thinking biotechnology company about utilizing the prototype system. The scientists have heard about other start-ups that have emerged from their academic institution, and, rather than license the technology to a large corporation, they work with their technology transfer office to form their own company. They license the technology, raise seed capital, and for a year or so everything goes extremely well. They develop the technology into an add-on product for NMR spectroscopes, and begin selling it to the customers they are most familiar with: other academic researchers. The company isn't making money, because it has embarked on an aggressive R&D effort to improve the analytical detail by another order of magnitude. The company constantly seems to be on the verge of a big sale to a biotechnology company, but after completing the initial testing work with their first contact, they find that the industrial customers are hesitant to commit to actual purchases. Funds begin to get tight, and difficult decisions will have to be made if the company is to survive.

We've seen this scenario at numerous early-stage technology companies across many fields: nanotechnology, biochemistry, drug discovery tools, medical devices, and so on. Academic research labs are often at the forefront of long-term research projects—they represent the "early adopters" in the lifecycle analysis. Cost-conscious, well-established academic programs often find funding for expensive research tools, based on the prospect of world-class research, but it's unlikely that the researchers are performing a cost-benefit analysis on the product acquisition, because the output of the research lab is papers, students, patents, and prestige—all difficult to value in dollars. Corporate purchasers utilize an entirely different calculation. Corporate research and production labs must justify significant capital expenditures—and even marginal technology investments—on the basis of how the acquired product (in this case, our hypothetical innovators' NMR add-on technology) will improve their own product innovation process and eventually their own revenues or costs. Using the "best" technology available isn't sufficient justification in the mainstream corporate environment.

We suspect that this phenomenon underlies the suggestions made by so many venture capitalists and experienced inventing entrepreneurs about the importance of bringing on experienced marketing and sales executives early in the process. Such hires provide leadership in ramping up revenue growth through sales to majority customers. In addition, bringing on experienced business management helps the founders *prepare* for the "chasm crossing" in advance. Acknowledging that the chasm exists is important, but implementing a process for crossing it requires highly specfic skills and expertise.

THE CHANGING ROLE OF THE INVENTING ENTREPRENEUR/FOUNDER

As the Entrepreneurial Journey Model shows (see Chapters 7 and 8), unique founder paths almost always involve change. *We believe that the nature of inventing entrepreneurship involves learning, growth, and transformation.* This lesson holds one of the most important keys for inventing entrepreneurs, whether you are considering a new venture or are already involved in one. *The successful venture will grow and change, the inventing entrepreneur will grow and change, and the inventing entrepreneur's role within the venture will also change over time.*

A few inventing entrepreneurs who take active management roles are unable to adapt as their commercialization venture evolves. In some cases, this can be detrimental to the venture. For example, if the inventing entrepreneur does not develop appropriate managerial skills, she may inadvertently promote incentives to key employees that conflict with the goals and prioritization set by other managers. Sometimes, the inventing entrepreneur has the appropriate managerial skills, but cannot transition from project management to business administration. In these situations, the inventing entrepreneur fails to participate in creating the necessary administrative infrastructure, effectively treating the business as her own development lab. In the end, this will create conflict with other managers.

The Entrepreneurial Journey Model only shows the *functional* role the inventing entrepreneur fulfills within the venture; it does not measure her *effectiveness* in that role. An inventing entrepreneur might argue that she has evolved from a product/research focus to a market/application focus as the company has grown, but an objective review of her activities (coupled with the likely difficulties and strains within the organization) might reveal discrepancies between the founder's functional role and the path of the venture. This is one argument against becoming a dual-role inventing entrepreneur. We believe that the academic researcher who retains half- or full-time employment at the university will face more challenges serving in an executive role in the commercialization business because of the role and identity distinctions (see Chapter 15). Clearly, some individuals are capable of managing both roles, but we presume that the pressures associated with maintaining divergent entities (especially since the growth of the commercial entity suggests an increasing divergence from the research laboratory) would be significant.

Some journeys, of course, require a less active transformation (if any at all) on the part of the inventing entrepreneur. When the founder participates primarily as an advisor to the venture (rather than in a leadership role within the venture), whether in an informal or formal capacity, it is generally understood that the inventor's position at the research lab remains his priority. Although his participation in the venture may be critical (or even in some ways controlling), he explicitly prioritizes his research laboratory over the venture. The sabbatical entrepreneur model usually results in a similar dynamic.

Most of our interviewees described an ongoing thought process in which they regularly reviewed their prioritization of research lab and commercial activities. This was especially relevant for individuals significantly involved in active commercialization ventures. Many of these inventing entrepreneurs participated directly in the process of evolving their responsibilities within the venture. For example, some hired CEOs to replace themselves; others worked with venture capital groups to recruit management talent to complement their own skills. A few chose to temporarily prioritize the venture during the critical start-up phase by negotiating special arrangements (such as a sabbatical or half-time allocation) with their academic institutions.

In fact, some inventing entrepreneurs create different prioritizations and personal roles for each commercialization effort. Professor Stonebraker, for example, has demonstrated versatility and creativity in his role development. He has been CTO, VP Engineering, or CEO of five different ventures, spanning a career in which he first served as a university professor at UC-Berkeley, retired, and then "un-retired" to become faculty at MIT. This reinforces our observation that every entrepreneurial journey is idiosyncratic. Individual inventing entrepreneurs can experience dramatically different journeys for each venture in which they participate.

Conclusions and Summary

The role of inventing entrepreneur is, by definition, a role that embraces change. The growth of the technology-based venture is a process that can generate rapid, even discontinuous change. Preparing for the growth of the venture may help inventing entrepreneurs adjust to these changes. Understanding certain strategic aspects of business growth enable this preparation. Growth businesses can be grouped into "types," which provide an over-arching structure for identifying key success characteristics. The inventing entrepreneur that objectively evaluates the likely strategic "type" can more effectively consider functional requirements for the business and his own role as the business grows.

Inventing entrepreneurs should also understand that growth businesses must be managed as business enterprises, not research projects. The transition from project management to business administration can pose special challenges to the inventing entrepreneur.

Inventing entrepreneurs have unique opportunities that are engendered by the juxtaposition of science and business. And at any such boundary, there are complex conditions, turbulence, risk, and rewards. We encourage inventing entrepreneurs to examine that boundary and the role they can play in shepherding technology to realization.

Endnotes

1. Churchill, N. C. & Lewis, V. L. 1983. The five stages of small business growth. *Harvard Business Review*, 61(3): 30.
2. Barringer, B., Jones, F., & Neubaum, D. 2005. A quantitative content analysis of the characteristics of rapid-growth firms and their founders. *Journal of Business Venturing*, 20: 663–687.
3. Bhide, A. 1996. The questions every entrepreneur must answer. *Harvard Business Review*, 74(6): 120.
4. For example, if the inventing entrepreneur believes that market and industry dynamics will require venture capital investments, then the license should be structured to be "venture capital" friendly. If the inventing entrepreneur anticipates a slow growth process that generates cash returns, the technology transfer office might require protective clauses to ensure that it can demand payments within a reasonable timeframe. These clauses would be extremely problematic for a venture capital firm to accept.
5. Many of these examples of business types were originally suggested by Professor Amar Bhide of Harvard Business School. "Note on Developing Start-Up Strategies," HBS 1993. We have taken the liberty of adding "enabler" and "evolutionary" on the basis of our own review of growth businesses.
6. This may seem counterintuitive, since one of the big advantages of licensing a technology out of the university structure is often the freedom to perform rapid, focused research and development. Start-up companies, however, are often underresourced, and the burden of managing all the necessary business functions can generate strain.
7. In the past 10 to 15 years, numerous outsourced service options have become available to start-ups, and high-tech growth companies have dramatically benefited by obtaining human resource (HR) services (among others), rather than attempting to build this capacity in-house from the start.
8. Summer and autumn of 2005.
9. Moore, G. 2002. *Crossing the Chasm*. New York: Harper Collins.
10. Moore, *Crossing the Chasm* (p. 20).
11. From Moore., G. 2002. *Crossing the Chasm*.

CHAPTER 14

EXIT

OVERVIEW

The concept of "exiting a business" may seem somewhat unnatural, and possibly even unappealing for the novice inventing entrepreneur to ponder. When researchers think long term about active scientific inquiry, they may have certain goals in mind, but it's unlikely they envision an exit event in which ownership of the research processes, resources, and outputs is transferred to someone else. The researcher might more instinctively define an exit as the point at which a scientific inquiry results in a dead end or when all the interesting questions have been exhausted; and the researcher moves on to pursue other intriguing research questions.

For technology ventures (and specifically for the external investors in technology ventures), the exit is literally the pot of gold at the end of the rainbow. But the exit can also mean something very different to the inventing entrepreneur. It may seem premature to consider the terminus before the start, but nearly every inventing entrepreneur we spoke with suggested that understanding the end point can provide helpful guidance throughout the journey.

First-time inventing entrepreneurs are usually focused on staying gainfully employed, rather than on pondering downstream financial rewards. John Devereux experienced this firsthand at the start of his entrepreneurial experience. As one of the inventing entrepreneurs we interviewed who had completed his entrepreneurial journey, Devereux provides an especially useful perspective. (His story is told more fully in Profile 14-1.) He eventually sold his bioinformatics business, Genetics Computer Group Corporation (GCG), to Oxford Molecular. But 15 years before that event, he was a junior scientist in a university genomics laboratory working on an innovative technology in a fast-moving field:

> We made a set of [software] tools for Oliver Smithies [recipient of the 2007 Nobel Prize in Physiology or Medicine] in the genetics department.

They were really [created] so he could write a major paper ... in the recombinant DNA game.... My career started off in professionalizing that work—[until] Reagan cut the budget in the early '80s, and obligations that the university had already made to people like me were going to be cut back ... Oliver said, "You will have to do one of two things with your career: You will have to learn to support yourself through this work you seem to love—or you will have to start work on some of my core grants because I don't have enough money to pretend you aren't there." And I was very excited about the [software] work; it was the first thing that had ever happened in my career where I'd been willing to put the amount of work in that was needed to succeed in a subject.

Every exit event can be traced back to a beginning like this one. Understanding basic information about exit events may give inventing entrepreneurs some additional tools for evaluating decisions relating to starting and growing commercialization ventures.

INVENTING ENTREPRENEUR PROFILE 14-1

John Devereux and GCG

In 1982, John Devereux led the development of genomic sequencing software while working as a postgraduate student for nationally recognized genetics professor Oliver Smithies at the University of Wisconsin–Madison. Professor Smithies is currently at the University of North Carolina, and was the recipient of the 2007 Nobel Prize in Physiology or Medicine. Because the software's initial customers were other academic researchers, the software was "sold" by Smithies' lab to other academic research labs at cost. Then corporations began purchasing copies, and Devereux found himself leading a small software and support organization from within the university. Devereux recounts: "I didn't know it at the time, but we were building a business, right inside the university." Eventually, pressure from within the university structure and from external sources forced the university to clarify its ownership of the GCG project.

Initially, Devereux had no intention of leaving the university. He describes his thought process at the time and the unexpected moment when his whole perspective changed:

My assumption was that if we got forced out [of the university] we would die a slow death.... I hadn't really thought about it that much, but it was kind of like being weaned.... The university provides, through its institutional framework, incredible service because it takes all employee risk. It's managing all your benefits, you know—it has a bunch of procedures that are bulletproof, and it gives you a nice set of ethical standards. The procedures are very rigorous. They're really terrific services and I was terrified to be without them. But I remember very precisely when it [happened].... I woke up one Sunday morning in February and realized that we could [start a company].

The success of the product required a commercial setting, and John made the decision to start Genetics Computer Group. The GCG story is indicative of an older, ad hoc approach to technology transfer. The GCG spin-out bears little resemblance to the more modern technology transfer process. The TTO chose not to get involved in the spin-out, and a favorable financial arrangement between the university and GCG allowed the new company to acquire the relevant capital equipment owned by the university to initiate operations. This helped Devereux and his cofounder to ramp up the business without private capital. Even so, as Devereaux explains, "The spin-off took an entire year." And there were some unexpected complications for the founders:

> I went from being a state employee making $50,000 a year to having made over $1 million in the first year—on paper, taxable—but [that $1 million] wasn't real money[1] and we had to find the money to pay the taxes.

Within five years, the company was supporting nearly 15,000 users worldwide. GCG was purchased by Oxford Molecular in 1997, and was reformed as Accelrys in 2000 when Oxford was bought by Pharmacopeia. For 18 years the software product was known simply as "The Wisconsin Package." Devereux summarized the transforming power of his entrepreneurial journey:

> Since our experience was so charmed, it's easy for me to say, "Go for it"—the rewards of private sector life are easily understated. If it begins to succeed, it's astounding how powerful it is.

For Devereux, the corporate exit event wasn't quite the end of the story. He stayed with Oxford Molecular after the acquisition for a transition period that lasted three years. When the second acquisition occurred, however, he knew his time with the business was completed. Devereux was able to retire on the profits from the sale of the company, completing his own personal exit. It's clear that he looks back on the business' growth process with enthusiasm and joy. He has retained a handmade book of professional photos of all the employees of the company, a collection that used to adorn the walls of the company's main office. And he talks about the map of the earth posted in one of the conference rooms that the team would refer to when they met to discuss "taking over the world."

As economies of scale became more critical in the genomics sequencing field, the GCG team recognized that they didn't have the internal resources to compete with bigger players. The GCG exit was not big enough to make headlines in the *Wall Street Journal*—there were no venture capitalists or investment bankers looking for an IPO. The corporate exit made sense for the business and the owners. For Devereux, an early example of the modern inventing entrepreneur, it was the end of a journey that had generated financial and personal rewards.

WHAT IS AN "EXIT"?

To an investor, the exit is the point at which the investment realizes financial returns. For a bank, the exit occurs when the loan is paid back or abandoned; for a private equity investor (shareholder), the exit occurs when the investor sells the stock or declares it worthless. Unlike an investor, however, the inventing entrepreneur may have multiple phases of exit. For example, the company might hire a professional manager to replace the inventing entrepreneur, ending his day-to-day involvement in the venture, though the inventing entrepreneur might stay on in a limited advisory role. Years later, the venture might be acquired by another company in an all-stock transaction, terminating that advisory role and reducing the inventing entrepreneur's ownership status to that of a small minority shareholder. Finally, the acquiring company might participate in an initial public offering, giving the inventing entrepreneur the opportunity to sell his shares on the open market. In this example, the company experiences two distinct exit events (the acquisition and the IPO), though investors in the original company might define only the IPO as a true exit. Whether the inventing entrepreneur sees any or all of these events as "exits" will depend heavily on how he perceives his role in the commercialization process.

In most cases, an exit is defined as a discontinuity—a significant change in participation, ownership, value, or activities. We'll discuss different types of exits, describe some "less than perfect" exits, and then talk about why these exits are of particular importance to the inventing entrepreneur.

TYPES OF EXITS

We're going to focus on exit events that are directly relevant to inventing entrepreneurs. Based on our interviews, as well as our observations of hundreds of early-stage companies, we can classify the relevant exit types as "financial," "participatory," and "ownership/control." We'll discuss financial exits first. Understanding financial exits will also help the inventing entrepreneur understand what drives investors. Then we'll consider participatory and ownership/control exits, which are relevant to the inventing entrepreneur.

FINANCIAL EXITS

An investor provides funds to an early-stage business with an expectation of generating certain financial returns. In many cases, early-stage investors derive other benefits from their investments. For example, angel investors often see private investing as an opportunity to support the local economy and the development of local high-tech infrastructure; they may also view the investing process as a "sport" played with friends and business associates that provides entertainment. Sometimes angels are particularly interested in the commercialization of a given product or solution (a cure for a disease that has affected family or friends, for example). In rare cases, these special-case investors may see an exit based on non-financial circumstances. The vast majority of the time, however, the exit is the point at which the investment is returned (or not) and profits or losses realized.

When investors loan money to a venture, their exit is relatively straightforward. Most loans have a defined term and regular (or accruing) interest payments. The lender's financial exit occurs when the loan and interest are paid back or when some or all of the loan is written off as a loss.

For equity investors, however, the exit process can be more complicated. We worked with a group of angels that in the year 2000 invested in a medical imaging software company called UltraVisual. In 2003, UltraVisual merged with a larger medical imaging systems business called Emageon. At the time of the merger, all the holders of UltraVisual stock received Emageon stock in exchange for their ownership stake in UltraVisual. Because both UltraVisual and Emageon were privately held companies, there was no public market for either company's stock, so the UltraVisual investors still had no mechanism to realize a financial gain (or loss). Technically, an "exit" had occurred—there had been a change in control and the investors now owned stock in a different company. From a more practical perspective, this could be considered an organizational exit, but not a financial exit.

In early 2005, Emageon participated in an initial public offering (IPO). Emageon stock was registered to trade on the NASDAQ, and after a (traditional) 180-day "lockup" period, the investors could sell their shares on the exchange. This event represented a true financial exit, but not an organizational exit (since the IPO event does not, intrinsically, change the management or control of the organization, other than by the sale of additional shares of stock). The relevant exit for investors is a financial exit, at which point they obtain the profits or losses associated with the success (or lack thereof) of their investment.[2]

The inventing entrepreneur (or other founder) may participate in multiple exits. The financial exit for the inventing entrepreneur is no different than for any other investor. If he loaned money to the company, the loan is paid off or defaulted on. If he was a shareholder, then he exits when he sells his stock or writes it off.[3]

PARTICIPATORY EXITS

Regardless of the specific role performed by the inventing entrepreneur for the company (CEO, CSO, advisory board member, etc.), the termination of that role will be a *participatory* exit. Such an exit may come in multiple stages, as described previously: The inventing entrepreneur may see any significant change in participation as an exit.

Participatory exits can be gradual, planned processes. The inventing entrepreneur who works closely with management on corporate and resource planning is less likely to be surprised by significant (or even forced) changes in his role. Realistically, however, some changes can't be predicted; even carefully planned transitions may be accelerated or retarded by changes in product strategy or financial circumstances. And, of course, a planned transition would likely include some period of limited involvement during which the inventing entrepreneur will have less information and authority—exactly the circumstances in which unexpected role changes are more common.

We have generally found that when first-time inventing entrepreneurs carefully evaluate their participation preferences, they almost always do so *through the lens of operating a start-up company*. It would be presumptuous to argue that inventing entrepreneur, especially first-time inventing entrepreneurs, should have enough foresight to envision their role throughout the life of the venture. But this is exactly what we recommend. Such providence, even while acknowledging the vast uncertainty inherent in the technology venture process, represents one of the most effective ways for the inventing entrepreneur to prepare for the journey itself. In particular, it requires exactly the type of self-assessment we described in Chapter 2 (and continued in Chapters 3–5). Having that baseline expectation, along with a preliminary hypothesis about personal exit, offers the inventing entrepreneur the only objective starting point to effectively monitor his goals, expectations, and satisfaction throughout the journey.

Serial entrepreneurs usually employ a much broader lens to the questions of role and exit. Regardless of whether they served as an advisor or executive (or even in a purely operational role), once they've seen the exit process (good or bad), they understand consciously that most participatory roles in growth businesses are transient. Even when the inventing entrepreneur is involved for an extended time, the dynamics and resource requirements of technology companies usually create transition and transformation.

Consider a few examples: Paul Reckwerdt at Tomotherapy started as CEO but remained at the company as president after significant venture capital funding prompted hiring an industry professional to serve as CEO.[4] Reckwerdt's role at Tomotherapy spans the full 10 years of the company's existence; he knows the value of being involved from start to exit.[5] In another example, Professor Blattner founded DNAStar 20 years ago and turned over the leadership role to a business manager. Following that manager's departure, Blattner assumed the top management role while he looked for another appropriate candidate. Michael Stonebraker prefers the CTO/VP of Engineering role because he feels it best matches his own skills and interests, but he has served as CEO during the launch of some of his start-ups.

Each of these individuals knows the reality of the personal exit process and understands his own expectations. But many of the inventing entrepreneurs we interviewed, especially the novices, appeared less clear about their expected participatory exit. This may exacerbate the potential for "founder's syndrome," especially in cases where the venture experiences difficulties.

Nesheim notes the emotional attachment founders can develop for their ventures:

> It would be an interesting and very useful study to learn how long founders last and why. Some leave because they have become independently wealthy. But few leave voluntarily; their lives seem to be so bound up in their start-up—their baby that they have given birth to and nourished from the first day they got the idea for the start-up.[6]

Participatory exits can happen earlier (or later) in a company's life, sometimes to the surprise of the inventing entrepreneur. In some cases, these transitions can be relatively painless and without much negative emotion or impact. For example, as NimbleGen Systems grew, the roles of its three founders (Blattner, Sussman, and Cerina) dramatically changed. Blattner and Sussman initially served as consultants, whereas Cerina served as CTO/VP Engineering. Cerina was eventually transitioned to a consulting role as well. The company obtained venture funding, hired professional management, and brought a high-speed genomic assay technology to market. In the meantime, however, all three founders' consulting contracts were cancelled by the company. None of the founders seemed particularly surprised, but all expressed disappointment. It's especially interesting to note that all three professors have moved on to found new companies, and their experiences at Nimblegen have clearly affected their strategic planning for those new businesses. Blattner is utilizing an organic growth process, funding the near-term research and development work with his own money to retain control of the business. Sussman and Cerina are focused on grant funding and angel investments, and are also utilizing a slower growth model to retain more control of the company.

OWNERSHIP/CONTROL EXITS

For inventing entrepreneurs that form a venture, license technology from their academic institution, and then raise funds to support operations, the inflection point at which they give up controlling stock interest (i.e., greater than 50% ownership) can be quite difficult. We have observed some inventing entrepreneurs who have attempted to carefully calculate valuations and financing events to try to ensure that they retain controlling interest as long as possible (or even indefinitely).[7] This mindset is often described as "founder's syndrome." This perspective is usually explained by the entrepreneur as follows: "I have to maintain control because I'm the only person who knows the technology, market, and/or business strategy well enough to lead the commercialization process."[8] Our own observations suggest that in the vast majority of cases, this statement simply is not correct. We have yet to see a start-up technology firm where a single researcher or scientist was the unique resource necessary to enable successful commercialization.

The reality is that few technology ventures reach a substantial exit event with the scientific founder still in control. Rather than discuss founder equity statistics in more detail, however, we refer you to Nesheim's *High-Tech Start-Up.*[9] Nesheim does an excellent job of discussing the reality of founder equity (p. 6 and elsewhere), and provides specific quantitative detail in the Saratoga Venture Tables, which show the relevant ownership percentages for founders, key employees, and venture investors for several companies that reached IPO.

In situations where control is ceded unwillingly, the transition can be very painful. We observed one start-up technology venture in the food pathology field, where the inventing entrepreneur (who served as full-time CTO) maintained a controlling interest through two rounds of financing, including a round of preferred stock. The company struggled to reach the market, however, and was forced to complete two additional rounds of financing under difficult circumstances. In the process, the inventing entrepreneur was required to give up controlling interest. The investors also replaced the original CEO (selected by the founder) with an industry professional. This was clearly a negative transition, both for the CEO and the inventing entrepreneur, as both felt they were betrayed by the investor group and the board of directors. The inventing entrepreneur temporarily went to part-time, primarily to help the company conserve cash. But the situation was exacerbated when the new CEO failed to get the company turned around. Eventually, the company was taken over by one of the investor groups. At that point, the CEO quit, and one of the investors stepped in to run the company on a pro bono basis. The inventing entrepreneur is still the CTO of the corporation and the single largest (though minority) shareholder, but the series of transitions has been especially difficult for him.

On the whole, serial entrepreneurs were less likely to demonstrate founder's syndrome or reluctance giving up ownership control; many openly discussed the low probability of maintaining control for any length of time. In many cases, where founders chose to participate in a nonexecutive role (e.g., by serving as a part-time CTO/CSO or as an advisor), the inventing entrepreneur either gave up ownership control immediately, or effectively never had it.[10]

Founder's syndrome represents the most significant problem in considering the "control/ownership" exit. In general, most inventing entrepreneurs we interviewed were comfortable ceding day-to-day authority within the commercialization process, especially once they fully appreciated the administrative requirements of a for-profit corporation. But many of these same individuals balked at giving up decision-making power for technology disposition and even company strategy.

A balance must be achieved between the innovator's technology expertise and the resources required to execute commercialization. As the inventing entrepreneur considers her own goals and the goals of the commercialization process, she will have to reach her own conclusions about the control/ownership exit.

LESS THAN PERFECT EXITS

We've focused primarily on positive exits, but statistics show that a significant number of technology-based ventures will fail.[11] Realistically, even some "successes" will involve corporate exits detrimental to investors, employees, and founders. Let's consider some possible negative outcomes, and how these eventualities could affect the inventing entrepreneur. The most obvious negative outcome is the failure of the business. Examples of underlying causes of failure include the following: The technology does not perform as expected, product is never brought to market, customers do not buy the product, products cannot be sold profitably, and so on. While companies fail for many reasons, ultimately companies fail when they run out of money to operate. Just as the ultimate cause of a person's death is lack of blood flow to the brain, which can be triggered by a heart attack or cancer or other ailments and traumas, the ultimate cause of the failure of a business is lack of cash. There are still many potential outcomes of failure, but the key ones for our interests have to do with control of the organization, control of the intellectual property, and long-term impact on inventing entrepreneurs. We'll start with a simplified example of a negative exit event.

A SIMPLIFIED NEGATIVE EXIT EXAMPLE

Before delving into this section, we remind inventing entrepreneurs to keep in mind that specific contracts executed by the company may impact the outcomes

TABLE 14-1 Hypothetical Capitalization after IP License Agreement				
	Stock Purchased	*Share Price*	*Investment*	*Percent Ownership*
Founder	900,000	$.01	$9,000	90%
TTO	100,000	N/A	N/A	10%
TOTAL	1,000,000			100%

of either success or failure. With this in mind, we're now going to walk through the dissolution of a hypothetical technology-based start-up company. This is dramatically simplified, though it is based on real-world observations.

At the start of Year 1, an inventing entrepreneur establishes a new venture. He purchases 900,000 shares of stock at par value ($.01/share). He owns 100 percent of the company. He negotiations a license to utilize the intellectual property (i.e., the underlying innovations he discovered and/or developed in the research laboratory, which were previously disclosed to the technology transfer office and are currently in patent prosecution) from his academic institution. Rather than make an up-front cash payment to the technology transfer office, he (i.e., the company) agrees to give the TTO 10 percent of the outstanding stock in the company in exchange for the license. Table 14-1 shows the current capitalization of the company.

The inventing entrepreneur then raises $1 million from private investors for 50 percent ownership of the venture. Table 14-2 shows the new capitalization.

Just for review, the theoretical value just prior to the financing event (the "pre-money valuation") was $1,000,000, because there were 1 million shares outstanding apparently worth $1/share (since investors were willing to pay this per share price). The financing adds $1 million in cash to the company's assets, so the valuation after the financing ("post-money valuation") is $2 million. This can be shown as either $1 million (pre-money valuation) + $1 million cash = $2 million, or by noting that the stock price is $1/share and there are 2 million shares outstanding, so the total firm value is theoretically $2 million.

The inventing entrpreneur now owns 45 percent of the company, the tech transfer office owns 5 percent, and the investors have 50 percent. As part of the investment arrangement, the investors demand preferential exit terms: Whenever an exit event takes place, they will have the right to recover their investment before any other shareholders get paid.[12]

In Year 2, it becomes clear that the venture's technologies and products do not present significantly more value-add to customers than existing products. The

TABLE 14-2 Hypothetical Capitalization after Angel Financing				
	Stock Purchased	*Share Price*	*Investment*	*Percent Ownership*
Founder	900,000	$.01	$9,000	45%
TTO	100,000	N/A	N/A	5%
Angel Investors	1,000,000	$1.00	$1,000,000	50%
TOTAL	2,000,000			100%

venture will be unable to compete effectively for sales and does not have an obvious alternative prospect. Although the company still has some cash left, the shareholders agree to close the company and distribute the assets.[13]

Let's say the company has $750,000 in cash and saleable assets as well as the intellectual property rights. The investors have first claim to $1,000,000, per their investment agreement. In this case, we assume they will simply draw out $750,000 from the company's bank account. All that remains is the disposition of the intellectual property.

Realistically, the most probable outcome is that the intellectual property will revert back to the university. This is, in some ways, ironic, in that the IP should have represented a significant amount of value in the company's capitalization. But without funds, the inventing entrepreneur probably has no commercialization path, and it is unlikely that the investors would want to make the effort to attempt to sell the IP on the open market. Retaining the license probably requires regular payments to the university, and most licenses have "performance clauses" that demand that the licensee demonstrate reasonable progress on commercialization. In this situation, it's almost certain that the license will be terminated.

Let's review the outcomes. The inventing entrepreneur has lost his $9,000 investment. If he was working unpaid for the company, then he has suffered an opportunity cost as well. The investors have lost $250,000. The university has suffered an opportunity cost associated with not having licensed the technology for cash to another firm.

Consider now, that when they made their investment, the investors had demanded only that they receive the first $500,000 at exit.[14] In this case, the investors get $500,000, and we again assume the IP reverts to the university. At that point, the remaining $250,000 will be returned to the owners of the company based on their stock ownership. So $125,000 will go back to the investors, $12,500 to the university, and $112,500 to the inventing entrepreneur founder. All things considered, this would be an extraordinarily generous outcome for the inventing entrepreneur, and, frankly, we've never seen something quite like this occur. The investors have lost $500,000, of which $125,000 went straight into the pockets of the inventing entrepreneur and the technology transfer office. This may provide a sense of why savvy investors carefully negotiate investment contracts.[15]

CONTROL OF THE ORGANIZATION AT FAILURE

When a company fails, control of the organization (and/or its assets) will default to various groups or individuals based on the capital structure of the firm and its contractual obligations. In the United States, a company in bankruptcy is obliged to pay back creditors prior to distributing assets to equity owners. In other words, if the business fails and the company owes a bank $20,000, the bank will get first rights to any remaining assets before investors (stockholders) receive anything. Once creditors' demands have been satisfied, remaining assets (if any) may be distributed to stockholders on the basis of the negotiated rights of those stockholders.

If the company has preferred stockholders (i.e., a certain class of stockholders have preferential exit terms), they may receive payout before common stockholders (most founders have common stock). This may seem counterintuitive, since it suggests that the individuals that have been involved the longest (usually the founders) may be the last to obtain rewards on exit (whether the exit is lucrative or the result of failure).

Actual "control" of the organization follows ownership and other contractual obligations. If, as is far more likely than our example, the company had operated until the cash was depleted, control would then presumably default to the investors. The entrepreneur and TTO might want to raise more funds, but if the company is bankrupt, the investors might have the right to demand liquidation of the assets to get some of their preferred payment. If the company owed money to creditors (suppliers, debtholders, etc.) at the time of bankruptcy, those creditors would have first say in asset liquidation, even before the investor group.

Of course, the situation could be significantly worse. The company may have spent all of its investment capital and accumulated additional debts and liabilities, including payroll liabilities and accounts payable for supplies, services, and inventory. In these situations, a third-party settlement or even bankruptcy court are possible—because these are situations in which all of the assets of the corporation go to pay off as much of the debt as possible. Stockholders (including the founder and the investors) may be left with nothing at all. We presume here that the corporation shields the founders and other stockholders from liabilities beyond the firm's asset base.[16] If the failure of the business is the result of (deliberate) wrongdoing, however, then other outcomes, including lawsuits and even criminal prosecution, are possible. This is true for any organization, no matter the size—Enron being the most prominent example.

CONTROL OF THE INTELLECTUAL PROPERTY AT FAILURE

With control over the organization goes control of the intellectual property,[17] which is, by default, an asset of the firm. It often merits special consideration because unlike other assets (e.g. cash, inventory, furniture, computer equipment), it often cannot be easily monetized. It bears more similarity to certain types of trade secrets, such as customer lists, than to hard assets. Regardless, unless special arrangements have been negotiated for the intellectual property, it will be treated as a firm asset, and the people or organizations that control the firm will dispose of the IP as they see fit.

We separate this from the issue of organizational control at failure, because there are other potential implications for the inventing entrepreneur. If, for example, the intellectual property were acquired by the investors, both the university and the inventing entrepreneur could experience difficulties in patenting or licensing related discoveries from that researcher's laboratory. Though the university would typically retain the right to practice the intellectual property, follow-on innovations might require access to the lost intellectual property to be practiced commercially. Consequently, without the earlier IP that was licensed to the company, it becomes difficult to protect and generate commercial value from downstream IP. In general this is a rare occurrence, but one that should be carefully considered in the licensing and financing processes.

LONG-TERM OUTCOMES FOR INVENTING ENTREPRENEURS

The long-term outcomes for founders and entrepreneurs associated with failed ventures vary dramatically. Every person who participated in some fashion in the dot-come boom of the late 1990s and early 2000s has multiple stories of brilliant successes and cataclysmic failures. Some failures involved entrepreneurs who were hardly daunted by bankruptcy and simply moved on to other opportunities; other collapses branded and scarred entrepreneurs, effectively blacklisting them indefinitely from new venture deals.

For the inventing entrepreneur, the long-term impact will depend heavily on three factors: The inventing entrepreneur's affinity for the technology and company, the dynamics within the ownership group, and the inventing entrepreneur's attitude towards failure and learning. We'll discuss each briefly.

If the inventing entrepreneur has high affinity towards his technology and the venture, it's very possible that the long-term impact of failure could be severe. He may see the failure as a personal failure. In addition, he may attribute negative perceptions to third parties, such as the technology transfer office, colleagues, and investors. While the failure of the organization could be tied, directly or indirectly, to the failure of the technology and the inventing entrepreneur, only the inventing entrepreneur in total control of a venture (including management control) could claim sole responsibility for failure. Even then, we would anticipate that there were external contributing factors. Komisar's comment about luck runs both ways: Success depends heavily on good luck, and failure is often caused by bad luck.

Regardless, for most of the inventing entrepreneurs we spoke with, the emotional toll associated with a negative exit seems to exceed the financial toll. Most of the inventing entrepreneurs had retained university positions or could reclaim an academic post if necessary. This matches our observation that the primary goal for inventing entrepreneurs is the commercialization of a novel technology rather than financial rewards or recognition. At the same time, because we believe that technology affinity is correlated with start-up formation (instead of direct licensing), it strongly suggests that inventing entrepreneurs may be surprised by the emotions generated if they are severed from the venture. In fact, we posit that inventing entrepreneurs respond with very strong emotions to such events, especially if they haven't previously envisioned some level of separation.

We encourage inventing entrepreneurs to pay close attention to the internal dynamics of the ownership group, including the technology transfer office and investors. Our observations and experiences suggest that founders who *partner* with other owners develop a relationship that buoys success and softens failure, both during the venture development process and after the venture has exited. To this end, we encourage inventing entrepreneurs to play an active role communicating with other owners, including keeping them apprised of both progress and setbacks. We've often heard experienced executives state: "Never surprise your investors, especially in a formal meeting." In other words, inventing entrpreneurs should help the other owners become part of the journey. If commercialization succeeds, they will believe they contributed to something powerful. If the venture fails, they are more likely to believe that the participants made every reasonable effort. It may seem counterintuitive that financiers will invest in entrepreneurs coming from failed ventures, including failed ventures in which that financier lost money. But we have repeatedly seen this happen. On the other hand, unhappy investors, especially surprised and unhappy investors, may remember the failings of the entrepreneur for many years, despite whatever milestones the venture achieved.

Finally, we believe that growth and learning mark the inventing entrepreneur who will recover from failure. This includes an honest assessment of failure, an analysis of the role that luck played, and acknowledgment of the mistakes made by the key participants. We have seen inventing entrepreneurs fixated on a single event or circumstance as the sole cause of failure; we have seen inventing entrepeneurs unable to accept responsibility for poor business decisions. But there are countless examples of inventing entrepreneurs with failed ventures on their resumes who gained experience and wisdom and moved on. Professor Stonebraker, for example, took useful lessons from the failure of Illustra and went on to start numerous other successful ventures. Not all of the companies that have licensed Professor Church's technologies have been runaway successes, but he remains tremendously successful innovator and advisor to many start-ups. Professor Farritor attempted to work with entrepreneurs to license a non-surgical technology from his laboratory, but ran into obstacles negotiating terms with the technology transfer office. He continues to be optimistic about that unlicensed technology, and fully expects to see it in commercial use within the next couple of years.

WHAT WILL I DO AFTER THE EXIT?

Inventing entrepreneurs often have a wide variety of options after exit events. Some return to the academic environment; some never left the academic environment in the first place. Some retire, while others move on to new ventures. On the whole, we found no clear pattern for inventing-entrepreneur behavior or goals after the participatory and/or financial exit. To close our discussion on exits as well as preface the issue of preserving identity, we provide additional information on where some of the inventing entrepreneurs we interviewed are now.

John Hennessy has gone on to become the current president of Stanford University. George Church is currently advising his twenty-second start-up while continuing his illustrious work at Harvard Medical School. Paul Reckwerdt anticipates getting involved in another technology venture when his tenure at Tomotherapy ends. John Devereux feels that he accomplished his goal—helping enable the emerging science of genomics with the software he originally developed for Professor Oliver Smithies:

> I always believed that this effort and technology would enrich the
> university, as well as provide tremendous benefits to researchers

worldwide.... I took a real love for our customers; we were helping them do better research and accomplish things.

The NimbleGen cofounders (Blattner, Cerrina, and Sussman) have continued their cutting-edge research and are turning their eyes toward new commercialization opportunities. Michael Stonebraker has worked with numerous other start-ups after Ingres was sold to Computer Associates and he "retired" from UC–Berkeley; but he's now an MIT professor and involved in new start-ups commercializing software prototypes developed in his MIT lab. It's hard to imagine Professor Fred Blattner will ever *not* be involved with a commercialization venture.

What inventing entrepreneurs do after their personal exit (regardless of whether that exit occurs quickly or after many years) is probably a function of three key factors:

1. *Does the inventing entrepreneur have an "entrepreneurial" personality?* If so, the odds are that he'll find himself actively looking for the next opportunity, whether from his own research or others. Michael Stonebraker appears to fit this description, even though he doesn't have the specific drive to be CEO of his ventures; he sees his value in the early commercialization stages, developing the technology and "bringing it to light." John Hennessy, on the other hand, has exceptional senior management talent but never wanted to leave the university in the first place. He seems to have found his true strength running a major research institution rather than scrappy start-ups. In general, we don't see that many "reluctant inventing entrepreneurs" converted into serial entrepreneurs.

2. *Does the inventing entrepreneur's research focus offer both a broad investigative regime and/or have extensive marketplace implications?* If the research represents the leading edge of a broad new area of scientific investigation then the inventing entrepreneur may have the rare opportunity to usher in multiple commercializable innovations. Alternatively, specialized technologies could be applied across varied markets. Professor Deluca's research focus is relatively specialized on the biochemistry of vitamin D, but the potential market for utilizing vitamin D analogs to target varied diseases is both enormous and mainly untapped. If, on the other hand, the scientist's expertise has focused on specialized phenomena with niche applications, the options to start additional ventures based on that research stream may be limited.

3. *What are the inventing entrepreneur's broader goals in life?* Those goals may be changed by the entrepreneurial experience, but this only emphasizes the need to consider them at the start of the venture as well as at the end of it. Most academic researchers didn't become scientists with the parallel intent of actively participating in commercial ventures. If those intentions and goals haven't changed significantly since the venture was started, then it may be safe to assume that the venture was an anomaly. An entrepreneurial adventure can reinforce non-entrepreneurial goals, leading some individuals to

focus on family or personal growth. Entrepreneurship, especially in the technology sector, is generally described as all consuming, leaving relatively little time or energy for other pursuits and goals. We expect that the personal fulfillment of the entrepreneurial journey, as measured by perceived learning and personal growth, will be the primary determinant of whether inventing entrepreneurs who return to academia will seek out additional entrepreneurial opportunities.

In *Angel Investing,* Robinson and Van Osnabrugge note: "The struggle to grow an idea into a smoothly operating entrepreneurial entity is not for those who lack courage and the conviction of their ideals."[18] And Nesheim comments:

> The toll of a start-up depends on how firm a foundation the employee has for his self-worth. A start-up is the most dangerous for the personality whose personal worth is wrapped up in the degree of his success or failure on the job.[19]

Exiting a venture, from either a financial or participatory perspective, can bring a sigh of relief and/or a sigh of regret. Some inventing entrepreneurs are more than ready to return to the relative security of the academic research laboratory; others don a new suit of armor and charge more windmills. In either case, we believe that the inventing entrepreneur will be transformed in profound ways.

Conclusions and Summary

Most inventing entrepreneurs anticipate some types of exit-event outcomes. These expectations may not be conscious—part of our goal in this chapter was to help the inventing entrepreneur explicitly consider his expectations.

In the world of early-stage companies, the exit event generally refers to either a change of corporate control or the return of funds to investors. The inventing entrepreneur, however, may experience numerous types of exits, including the transition from active involvement with the venture to passive involvement or even non-involvement. Only with conscientious self-examination and honest appraisal of his goals and purpose will the inventing entrepreneur approach the entire issue of exit with confidence. Exits can be good or bad, and it is the relatively rare inventing entrepreneur whose consistent, active leadership role at a high-growth technology-based venture can be maintained from start-up all the way until the company experiences a true exit event (such as acquisition or IPO). Regardless, participation in commercialization activities has a profound impact on the identity of the inventing entrepreneur. In the final chapter of this book, we'll discuss how inventing entrepreneurs preserve their scientific identity.

Endnotes

1. Author's note: We can to try to clarify Devereux's comment. When GCG was formed, Devereux and his co-founder became the two sole stockholders. If, for example, they did not *purchase* the stock, but were simply *granted* the stock by the

company (which is a common mistake made by first time entrepreneurs), then the value of that grant is treated by the U.S. Internal Revenue Service as *taxable compensation*. In this case, for example, Devereux's stock might have have been worth, on paper, $1 million (because there were capital assets, customers, and ongoing revenues and net income that might suggest the company was worth, in total more than $1 million). If the IRS had assessed taxes on that amount, treating it as income, Devereux could have owed hundreds of thousands of dollars in federal income taxes, *despite the fact that he did not receive a single dollar in cash*. There are appropriate legal mechanisms to avoid this problem. We did not ask Devereux to go into explicit details about the financial structure of GCG, so we don't know for certain if these were the circumstances (or how they were resolved), but inventing entrepreneurs are strongly advised to discuss this issue with corporate counsel and possibly even tax specialists at the time of start-up.

2. Stuart, T. E. & Sorenson, O. 2003. Liquidity events and the geographic distribution of entrepreneurial activity. *Administrative Science Quarterly*, 48(2): 175–201.

3. For the founders of some companies, the financial exit of selling stock may occur very differently than for external investors. For example, if the founder's management role ends, the company might offer to buy some or all of the founder's stock. In some cases, founders may have opportunities to sell stock to third parties in private transactions, usually approved by the company. Again, these circumstances can get very complicated; we recommend that inventing entrepreneurs speak to a competent attorney to discuss these and other potential outcomes.

4. Reckwerdt stayed on in the president position when that CEO was replaced.

5. It is appropriate to note that Reckwerdt participated in the Geometrix exit, so he had seen the process previously.

6. Nesheim, J. P. 150.

7. This is usually only possible if the company either generated enough cash from operations to cover the cost of growth or raised angel funds at high valuations. In the former case (organic growth), the inventing entrepreneur (owner) may have legitimate concens about transitioning to venture-funded growth. Most of our observations of the latter scenario strongly suggest that the early financing valuations may have been too high, enabling the inventing entrepreneurs to retain artificial expectations. Although inventing entrepreneurs struggle with this issue even when it occurs in the first financing (which is often appropriate), we suggest that the longer the "illusion" of control lasts, the more intense the inventing entrepreneur's struggle to give it up.

8. As we've discussed, although final authority may reside with the majority stockholders, founding scientists often maintain special power within start-up technology ventures. Their participation and/or approval may be fundamental to the success of the business, regardless of their ownership stake. We found, in most cases, that inventing entrepreneurs seemed to understand this, whether they stated it explicitly or not. A few inventing entrepreneurs, however, hoped to maintain a controlling ownership interest in the venture, specifically to ensure that their vision is fully implemented. In rare cases this seemed to stem from an internally driven sense that the founder/scientist had an inherent right to the largest financial rewards.

9. Nesheim, J. 1992. (especially Appendix A, pp 268–288).

10. In some cases, for example, the inventing entrepreneur worked directly with a venture capitalist to establish the venture. In such situations, we generally assume that, given the ownership stakes of the VC and the technology licensing office, the innovator would start out with less than 50 percent ownership of the venture.

11. "Most entrepreneurs are certain that their venture will succeed—despite the fact that nearly half of all venture-capital-backed companies don't fulfill their potential, and nearly one-third go out of business. For newly launched enterprises without venture-capital backing, failure is almost assured: Nearly 90 percent fail within three years." Gompers, P. & Lerner, J. 2001. *The Money of Invention: How Venture Capital Creates New Wealth*. HBS Press. Cambridge. P. 28

12. This is not an uncommon demand; in some situations investors might demand that twice (or a higher multiple of) their investment be paid to them before any other shareholders are paid out. It is important to consult legal counsel for the appropriate class of shares and its impact on the business.

13. This outcome, in our experience, is highly unusual—our experience suggests that most ventures end up bankrupt or significantly in debt before dissolution occurs. In some cases, this is due to the inventing entrepreneur and/or the investors being unwilling to accept defeat.

14. We've never seen an agreement in which the preferential payback is less than the investment, for reasons about to be explained.

15. To drive this point even further—imagine if the investors did not have a payout preference at all. In that case, the inventing entrepreneur would receive $337,500, an absurd outcome, though potentially legal. The investors, having apparently decided that such a loss was better than continuing the venture, might still be prompted to lead a shareholder lawsuit against the founder.

16. For example, it's quite possible that liquidating the firm's assets might not generate enough cash to pay back all of the company's debts. Under U.S. law, it is very difficult for creditors to attempt to recoup losses from the owners' personal funds. There can be exceptions, such as payroll liabilities, in some U.S. States.

17. Unless, as in some cases, the license agreement with the university specifically provides for outcomes in specific circumstances, such as bankruptcy.

18. Robinson, R. & Van Osnabrugge, M., p. 16

19. Nesheim, p. 150

PART V

PRESERVING IDENTITY

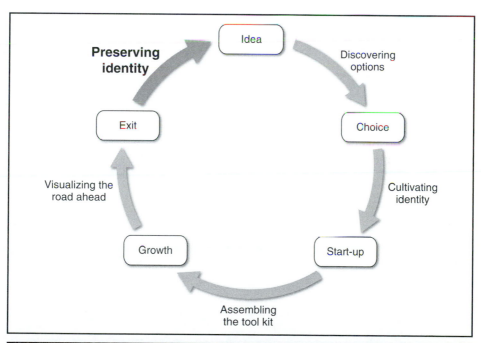

Stages of the Entrepreneurial Process

CHAPTER 15

IDENTITY, GROWTH, AND LEARNING ON THE JOURNEY

OVERVIEW

In this final chapter, we return to the central concept of role identity and revisit how the entrepreneurial journey transforms the inventing entrepreneur. Throughout our interviews, inventing entrepreneurs were eager to share what they had learned from their experiences. Nearly all had transforming journeys; they emerged with new perspectives, new role identities, new beliefs, and often, new personal and professional goals. We believe that entrepreneurship transforms its willing participants, but that inventing entrepreneurs tend to have an unusually intense experience for two reasons.

First, their scientific training provides a framework for appreciating, understanding, and internalizing the breadth and depth of information associated with entrepreneurial ventures. Second, because most inventing entrepreneurs approach the commercialization process (at least at the very start) from a problem solving perspective rather than a profit-generating perspective, immersion in the world of corporate ventures provokes new thinking. Some will conclude that they prefer the research laboratory of the university; others find the rapid-fire world of the start-up venture exciting and challenging.

Regardless, we hope to provide even the nascent inventing entrepreneur with a long-term perspective on the impact of the journey.

SCIENTIFIC IDENTITY: BACK TO THE BASICS

Entrepreneurship represents a mechanism by which researchers can convert the promise of a novel technology into realized societal benefit. But researchers *become* inventing entrepreneurs for many different reasons. Some see it as the logical way to bring technology to the marketplace. Some see it as the next logical step in a long-term growth and learning process. A few others are driven to entrepreneurship because they perceive no alternatives for commercialization.

When a researcher chooses to become an inventing entrepreneur as a logical step in the long-term evolution of his role identity, the start-up is a vehicle through which he hopes to realize the impact of his inventions. This decision, however, leaves open the option to retain a primarily scientific identify. Professor Mackie, for example, maintained his scientific identity throughout the commercialization process of the TomoTherapy technology. On the one hand, he's well aware of the power of corporate commercialization, as he describes technology adoptions:

> If you start a company that can take your ideas out from one site to multiple sites, it's a tremendous lever. Rather than just affecting 1,000 patients a year (or less), because not everything we do would be used on every patient, the impact is multiplied by the number of clinics that have the equipment. For example, the Geometrix software to calculate dosage in radiation therapy for cancer has been used to treat millions of patients throughout the world.

But when we asked him about his role in the commercialization process, and why he chose to remain at the university even when it became clear that first Geometrix and then TomoTherapy were going to be the vehicles for technology adoption, he responded: "It was more of a lifestyle thing. I really enjoy being a professor."

Another inventing entrepreneur we interviewed described the self-actualization that accompanies success:

> The way professors view their career accomplishments is through their publications or graduate students. By the time a student graduates and sets up a lab and conducts high-quality research—it becomes, say, 10 years later or more. That is when we can say, "See what we've done ... there is good in that." But for a company, we can perhaps do that in 5 years or so. They are not the same thing and they do not compete—but they are both ways in which we can realize that what we are working on is useful to humanity in some way.

At the same time, he qualified his response by noting that the decision to become an inventing entrepreneur should be conscious and deliberate. This is sobering advice, even for researchers who agree that academic research with proven value should be made available to the broad market.

> Don't start a company unless you really want to start a company. There is a lot more than you think there is, and there is a lot more that can go wrong than you think it could, but the way I looked at the new company was that it allowed me to bring the technology out of my lab. It is no use [to do] academic research if it is not put to the test or to good use in society.

However, for a significant proportion of inventors-turned-entrepreneurs, start-ups represent a course of action selected after a number of other commercialization options have been exhausted. This is particularly pertinent in situations where existing industry players are reluctant to adopt novel technologies, often because their level of investment in an existing technology precludes the introduction of radical changes to their platform. Inventing entrepreneurs often described two key factors that drove their entrepreneurial behavior: The desire to prevent their nascent technologies from languishing and the aspiration to have a broader societal impact. When other commercialization options reached dead-ends, some inventors reluctantly initiated entrepreneurial activity as a last recourse.

The plurality of motives for becoming an inventing entrepreneur suggests that there is considerable variance with regard to scientists' inclination to change their scientific role identity. Attitudes range from unwillingness, which results in noninvolvement in commercialization activity, to enthusiasm, which may result in a complete role-identity transformation (sometimes leading the scientist to become a full-time entrepreneur as discussed in Chapter 8). Studies suggest that a majority of scientists who are involved in commercialization activity fall somewhere in between these two extremes. These inventing entrepreneurs embrace more than one role identity for some period of time. Most scientists in these situations recognize the need to actively manage multiple identities (i.e., the identity of a scientist versus that of an entrepreneur).

Finally, we have observed that most inventing entrepreneurs place high importance on retaining the extant role identity of being a scientist, even in cases where the inventing entrepreneur has taken on a primarily commercial role, temporarily or permanently. These individuals, can be further categorized based on whether they maintain their affiliation with an academic research institution. There are significant advantages to maintaining academic identity and the benefits that accrue from it. One scientist described the advantages of academic status this way:

> A lot of investigators make a serious mistake of seeing this lucrative bunch of money, and they make all kinds of agreements, even before they talk to people knowledgeable about intellectual property at the university or [TTO]. And they sometimes give that all away. But even worse, they make agreements as to what they're going to work on. And

that's a mistake because if you're an inventor or a university innovator, you want the freedom—that's why we're here at the university—you want the freedom to go whichever direction your mind tells you, and not some CEO at a company.[1]

But even the scientists who have given up all ties to the academic world tend to maintain some level of scientific identify. Paul Reckwerdt noted, almost wistfully, "My software is still the basis for what the [Tomotherapy] machine is running. But in business you get further and further away from technology development." And Virginia Deibel, who has been CEO of her start-up for more than 5 years, still attributes some of her success to her underlying identity as a scientist: "It has been extremely beneficial in putting together experimental design, scientific design—helping customers think through their problems critically."

Another inventing entrepreneur indicated that though he had been a scientist for more than 30 years and had encouraged others to start companies, "Neither [I nor my venture partner] wanted to leave the university to join the business." For these individuals, the decision to initiate or participate in start-ups clearly did not come at the expense of forgoing their extant role identity as scientists. Indeed, many inventing entrepreneurs go to great lengths to maintain their academic role identity even while engaging in commercialization activity. These inventing entrepreneurs view their multiple identities in terms of a hierarchy comprised of a focal scientific identity overlaid with a secondary entrepreneurial identity.

As we reviewed the comments from inventing entrepreneurs, along with our direct observations of the research discovery to technology commercialization process, we noted that inventing entrepreneurship tends to be cyclical (as shown in the "Stages of the Entrepreneurial Process" graphic shown throughout the book). From our research, we concluded that for the inventing entrepreneur, *a critical component of this cycle is the preservation of the scientific identity* to ensure a continual supply of new ideas that generate societal and economic benefits.

This can be seen, at some level, in the experiences of nearly every inventing entrepreneur we've observed, including those profiled in this book. An excellent example is Professor Jamie Thomson of the University of Wisconsin–Madison, whose stem-cell discoveries and innovations have generated worldwide attention (see Profile 15-1). Thomson's technologies have been licensed to numerous corporations and he has had the opportunity to serve in scientific advisory roles for some of those firms. These experiences exposed him to the entrepreneurial cycle, in a less intensive role before the formation of Stem Cell Products, Inc. and Cellular Dynamics, Inc. It is useful to contrast Thomson's perspective with that of David Sneider, the business manager currently running these two companies. The contrast highlights key differences between the inventing entrepreneur and the serial business entrepreneur.

Professor James Thomson and David Sneider

Stem-cell research is one of the most innovative and controversial technologies ever developed in an academic research lab: a fact that has made Professor Jamie Thomson a well-known academic researcher worldwide. Thomson fits the journey model of the "research transfer entrepreneur." He has retained his primary role identity as a research professor at the University of Wisconsin–Madison, but he is also one of the scientific founders of two start-up companies that are commercializing stem-cell technology: Cellular Dynamics, Inc. and Stem Cell Products, Inc. The person managing those companies, on the other hand, isn't as well known—unlike Thomson, David Sneider has not been on the cover of *Time* magazine.

Throughout this book we have talked about "professional management," a general term that refers to experienced business professionals who bring expertise, experience, and connections to the challenging process of growing a technology-based company. Sneider has become a consummate growth-company executive. As CFO of Tellabs, Inc., he took the company public in 1980. As CFO of Third Wave Technologies, he negotiated the acquisition of the company by Applied Biosystems, though this acquisition fell through after Sneider left Third Wave (Third Wave subsequently completed an IPO). He was the CFO of NimbleGen, another company profiled in this book, raising seven rounds of financing before leaving for other opportunities. He is now the chief business officer of both Cellular Dynamics and Stem Cell Products, having been brought in by the seed investors to get those companies off the ground.

Thomson and Sneider have dramatically different backgrounds and skill sets. In this final profile, we want to show how differing perspectives and goals come together in an early-stage venture, and to hint at the identity differences between an inventing entrepreneur and an established professional manager.

The entire inventing entrepreneurship cycle starts, of course, with fundamental research begun at the university. When Thomson was at the university, he wasn't even sure what was patentable:

> At the time that we derived primate embryonic stem cells it really was not obvious to me that that was a patentable thing. But we went to the technology transfer office and described what we did and described it to the patent attorney.... It turned out that a few years later they were successful in getting that original primate patent.

For Thomson, there are two important lessons about innovation disclosure. First, technology transfer patent agents could understand and evaluate the patentability and commercial potential of innovations, even early in the process. Second, it made sense to go to the tech transfer office early:

> The easiest time to go to [the technology transfer office] and talk about [an invention] is when you've already written a manuscript [for a publication] about it—because it's quite easy just to give the manuscript to the patent attorneys and they'll do the patent and your involvement is just to proof it and see that it's appropriate.... You have to think about whether there's practical

(continues)

utility in what you've just done, whether a company might want to do that for some reason, and whether it really is novel and unexpected and the things you need in a patent. Then you take it to [the technology transfer office] and they have to decide not only whether it is patentable but whether they think they can make money on it someday—because it's a considerable investment to get the patent.

Like many academic researchers, Professor Thomson has begun thinking about commercialization issues relatively early in the process. Decades ago, disclosing inventions to a technology transfer office was often a "hands-off" process in which the researcher turned over responsibility for any commercial activities to another, almost foreign department of the university. That perspective has changed dramatically, as Thomson notes:

> It's very good to keep track of the fact that what you do does have commercial interest, and it's important when you're about to publish that you actually think it through and say, "Does this have commercial value?

Thomson's and Sneider's paths would cross when Thomson made the decision to participate more actively in commercialization. He was introduced to seed investors prepared to finance early-stage development outside the university. The formation of Cellular Dynamics and Stem Cell Products (and the licensing of the technology from the university) represented the critical events required to initiate commercialization. As is often the case, the investors wanted to hire a professional manager they already knew—someone with a successful track record. David Sneider fit the description.

Sneider had developed a strong resume of executive management roles at rapidly growing biotechnology companies. His experience at Third Wave led directly to his role at NimbleGen: The CEO of NimbleGen, Mike Treble, has been Chief Operating Officer at Third Wave while Sneider was CFO at Third Wave. With a background in both accounting and law, Sneider's breadth of knowledge makes him a valuable asset to an early-stage technology company. He describes the broad range of activities that the senior managers of an early-stage venture must navigate, often with limited resources:

> Mike Treble [the CEO of Nimblegen] was hired to put together a team that would ultimately develop this idea into an instrument that could be sold independently or would be used for producing arrays.... Mike brought me in on a part-time basis; I went full time three or four months later. I was more than a finance officer; I have a law degree—I was responsible for looking at terms and conditions, negotiating contracts, hiring, setting up human resources, purchasing terms and conditions, and even [managing] the legal structure for the company as well.

The investor group had very specific ideas about the type of person they were looking for, and they had experience putting academic founders together with professional managers. David Sneider explains the connection, and also talks about the type of manager he believes is necessary for this type of venture:

> The initial seed investors [in Stem Cell Products and Cellular Dynamics], who were the seed investors for NimbleGen, thought that I would be a strong candidate for a start-up company in the initial stages—to get the company viable.... If it were me [looking to hire start-up management], I would look for somebody who has gone through the process and done it successfully. I wouldn't want to hire somebody or use somebody as a trainee. I would like somebody who has taken a company from inception (or close to it) and has run it, if possible, to IPO or acquisition. And they are available. I don't know if you could run a newspaper ad, but they exist and they are well known in the venture-capital community, so I would network through there to find that type of person.

Unlike some of the inventing entrepreneurs we interviewed, who chose to take an active executive role within the commercialization vehicle, Professor Thomson knew he planned to stay at the university. Like Professor George Church, Thomson sees his primary value in his academic research role. He understands the potential tension between pure research and commercialization issues, but he also has relatively firm beliefs about his rationale for his scientific role identity:

> I went into science having no clue that you could actually make money doing it. When I was in high school, that was when recombinant DNA came out and nobody started biotech companies. Ultimately you go into academics because you love a certain area.

In some ways, the match between the investor group, Thomson, and Sneider covers all the major functional criteria for an early-stage technology venture. Thomson brings world-renowned scientific research and inventions. Sneider has the business expertise, savvy, and connections; the investors provided the initial capital and performed the preliminary market diligence. Sneider expects the investors and business managers to provide the knowledge to help evaluate that commercial potential:

> The business partner or the investor should be able to assess the value of the technology. Unless I'm naïve or foolish, it would be rare to find a scientist who has the ability or knowledge [to value technologies], other than on a cursory basis.

We've talked about the interaction between inventing entrepreneurs and corporate management, and about how inventing entrepreneurs can prepare for the long term. Sometimes it's helpful to hear it from someone who's been through the entire process. Sneider provides that perspective, having been through the process numerous times. He's generally optimistic about how inventing entrepreneurs and professional management interact, especially when savvy seed investors are involved to ensure that everyone's incentives are aligned. While he notes that scientific founders may not be involved forever, he is at least encouraging about the financial rewards available for successful endeavors:

> At some point the technology might develop to the extent that the original founders might not recognize it anymore.... One has to realize that there might be a time to separate—and the founding scientists might have to take the role of more passive shareholders. In any company that has to go through multiple rounds of financing, all of the early people, both the founding scientists and early investors, are going to get diluted along the way. I don't know how that can be avoided—[but] if you get to the final goal line, be it IPO or acquisition—there's enough money to go around to make everybody happy.

In Thomson and Sneider we have two experts in disparate fields working together to lead entrepreneurial activities. Understanding what motivates them helps highlight the challenges and opportunities that every inventing entrepreneur faces. Thomson describes this motivation in terms of his primary role as an academic researcher:

> The joy of academics is the freedom of academics. If you deal with a company and have a confidentiality agreement, you have to divide your brain in some way and just not talk freely about things. For me that wasn't worth it, because I like to be able to talk about what I care to talk about.

(continues)

Sneider describes his own motivations, and explains why he keeps coming back to lead entrepreneurial ventures:

> After Tellabs I had a seven-year hiatus from start-up companies. I was working for a company in an unrelated industry, I was making a fantastic salary, I had a company car and all kinds of benefits, but I didn't have any equity in the company. The bottom line for me was I gave that up and took a job with a start-up in Madison [Third Wave], making a salary that was well less than half of what I had been making, without any of the perks, for the opportunity to have stock and stock options.... I got tired or bored of working as a salaried employee; I didn't have any skin in the game and I lost interest. When companies get to be a certain size, they get to be a lot less fun. Now that I've been doing it for the last decade, I like working in a smaller environment than a big corporate environment; I like making a difference—my decisions greatly impact the company.... It's nice putting your seal or your stamp on and growing something.

THE UNDERLYING CHARACTERISTICS OF INVENTING ENTREPRENEURS

We believe that all inventing entrepreneurs, at some point, manage multiple role identities; this includes preserving a scientific identity. This appears to be true despite dramatic differences in goals, interests, and perspectives across inventing entrepreneurs.

We have also been struck by the similarities of the underlying characteristics of inventing entrepreneurs. We cannot speak to whether these characteristics are self-selected via the mechanism of competitive research and commercial opportunities, or whether the combined processes of research methodology and business experience encourages and enables these characteristics. We describe three of these characteristics in this section: *analytical optimism, pride in craftsmanship* and *self-reflection*. Though inventing entrepreneurs share many attributes with other entrepreneurs (such as strong motivation for success and the propensity for taking calculated risks) we believe these three attributes are more specific to inventing entrepreneurs and provide additional insight into their experiences.

Analytical optimism is a sense of optimism engendered by data or research experience–based intuition. Like all entrepreneurs, inventing entrepreneurs start with the mindset that problems can be solved. In addition, inventing entrepreneurs see research and technology as fundamental tools for solving problems. Finally, the inventing entrepreneur sees inherent value in the problem solving process; *he is motivated by the problem-solving process itself, regardless of the outcome.* This optimism seems to hold even in situations when the "problem" itself has changed, or even when the technology solution turns out to be completely different from the original research. Consider this perspective from Professor Blattner, who is involved in his third research-based start-up:

> I have found that I am very optimistic. I think that always counts. I don't propose I've pursued every idea that I have had, but I am always thinking that things are going to work.

Pride in craftsmanship is the pleasure that inventing entrepreneurs obtain from direct ownership of their accomplishments, both academic and commercial. Given their strong scientific identity, inventing entrepreneurs tend to focus on the systematic process by which they address a scientific or technological challenge, including challenges in the start-up environment. Certainly, many attribute an element of their success to luck, such as being in the right place at the right time, or having serendipitously identified critical coworkers or mentors, without whose unique abilities the work might not have succeeded.

Unlike many traditional entrepreneurs, however, who strive to succeed measured strictly by the yardstick of customer adoption and/or profits, inventing entrepreneurs often perceive the inherent value of the journey experience and take pride in their involvement in the process, independent of the outcomes. We divide this personal satisfaction into three categories: pride in personal creative/learning activities, pride in others' creative/learning activities, and pride in personal involvement.

Throughout our interviews, inventing entrepreneurs discussed their learning experiences. This love of learning and creativity almost always extended to the opportunities inventing entrepreneurs wanted to create for students, colleagues, and subordinates. Virginia Deibel talked about creating an environment at TRAC Micro where scientific employees would have opportunities to grow and learn. Professor Burgess spoke about a similar pride associated with creating that type of environment within the academic environment:

> I've always believed that my students should develop their independence and their ability to be self-motivating; I shouldn't be there with a whip. I think my students have enjoyed their graduate degree more and I think the fact that all 26 of my students are still doing science suggests that maybe I did something right.

The pride associated with personal involvement, especially successful personal involvement, was a recurrent theme. In some cases that likely reflects a strong personal sense of curiosity, as with Professor Sussman, who has a preference for tackling problems hands-on:

> I always like to do things myself in the lab. If I see something cool, I like to try to do it myself, if at all possible.

Professor Church reflected on a longer-term personal success. It's useful to note that this success wasn't defined by market adoption or financial outcomes. Church takes pride that some of his earliest technologies are still under license and in use, and that in fact he had at least one repeat customer:

> The multiplex technology (licensed to Agincourt) is still out there. Agincourt is one of the major sequencing companies in the world. They just did a new license with me, 14 years after the first one, so I guess that's successful.

The inventing entrepreneur usually grasps his or her role and value within the context of progress and technological development. And, in the case of nearly every inventing entrepreneur we interviewed, this was true both for work within the academic environment and in the commercial frame. We consistently saw in the inventing entrepreneurs a capacity for **self-reflection;** in other words, the ability to identify within themselves areas of weakness or inexperience. Time and time again inventing entrepreneurs told us about specific activities they didn't like or didn't feel comfortable performing. Professor Stonebraker was very explicit:

> Taking on a bigger role [at the firm that acquired one of his start-ups] would have meant becoming vice president of engineering [at a large corporation], and that would have meant running engineering, salary reviews, pushing a lot of paper, justifying budgets — and by and large I consider all of that no fun.

Professor Handelsman reflects on the same issue, comparing herself with a colleague who did start a company:

> I think he liked the commercial challenge more than I ever have — the intrigue of going from idea to product. He can make a lot of contacts and have a lot of involvement and that doesn't bother him. It would drive me completely crazy.

COMMON EXPERIENCES OF INVENTING ENTREPRENEURS

Not only are there perceived patterns in the role identities and characteristics of inventing entrepreneurs, there are also patterns in what these entrepreneurs have experienced and learned through the process. We do not intend to summarize the many experiences of the inventors discussed in earlier chapters; instead, we highlight three common learning experiences: the importance of luck, the value of people and the everpresent challenge of technology commercialization.

THE IMPORTANCE OF LUCK

The inventing entrepreneur realizes that serendipitous events occur in start-ups as well as in science. Few entrepreneurs will deny that desirable discoveries or outcomes are aided by unpredictable events or pure accidents. There is an element of luck involved in technology-based start-up companies. Professor Burgess spoke about timing and luck:

> If you were to plot the number of days in which we felt optimistic against the number of days we felt pessimistic, so far it's not been too traumatic — but there was still a lot involved [in getting a company started that] I had no idea about. We were fortunate to get Sal [start-up COO]; we were fortunate to find about Chris [start-up CEO] and get him aboard ... because the timing [of identifying key resources when needed] doesn't always work out.

Unfortunately, luck runs both ways. Professor Stonebraker described an external circumstance over which his start-up had limited control. The outcome of that situation had a significant negative effect on his first start-up:

> For instance, Ingres was competing head to head with Oracle in the relational database market, and in 1984 IBM blessed Structure Query Language (SQL) as the relational query language. And that happened to be what Oracle implemented and not what Ingres implemented, and Oracle shrewdly capitalized on that one fact to leap ahead of Ingres. If IBM had selected a different query language, the positions of Oracle and Ingres could be reversed. There's a lot of luck involved; you have to be in the right place at the right time.

THE IMPORTANCE OF THE TEAM

Nearly every inventing entrepreneur we interviewed emphasized that team member selection was critical. In some cases, scientists maintained their scientific role identity by hiring managers who would handle the operational side of entrepreneurial activities. For Professor Burgess, finding first the right short-term leader and then a CEO was critical. Professor Raines brought in a seasoned executive. Professors Stonebraker and Church emphasized the importance of experienced financiers and scientific advisors. Professor DeLuca elaborated further:

> Handling personnel is key. Knowing, evaluating, and handling personnel is extremely important because you can't do it all; you've got to hire the right people and you have to have a pretty good nose to figure out who is going to do the job.

Paul Reckwerdt and Professor Mackie also discussed the importance of hiring, retaining, and managing good team members. They also emphasized their own values and responsibilities towards those team members, including matching the right people with the right responsibilities:

> Reckwerdt: There are so many stages in company growth. How do you get people through those stages? And how you transition your key people through the stages? You learn who the key people are, and you raise them up and grow them up to the situation you want to be in. There are some people who can't make the transition from a start-up to a real company. We nursed along a lot of our original people [from the university laboratory]—we found places for them and fit them in. Something that's a skill you can bring in is balancing multiple requirements. There's a thousand things happening here, and you have to balance them off each other and do triage and balance their impact.
>
> Mackie: It is a different world, and just because you are smart as a scientist doesn't mean you do know business. That doesn't mean you can't learn business. As Paul says, it's not rocket science; you don't have

that knowledge yet, but you can learn it. One of the key things is realizing that anything you're going to do is about the people. People made this company, employees made the company. We feel that's important. A high-tech company is about the people.

THE SEARCH FOR CHALLENGE AND GROWTH

But of all the common experiences shared by inventing entrepreneurs, we'd like to conclude with the joy of the challenge and the personal growth that these individuals achieve. Some inventing entrepreneurs gave up their academic careers (permanently or temporarily), whereas others chose to focus on their long-term research efforts. Some have managed to do both. Some have helped develop commercial products; some have watched experienced professionals bring their innovations to market (sometimes in almost unrecognizable variations). And each inventor took away something slightly different from the experience. Professor Sussman talked about the pride he takes in seeing his technology in use:

> The other day I'm watching PBS—a cancer program. There's [a research scientist] describing his experiments on finding the gene disruptors, and he did it all with Roland [NimbleGen's chief technology officer], and it's very satisfying.

Professor Rao talks about how the business side has unexpectedly increased his research output:

> It's interesting.... That was the other concern I had about forming a company: I thought my scientific productivity would go down as a result of all the time I spend on the business. But what I'm finding is that I have a lot of data that's very relevant in terms of supporting fMRI as a clinical tool—so actually I have a greater impetus to get a lot of the stuff that I have published and validated. I've been probably more scientifically productive in the last two years than I have at any other two-year period of my life.

Professor Livny, who effectively commercializes his technology from within the university structure, describes a clear sense of accomplishment from seeing Condor adopted by corporations to solve real problems:

> The advantage of working with real companies is we don't have to dream up problems—they are coming at you faster than you can think about it. As long as we don't see someone who can do it better than we do, we plan on going forward. The important part is to continuously examine what we are doing.

Conclusions and Summary

Inventing entrepreneurs share many characteristics with traditional entrepreneurs. They demonstrate motivation, optimism, and strong goal-orientation. Some of these characteristics are intensified by their scientific training; other characteristics emerge with distinctions from traditional entrepreneurial traits (such as inventing entrepreneurs' focus on the learning aspects of the journey).

The entrepreneurial journey itself transforms inventing entrepreneurs. While the transformation tends to reinforce certain key lessons about entrepreneurship, every inventing entrepreneur undergoes an idiosyncratic change, taking away unique lessons from the process. The outcome of this personal growth is unpredictable, though we believe that certain entrepreneurial journeys are more common than others.

We started this book by discussing the experience of John Hennessy, the president of Stanford University. As we spoke with other inventing entrepreneurs and integrated everything we'd learned, Hennessy's words kept coming back to us. So it seems appropriate to conclude the book with his own summation of his inventing entrepreneurial experience. Professor Hennessy is a respected scholar who founded a successful high-technology company and then went on to become president of one of the most successful research universities in the world. His simple description of the impact of his entrepreneurial journey carries more weight than any advice or direction we could provide:

> I learned more in that year than I learned in any five years of my life.
> And it's fun!

Endnote

1. Cook, M. 2004. *Inventing Wisconsin: Succeeding at Technology Transfer at UW–Madison,* video. Edited by G. George. Madison, Wisconsin: Wisconsin Alumni Research Foundation.

NAME INDEX

A

Aguilar, F. J., 141n1
Ahuja, G., 142n23
Aldrich, H. E., 67n8, 94n8
Arora, A., 55n16
Audretsch, D. B., 132, 143n24

B

Baird, M., 227n2
Baker, T., 68n14
Barringer, B., 67n8, 242n2
Batenburg, R., 115n2
Bates, T., 202n10
Baum, J. R., 30n10
Beckman, C., 94n7, 228n11
Bell, C. Gordon, 2
Bercovitz, J., 54n5
Bhide, Amar, 181n6, 202n8,
    230, 242n3, 242n5
Binks, M., 227n6
Birkinshaw, J., 115n2
Bisceglie, Gianluca, 142n10
Blattner, Fred, 58–60, 63,
    104–105, 172, 230,
    236–237, 248–249, 256, 270
Bok, D., 80n1
Bosma, N., 202n6
Bourke, S., 67n8
Braico, Sal, 27, 216–217
Bresee, J. S., 143n31
Brill, Winston, 196
Brin, Sergei, 216
Burgelman, R. A., 115n2
Burgess, Richard, 27, 66, 73,
    195–198, 271–273
Burton, D., 228n11
Burton, M. D., 94n7
Burton, R., 54n5

C

Campbell, A., 115n2
Carland, J. C., 68n10

Carland, J. W., 68n10
Carter, N., 181n1
Carter, N. M., 94n8
Ceccagnoli, M., 55n16
Cernohaus, Jeff, 26, 105–107
Cerrina, Franco, 59, 65–66,
    230, 236–238,
    248–249, 256
Chambers, Matthew, 133
Chapple, W., 54n1
Christensen, C., 131–132,
    142n15
Church, George, 40, 41n12,
    43–45, 51, 72, 74, 79, 96–97,
    215–216, 231, 255, 269,
    271, 273
Churchill, N. C., 242n1
Clarysse, B., 29n2
Cohen, B. D., 227n4
Cohen, W., 143n28
Cook, M., 275n1
Cooper, A. C., 227n5
Cortwright, Randy, 72, 101,
    131–132, 207–211
Covin, J. G., 181n3
Cullinane, John, 94n11

D

Daily, C. A., 181n3
Dalton, D. R., 181n3
Dean, T. J., 227n4
Deibel, Virginia, 73–74, 109,
    223–226, 266, 271
De Janasz, S. C., 80n4
Dell, Michael, 216
Delmar, F., 68n9, 181n5
DeLuca, Hector, 23, 73, 95,
    101–103, 113, 256, 273
Devereux, John, 27, 63,
    99–101, 243–245, 255–256,
    257n1
De Wit, G., 202n6
Dietz, V., 143n31

Di Gregorio, D., 54n5
Ding, W. W., 54n2, 54n5
Doerr, John, 142n17
Dubos, Rene, 9n5
Duderstadt, J. J., 80n5
Dushnitsky, G., 115n2

E

Eckhardt, J. T., 181n5
Edwards, M., 55n12
Etzkowitz, H., 54n1

F

Farritor, Shane, 75, 124–125,
    147–149, 155, 182n19, 195,
    209, 255
Feldman, M., 54n5
Feldman, M. P., 132, 143n24
Feller, I., 54n5
Filutowicz, Marcin, 196
Fleishman, Martin, 6
Ford, Henry, 5
Fosfuri, A., 55n10
Fouche, Mike, 107–108, 127,
    145–146, 170–172

G

Gartner, W., 181n1
Gates, Bill, 5, 216
Gecas, V., 94n2
Gehring, Mark, 37
George, G., 9n6, 30n14, 40n4,
    54n4, 54n5, 68n9, 68n14,
    275n1
Gilbert, Wally, 44
Gimenogascon, F. J., 227n5
Goe, W. R., 80n3
Gompers, P., 259n11
Grady, Denise, 142n6
Griffin, P. M., 143n31
Gulbrandsen, Carl, 49

H

Hambrick, D. C., 141n2
Handelsman, Jo, 51, 71–72,
    77–79, 113, 145, 217, 272
Handlesman, J., 80n7
Hanel, P., 41n10
Harrell, Wilson, 213, 222, 226,
    227n8
Heath, C., 55n14
Hendee, Bill, 128–129
Henderson, R., 54n2
Henkel, J., 55n14
Hennessy, John, 1–3, 24, 35,
    113, 255, 256, 275
Hitt, M. A., 115n2
Holtz-Eakin, D., 30n15, 202n5
Hsu, D. H., 202n3
Huse, M., 115n2

I

Ibarra, H., 94n3
Ireland, R. D., 115n2

J

Jacobson, Joe, 44–45
Jaffe, A. B., 54n2
Jain, S., 9n6, 30n14, 40n4
Jeffrey, Stephen, 142n7
Jones, F., 67n8, 242n2
Joulfaian, D., 30n15, 202n5

K

Katila, R., 142n23
Kauten, Ralph, 97
Kawasaki, Guy, 181n4
Keister, L. A., 67n8
Kenney, M., 80n3
Khessina, O., 143n25
Khurana, R., 94n9
Kiessling, Laura, 98
Kim, P. H., 67n8
Kinchy, A., 80n7
Kirzner, I., 9n3
Kleinman, D., 80n7
Komisar, Randy, 213, 214, 220,
    227n9, 228n14, 254

L

Lenox, M. J., 115n2
Lerner, J., 259n11
Levinthal, D., 142n21, 143n28

Lewis, V. L., 242n1
Link, A., 30n4, 54n1
Livny, Miron, 15–19, 274
Locke, E. A., 30n10
Lockett, A., 29n2, 54n1, 68n9
Lounsbury, M., 228n11

M

Mackie, Thomas Rockwell
    (Rock), 32–33, 37–39, 72,
    88–90, 94n14, 231, 264,
    273–274
Maltarich, M., 9n6, 40n4
March, J., 142n21
Mazess, Dick, 102
McCaig, L. F., 143n31
McCall, G. J., 94n4
McDougall, P. P., 181n3
Mead, P. S., 143n31
Merton, R. K., 9n1, 94n1
Meth, Sheldon Z., 142n18
Moore, G., 30n9
Moore, Geoffrey, 238, 242n9
Morrison, A., 115n2
Mowery, D. C., 54n2, 80n8
Mullins, John, 137, 143n32,
    143n33
Murray, F., 54n2, 55n12, 80n2
Murray, J. A., 67n8
Mustar, P., 29n2

N

Nelson, R., 54n2, 68n14
Nelson, R. R., 80n8
Nerkar, A., 142n22
Nesheim, John, 15, 29, 30n6,
    178, 212, 222, 227n7, 248,
    249, 257, 258n6, 258n9,
    259n18
Neubaum, D., 67n8, 242n2
Neubaum, D. O., 115n2
Nicholson, N., 94n6
Noffke, T., 142n12

O

O'Gorman, C., 67n8
Oleynikov, Dmitry, 147–149
Owen-Smith, J., 54n2

P

Page, Larry, 216
Penrose, E. G., 68n14

Platt, Steve, 149
Pons, B. Stanley, 6
Porter, Michael, 134, 141n3,
    142n11
Powell, W. W., 54n2
Pricer, Bob, 222

R

Raines, Ron, 20–21, 97–99, 134,
    273
Rao, Steven, 35, 119–120,
    128–130, 274
Razgaitis, R., 41n10, 54n3
Reckwerdt, Paul, 32–33, 37–39,
    72, 88–90, 94n14, 99, 137,
    231–232, 248, 255, 266, 273
Reitzig, M., 55n14
Reynolds, P., 181n1
Roberts, E., 54n1
Robinson, R., 178, 182n9, 257,
    259n18
Romanelli, E., 131, 142n14,
    143n25
Rosen, H. S., 202n5
Rosenkopf, L., 142n22
Ruef, M., 94n8
Rutter, Bill, 20

S

Sampat, B. N., 54n2, 80n8
Samsom, K., 40n3, 94n10
Sanders, Cam, 37
Schein, E. H., 94n5
Shane, S., 9n4, 29n1, 29n3,
    54n5, 68n9, 94n9, 181n5
Shapiro, C., 143n31
Shepherd, D., 68n10
Siegel, D., 30n4, 54n1
Simmons, J. L., 94n4
Sirmon, D. G., 115n2
Slutsker, L., 143n31
Smithies, Oliver, 99, 243–244,
    255
Sneider, David, 266–270
Sorensen, J., 228n11
Sorenson, O., 143n27, 258n2
Soros, George, 5
Staw, B. M., 94n5
Stewart, W. H., 68n10
Stonebraker, Michael, 81–84,
    136, 202n7, 221–222, 234,
    241, 248, 255, 256, 272, 273
Strong, Laura, 21

Stuart, T., 143n27
Stuart, T. E., 54n2, 54n5, 258n2
Sullivan, S. E., 80n4
Sussman, Michael, 7, 59, 230,
    236–238, 248–249, 256,
    271, 274
Swanson, J., 227n2

T

Tauxe, R. V., 143n31
Teece, D., 55n16
Thomson, James (Jamie), 22,
    25–26, 266–269
Trajtenberg, M., 54n2
Treble, Mike, 268
Tushman, M., 131, 142n14

U

Ucbasaran, D., 227n6

V

Van Maanen, J., 94n5
Van Osnabrugge, M., 178,
    182n9, 257, 259n18
Van Praag, M., 202n6
Ventresca, M., 228n11
Vohora, A., 68n9

W

Waldinger, R., 67n8
Waldman, D., 30n4, 54n1
Watson, W. E., 68n10

Westhead, P., 227n6
Wiklund, J., 68n9, 68n10
Woo, C. Y., 227n5
Wood, D. R., 54n5
Wright, M., 29n2, 54n1, 68n9,
    227n6

Y

Yu, R., 55n12

Z

Zahra, S. A., 54n5, 68n9, 115n2
Ziedonis, A. A., 54n2, 80n8

SUBJECT INDEX

A

Academia
  business versus, 2, 17, 74, 79
  changes in culture of, 80
  entrepreneurs in, 71–80
  research leaked from, 67n2
  start-ups based in, 14–18,
    57–58, 133
Accelrys, 245
Accountants, 153–154
ADAC Laboratories, 37, 88
Advanced Technology
    Program (ATP) grants,
    176, 177
Advisors, 154–155
Affinity, of inventing
    entrepreneur for project,
    24–25, 92, 113, 124,
    219–220, 223, 254
Affymetrix, 111, 136
Agincourt, 271
Agricetus, 196
Akamai, 231
Amyotrophic lateral sclerosis
    (ALS), 36
Analyses, realistic, 169–170,
    172–176
  budget, 175
  competition analysis,
    174–175
  customer analysis,
    172–173
  market analysis, 173–174
  revenue projection, 176
Analytical optimism, 270
Angel Investing (Robinson
    and Van Osnabrugge),
    178, 257
Angels, 194*t*, 195,
    203n18, 246
Applied Biosystems, 267
Attorneys. *See* Legal issues

B

Banking, 154
Bankruptcy, 252–253
Barriers to entry, 141n4
Bay Area, California, 132, 133
Bayh-Dole Act, 78, 80
Bessemer Venture Partners,
    202n7
Biogen, 44
Bio-Rad, 43
Birmingham, Alabama, 134
Boards of directors, 151–152
Boeing, 107, 170
Bone Care International, 23,
    30n11, 102–103, 113
Bootstrap finance, 26, 63, 190
Boston, Massachusetts, 132,
    133
Budgets, 175
Business
  academia versus, 2, 17, 74, 79
  challenges of, 74–76
  See also Industry
Business administration,
    234–236
Business failure. *See* Failure
Business-focused inventing
    entrepreneurs, 108–109,
    109*f*
Business formation, 146–155
  officer and director
    selection, 151–152
  ownership allocation, 150,
    150–151*t*
  service providers, 152–153
  timing of, 147–150
  types of legal entity, 147–150
Business plans, 155–169
  appendices for, 168, 169*t*
  components of, 158–166
  development of,
    156–157, 157*f*

documentation of, 168–169
exit strategies in, 166–167,
    167*t*
help for writing, 168
purpose of, 156
realistic analyses in,
    169–170, 172–176
value of, 155
Business value, 67n7
  See also Valuation of
    companies

C

Cambridge, England, 133
Capital intensity, 112–113
Cargill, 132, 209, 211
C corporations, 149–150
Cellular Dynamics, 266–268
Centers for Disease Control
    (CDC), 36
Change
  entrepreneurs as agents of,
    3–4
  punctuated equilibrium
    model of, 131
Chiron, 20
Cisco, 3, 231
City of Hope, 59
Cleveland Clinic, 130
Codon Devices, 44, 72
Cohera, 84
Commercialization of venture
  administration versus, 145
  benefits of, 25–26
  decision process for,
    140–141, 140*t*
  inventors' involvement
    with, 216, 221,
    226, 265
  licensing and, 28
  revolutionary technologies
    and, 231–232

Commercialization
of venture (*Continued*)
typology of technology
entrepreneurs and, 32*f*,
34–36
university start-ups and,
14–18
value dependent on, 209
Commercial roles, 85, 86*t*
Common stockholders, 253
Company operations
disposition of company, 29
disposition of technology,
28–29
long-term strategy, 27–28
management, 27
Competition, analysis of,
159–160, 174–175, 181n7
Competitive advantage, 134*f*
Complementary assets, 52, 140
Computer Associates, 83, 256
Condor distributed computing
technology, 15–17, 30n8,
274
Confederate Motorcycles, 133
Confidentiality, 162–163,
182n10, 198
Conflicts of interest, 77, 79,
220–221
ConjuGon, 27, 195–198, 216
Consultants, 154–155
Control, entrepreneurial,
26–29, 45, 215, 258n8
Control exits, 249–250, 258n7
Corporate entrepreneurs,
105–108, 106*f*, 108*f*
Crossing the Chasm (Moore),
238
Cullinane, 83
Culture, corporate, 217
Customer analysis, in business
plan, 158–160, 172–173

D

Debt. *See* Loans
Deltanoid Pharmaceuticals, 73,
102–103
Digital Equipment
Corporation, 2
Dilution, ownership versus
value, 199–201
Directors, 151–152
Disclosures, 45, 46*t*

Disposition of company, 29
Disposition of technology,
28–29
Disruptive technologies,
131–132, 142n16, 142n20
Distribution analysis, in
business plan, 163, 164*t*
DNAStar, 58–59, 63,
104–105, 248
Down rounds, 200
Dual-role inventing
entrepreneurs, 101–105,
104*f*, 105*f*, 223–224, 241
Due diligence, 182n20
Dyneon, 106–107

E

Early adopters, 238
Early-majority buyers, 238
Early-stage growth-based
start-ups, 165–166,
188–189, 189*f*
E. coli genome, 60
Emageon, 246–247
Enable Fuel Cell
Corporation, 210
Enabler model of company
growth, 234
Enron, 253
Entrepreneurial academics,
71–80
Entrepreneurial capacity, 32,
40n1
Entrepreneurial intent, 32–34
Entrepreneurial journey, 81–94
affinity as influence on, 92
business-focused inventing
entrepreneur, 108–109, 109*f*
case study of, 88–90
commercialization path
versus, 110
corporate entrepreneur,
105–108, 106*f*, 108*f*
dual-role inventing
entrepreneur, 101–105,
104*f*, 105*f*, 223–224, 241
final outcome of, 92–93
growth of company and,
240–241
identity and, 8, 82–83
initial conditions of, 92, 93*t*
lessons learned from,
109–114

matrix for, 86–88, 87*f*, 89*f*
milestones in, 7–8, 8*f*
model of, 85–88, 90–93
personal evaluations of, 18
realistic model of, 91–92, 92*f*
research-driven inventing
entrepreneur, 99–101, 100*f*
research transfer
entrepreneur, 96–97, 97*f*
research versus commercial
roles in, 85, 86*t*
sabbatical entrepreneur,
97–99, 98*f*
simple model of, 90, 91*f*
technology-based versus
market-based identities
in, 85, 86*t*
as transformative
experience, 113–114, 263,
275
types of, 95–114
uniqueness of, 110–112
Entrepreneurial options,
31–40, 66*t*
"file drawer idea," 34
inventing entrepreneurs, 36
lifestyle entrepreneurs,
35–36
reluctant entrepreneurs, 35
Entrepreneurial purpose,
13–29
affinity threshold and, 24–25
assessing market
opportunities, 22–24
benefits of
commercialization, 25–26
control issues, 26–29, 45,
249–250
foundations of, 18–29, 19*t*
goal visualization, 20, 22,
256–257
origin of, 13–14
Entrepreneurs
as change agents, 3–4
defined, 5
popular conception of, 4
serial, 248, 250
traditional versus inventing,
5–6
See also Inventing
entrepreneurs;
Technology entrepreneurs
Entrepreneurship
defined, 6

as transformative
experience, 2–3, 6,
113–114, 172, 263, 275
See also Entrepreneurial
journey
Equity investment, 177,
190–191, 190t, 246–247
Evolutionary technologies,
231–232
Exits, 243–257
actions/options after,
255–257
business plans and, 166–167,
167t
defined, 245–246
financial, 246–247, 258n3
importance of
understanding, 243
negative, 250–255
ownership/control, 249–250,
258n7
participatory, 247–249
types of, 246–250

F

Failure
control of intellectual
property at, 253–254
control of organization at,
252–253
exits caused by, 250–255
growth/learning from, 255
long-term outcomes for
inventing entrepreneurs
at, 254–255
management experience
with, 212
rates of, 259n11
Feasibility plan, 139t
"File drawer ideas," 34
Financial exits, 246–247, 258n3
Financial information, in
business plan, 163–166
Financing, 177–180, 185–201
angels and, 194t
expansion-related, 186–188,
187f, 187t, 199–201
at founding, 177–178,
190–191, 190t
help for obtaining, 180
information and
documentation on, 179
layers of funding, 190–192

long-term, 178
milestone-based, 179,
192–193
necessity of, 186
private, 193–199
recommendations on,
178–180
sources of, 177–178
valuation and, 178–179,
188–189, 191–193,
199–201, 202n13
venture capitalists
and, 194t
Firing, of employees, 217
Flagship, 45
Ford Aerospace, 107, 170
Founder's syndrome, 25, 220,
248, 249, 250
Functional magnetic
resonance imaging
(fMRI), 35, 120,
128–130
Fundraising, 186

G

Genentech, 231
General Electric (GE), 32, 38
Genetics Computer Group, 24,
27, 63, 100–101, 243–245
Genomic sequencing, 41n12,
44–45, 231, 244
Genzyme, 101–102, 113
Genzyme Transgenics, 126
Geometrix, 32, 37–38, 88–90,
264
Goals, entrepreneurial, 20, 22,
256–257
Going it alone, 140–141
Google, 3, 173, 174
Grant-based funding, 186,
202n2
Growth, 229–242
and adoption lifecycle,
238–240, 239f
and inventing entrepreneur's
changing role, 240–241
and project management to
business administration
transition, 234–236, 235t
types of, 230–232,
233t, 234
Growth financing. *See*
Financing

H

Harvard Medical School, 255
Harvard University, 57
Hectorol, 101
Helicopters, 107, 127, 170–172
Herceptin, 125
Highland Capital Partners,
202n7
High-Tech Start-Up
(Nesheim), 178, 222, 249
Hiring, 217
Honda, 132, 211
Human genome project,
41n12, 44–45
Human resource management,
217, 235–236, 242n7,
273–274
Hustle, growth strategy based
on, 232, 234
Hydrogen fuel, 209–211

I

IBM, 16, 273
Identity
defined, 82
entrepreneurial journey and,
8, 82–83
role, 82
scientific, 264–266
technology-based versus
market-based, 85, 86t
Illustra, 83, 222, 255
Imperial College, London, 14, 57
Imperial Innovations, 14
Industry
analysis of, 122–131
cost and differentiation
strategies in, 134–137
defined, 120
Five Forces model and
analysis, 122f, 123t, 128t
Informix, 83
Ingres Corporation, 83, 222,
256, 273
Initial public offerings (IPOs),
247
Innovations
disruptive, 131–132, 142n16,
142n20
revolutionary, 231–232, 234
Innovator's Dilemma, The
(Christensen), 131

Intellectual property
 business plan description
  of, 162
 confidentiality and, 162–163,
  182n10, 198
 control of, at business
  failure, 253–254
 costs associated with, 153
 legal counsel for, 152
 publication and, 77, 80n6
 types of legal entity and, 147
 valuation of, 39–40
Interfacial Solutions, 26, 107
Inventing entrepreneurs
 affinity of, for project, 24–25,
  92, 113, 124, 219–220,
  223, 254
 business challenges for,
  74–76
 business-focused, 108–109,
  109f
 and business skills
  acquisition, 221–222
 changing role of, as company
  grows, 240–241
 characteristics of, 270–272
 cognitive models for,
  86–88, 87f
 and commercialization
  process, 140–141, 140t,
  216, 221, 226, 265
 common experiences of,
  272–274
 and conflicts of interest,
  77, 79
 defined, 1, 5
 dual-role, 101–105, 104f,
  105f, 223–224, 241
 entrepreneurial options for,
  36
 exits for, 245–250, 258n3,
  258n7
 intellectual challenges for,
  73–74
 and interactions with
  management, 216–220,
  269
 inventors versus, 30n13
 long-term outcomes for,
  upon business failure,
  254–255
 and love of learning, 271
 management models for,
  214–216, 215t

 as managers, 220–224, 226
 motivations of, 4, 7, 15, 20,
  264–265
 optimism of, 270
 paths available to, 5
 personal challenges for,
  76–77, 79
 personal issues of, 219–220,
  248
 preconditions for, 6–7
 pride of, in craftsmanship,
  271
 relations of, with other
  owners, 254–255
 research-driven, 99–101,
  100f
 and research needs, 66
 satisfaction of, 226, 274–275
 self-evaluation questions
  for, 230
 self-reflection capacities of,
  40n1, 272
 skepticism of, 5–6
 and stress, 222–223
 study of, 4–5
 traditional entrepreneurs
  compared to, 5–6
 transformative experiences
  of, 263
Investors
 business contributions of,
  180
 partnership with, 201,
  254–255

J

Johns Hopkins University,
  49–50
"Just-in-time" manufacturing,
  219

L

Lawyers. *See* Legal issues
Learning, inventing
  entrepreneurs' love of,
  271
Legal issues
 corporate counsel, 152
 costs of counsel, 146,
  152–153, 181n4
 counsel selection criteria,
  153t

 for financing, 198
 formation of legal entity, 146
 intellectual property
  counsel, 152
 types of legal entity, 147–150
 See also Intellectual
  property
Lexus, 135
Licensing
 commercialization purpose
  defined by, 28
 considerations in, 51–53,
  52–53t
 growth types and, 242n4
 likelihood of, 50f
 patenting and, 47
 performance clauses
  in, 252
 TTO perspective on, 49–50
 See also Technology transfer
Lifecycle of companies,
  238–240, 239f
Lifestyle businesses, 57–67
 benefits of, 66–67
 considerations for, 63–65,
  64–65t
 defined, 61
 market analysis for, 61–62
 start-ups as, 58
 TTOs and, 62–63
 university-based start-ups as,
  58
Lifestyle entrepreneurs, 35–36
Limited liability corporations
  (LLCs), 149–150, 181n2
Loans, 177, 190–191, 190t, 246
Location, of start-ups, 132–134
Lou Gehrig's disease, 36
Luck, 272–273

M

Management, 207–227
 business plan description of,
  160–161
 characteristics of, 212–213
 commercialization effort
  versus, 145
 difficulties in identifying,
  68n13
 entrepreneurial purpose
  and, 27
 as financing factor, 195
 importance of, 208–209

interactions with, 216–220, 269
inventing entrepreneurs in, 220–224, 226
models of, 214–216, 215*t*
and risk reduction, 213–214
vision and implementation, 211
Market analysis
in business plan, 158–159, 173–174
entrepreneurial purpose and, 22–24
lifestyle businesses and, 61–62
realistic, 173–174
target markets and, 127–129
trend evaluation, 121*t*
See also Opportunity analysis
Market-based identity, 85, 86*t*
Marketing analysis, in business plan, 163, 164*t*
Markets, defined, 120
Massachusetts Institute of Technology (MIT), 44, 57, 80
Master of Business Administration (MBA)–level resources, 76
Medical College of Wisconsin, 120, 129–130
Medical robots, 148–149
Mentors, 75, 154, 168, 222
Microarray chips, 59
Microsoft, 40
Milestones, financing based on, 179, 192–193
MIPS Technologies, 1–2
Mobile telephony, 126, 127*f*
Moore's Law, 16, 30n9

N

Nanopositioning systems, 128, 128*t*
National Institutes of Science and Technology (NIST), 101
National Medal of Technology, 48–49
Nebraska Surgical Solutions, 75, 125, 132, 149, 195, 208

Neural Robotics Inc. (NRI), 107, 136, 145, 172
Neurognostics, 35, 128–130
New Business Road Test, The (Mullins), 137–138
New York University, 57
NimbleGen Systems, 7, 58–59, 104–105, 111–112, 136, 230, 236–238, 248–249, 256, 267–268, 274
Non-disclosure agreements (NDAs), 163
Northrup-Grumman, 107, 170

O

Office actions, 46
Officers, 151–152
Opportunity analysis
in business plan, 158–159
for new businesses, 137–138
seven domains of, 138*f*
See also Market analysis
Optimism, analytical, 270
Oracle, 83, 273
Orphan drugs, 36, 41n7
Ownership dilution, 199–201
Ownership exits, 249–250, 258n7
Ownership of companies, 150, 150–151*t*, 199–201, 217
Oxford Molecular, 28, 63, 100, 243, 245

P

Participatory exits, 247–249
Patents, 46–48, 50*f*, 55n11, 153, 232
Patent searches, 160, 174
Patent trolls, 48
PeachTree, 154
PeopleSoft, 84
Performance clauses, 252
Pharmacopeia, 245
Phillips Plastics, 26, 88
Pinnacle picture archiving and communication system (PACS), 32–33, 37, 88, 174
Preferred stockholders, 253
Pride in craftsmanship, 271
Private placement memorandum (PPM), 179, 182n21, 198
Problem solving, 270

Product/service description, in business plan, 161–162
Proteomics, 239
Publication, intellectual property rights as issue in, 77, 80n6
Punctuated equilibrium, 131

Q

Quickbooks, 154
Quintessence Biosciences, 21, 97–98, 134

R

Raleigh–Durham, North Carolina, 132
Reluctant entrepreneurs, 35
Research-driven inventing entrepreneurs, 99–101, 100*f*
Research roles, 85, 86*t*
Research transfer entrepreneurs, 96–97, 97*f*
Revenue projections, 176
Revolutionary technologies, 231–232, 234
Ribonucleases (RNases), 97
"Risk and reward" concept, 202n11, 203n17
Risk reduction, 213–214
Robots, for surgery, 148–149
Roche, 58–59, 238
Role identity, 82
Roles, 82, 85
Rosetta Partners, 197

S

Sabbatical entrepreneurs, 97–99, 98*f*
Sales analysis, in business plan, 163, 164*t*
San Diego, California, 133
Saratoga Venture Tables, 249
Scarab Genomics, 60, 105, 172
Scientific identity, 264–266
S corporations, 149
Securities Act (1933), 203n21
Securities Act (1934), 203n21
Securities and Exchange Commission (SEC), 198, 203n20, 203n21
Seed-stage technology-based start-ups, 164*t*, 188–189, 189*f*

Self-reflection, 40n1, 272
Serial entrepreneurs, 248, 250
Service Corps of Retired
   Executives (SCORE), 168
Service providers, 152–155
Skin in the game, 201
Small Business
   Administration, 168
Small Business Development
   Centers, 222
Small businesses, 61, 67n7
Small Business Innovation
   Research (SBIR) grants,
   176, 177, 186
Sole proprietorships, 61
Solera, 40
Stanford University, 80
Start-ups
   basic premise of, 138,
      140–141
   early-stage growth-based,
      165–166
   feasibility plan for, 139t
   financing of, 177–180,
      185–201
   formation of, 146–155
   growth of, 229–242
   innovation-resource
      relationship in, 23f
   location choices of, 132–134
   opportunity analysis for,
      137–138
   seed-stage technology-
      based, 165
   and technology transfer, 2
   timing of, 146–147
   university-based, 14–18,
      57–58, 133
Stem Cell Products, 266–268
Stem-cell research, 25–26, 34,
   267–268
Stockholders, preferred versus
   common, 253
StreamBase, 84, 202n7
Stress, 222–223
Structure Query Language
   (SQL), 273
Sweat equity, 201

T

Tax issues, for stockholders,
   257n1
Team, importance of, 273–274

Technology-based identity,
   85, 86t
Technology entrepreneurs
   "file drawer idea," 34
   inventing entrepreneurs, 36
   lifestyle entrepreneurs,
      35–36
   reluctant entrepreneurs, 35
   typology of, 32f
Technology transfer
   for academic researchers,
      43–44
   and conflicts of interest, 78
   defined, 43
   entrepreneurial journey
      based on, 96–97
   intellectual property and, 39
   process of, 45–48, 47f
   start-ups and, 2, 14
   WARF and, 48–49
Technology transfer offices
   (TTOs)
   evaluative role of, 54n8
   and legal formation of
      entities, 147
   and licensing, 49–50
   and lifestyle businesses,
      62–63
   and technology transfer
      process, 45–48
   university, 14, 54n7, 129
   WARF as example of, 48–49
TechStar, 35
Tellabs, 267, 270
Term sheet, 198, 203n23
Tetrionics, 102–103
Third Wave Technologies,
   267–268, 270
3M, 105–107
Time management, 223
Tolerance for failure, 212
TomoTherapy, 33, 37–39, 41n9,
   72, 88–90, 99, 131, 195,
   231–232, 248, 255, 264, 266
Toyota, 134–135
TRAC Microbiology, 73, 109,
   223–226, 271
Tranching, 198–199
Transgenic technologies,
   125–126
Trust, 201
TTOs. See Technology transfer
   offices (TTOs)
Tyler Research, 35–36

U

UltraVisual, 246–247
United Kingdom, 133
Universities. See Academia
University of California, 57
University of Nebraska-
   Lincoln, 147–149
University of Nebraska
   Medical Center, 147–149
University of North Carolina,
   57
University of
   Wisconsin–Madison, 15,
   20, 37, 58, 80, 244–245, 267
   See also Wisconsin Alumni
      Research Foundation
U.S. Agriculture Department
   (USDA), 211
U.S. Energy Department
   (DOE), 211
U.S. Food and Drug
   Administration (FDA), 126

V

Valuation of companies,
   178–179, 188–189,
   191–193, 199–201,
   202n13
   See also Business value
Value creation
   potential, 31–34
Value dilution, 199–201
Venture capitalists
   angels versus, 194t, 195
   business plans reviewed by,
      203n18
   and location of businesses,
      133
   opportunity analysis
      by, 62
   valuation by, 202n16
Vertica, 83, 136, 202n7, 234
Virent Energy Systems, 72,
   101, 131–132, 136, 207,
   209–211
Vision, 211
Vitamin D, 101–102, 256

W

Wisconsin Alumni Research
   Foundation (WARF), 21,
   48–49, 71